A Guide to
Psychotherapy
and Aging

A Guide to Psychotherapy and Aging

Effective Clinical Interventions in a Life-Stage Context

Edited by

Steven H. Zarit

and

Bob G. Knight

AMERICAN PSYCHOLOGICAL ASSOCIATION

WASHINGTON, DC

First printing August 1996
Second printing September 1998

Published by
American Psychological Association
750 First Street, NE
Washington, DC 20002

Copies may be ordered from
APA Order Department
P.O. Box 2710
Hyattsville, MD 20784

In the UK and Europe, copies may be ordered from
American Psychological Association
3 Henrietta Street
Covent Garden, London
WC2E 8LU England

Typeset in Goudy by PRO-Image Corporation, Techna-Type Div., York, PA

Technical/Production Editor: Molly R. Flickinger
Printer: Braun-Brumfield, Inc., Ann Arbor, MI
Cover Designer: Minker Design, Bethesda, MD
Cover photographs by Sunny Reynolds

Library of Congress Cataloging-in-Publication Data
A guide to psychotherapy and aging : effective clinical interventions in a life-stage
    context / edited by Steven H. Zarit and Bob G. Knight.
        p.   cm.
    Includes bibliographical references and index.
    ISBN 1-55798-373-9 (hardcover) 1-55798-569-3 (softcover) (acid-free paper)
    1. Psychotherapy for the aged.   I. Zarit, Steven H.   II. Knight,
Bob.
RC480.54.G85   1996
618.97'68914—dc20   96-20258
                                                                                             CIP

British Library Cataloguing-in-Publication Data
A CIP record is available from the British Library

Printed in the United States of America

CONTENTS

PART II: SPECIAL ISSUES FOR WORK WITH THE ELDERLY

CONTRIBUTORS

Dolores Gallagher-Thompson, Veterans Affairs Palo Alto Health Care System and Stanford University School of Medicine

William E. Haley, University of South Florida

Alfred W. Kaszniak, University of Arizona

Bob G. Knight, University of Southern California

Mark D. Miller, Western Psychiatric Institute and Clinic, University of Pittsburgh

Sara Honn Qualls, University of Colorado at Colorado Springs

Vicki Granet Semel, Psychoanalytic Center of Northern New Jersey

Rebecca L. Silberman, Western Psychiatric Institute and Clinic, University of Pittsburgh

Michael A. Smyer, Boston College

Catherine Selth Spayd, Geriatric Mental Health Unit, Mercy Regional Health System, Altoona, PA

Ann Steffen, University of Missouri—St. Louis

Larry W. Thompson, Veterans Affairs Palo Alto Health Care System and Stanford University School of Medicine

Judy M. Zarit, Child, Adult, and Family Psychological Services, State College, PA

Steven H. Zarit, Pennsylvania State University

Antonette M. Zeiss, Veterans Administration Medical Center, Palo Alto, CA

PREFACE

With the dramatic growth of the older population during the second half of the twentieth century, there is an increasing need for trained mental health professionals to provide treatment for this age group. Timely psychological interventions can help older people and their families with many of the complex and pressing problems they encounter in later life and can be cost effective by reducing inappropriate use of other services. Despite the historic pessimism about treating the elderly, a growing body of research and clinical reports has documented that psychotherapy is frequently effective with older people. Geropsychology is emerging as an important and fulfilling specialization that addresses the extensive unmet needs of older people.

This book presents a variety of psychotherapy systems that have been used with older clients. The chapter authors are clinicians practicing psychotherapy with older adults, and this book offers a variety of therapeutic perspectives. Each chapter considers how a particular approach is similar and different when used with older clients. The book also reviews the various settings in which interventions can be offered, such as the hospital and nursing home, and provides information on special issues that are central to practice with older people, including assessment, how medical and psychological problems often interact, and ethical considerations.

We want to thank the many people who supported us in development of this book. The idea for the book developed from a series of two conferences on psychotherapy and aging that were organized by us under the auspices of Division 20 (Adult Development and Aging) of the American Psychological Association (APA) and held in Pittsburgh in October 1994 and San Francisco, in February 1995. These conferences were made possible through generous support from the Retirement Research Foundation. Additional support from the Psychological Corporation is gratefully acknowledged. Cosponsors also played an important role in making the conferences a success, including Division 12, Section 2 (Clinical Geropsychology) of the APA, the Geriatric Education Center of Pennsylvania, the Gerontology Center at the Pennsylvania State University, the Andrus Gerontology Center of the University of Southern California, and the Aging Task Force of the American Society on Aging. Special thanks go to Pat Hansen and Wayne Friedlander, whose exhaustive efforts made the conferences a success, to Alvin Hall who oversaw the administration of the conferences in his usual calm and efficient way, and to Melissa Strouse, who assisted with manuscripts and correspondence for this book. John Santos, whose vision of the importance of making education in clinical geropsychology available to practicing clinicians, has been a key to our efforts.

We also want to express our indebtedness to Gary VandenBos, Executive Director of Publications and Communications at APA, who helped us in the initial design of the conference and supported our efforts to bring this book to press, and to Ron Wilder and Beth Beisel of APA Books, who provided ongoing encouragement and assistance.

STEVEN H. ZARIT
BOB G. KNIGHT

INTRODUCTION

PSYCHOTHERAPY AND AGING: MULTIPLE STRATEGIES, POSITIVE OUTCOMES

STEVEN H. ZARIT and BOB G. KNIGHT

Treatment of older people represents an important and growing challenge to mental health practitioners. Interest in psychotherapy with older people dates back at least to the 1920s (Knight, Kelly, & Gatz, 1992), but treatment of older adults was rare. With the convergence of several sweeping social changes, aging has been brought to the forefront in society as a whole and in mental health practice. Clinicians can expect that the opportunities to work with older people will increase dramatically in the coming years and that they will need specific knowledge and skills to work creatively and effectively with this population.

This book is designed for clinicians and students who want to develop or enhance their knowledge in clinical geropsychology. Our goal was to present in one volume a variety of psychotherapy systems that have been used with older clients. To our knowledge, this is the first book that addresses psychotherapy with older adults from several different perspectives rather than from one theory or viewpoint. In each chapter, the authors consider how a particular approach is similar and different when used with older clients. They also examine the practical decisions that clinicians make when treating older people. Toward that end, the chapters have been contributed by practicing clinicians. The book also examines the application of psychotherapy for different types of problems in later life and how psychotherapeutic interventions can be implemented in different settings.

1

THE CHALLENGES OF AN AGING SOCIETY FOR CLINICAL PRACTICE

We begin the exploration of treatment of older people by providing an overview in this chapter of aging issues and why late life is increasingly important for clinicians. Four social trends have dramatically altered the age distribution of the population and have led to new opportunities for working with this age group. These trends are as follows: the aging of the population, the changing character of aging, the effectiveness of treating older people, and coverage of outpatient mental health benefits by Medicare.

The Aging of the Population

The first and most important of these social trends is that the number of older people in the population has grown dramatically. In the past, the proportion of elderly in the population was relatively small; for example, in 1900 only 4% of people living in the United States were older than 65. By 1990, 13.5% of Americans were older than 65, with that figure projected to increase to as high as 17% by the year 2010 (Treas, 1995). Much of this growth is attributable to better control of infectious diseases and other causes of mortality in childhood and adulthood. As a result, a bigger proportion of people in any birth cohort can expect to survive to age 65 and beyond. The life expectancy is now almost 73 years for men and almost 80 years for women. People who survive to age 65 actually have even longer life expectancies: another 15 years for men and 19 years for women (U.S. Bureau of the Census, 1992). When fewer people lived beyond age 65, it was easier to ignore the mental health needs of the aged. Now, turning 65 is an expected occurrence, and people reaching that age may have one fourth or more of their life ahead of them.

The Changing Character of Aging

The second trend is that characteristics of the older population have changed. Current generations of older people are healthier and better educated than previous cohorts. In comparison with past generations, they have greater economic security. These trends will continue as the baby boomer generation begins reaching old age in the year 2010. One consequence of these changes is that older people are more psychologically minded and open to the possibility of psychotherapy. Opportunities exist not just for assisting in management of significant problems but also for making interventions that promote and extend the period of productive and healthy life (Park, Cavanaugh, Smith, & Smyer, 1993).

The Effectiveness of Treating Older People

A third factor leading to increased opportunities for treating older people is that psychotherapy is clearly and unequivocally successful. Despite historical pessimism about the ability of older people to change or to benefit from psychotherapy, the preponderance of the evidence suggests that older clients improve when given appropriate treatments by competent clinicians (Scogin & McElreath, 1994; Smyer, Zarit, & Qualls, 1990; see also chapter 3 in this book). Rates of improvement and the extent of gains are often similar to those found among younger clients. Psychotherapy can improve outcomes when used in conjunction with medications and in many situations when medication is not appropriate or is contraindicated because of health problems. Psychotherapy is effective in traditional one-to-one sessions and in other modalities, such as couples and family therapy (see chapter 6 in this book). Even in circumstances in which older clients cannot benefit from a talking therapy (e.g., if they are suffering from moderate or severe symptoms of dementia), interventions that focus on family members or on hospital or nursing home staff can make significant improvements in the patient's condition and in how family or staff are coping (see chapters 7, 9, and 10 in this book).

Including Outpatient Mental Health Benefits in Medicare

In the past, cost was a major barrier to treating older people. Since 1989, however, outpatient mental health services, including assessment, consultation, and psychotherapy, have been covered by Medicare. This change has reduced but not eliminated financial concerns because Medicare covers only 50% of the cost of these services, compared with 80% of medical charges. Nonetheless, this change has made mental health services more affordable for a greater number of older people.

The cost of care for the growing number of elderly is, of course, a major social concern. Although a great deal of attention has been paid to slowing the increase in the cost of Medicare, psychotherapeutic interventions may actually be cost effective. Timely interventions can reduce the use of inappropriate and often more expensive medical services while restoring older people to their maximum level of functioning. For example, many depressed older people visit their primary care physicians frequently with a variety of minor complaints that are often related to their mood. The treatment of depression can reduce the use of physician visits, medical tests, and even hospitalization.

The convergence of these social trends has created opportunities for clinicians to assess and treat older people in many different settings: inpatient psychiatric hospitals, outpatient clinics, the aging services network, private practice, and, increasingly, hospitals and nursing homes. It is clear that the demand for treatment greatly exceeds the number of clinicians with formal training in geropsychology. Few clinical training programs have offered specializations in geropsychology in the past, and even now most programs do not even offer a basic course in aging. To meet the needs of the growing population of older people, clinicians will need to develop competencies and expertise through their own ongoing education.

THE SOCIETAL CONTEXT FOR PSYCHOTHERAPY WITH THE ELDERLY

The social context of aging is complex and varied. Many older people live in a somewhat separated portion of society that has its own social settings. The set of residential settings, social services, and health services that make up that world is often referred to as the *aging network*. Some familiarity with the social context of older adults is helpful for any psychotherapist who works with elderly clients. The greater the proportion of older clients in one's practice, the greater the need to be familiar with these settings. Having a practice with older adults that is largely centered in one part of this network also makes an appreciation of the whole network and the position of the setting in which therapy is taking place helpful in understanding the particular subset of the elderly with whom psychotherapy is being done.

Residential Settings

The range of residential settings in which older adults live starts with independent living (both age integrated and age segregated) and includes increasingly supportive and restrictive settings such as supported independent living, assisted living, residential care, locked residential care, intermediate care, skilled nursing care, and locked skilled nursing care. Each of these levels of care has its own rules and social characteristics. Specific categorizations of levels of care can vary somewhat from state to state depending on licensing laws and local customs. There also is, of course, considerable variation within levels. Age-segregated independent living can include high-priced retirement communities, Housing and Urban Development-subsidized housing for the elderly, mobile home parks, and so on. Retirement communities may or may not make provision for people who develop disabilities or need assistance for other reasons. Similarly, skilled nursing care varies widely in cost, the care provided, and the restrictiveness of the rules imposed on residents.

Social Services for the Elderly

During the 1960s and 1970s, a variety of community-based programs for older adults developed that are funded by or at least encouraged by the Older Americans' Act and the set of planning and coordination agencies created by that act (the Administration on Aging, state Units on Aging, and local Area Agencies on Aging). Senior recreation centers, multipurpose centers, congregate and home-delivered meals, social model day care for adults, legal aide, in-home supportive services, volunteer support, and the long-term care ombudsman programs all are part of this system.

The array of services is diverse and can be confusing to the outsider. There has been relatively little formal or informal cooperation between the aging services system and the mental health services, although there are model programs that are exceptions to this general rule (Fleming, Richards, Santos, & West, 1986; Lebowitz, Light, & Bailey, 1987; Raschko, 1991). In part, the problems are due to differences in the definitions of target populations in that mental health services are for people with diagnosable disorders, whereas aging services are based on age rather than need. The mental health professional working with older adults needs, at a minimum, to be able to refer intelligently within this range of services.

In recent years there has been growth in another portion of this network: dementia care services. Although the need for segregated services for elderly people with dementia is far from clearly established, policies and services in some states have moved toward a separate system of care for this population. Dementia care services can include specialty diagnostic centers, special care units within nursing homes and residential care homes, specialized day care, in-home care and supervision, and supportive services for the caregiving family. Knight and Macofsky-Urban (1990) summarized these developments and discussed needs that are similar (e.g., accurate diagnosis and intervention for behavior problems) and needs that are more specific to the older adult with dementia (e.g., surrogate decision making).

Medical Care

Although not specifically designed to be part of the social context of older adults, the medical care system occupies an important place in the life space of older people with chronic illnesses or functional disabilities. This system includes physician's offices and outpatient clinics, outpatient surgery centers, in-home health services, and hospitals. The rules, regulations, and social norms of medical care settings have an important impact on the emotional and social lives of many older adults. Probably of most importance is the understanding that Medicare does not cover most long-term care services for disabled elderly, such as nursing homes, adult day care, or in-home care. These services must be paid out-of-pocket in most cases. People who spend down their available assets may qualify for long-term care benefits under the Medicaid program. Another critical development in medical care is shorter hospital stays, which can result in discharging older people who have significant acute care needs. Brief post-hospitalization stays in nursing homes and more intensive in-home health care services are becoming more common as a result.

Navigating the Aging Service System

Local Area Agencies on Aging are a good starting point for obtaining information about the available services within a locale. Other possible sources of information on long-term care or health services include the aging service section of public social services, ombudsman programs, adult protective services, self-help groups, and hospital discharge planners. Remember that both public and private resources must be considered. Many older clients will be simultaneously involved with, or will need referrals to, several different sources of help. Coordination of services is often a tricky issue, and sometimes the psychotherapist must help clients through the maze of services or be an advocate for them to get the help they need.

COMMON PROBLEMS THAT BRING OLDER PEOPLE INTO PSYCHOTHERAPY

A wide range of concerns and problems can bring an older person into treatment. There are, however, certain patterns that are encountered with more frequency in this age group. The psychological problems of this population are likely to include depression, anxiety, and adjustment disorders. These psychological problems are likely to be comorbid with medical illness and may therefore complicate medical treatment. This interaction of physical and psychological problems is a common issue in psychotherapy with older adults and a common motivation for referrals from physicians and clinics. Grieving for loved ones, especially when the grief is for several people who have died, also may be linked to depression, anxiety, and other psychological disorders that bring older adults to therapy.

Physical frailty and cognitive frailty caused by dementia-related illnesses in later life affect family members as well as the identified patient and the treatment team. Caregivers of older people with dementia and a variety of physical problems are at risk for developing clinical syndromes of depression and anxiety and may need psychotherapy in addition to or instead of the supportive services that are available in many communities.

As diagnosis improves and people with progressive cognitive impairment are identified at the earlier stages of the disease process, a group of potential clients is created who still have sufficient cognitive functioning to participate in psychotherapy but who are at significant risk of depression and other psychological problems as they accept their diagnosis and learn to cope with more limited cognitive functioning. These early-stage older adults with dementia may benefit from psychotherapy.

Finally, older adults come to psychotherapy for the same variety of reasons that bring younger adult clients to therapy: the full range of potential diagnoses for adults. Common issues can include marital problems, sexual dysfunction, family conflicts, personality disorders, and substance abuse.

DEVELOPING EFFECTIVE TREATMENT WITH OLDER PEOPLE

The key to developing competencies in clinical practice with older people is to understand the similarities and differences as compared with other age groups. A sound foundation in modern clinical practice is needed to begin working with older people, one that will contribute considerably to effective practice. However, there are specific types of knowledge about older people, their problems, their families, and the settings in which they reside that are integral to clinical geropsychology. In particular, competency in clinical geropsychology incorporates the following areas: knowledge of the aging process; the diversity of the older population; assessment; and differences in the process of psychotherapy, the goals and issues of treatment, and treatment settings between younger and older clients.

Knowledge of the Aging Process

Most older people are healthy, competent individuals who live independently. Most do not fit the stereotypical characterizations of old age. They are not senile or rigid, nor have they become increasingly neurotic, emotionally dependent, or childlike as they age. Clinicians need to be familiar with these normal aging patterns and their differentiation from disease. An understanding of the aging process will help clinicians identify appropriate goals for the clients and to counteract negative views of aging.

Diversity of the Older Population

The older population is not a homogeneous group with one pattern of functioning or set of needs. Like any other broad social group, older people encompass a wide range of people who differ as much from one another as they do from younger people. Social characteristics such as education, occupation, wealth, and ethnicity are usually more important than age in shaping current attitudes and beliefs, as well as the types of problems older people might have and the resources available for addressing those problems.

A major consideration in later life is gender. Because of women's greater life expectancy, they outnumber men in the population over 65 by a ratio of 3:2 (U.S. Bureau of the Census, 1992). This difference becomes greater at advancing ages. At age 65, there are 81 men for every 100 women, but, by age 90, there are only 33 men per 100 women. As a result, communities of older people are predominantly female.

The older population is frequently divided by age into "young-old," "old-old," and sometimes "oldest-old." The ages these categories refer to are roughly 55–74 for young-old, 75–84 for old-old, and 85+ for oldest-old. These categories, however, are not precise and do not indicate stages of development. In fact, the original formulation of young-old and old-old by the social psychologist Bernice Neugarten (1974) emphasized functioning rather than chronological age. Young-old people lived independently and were capable of functioning at a high level, whereas old-old individuals had chronic disabilities and needed help and assistance. Disability becomes more common with advancing age, but even in the 80s and 90s, significant numbers of older people remain independent and active (Zarit, in press).

Assessment

Although important with any age group, assessment has perhaps an even more central role in geriatrics. Because of stereotypes about aging, there is a tendency to view any problem as being due to aging or senility. As a consequence, many potentially treatable problems may be overlooked. Even conditions that are largely irreversible, such as Alzheimer's disease, may have treatable components. Clinicians, then, need to know how to identify the common disorders of aging, such as dementia and depression, and to use the results of assessment to build a strong treatment plan.

The Process of Psychotherapy Is Sometimes Different

Although psychotherapy with older people often is similar to that for younger people, clinicians should be prepared to make modifications in their approaches. In subsequent chapters, many such changes are described, including conducting sessions at a slower pace, talking clearly and slowly for people with hearing loss, and using written notes to help clients with mild memory problems. On a different level, clinicians need to be aware of their own feelings and attitudes toward older clients and to recognize instances of both negative and positive countertransferences. Some examples of negative countertransferences occur when clinical material stimulates the clinician's own fears about aging or unresolved issues with a parent or grandparent. Although the clinical geropsychology literature has tended to emphasize these negative countertransferences, there also are instances in which clinicians' enthusiasm about working with older people caused them to overlook or excuse their clients' problems and limitations.

The Goals and Issues of Treatment Are Sometimes Different

Clinicians need to understand the special concerns and issues that can arise in later life. Old age is a long and varied time of the life cycle. It cannot be understood through simple formulas, such as Erikson's (1963) famous dichotomy of "ego-integrity or despair." The period of late life covers a long period of time during which many different stressors and problems can be experienced by people who have vastly different psychological and social resources available for coping. Certainly, clients will present problems related to concerns about aging or decline, as well as how to cope with the consequences of chronic and debilitating conditions. Loss is a common theme, but often in subtle and varied ways, so that it is difficult to characterize all older people within a few categories. Of particular importance for therapists is to understand the implications of losses, whether it is the death of a spouse, an illness, or other problem. A loss may present opportunities for rehabilitation and recovery, which an inexperienced clinician can overlook. Concerns about death and dying occur, but most often these occur in the face of a life-threatening illness, not as a general preoccupation. Many of the clinical problems presented by older clients are familiar, such as marital or family conflict, but they may present in later life with a different twist or focus.

The Settings for Treatment Are Sometimes Different

Treatment of older people may take place in an office or outpatient clinic. However, clinicians may find that they are seeing older clients in a variety of settings. Home visits are often important when working with physically frail or disabled older clients. Hospitals, nursing homes, and other specialized institutional settings are frequently places in which older people or their families or advocates seek assistance. In those settings, the geropsychologist needs to combine a knowledge of the problems of aging with an understanding of how that institution functions in order to make effective interventions. In a nursing home, for example, interventions are often made through the staff or family rather than directly with an older patient. The clinician must sometimes subtly and tactfully redirect or educate staff so that they can manage more effectively a troublesome patient.

AN OVERVIEW OF *PSYCHOTHERAPY AND AGING*

We have organized the chapters in this book to expand on these themes and to identify other important issues in clinical practice with older people. We have divided the book into two main sections. In Part I, the central question of how to adapt psychotherapeutic approaches for older people and their families is addressed. Each chapter provides practical suggestions and case examples, as well as information on theoretical and research issues in the treatment of older people. Part II addresses a series of special concerns that are critical for psychotherapists working with this population.

The first chapter, by Bob Knight, is an overview of aging and aging issues in psychotherapy that provides a foundation for understanding the older client. In this chapter Knight presents a model of psychotherapy with older people that incorporates an understanding of the aging process and the specific problems and challenges faced by the older population. Knight argues that a lifelong process of maturation can offset age-associated losses. As a consequence, older clients may be both interesting to work with and able to benefit from psychotherapeutic interventions.

The next two chapters focus on different aspects of behavioral and cognitive–behavioral therapy. These two chapters were included because they address the most widely used and researched interventions with older people. In the first chapter, Antonette Zeiss and Ann Steffen use case examples to illustrate how a wide range of problems can be treated with cognitive and behavioral approaches, including depression, anxiety, insomnia, sexual dysfunction, and the problems of family caregivers of people with dementia. Dolores Gallagher-Thompson and Larry Thompson present a model of short-term cognitive–behavioral therapy for use with older clients and review research on its effectiveness. Both chapters emphasize the types of modifications that clinicians must make when adapting these techniques with older people.

An emerging treatment that has developed from a solid foundation in research is interpersonal psychotherapy. Specifically designed for treatment of depression, this approach focuses on the social interactions of depressed people, an area that is often a significant problem for older clients. In their chapter, Mark Miller and Rebecca Silberman discuss the basic approach used in interpersonal psychotherapy and its adaptation for use with older people.

Despite Freud's early pessimism about the effectiveness of treating anyone over the age of 50, psychoanalysis includes a small but rich tradition of work with older people. In her chapter, Vicki Granet Semel discusses how one psychoanalytic approach, modern psychoanalysis, can be adapted for work with older people. Using case examples, she demonstrates the use of a psychoanalytic perspective and therapy approach for treatment of long-standing personality characteristics in an aging context.

Families are one of the most critical sources of emotional support and assistance for older people. Conflict within families can be one of the most distressing events for the elderly. Sara Honn Qualls describes family relationships in later life and the application of family therapy approaches. She discusses how a family-systems perspective allows therapists to use information about family history, structure, and functioning in addressing current problems and difficulty. A particularly difficult family transition involves caring for an older person with a disability. Steven Zarit describes the stresses associated with caregiving and how clinicians can make interventions that lower stress. Even in the face of irreversible disorders such as Alzheimer's disease, there often are modifiable features of the situation that can be addressed through interventions with the family caregiver and extended family system.

Part II of the book focuses on special issues for clinicians conducting psychotherapy with older people. Alfred Kaszniak provides an overview of assessment issues and procedures used when working with older people. This chapter provides extensive information on tests and testing procedures, including references to the most commonly used psychological tests. Kaszniak also provides a clear and concise discussion of the most important questions of differential diagnosis facing clinicians who work with older clients.

One of the most important features of clinical practice with older people is the intersect between psychological and medical problems. William Haley illustrates the problem of comorbidity of medical and psychological problems and presents a framework for psychological interventions. He describes both the substantive knowledge needed when making interventions and how nonphysicians can work effectively with medical personnel in hospitals.

In many ways, nursing homes have become the mental hospitals of the 1990s. In most facilities, a majority of residents have significant psychiatric symptoms, but typically little or no treatment is provided. Catherine Selth Spayd and Michael Smyer describe nursing homes as settings for psychological intervention, including what type of interventions have been successful and how to work within the nursing home setting and with different types of staff.

In the final chapter, Judy and Steven Zarit discuss some of the specific ethical dilemmas that psychotherapists can encounter when working with older clients and their families. Two ethical issues are highlighted: confidentiality and end-of-life decisions. Confidentiality of client–therapist interactions is a central tenet of mental health practice, but situations can arise with older patients that have more ambiguity or complexity than is typically encountered. End-of-life issues address the problem of preserving a patient's rights to autonomy in the face of usual medical practices, which sometimes can make the dying process unnecessarily painful and prolonged. As with other aging issues, therapists need to supplement their fundamental training in ethics with an understanding of the unique ways these problems are manifested with older clients.

Our intended audience in planning and editing this book is the full spectrum of psychotherapists of the various mental health professions and students training to become psychotherapists. The unique contribution of this book is bringing together discussions of psychotherapy with older adults from a variety of theoretical system perspectives. It should be of interest to psychotherapists specializing in work with older adults and to psychotherapists who see older clients occasionally as part of a general practice.

We also hope that this book will be useful to members of the aging network who regularly come into contact with older adults who are, or who they suspect might be, clinically depressed, anxious, or suffering from other problems that might benefit from psychotherapy. Physicians, nurses, social workers, rehabilitation therapists, nursing home administrators, and others who have wondered whether psychotherapy might be helpful to older clients in distress can read this book and make a more informed judgment about the appropriateness of a referral to psychotherapy.

SUMMARY

The aging of the population presents new challenges and opportunities for the practice of psychotherapy. Well-planned psychological interventions with older people, their families, and, sometimes, the professionals and service personnel they interact with, can make substantial differences in well-being and quality of life. We hope that this book contributes to the growth of a cadre of clinicians who are sensitive to and informed about the psychological issues of later life.

REFERENCES

Erikson, E. (1963). *Childhood and society* (2nd ed.). New York: Norton.

Fleming, A. S., Richards, L. D., Santos, J. F., & West, P. R. (1986). *Mental health services for the elderly* (Vol. 3). Washington, DC: Retirement Research Foundation.

Knight, B., Kelly, M., & Gatz, M. (1992). Psychotherapy and the older adult. In D. K. Freedman (Ed.), *The history of psychotherapy* (pp. 528–551). Washington, DC: American Psychological Association.

Knight, B., & Macofsky-Urban, F. (1990). Toward a policy for Alzheimer's disease in California. In P. Liebig & W. Lammers (Eds.), *California policy choices for long term care* (pp. 145–170). Los Angeles: Andrus Gerontology Center.

Lebowitz, B. D., Light, E., & Bailey, F. (1987). Mental health center services for the elderly: Impact of coordination with Area Agencies on Aging. *The Gerontologist, 27,* 699–702.

Neugarten, B. L. (1974). Age groups in American society and the rise of the young-old. *Annals of the American Academy of Political and Social Science, 415,* 187–198.

Park, D., Cavanaugh, J., Smith, A., & Smyer, M. (1993). *Vitality for life: Psychological research for productive aging.* Washington, DC: Public Policy Office, American Psychological Association.

Raschko, R. (1991). Spokane community mental health center elderly services. In E. Light & B. D. Lebowitz (Eds.), *The elderly with chronic mental illness: Directions for research* (pp. 232–244). New York: Springer.

Scogin, F., & McElreath, L. (1994). Efficacy of psychosocial treatments for geriatric depression: A quantitative review. *Journal of Clinical and Consulting Psychology, 62,* 69–74.

Smyer, M. A., Zarit, S. H., & Qualls, S. H. (1990). Psychological intervention with aging individuals. In J. E. Birren & K. W. Schaie (Eds.), *Handbook of the psychology of aging* (3rd ed., pp. 375–403). San Diego, CA: Academic Press.

Treas, J. (1995). Older Americans in the 1990s and beyond. *Population Bulletin, 50* (No. 2), 1–46.

U.S. Bureau of the Census. (1992). Sixty-five plus in America. *Current Population Reports: Special Studies* (Series No. P23-178). Washington, DC: U.S. Government Printing Office.

Zarit, S. H. (in press). Continuities and discontinuities in very late life. In V. Bengtson & P. K. Robinson (Eds.), *Continuities and discontinuities in adulthood and aging: Research contributions in honor of Bernice Neugarten.* New York: Springer.

I

ADAPTING THERAPEUTIC APPROACHES FOR THE ELDERLY

1

OVERVIEW OF PSYCHOTHERAPY WITH THE ELDERLY: THE CONTEXTUAL, COHORT-BASED, MATURITY–SPECIFIC-CHALLENGE MODEL

BOB G. KNIGHT

Psychotherapy with older adults has been done, discussed, and studied for about 8 decades. In general, both the case studies and the controlled research on outcomes have been positive (Knight, Kelly, & Gatz, 1992). For the most part, people who have experience doing psychotherapy with older adults have described it as valuable for clients and rewarding for the therapist, whereas those who have not worked with older adults have argued that the aged cannot benefit from psychotherapy. Since the 1970s, writing about therapy with older adults has increasingly drawn on scientific gerontology (Knight et al., 1992).

Gerontology is a multidisciplinary field of study to which scholars have traditionally come after completing training in one of the constituent disciplines. However, in the past 10 years or so, increasing numbers of people have received degrees in gerontology. The constituent disciplines have included biology, medicine, nursing, psychology (mainly developmen-

This chapter was adapted from chapters 1 and 2 of *Psychotherapy With Older Adults* (Knight, 1996; pp. 1–41, copyright 1996 by Sage, adapted with permission). Those chapters drew on material published previously as the concluding chapter of *Older Adults in Psychotherapy: Case Histories* (Knight, 1992). The current chapter also incorporates material published in *Generations* (Knight, 1993a; pp. 61–64, copyright 1993 by the American Society on Aging, 833 Market St., Suite 511, San Francisco, CA 94103; adapted with permission) and reprinted as chapter 12 of *Mental Health and Aging* (Knight, 1993b; pp. 125–134, copyright 1993 by Springer Publishing Company, Inc., New York; adapted with permission).

tal, cognition, and sensation–perception), social work, and sociology. Services to the elderly have been largely delivered by social workers and nurses, who have been joined in more recent years by social planners in the aging network, nursing home administrators, various kinds of rehabilitation and recreation therapists, paraprofessionals involved in senior centers and nutrition sites, and most recently by physicians and psychologists. The complex array of perspectives, persons, and disciplines in gerontology obviously generates a body of knowledge of considerable complexity that cannot be well summarized in a large book, much less in a short chapter. However, there are within the discipline some general perspectives, trends in findings, and key sources of information that can present the therapist with different concepts of aging and of the elderly than he or she is likely to have gotten from coming of age in American culture. It is these novel ways of thinking about aging that I discuss in this chapter.

The early history of gerontology as a discipline was characterized by a split between researchers who were discovering that aging is a more positive experience than society presumably believed and practitioners who were struggling with the problems of selected elderly and who generalized the real problems of frail older adults to all aging persons. The loss–deficit model of aging, which portrays the normative course of later life as a series of losses and the typical response as depression, has been an integral part of the practitioner heritage.

On the other side, life span psychology has brought important conceptual and methodological advances to the study of adult development and aging. Chief among these has been the insistence on using longitudinal methods to study the aging process, as opposed to the inexact but common practice of comparing older adults and younger adults at one point in time and drawing developmental conclusions from the observation of differences between young and old people. The development of mixed designs that use aspects of cross-sectional and longitudinal methods has brought greater sophistication to the study of adult development and has called attention to two competing influences that are often confused with aging: cohort differences, which are the ways that successive generational groups differ from one another, and time effects, which can be related to social influences that affect everyone at about the same time or which can be specific to changes in the research study itself.

In my own work on psychotherapy with older adults, I have attempted to bridge this gap between science and practice. This attempt was motivated partly by being puzzled over the discrepancy between the loss–deficit model followed by most practitioners prior to 1980 and the emerging view of life span developmental psychology of the 1970s, which focused on normal aging and was more positive. In recent years, this has led to the proposal of a contextual, cohort-based maturity–specific-challenge model (Knight, 1992, 1993b, 1996; see Table 1), much of which is repeated and

TABLE 1
The Maturity–Specific-Challenge Model

Element of maturity	Specific challenge	Cohort effect	Context

Cognitive complexity
Postformal reasoning
Emotional complexity
Androgyny
Expertise
  Areas of competency
  Multiple family ex-
    periences
  Accumulated inter-
    personal skills
	Chronic illnesses
	Disabilities
	Preparation for
	  dying
	Grieving for loved
	  ones
		Cognitive abilities
		Education
		Word usage
		Values
		Normative life paths
		Social historical life
		  experience
			Age-segregated
			  communities
			Aging services
			  agencies
			Senior recrea-
			  tion sites
			Medical set-
			  tings
			Long-term care
			Age-based law
			  and regula-
			  tions

expanded in this chapter. In this view, older adults are seen as being more mature than younger ones in certain important ways, but they also are recognized to be facing some of the hardest challenges that life presents, including adjusting to chronic illness and disability as well as frequent grieving for others. The special social context of older adults and the fact that they are members of earlier-born cohorts raised in different sociocultural circumstances may require adaptations that are not dictated by the developmental processes of aging. In what follows, maturation is discussed first, followed by cohort differences and contextual factors as important potential sources of difference in working with older adults in therapy. Finally, specific challenges that are not unique to later life but are experienced more commonly in old age are introduced.

MATURITY

Cognitive Changes With Aging

Slowing

The most pervasive cognitive change with developmental aging is the slowing that occurs in all cognitive tasks in which speed of response is a factor (Botwinick, 1984; Salthouse, 1985). Although reaction time can be speeded up in older adults by practice, exercise, and other interventions, the age difference is seldom completely eliminated. In a thorough review of this literature, Salthouse (1985) argued convincingly that the probable locus of slowing is in the central nervous system.

Intelligence

Intelligence can be divided up in a number of ways. A useful two-factor distinction was proposed by Cattell and elaborated on by Horn (see Labouvie-Vief, 1985, for a review). In the study of aging, fluid intelligence, which is usually measured by tasks that involve a speeded or timed component, shows clear evidence of change with developmental aging. Inferential reasoning (e.g., as assessed by questions that ask what comes next in a series), is a part of fluid intelligence in this sense. Crystal intelligence, which involves the types of tasks most often associated with intelligence in adults (e.g., a general fund of information, vocabulary, and arithmetic skills), shows little change as a result of the aging process until age 75 or later (Schaie, 1983). Changes after age 75 have been less frequently studied and are difficult to untangle from changes that could be signs of the early stages of Alzheimer's disease or other dementias.

Rybash, Hoyer, and Roodin (1986) advanced some intriguing notions about the course of cognitive development across the adult life span. Drawing on the information-processing "mind as computer" metaphor, they argued that increased experience can be seen as operating like an "expert system" program. With the accumulation of experience, older adults have a considerable store of knowledge about how things are and how things work, especially in their individual area of expertise, which is in turn informed by work experience and family experiences. In these expert domains, the more mature may tend to outperform the young. By contrast, the excess speed and energy of the young may be helpful in processing large amounts of new information without the aid of an expert system. In a somewhat related vein, Salthouse (1985) speculated that slowing with age could be attributable to older adults having developed a machine language (the internal control language of the "mind as computer") that handles abstract material better and faster but at the cost of slowing down in the lower level tasks typically measured in reaction time experiments (e.g., speed of hitting a lever after hearing a tone).

Rybash et al. (1986) also argued for the existence of a postformal stage of cognitive development for more mature adults. Beyond the abstract thinking, deductive ability, and symbol manipulation of the formal stage, the postformal stage would include dialectical thinking, an appreciation of the truth of ideas depending on context, and the ability to hold two opposing viewpoints in mind at the same time. They acknowledged evidence that many adults have not reached the formal stage and that both formal and postformal stages seem to be confounded with level of education. The notion is intriguing and consistent with clinical observations of greater complexity of thinking among older clients.

Learning and Memory

Memory is perhaps the most difficult topic in the study of cognitive changes in late life. In sharp contrast to the methodological sophistication of studies of intellectual change in aging, most memory studies are cross-sectional and so compare older adults with younger adults at one point in time, confounding aging effects and cohort differences. Longitudinal studies with the Wechsler Memory Scale show little developmental change in memory when health is statistically controlled (Siegler, 1983). In a more recent longitudinal study, Zelinski, Gilewski, and Schaie (1993) found no evidence of age effects on longitudinal change in memory when reasoning (an aspect of fluid intelligence) was statistically controlled. Reisberg, Shulman, Ferris, de Leon, and Geibel (1983) identified older adults with memory problems and followed them over time. They reported that most older adults with memory changes, even changes that interfere with complex work or social activities, do not develop progressive memory loss. Although there clearly are increasing numbers of older adults with dementia with each decade of advanced age, it is unclear whether there also are benign memory changes in normal aging. The problem is methodologically challenging and has important implications for the understanding of normal aging and researchers' ability to estimate the prevalence of disorders such as Alzheimer's disease in very late life. In general, what is known about memory now would suggest that even differences between current younger and older adults in memory performance are not large when the material is meaningful and relevant to the older adult and the older adult is motivated to learn (Botwinick, 1984; Craik & Trehub, 1982; Hultsch & Dixon, 1990; Poon, 1985). By contrast, younger adults do better on novel information and learning tasks with no intrinsic meaning (e.g., learning lists of nonsense words).

An intriguing problem in this area is that older adults do not spontaneously use mnemonic aids. They can be taught to do so and will improve their memory performance substantially. However, they have to be reminded to use the mnemonic aids at the next session (cf. Botwinick, 1984). If this tendency to need prompting to use newly learned strategies generalizes to the therapeutic context, it would be important even if it is specific to current cohorts of the elderly.

There is recent evidence that working memory typically declines with age (see Light, 1990, and Salthouse, 1991, for reviews). Working memory is the limited-capacity resource through which information must be processed before being registered in long-term memory. This limitation could influence the pace and effort of new learning as well as affect language comprehension (Light, 1990). This finding would suggest yet another reason to slow down and use simpler phrasing when working with older clients.

Personality and Emotional Development

There is much more available research on personality development in adulthood and later life than there was 9 years ago. The work of Costa, McCrae, and associates in the Baltimore Longitudinal Study on Aging (Costa & McCrae, 1988; McCrae & Costa, 1984), using self-report measures of personality and a nomothetic model of personality measurement, has supported the stability of personality across the adult life span, with the greatest certainty of stability from age 30 to age 60. Their sample was mostly male and middle class to upper middle class. The dimensions on which they found stability included introversion–extraversion, neuroticism, openness to experience, dependability, and agreeableness. These results are not trivial: They support the concept that these personality dimensions are stable across years and even decades and that personality traits stay roughly the same through much of adulthood and into at least the early part of old age. On the basis of their data, Costa and McCrae (1985) argued against the concepts that older adults become more hypochondriacal and that a midlife crisis is normal. These concepts of stability refer to correlational stability (i.e., mean-level changes do occur, although Costa and McCrae, 1988, did not consider them large enough to be important).

Using a different methodology that included interviewer ratings rather than self-reports and an ipsative model of personality that leads to description of the relative salience of dimensions within the individual rather than the person's ranking in the group on predetermined scales, Haan, Millsap, and Hartka (1987) reported on the Oakland Guidance Study of both men and women from age 7 to about age 60. They found stability for cognitive commitment, dependability, and outgoingness, dimensions that are conceptually similar to openness to experience, dependability, and introversion–extraversion in the Costa et al. studies. They found self-confident–victimized (similar to neuroticism) to be stable across the adult years for men but not women. In general, they found women to be more flexible in their organization of personality across the life span than were men. They concluded that in spite of considerable stability across many transitions, the organization of personality in late life was much different from that of childhood. They found childhood to early adolescence to be the most stable period of life, followed by considerable flux and reorganization in adolescence and early adulthood, followed by moderate stability in adulthood (the period for which Costa and colleagues have data). The transition into later life is highly stable for men but marked by considerable personality reorganization for women.

These two research programs show remarkable convergence of the traits found to be stable in men and the Oakland studies provide a rare report of empirical data on personality development in women. Field and Millsap (1991), in a follow-up on the Oakland/Berkeley studies, reported declines in energy level and a tendency to become somewhat more intro-verted as people aged into their 80s. Satisfaction (the inverse of neuroti-cism) remained stable and agreeableness increased in the 70s and then remained stable. More guidance in what to expect of people as they develop past the age of 60 is clearly needed. Of interest to therapists, it also is known that in spite of objective stability in personality, people report be-lieving that they have changed and grown (Bengtson, Reedy, & Gorden, 1985).

Another intriguing discussion in the study of personality development is the question of changes in gender role and stereotypic gender-based at-titudes across the life span. Gutmann (1987), using projective testing in several cultures, has long argued that men and women cross over in later life, with women becoming more self-assertive and independent and men becoming more nurturing and caring. In a masterful review of the literature on self-concepts, Bengtson et al. (1985) concluded that findings depend on the method used to study the question: Objective personality measures tended to show more gender-stereotypic patterns in earlier-born cohorts, whereas self-concept measures (e.g., the Bem Androgyny Scale) showed more androgyny in the older respondents. Those authors also noted that age-graded social roles and cohort effects were the probable reasons for the reported differences and were difficult to disentangle. For example, there is some reason to believe that gender-based stereotyping in self-concept is strongest during the child-raising years and that androgyny may be more common both before and after these years. In work with older adults, one should keep an open mind about the possibility of naturally occurring change in long-held behaviors and beliefs about gender-related issues. In fact, contrary to the popular image of older adults as holding fast to tra-ditional gender roles and values, there may well be a tendency for men to become more interested in children and relationships and for women to become more interested in self-assertion, politics, and career.

Emotional changes over the adult life span are a topic of considerable importance for psychotherapists working with older adults. Gynther (1979), in a review of Minnesota Multiphasic Personality Inventory re-search with older adults, noted that older adults scored lower on scales associated with anger, impulsivity, and confusion and argued that people may become less impulsive with maturity. At the psychobiological level, Woodruff (1985) concluded that older adults are more difficult to arouse but that they also have more difficulty returning to a state of calm once aroused. This finding might suggest a different timeline for anxiety and anger in older adults than in younger ones. Schulz (1982) argued that the accumulation of experience leads to more complex and less extreme emo-tional experiences in later life. Each new experience reminds the older adult of previous experiences that may have a mix of negative and positive emotional connotations, whereas earlier in life it is possible to have simpler and more intense reactions with little or no prior experience to moderate reactions to new events (e.g., falling in love) or losses (e.g., a friend moving away).

Labouvie-Vief, DeVoe, and Bulka (1989) proposed a developmental model for the development of understanding of the emotions and controlling the emotions that moves from a simple physical reaction and naming of feelings in early adolescence up to an integrated physical and emotional experience combined with an appreciation of situational determinants of the emotion and the reactions of others. This latter stage is reached in midlife according to their model. Malatesta and Izard (1984), reporting on the study of facial expression of emotions, discussed evidence that older people's expressions convey elements of several feelings at once. As a cautionary note to younger adults working with the elderly, they also reported that younger people are much less accurate in identifying emotion in pictures of older faces. Taken as a whole, this body of work argues that emotionality in older adults will be more complex and more subtle than that of younger adults.

Summary: Evidence of Increasing Maturity Through Adulthood

In a now-classic discussion of personality across the life span, Neugarten (1977) suggested that there is an increase in interiority with age, in which interiority is a tendency to turn inward and to become more reflective, psychologically oriented, and philosophical about life. This change would, of course, make older adults more suited for psychotherapy.

Although speed of processing and other components of fluid intelligence decline with age, crystal intelligence likely remains stable. Cognitive maturation throughout adulthood and into later life also may be characterized by the development of expert systems depending on the individual's experiences in adult life (Rybash et al., 1986) and on movement to a stage of postformal reasoning with an appreciation of the dialectical nature of argument and social change and a greater appreciation that people hold differing viewpoints (Rybash et al., 1986).

On the emotional side, older adults have been seen as becoming less impulsive and driven by anxiety (Gynther, 1979) and more emotionally complex, with more complex reactions to events (Schulz, 1982) and more complex experience of and ability to control emotional states (Labouvie-Vief et al., 1989). De Rivera (1984) argued for the development of a greater range of emotions and greater experience of the transformation of emotions as a likely outcome of increased experience throughout life. Increased androgyny (Bengtson et al., 1985; Gutmann, 1987) also can be seen as increased psychological maturity. As one moves into the second half of life, behavior and social skills can become less constricted by sex role stereotypes and therefore more fully human. At least in the context of heterosexual relationships, men and women learn skills and behaviors from one another over a period of decades.

The mechanism for such improvement can be as simple (and as complex) as the accumulation of life experiences, which can be understood as an increasingly complex database of human interaction. Breytspraak (1984) summarized sociological and social psychological thought on the development of the self and noted that social comparison processes, reflected appraisals, and the role of person–environment interactions provide input for a dynamically evolving self-concept. Assuming that such input is continual throughout life implies that with increasing years, there is at least the potential for greater self-knowledge and the development of a more complex self (see also Markus & Herzog, 1991; Sherman, 1991).

Attacking the same notion from a somewhat different theoretical position, Bowen's family systems theory (cf. Hall, 1981) relates the development of the differentiated self to experience with one's family context. Bowen's concept of multigenerational transmission implies a general consistency from family of origin to family of marriage. Working with older families drives home the point that almost all older adults have experienced several family constellations: the family of origin, the family of marriage and small children, the extended family with adult children and grandchildren, and the dispersed family of later life. If one adds the knowledge gained of the spouse's family and the families of the spouses of the client's children, almost every older person can be something of an expert on family dynamics.

In summary, these trends in gerontological thinking suggest a potential for continual growth toward maturity throughout the adult life span. In this sense, maturity means increasing cognitive complexity, possibly including postformal reasoning; development of expertise in areas of experiential competence including work, family, and relationships; androgyny, at least in the sense of acquiring role competencies and interests stereotypically associated with the opposite gender; and a greater emotional complexity with better comprehension and control of emotional reactions.

COHORT DIFFERENCES

As described earlier, another dimension of understanding older adults from life span development is the ability to separate the effects of maturation from the effects of cohort membership. Much of social gerontology could be summarized as the discovery that many of the differences between the old and the young that society has attributed to the aging process are due, in fact, to cohort effects. Cohort differences are explained by membership in a birth-year-defined group that is socialized into certain abilities, beliefs, attitudes, and personality dimensions that will stay stable as it ages and that distinguishes that cohort from those born earlier and later. For example, later-born cohorts in twentieth-century America have more years of formal schooling than earlier-born groups.

For example, cohort differences in intellectual skills have been identified. In general, Schaie's (1990) Seattle study shows that later-born cohorts tend to be superior in reasoning ability. On the other hand, some earlier-born cohorts (people who are now older) are superior in arithmetic ability and verbal fluency (Schaie, 1990). These examples illustrate the important point that the absence of developmental change does not necessarily mean that older people as they exist today are not different from today's younger people. This example also shows that some differences between cohorts favor the older cohort.

In studies of learning and memory, one aspect of the familiarity of materials to be learned is the discovery that older adults learn word lists better when the lists are made of "old words" (e.g., fedora) as opposed to "new words." This finding demonstrates that word usage changes over time and suggests that therapists need to consider using appropriate word choices when communicating with older adults (Barrett & Wright, 1981).

Costa and his associates found cohort effects in personality; for example, later-born cohorts are less restrained and higher in dominance than those born earlier in this century (Costa, McCrae, & Arenberg, 1983). In general, their results argue that observed personality differences between young people and older adults are more likely to be cohort differences than attributable to aging as a developmental process.

With regard to changes in life satisfaction, Costa et al. (1987), using a large national sample, found that average levels of life satisfaction stay stable with aging and across cohorts but that earlier born cohorts tend to express both less positive and less negative affect.

In other domains, social change that occurs before or during childhood years may be taken for granted, that which occurs during the adult years will be truly experienced as change. These cohort differences are the reasons that older people seem "old-fashioned."

Cohort differences, although not developmental, are real. Working with older adults involves learning something of the folkways of members of earlier-born cohorts, just as working with adolescents or young adults demands staying current in their folkways and worldviews. During times of rapid social and technological change (e.g., the twentieth century), cohort effects may overwhelm advantages of developmental maturation. Preparation to do therapy with older people has to include learning what it was like to grow up before the therapists were born.

Understanding aging is about understanding maturation; working with old people is about understanding people who matured in a different era. Perhaps one of the most undeveloped aspects of understanding psychotherapy with older adults, comprehending psychologically significant cohort effects is not essentially different in quality or difficulty from learning to work with clients from other cultures or from the other gender.

THE SOCIAL CONTEXT OF OLDER ADULTS

Another complication for understanding older adults in psychotherapy is the need to understand the distinctive social milieu of older adults in the United States of the late twentieth century. This context includes specific environments (age-segregated housing, age-segregated social and recreational centers, the aging services network, age-segregated long-term care, etc.) as well as specific rules for older adults (Medicare regulations, Older Americans' Act regulations, conservatorship law, and so forth). The network of aging services is yet another element of this context. An understanding of this social context that is based on both knowledge of what is supposed to be and experience of actual operations is important to the understanding of what older people say about their experiences in these settings. A danger of selective exposure of professionals to these environments for older adults is that many people who are expert about a given context (e.g., skilled nursing facilities) imagine that they are expert about older adults in general.

This type of work requires some knowledge of the social worlds of the elderly. The knowledge does not have to be extraordinarily extensive, but it does need to go beyond the commonly believed but entirely false assumptions of many younger adults. The assumption that living in an age-segregated environment will lead to increased friendships is something that only a naive outsider to that world can believe. Many age-segregated environments are intolerant of frailty and of social deviance of any sort (cf. Frankfather, 1977).

Each senior recreation center and meal site tends to have its own particular social ecology. Recommending that clients go to such places to find activity or friendship is risky if one does not know the particular range of activity or the degree of openness to newcomers at that site. In one locale in which I have worked, the range of settings went from one site that attracted retired professionals with a wide range of activities to another that mostly served former state hospital patients and that had an environment similar to the day room in a chronic ward. Often part of initial rapport building has been showing that I understand and agree with the client's perception of why finding appropriate activity or help has been so difficult.

Although this understanding is not terribly difficult to acquire, the lack of it among psychotherapists working with a general population may be one reason why older adults can seem difficult to understand. The formal network of health and social services for older adults and the formal distinctions between different levels can be learned in a lecture or two. Some informal visiting at such places can do a great deal toward providing a more experiential framework for understanding the environments of the elderly. These environments are unfamiliar territory for most younger adults.

People acquire some experience of school, work, military, sports, and family settings through their own lives, and this forms a background for understanding what clients tell therapists. The settings of the elderly (e.g., senior recreation centers, retirement hotels, hospitals, nursing homes, doctor's offices, senior meal sites, volunteer programs, and mobile home parks) are unfamiliar ground for most adults, including psychotherapists. Unfortunately, therapists often seem to confuse this unfamiliarity with the settings of older adults with inability to understand the older adults themselves. When older adults tell therapists strange things about the settings in which they live, therapists should perhaps be more ready to trust their psychotherapeutic skills in understanding others and in working within the client's point of view.

THE SPECIFICITY OF CHALLENGES IN LATE LIFE

Practitioners working with older adults may well be thinking at this juncture that this view of aging is overly optimistic. In this outline of evidence for increasing maturation, I have intentionally focused on normal development through the life span. Many elderly clients seeking help in therapy are struggling with problems that threaten psychological homeostasis at any point in the life span: chronic illness, disability, and the loss of loved ones to death. These problems are not unique to late life but are more likely in the latter third of life. In addition, late life is not immune to the usual vicissitudes of all of life: disappointment in love, arguments with family members, and failing at the tasks we set for ourselves. Finally, many people who have struggled with depression, anxiety, substance abuse, or psychosis all of their lives eventually become older adults who continue to struggle with these problems.

The specific nature of these problems is important to the practice of psychotherapy with older individuals. Just as the deficit side of the loss–deficit model ignores evidence for maturation, the perception that generic losses are normative in late life fails to do justice to the specific nature of the losses incurred. Clinical experience suggests that it matters whether what is lost is one's spouse, one's vision, or the use of one's legs. Recognizing the specificity of loss and reconceptualizing losses as challenges implies that some losses can be overcome through rehabilitation counseling as well as adjusted to through grief counseling. Turning from a loss–deficit model to a maturity–specific-challenge model also helps therapists to recognize when depression is not normative for a given life experience. For example, depression after retirement may be seen in this model as atypical (because many older adults enjoy freedom from the demands of work) and therefore in need of careful therapeutic assessment.

Chronic Illness and Disability

Continued work with older adults and the writing of the case histories volume has made it clear to me that working with emotionally distressed older adults often means working with older adults who are chronically ill, physically disabled, or both and who are struggling to adjust to these problems. In setting out to do psychological work with older adults, I have learned about chronic illnesses and their psychological impact, pain control, adherence to medical treatment, rehabilitation strategies, and assessing behavioral signs of medication reactions. I have gone to hospitals, nursing homes, cardiac rehabilitation programs, emergency rooms, and the bedside of many severely disabled older adults.

In doing this work, I have become acquainted with physicians and nurses and have learned how to talk to and with them. I have learned much about the limitations of medicine and about the demands that patients place on doctors. I have learned to think about hospitals and other medical settings as organizational systems inhabited by human beings but operating within distinctive social rules. I have come to better appreciate my own expertise by observing that many people with medical training are as uncomfortable with emotionality, psychosis, and suicidal threats as I am with blood, physical symptoms, and medical emergencies.

This aspect of working with older adults involves specialized knowledge and specialized skills compared with other areas of psychotherapeutic practice in which physical problems and the physical dimension of the person can be more safely ignored. The increased proportion of chronic illness and disability with each decade of life and the increased correlation of the physical and the psychological in later life make it impossible to function without the ability to discuss physical problems and to understand when a problem may have physical causes. This principle does not mean that every psychotherapist working with the elderly must be a physician. It does mean that therapists must be able to talk intelligently and cooperatively with physicians and with older clients who need to discuss the real physical problems they face.

The specific challenges part of this model differs from the loss–deficit model in that the loss–deficit model argues that the work of therapy with the elderly is adjustment to the natural losses of late life and grieving for them. This model is wrong on two counts: First, there is nothing especially natural about blindness or heart disease or cancer. The fact that they happen more frequently to older adults does not make these diseases and disabilities part of normal development. It certainly does not make the individual older person experience these problems as normal or as less of a crisis than they would be for a younger adult.

Second, the loss–deficit model fails to suggest the next step of optimizing functioning. Rehabilitation may start by accepting the deficit in functioning, but it does not end there. The next step is to consider how life may be improved. The goal may not necessarily be a return to premorbid levels of functioning and mood; however, there is always room for improvement over the initial level of mood and functioning.

Grief

In a similar manner, working with older adults in outpatient therapy often involves grief work. Although loved ones die throughout people's lives, the experience is more common in later life. Older adults seeking help for depression frequently have experienced several deaths of loved ones in the preceding months or years. Much of psychotherapy with older adults is grief work.

As is true for chronic illness and disability, older adults do not seem to experience grief as a normal and expected part of later life. Losing a loved one, even a loved one who has been ill for some time, is often experienced as surprising and tragic. The loss may be experienced more deeply because of the length of the relationship.

Unlike the loss–deficit model, the maturity–specific-challenge model goes beyond emotional grief work and the acceptance of loss to explore the question of what the remainder of the grieving client's life will be like. Grief work is not only about accepting loss but also about finding a new way of living without the deceased.

In brief, the specific challenge part of this model recognizes the gravity of the problems faced by older adults. It emphasizes the specificity of the problems and assumes that problems in later life can be overcome. In fact, one implication of the specific-challenge model is that work with older adults facing a specific problem should draw on the available knowledge about helping all adults with similar problems. Therapy with older adults should not become so specialized that techniques and concepts developed for other clients are not readily generalized to older adults and that techniques and concepts developed in gerontological counseling are not tried with younger adults as appropriate.

SUMMARY

The contextual, cohort-based, maturity–specific-challenge model portrays older adults in a complex light that draws on scientific gerontology.

The process of maturation is seen as making older adults more mature in some ways and as producing mild deficits in other cognitive processes. Cohort differences and the specially created social context in which many older adults live invite therapists to understand older adults in a specific context and a context that changes as new cohorts become old and as the social context of older adults changes over time in response to social, economic, and political influences. Finally, some of the problems faced by older adults are encountered more frequently in later life and have come to be identified with old age. Although the problems require specific expertise, the problem should not be overidentified with the age of the client: Younger adults also have chronic illness, disabilities, and grief.

The discussion of these sources of change has laid a groundwork for arguing that the major adaptations to therapy with the elderly will arise from cohort effects and social context effects rather than from developmental changes. This perspective makes the therapist's task in approaching work with the older client easier in that comprehending persons of different backgrounds is easier than comprehending stages of life that one has not yet experienced. It also brings the work of understanding the elderly within the range of familiar skills: Most therapists have had exposure to different cohorts and to people of different social backgrounds. In addition, reflection on therapeutic experience suggests positive characteristics of older clients that may make them well suited to the work of therapy.

This spirit of optimism about the possibility for change in late life runs counter to much of both common folk wisdom about aging and much of clinical lore about older adults. It is, however, based on an understanding of aging gathered from gerontological knowledge and clinical experience with a large number of older adults in various community settings. In the absence of ill health, there is no block to normal therapeutic work with the elderly and these positive actors can make working with the elderly a rewarding experience for the therapist.

REFERENCES

Barrett, T. R., & Wright, M. (1981). Age-related facilitation in recall following semantic processing. *Journal of Gerontology, 36,* 194–199.

Bengston, V. L., Reedy, M. N., & Gorden, C. (1985). Aging and self-conceptions: Personality processes and social contexts. In J. E. Birren & K. W. Schaie (Eds.), *Handbook of the psychology of aging* (2nd ed., pp. 544–593). New York: Van Nostrand Reinhold.

Botwinick, J. (1984). *Aging and behavior* (3rd ed.). New York: Springer.

Breytspraak, L. M. (1984). *The development of self in later life.* Boston: Little, Brown.

Costa, P. T., & McCrae, R. R. (1985). Hypochondriasis, neuroticism, and aging: "When are somatic complaints unfounded?" *American Psychologist, 40,* 19–28.

Costa, P. T., & McCrae, R. R. (1988). Personality in adulthood: A six-year longitudinal study of self-reports and spouse ratings on the NEO Personality Inventory. *Journal of Personality and Social Psychology, 54,* 853–863.

Costa, P. T., McCrae, R. R., & Arenberg, D. (1983). Recent longitudinal research on personality and aging. In K. W. Schaie (Ed.), *Longitudinal studies of adult psychological development* (pp. 222–265). New York: Guilford Press.

Costa, P. T., Zonderman, A. B., McCrae, R. R., Cornoni-Huntley, J., Locke, B. Z., & Barbano, H. E. (1987). Longitudinal analysis of psychological well-being in a national sample: Stability of mean levels. *Journal of Gerontology, 42,* 50–56.

Craik, F. I. M., & Trehub, S. (1982). *Aging and cognitive processes.* New York: Plenum.

de Rivera, J. (1984). Development and the full range of emotional expression. In C. Z. Malatesta & C. E. Izard (Eds.), *Emotion in adult development* (pp. 45–63). Beverly Hills, CA: Sage.

Field, D., & Millsap, R. E. (1991). Personality in advanced old age: Continuity or change? *Journals of Gerontology: Psychological Sciences, 48,* P299–P308.

Frankfather, D. (1977). *The aged in the community.* New York: Praeger Press.

Gutmann, D. (1987). *Reclaimed powers: Toward a new psychology of men and women in later life.* New York: Basic Books.

Gynther, M. D. (1979). Aging and personality. In J. N. Butcher (Ed.), *New developments in the use of the MMPI* (pp. 39–68). Minneapolis: University of Minnesota Press.

Haan, N., Millsap, R., & Hartka, E. (1987). As time goes by: Change and stability in personality over fifty years. *Psychology and Aging, 1,* 220–232.

Hall, C. M. (1981). *The Bowen family theory and its uses.* Northvale, NJ: Jason Aronson.

Hultsch, D. F., & Dixon, R. A. (1990). Learning and memory in aging. In J. E. Birren & K. W. Schaie (Eds.), *Handbook of the psychology of aging* (3rd ed., pp. 259–274). San Diego, CA: Academic Press.

Knight, B. G. (1992). *Older adults in psychotherapy: Case histories.* Newbury Park, CA: Sage.

Knight, B. G. (1993a). Psychotherapy as applied gerontology: A contextual, cohort-based, maturity–specific challenge model. *Generations, 17,* 61–64.

Knight, B. G. (1993b). Psychotherapy as applied gerontology: A contextual, cohort-based, maturity–specific challenge model. In M. Smyer (Ed.), *Mental health and aging* (pp. 125–134). New York: Springer.

Knight, B. G. (1996). *Psychotherapy with older adults* (2nd ed.). Newbury Park, CA: Sage.

Knight, B. G., Kelly, M., & Gatz, M. (1992). Psychotherapy with the elderly. In D. K. Freedheim (Ed.), *The history of psychotherapy* (pp. 528–551). Washington, DC: American Psychological Association.

Labouvie-Vief, G. (1985). Intelligence and cognition. In J. E. Birren & K. W. Schaie (Eds.), *Handbook of psychology and aging* (2nd ed., pp. 500–530). New York: Van Nostrand Reinhold.

Labouvie-Vief, G., DeVoe, M., & Bulka, D. (1989). Speaking about feelings: Conceptions of emotion across the life span. *Psychology and Aging, 4*, 425–437.

Light, L. L. (1990). Interactions between memory and language in old age. In J. E. Birren & K. W. Schaie (Eds.), *Handbook of the psychology of aging* (3rd ed., pp. 275–290). San Diego, CA: Academic Press.

Malatesta, C. Z., & Izard, C. E. (1984). The facial expression of emotion: Young, middle-aged, and older adult expressions. In C. Z. Malatesta & C. E. Izard (Eds.), *Emotion in adult development* (pp. 253–273). Beverly Hills, CA: Sage.

Markus, H. R., & Herzog, A. R. (1991). The role of the self concept in aging. *Annual Review of Gerontology and Geriatrics, 11*, 110–143.

McCrae, R. R., & Costa, P. T. (1984). *Emerging lives, enduring dispositions: Personality in adulthood.* Boston: Little, Brown.

Neugarten, B. L. (1977). Personality and aging. In J. E. Birren & K. W. Schaie (Eds.), *Handbook of the psychology of aging* (pp. 626–649). New York: Van Nostrand.

Poon, L. W. (1985). Differences in human memory with aging: Nature, causes, and clinical implications. In J. E. Birren & K. W. Schaie (Eds.), *Handbook of the psychology of aging* (2nd ed., pp. 427–462). New York: Van Nostrand Reinhold.

Reisberg, B., Shulman, E., Ferris, S. H., de Leon, M. J., & Geibel, V. (1983). Clinical assessments of age-associated cognitive decline and primary degenerative dementia: Prognostic concomitants. *Psychopharmacology Bulletin, 19*, 734–739.

Rybash, J. M., Hoyer, W. J., & Roodin, P. A. (1986). *Adult cognition and aging.* Elmsford, NY: Pergamon Press.

Salthouse, T. A. (1985). Speed of behavior and its implications for cognition. In J. E. Birren & K. W. Schaie (Eds.), *Handbook of the psychology of aging* (2nd ed., pp. 400–426). New York: Van Nostrand Reinhold.

Salthouse, T. A. (1991). *Theoretical perspectives on cognitive aging.* Hillsdale, NJ: Erlbaum.

Schaie, K. W. (Ed.). (1983). *Longitudinal studies of adult psychological development.* New York: Guilford Press.

Schaie, K. W. (1990). Intellectual development in adulthood. In J. E. Birren & K. W. Schaie (Eds.), *Handbook of psychology and aging* (3rd ed., pp. 291–310). San Diego, CA: Academic Press.

Schulz, R. (1982). Emotionality and aging: A theoretical and empirical analysis. *Journal of Gerontology, 37*, 42–51.

Sherman, E. (1991). *Reminiscence and the self in old age.* New York: Springer.

Siegler, I. C. (1983). Psychological aspects of the Duke Longitudinal Studies. In K. W. Schaie (Ed.), *Longitudinal studies of adult psychological development* (pp. 136–190). New York: Guilford Press.

Woodruff, D. S. (1985). Arousal, sleep, and aging. In J. E. Birren & K. W. Schaie (Eds.), *Handbook of the psychology of aging* (2nd ed., pp. 261–295). New York: Van Nostrand Reinhold.

Zelinski, E. M., Gilewski, M. J., & Schaie, K. W. (1993). Individual differences in cross sectional and 3-year longitudinal memory performance across the adult life span. *Psychology and Aging, 8,* 176–186.

2

BEHAVIORAL AND COGNITIVE–BEHAVIORAL TREATMENTS: AN OVERVIEW OF SOCIAL LEARNING

ANTONETTE M. ZEISS and ANN STEFFEN

In this chapter, we present basic concepts of cognitive and cognitive–behavioral approaches to treatment. We also discuss adapting this approach to treatment, with an emphasis on responding to potential changes in the way older adults learn, because these approaches use a psychoeducational format. Next, we review data and clinical experience of using cognitive–behavioral therapy (CBT), with particular attention to anxiety and depression. Using a case example, we illustrate the CBT approach to the treatment of mixed depression and anxiety in a homebound older woman. In brief reviews, we also cover CBT for treatment of insomnia, sexual dysfunction, and problems related to dementia. Finally, we provide suggestions for further training in CBT with older adults.

Behavioral therapies and CBTs are based on theoretical approaches that emphasize lifelong learning and the optimistic belief that people can make important changes in their thoughts, feelings, and actions at any point in their lives (e.g., Bandura, 1969; Beck, Rush, Shaw, & Emery, 1979; Goldfried & Davison, 1994). These approaches recognize the influence of learning history, including early childhood experience, but do not posit critical periods that play formative roles in relation to particular issues. Similarly, behavioral therapies and CBTs do not assume that a fixed pattern of responding, thought of as character structure or personality in other approaches, develops during early experience. Rather, they emphasize the continual interaction, over the life span, of personal qualities and environmental demands (e.g., Mischel, 1968, 1973). Thus, the expression of personal style is continuously evolving, and different aspects of anyone's complex personal abilities and limitations may be apparent in different situations.

Cognitive and behavioral therapists define the term *behavior* broadly as encompassing thoughts, feelings, and actions. These three aspects of behavior are seen as being interrelated in that they reciprocally influence each other. Cognitive therapists emphasize the role of cognition in generating actions and feelings, whereas behavioral therapists emphasize the role of actions as an influence on thoughts and feelings. However, thoughtful examination shows that each of the therapies recognize and use the reciprocal interactions among thoughts, actions, and feelings.

Behavioral therapies and CBTs emphasize the relationship between the therapist and the client as being key to the progress of therapy, but not the vehicle in itself of therapeutic change. Cognitive–behavioral therapists develop a collaborative therapeutic alliance with their clients, in which the therapist and client work as colleagues. The therapist brings expertise and a nurturing, supportive stance to this alliance. The client brings expertise on his or her daily experience and personal history, particularly a recognition of personal strengths and weaknesses. The therapist and client set explicit goals together that define the purpose of their work. These goals describe how the client would like his or her behavior (i.e., thoughts, actions, feelings) to be different. To accomplish the goals, the therapist and client use interventions that will increase the client's effectiveness in order to improve affect, quality of life, personal effectiveness, or satisfaction with relationships. The interventions might focus on changing thought patterns, skills in carrying out actions, or changing emotional level (e.g., through relaxation training). The "client" in CBT might be an individual, a couple, or a family, and the therapy might be offered in individual, couples, family, or group modalities. The underlying principle nevertheless remains the same: The therapist and client work together to bring about change in the client's behavior and accomplish identified goals.

The elements that represent the core of the approach to therapy and are presumably some of the reasons for its demonstrated effectiveness are as follows: collaborative therapeutic relationship, focus on a small number of clearly specified goals, emphasis on change, psychoeducational, length of therapy contracted and linked to goals, agenda set at each meeting, and skill training (cognitive, behavioral, and interpersonal).

HISTORICAL USE OF THIS APPROACH WITH OLDER ADULTS

Carstensen (1988) reviewed the progress of behavioral therapy with older adults. The first focus for behavioral work was on nursing home residents (e.g., Blackman, Howe, & Pinkston, 1976; Hussian, 1981; McClanahan & Risley, 1974); behavioral approaches continue to be effectively used in long-term care settings. Therapeutic applications in nursing homes are discussed in chapter 10 of this book; in this chapter we focus on outpatient approaches. The history of outpatient approaches, and the history of the use of cognitive therapy strategies with older adults, is more recent. Lewinsohn and Teri contributed important early work reviewing behavioral treatment approaches, particularly in outpatient settings (Lewinsohn & Teri, 1984; Teri & Lewinsohn, 1986). Carstensen and Edelstein (1987) published what is thought to be the first handbook for clinical geropsychologists, which emphasized cognitive–behavioral approaches. There is research demonstrating the effectiveness of CBTs for the treatment of depression (e.g., Thompson, Gallagher, & Breckenridge, 1987), sexual dysfunction (e.g., R. A. Zeiss, Delmonico, Zeiss, & Dornbrand, 1991), sleep problems (e.g., Lichstein & Johnson, 1993), and tension (e.g., Scogin, Rickard, Keith, Wilson, & McElreath, 1992), and the pace of literature has expanded greatly through the late 1980s and early 1990s.

One reason for the rapid, seemingly exponential, expansion of literature on CBT is that there has not been theoretical bias against work with the elderly within this approach, unlike in some other theoretical perspectives. Because learning is seen as a lifelong process in the philosophical underpinnings of CBT, it is expected that therapy can be helpful for people of any age. As Knight (1986) stated, "By its very nature, behavior therapy is committed to a spirit of optimism about the possibility for change in older people" (p. 28).

BENEFITS OF USING THIS APPROACH WITH OLDER ADULTS

There are many reasons to advocate the use of behavioral and cognitive–behavioral interventions with individuals over the age of 60. Most important, this collection of therapies has been shown to be effective in reducing a number of behavioral, emotional, and psychosocial problems. Although there is not as rich a literature on the use of cognitive–behavioral techniques with older adults as there is with younger clients, we do not think there would be radically divergent results attributable to age differences. We believe that as the therapy outcome literature expands, an increasing number of conditions will be creatively treated with behavioral and cognitive–behavioral applications.

Although the use of cognitive–behavioral interventions has many of the same advantages with older as with younger clients, there also are some reasons why this orientation is particularly conducive to treating older adults. The collaborative stance advocated by this approach is appealing to older adults; the nature of the therapy automatically provides therapists with a number of opportunities to communicate their respect for clients' experiences and strengths. Because of the behavioral and psychoeducational features of these therapies, clients do not have to be especially "psychologically minded" in order to benefit. Similarly, clients do not necessarily have to think of themselves as being "mentally ill" or as receiving care for "mental illness" because cognitive–behavioral therapists generally emphasize a nonpathologizing approach to assessment and goal setting. Group interventions often are framed as "classes" rather than as "therapy groups." Individual interventions emphasize learning to adapt to challenges of aging rather than emphasizing treatment of a specific diagnosis.

The core features of cognitive–behavioral interventions can be tracked easily on paper, making the therapy adaptable to clients with age-related changes in memory or actual memory impairment. These time-limited approaches also are likely to be compatible with the economic concerns of most older adults and their insurance providers. Improvements often can be linked to clients' ability to remain active and independently functioning in the community (Kemp, Corgiat, & Gill, 1992).

In addition to maximizing a client's potential for involvement in treatment, cognitive–behavioral approaches take advantage of factors related to the client's natural environment or service settings. For example, the time-limited approach fits the settings in which many mental health professionals have contact with clients (e.g., hospitals, outpatient medical clinics, comprehensive senior services). The therapy techniques can be used anywhere, including at a hospital bedside, in the patient's home, or in a nursing home day room. The biopsychosocial model endorsed by most cognitive–behavioral practitioners, as well as the focus on resolving present difficulties, is compatible with the problem-solving stance of the other health care professionals involved. This provides an opportunity to identify overlap in conceptualization of problems and for professionals from different disciplines to collaborate with each other and provide better patient care (A. M. Zeiss & Steffen, in press).

In addition to improved communication and collaboration with other disciplines, this approach can improve communication in the client's family and allow the resources of family members to be used. Families often are involved in the health care of older adults (e.g., providing transportation, sitting in on medical examinations) and are sometimes the primary force behind an older adult seeking mental health care. Some therapeutic orientations view family involvement as being intrusive and as a likely contributing cause of the client's problems. By contrast, many cognitive–behavioral treatments emphasize the role of the family in serving the client, some to the extent of training family members to administer the therapy (Teri & Uomoto, 1991).

Finally, we believe that there are several features of a cognitive–behavioral orientation that are highly beneficial to those involved in training mental health professionals. One obvious advantage is the growing number of treatment manuals available to facilitate training. For example, there are manuals that detail group (Lewinsohn, Antonuccio, Steinmetz, & Teri, 1984; Yost, Beutler, Corbishley, & Allender, 1986) and individual (Beck et al., 1979; Burns, 1980; Gallagher et al., 1981; Lewinsohn, Muñoz, Youngren, & Zeiss, 1986) approaches to therapy for depression. Additional guides are available for pain management (Saxon, 1991), psychosexual dysfunction (Spence, 1991), problem drinking (Miller & Munoz, 1982), behavioral problems in patients with dementia (Teri, 1990), and anger in family caregivers of patients with dementia (Gallagher-Thompson et al., 1992). In addition, Glasgow and Rosen (1978) provided a detailed review of earlier manuals describing bibliotherapy approaches. The majority of these manuals have been developed in the context of conducting rigorous outcome studies, and they are thorough in their description of the ingredients for successful treatment. Just as important to training, however, is that time-limited approaches necessitate careful assessment and conceptualization early in the therapeutic relationship. This means that trainees are required to be clear and sure about their assessment and conceptualization strategies, something that we believe will improve the quality of mental health care available for older adults.

DISADVANTAGES OF THE APPROACH

Although we believe that there are few problems in using behavioral therapies or CBTs with older adults, there are some disadvantages worth mentioning. We are concerned that the role of specific techniques in this orientation (e.g., relaxation training, self-monitoring procedures) may increase the probability of professional misuse of the cognitive–behavioral approach. For example, poorly trained therapists may see the orientation merely as a collection of simplistic techniques to be used when convenient and omit the careful assessment, conceptualization, collaborative relationship development, and focused treatment planning that are required. Some professionals who practice from a cognitive–behavioral framework have known others who oversimplified the approach, ignored the crucial elements of establishing rapport and collaboration, or focused on clients' thoughts about an event during one session and called it *cognitive therapy*.

We hope that an increase in training opportunities for professionals will reduce this problem.

There are some older clients who may not benefit as much from cognitive–behavioral approaches. For those with little education, the psychoeducational perspective and assignments involving paperwork may be uncomfortable. Other clients may come in looking for insight-oriented or supportive psychotherapy and may be taken aback by an approach as detail oriented as CBTs.

WHAT WE DON'T KNOW

There are some limits to the known benefits of CBTs that cannot be thought of as "disadvantages" of the approach but could be considered disadvantages in trying to use the approach with complete confidence. For example, innovative service delivery systems (e.g., home-based therapies) seem to be excellent settings for cognitive–behavioral interventions, but they have not been studied formally. Most research protocols take place in traditional outpatient settings or medical center settings that may be alien or harder to access for many older adults. This means that researchers know less about serving older adults in their naturally occurring environments in the settings most comfortable for them. These setting factors may influence clients' ability to generalize skills learned in therapy to other life situations and maintain gains over a longer period of time.

For clinicians, there also is the familiar problem of applying intervention techniques used successfully in research when working in clinical settings: Multiproblem patients are excluded in research samples but are common in typical practice settings. Patients have greater cognitive problems than the research samples or more health problems, or they have less education and more limited resources. This may limit the therapist's ability to choose the most effective treatment strategies for these clients. Research settings also have used restricted age ranges of "older adults," so less is known about treating old-old (>85 years) clients. Research has rarely used ethnically or culturally diverse samples, so most support for the cognitive–behavioral approach has been obtained using White older adults.

Although these are real constraints on the strength of empirical support for CBTs, they should be kept in perspective. In particular, no other therapy approach, to our knowledge, has demonstrated effectiveness in widely generalized settings or populations. CBTs and the other approaches presented in this book need to continue adapting the basic therapeutic model to the needs of diverse elders and testing the effectiveness of those adaptations.

ADAPTATIONS FOR USE WITH OLDER ADULTS

Using CBTs with the elderly can require some adaptation of strategies with younger adults. However, chronological age is not a good marker for how much adaptation may be needed. People age at different rates according to their genetic background, childhood and adult nutrition, health habits, presence of chronic illnesses, how stimulating their environment is, and so on. A fundamental principle of aging is that, although there may be decrements in function in many abilities on average, the range of abilities in older people will be broader than the range of abilities in younger people (Fries & Crapo, 1981). For example, if we consider short-term memory function, the younger population will include people with a fairly broad range of ability, particularly if we include those with mental retardation and brain injuries. However, the average level of function will be high and a fairly large proportion of the population will function at a level close to the average performance. In older adults, the average level of function will be lower, but, more important, the distribution of scores will be much more broadly dispersed: Scores will range from extremely capable performance to the almost total absence, in older people with dementia, of ability to maintain short-term memories.

The direct clinical implication of this increased variability is that, when working with older adults, it is important not to assume that specific adaptations of CBT will be needed. Each individual in therapy will function in a unique way. The adaptations that follow therefore represent a mental checklist of adaptations that might be helpful or even necessary. Assessment of each client should include information not only on the presenting complaint, but also on cognitive strengths and deficits in order to determine which of these adaptations will be appropriate (see chapter 8 in this book for additional information on cognitive assessment).

The basics of CBTs, as discussed earlier, are not changed with older clients, even those with cognitive or physical impairments. Most of the changes that are needed in CBTs when they are adapted for the elderly are a result of the cognitive changes that can be part of normal aging or that can occur with more dramatic brain changes as a result of trauma or a dementia-related process. These changes can affect the process of learning, and because the psychoeducational component is central to both cognitive and behavioral therapies, attention to how older adults learn is vital. There is an extensive literature on cognitive changes with age (see Craik, 1994, and Verhaegen, Marcoen, & Goossens, 1993, for more detail).

Verhaegen et al. (1993) relied on meta-analytic strategies to examine age-related changes. These analyses confirmed that there are significant age decrements in short-term memory, memory span, recall of lists of information, recall of paired-associates learning, and recall of prose material.

These changes suggest that older adults in CBT might have more difficulty learning new material, particularly when they are asked to use recall memory to retrieve information discussed in sessions or to carry out assignments generated in sessions. Recognition memory is generally not as impaired; older adults also benefit from the possibility of reviewing lists or texts, particularly when they can set their own pace for review. Older adults did not show poorer ability than younger adults in semantic processing, strategies for making associations, imagery, or extracting main points from prose material.

These results suggest relatively straightforward adaptations of therapy procedures designed to enhance memory and therefore skill acquisition. These are summarized in Table 1.

In addition, some changes in therapy need to be made to respond to the relative strengths of older adults. These strengths can be thought of as wisdom (Baltes & Staudinger, 1993; Baltes, Staudinger, Maercker, & Smith, 1995), which is an age-related but not inevitable consequence of life experience. Even clients who might not meet criteria for wisdom have faced many difficult life challenges and have coped with a diversity of difficult experiences. Most older adults can abstract helpful information from those experiences and describe personal skills that have helped them handle adversity. Showing respect for the client and his or her accumulated experience can enhance therapy. Ways that such an approach lead to modifications in the cognitive–behavioral approach also are shown in Table 1.

There are few major content differences in therapy with older than younger adults. One important area is that older adults have more health problems, and their psychological status is therefore closely bound to their physical status (A. M. Zeiss, Lewinsohn, & Rohde, in press). In addition, older adults may face obstacles in terms of resources for supporting an adequate quality of life. They may have limited financial resources or transportation, or they may be experiencing the loss (through death, illness, or

TABLE 1
Adaptations of Cognitive–Behavioral Therapy With Older Adults

Adaptations to cognitive deficits in older adults	Qualities representing relative strengths of older adults
Slower pacing of material	Right to be respected
Multimodal training (say it, show it, do it)	Patient's knowledge of personal strengths
Memory aids (tapes, written assignments, notebooks)	Experience of handling past problems
Strategies for staying on track in session	Wisdom
Planning for generalization of training	

moves) of friends and family. The problems older adults face are not all appropriate targets for CBT, but they may be important targets for the services of other health care professionals, such as geriatricians, social workers, and occupational therapists. Thus, CBT with the elderly often is part of a comprehensive, interdisciplinary treatment plan (see chapter 9 in this book; A. M. Zeiss & Steffen, in press).

The changes due to cognitive deficits, strengths of the elderly, and the intrinsically interdisciplinary nature of work with older adults are summarized in the mnemonic MICKS to help therapists remember the key adaptations of CBT that should be considered with each older client: (a) use multimodal teaching, (b) maintain interdisciplinary awareness, (c) present information more clearly, (d) develop knowledge of aging challenges and strengths, and (e) present therapy material more slowly.

APPLICATIONS OF BEHAVIORAL AND COGNITIVE–BEHAVIORAL APPROACHES

In the following section, we describe the literature on cognitive–behavioral approaches with older adults and provide more detailed examples of the use of some of these treatments in clinical practice. Depression is discussed in the most detail because of the attention it has received from researchers, but we also discuss the treatment of anxiety, insomnia, sexual dysfunction, and problems secondary to dementia. Because we want to highlight recent additions to the literature, we focus on studies published since Carstensen's (1988) review of the field of behavioral gerontology. Case examples are used to illustrate the cognitive–behavioral techniques described.

Depression

If one decides to work with a depressed older client in individual psychotherapy, there are several options that have demonstrated efficacy. There is evidence that either a behavioral approach, a cognitive approach, or an approach combining the two can be effective. There also is some limited evidence to suggest that combining CBT with antidepressant medication may be more effective than either CBT alone or medication alone (Thompson, Gallagher, Hanser, Gantz, & Steffen, 1991). Decisions on the combination of cognitive, behavioral, and pharmacotherapy elements are made on a case-by-case basis.

Behavioral approaches typically include assessing the client's daily activities and participation in meaningful events, using daily self-monitoring to establish that events are mood related, and helping the client change the frequency of key activities and events. The Daily Mood Rating Form (see Figure 1) is often used as a simple way for clients to track mood on a daily basis, using a 9-point scale (1 = *very depressed*, 9 = *very happy*). The form also encourages clients to begin developing hypotheses for events and experiences that are mood related. Later in treatment, it can be used to evaluate the impact of specific changes that the client is making in frequency of pleasant events. Along with this form, the Older Person's Pleasant Events Schedule (Teri & Lewinsohn, 1986) is used to obtain the frequency and pleasure of engaging in a variety of activities. The client is

Daily Mood Rating Form

Please rate your mood for each day (i.e., how good or bad you felt) using the 9-point scale shown below. If you felt good, put a high number on the chart below. If you felt "so-so," mark it a 5. And if you felt low or depressed, mark a lower number.

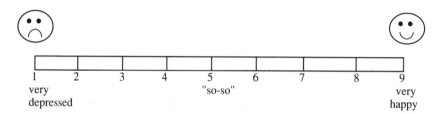

On the two lines next to your mood rating for each day, please briefly give two major reasons why you think you felt that way. Try to be as specific as possible.

Date	Mood Score	Why I Think I Felt This Way
		1. 2.
		1. 2.
		1. 2.
		1. 2.
		1. 2.
		1. 2.
		1. 2.

Figure 1. The daily mood rating form.

asked to go through a list of 66 items and indicate how often the event occurred in the past month and how enjoyable it was. By identifying categories of activities (e.g., nature activities, social interactions, and provision of help to others) in which pleasure ratings are high but rates of engagement are low, the therapist and client can begin to identify areas that would be appropriate for intervention. Over the course of treatment, the client monitors frequency of involvement in specific activities that are closely linked to mood for that individual.

The therapist and the client also may focus on enhancing other skills that are related to the client's ability to enjoy specific activities (i.e., problem-solving or social skills, relaxation training, and pain management). On the other hand, the therapist may decide to use cognitive approaches that focus on clients' self-talk and negative interpretations of life events. In cognitive therapy, the therapist would assist a client in identifying thought patterns that are likely to result in a depressed mood. The client becomes skilled in identifying and labeling negative distortions and then substituting these thoughts with more adaptive cognitions. Dysfunctional thought records (Beck et al., 1979) are used in this process to help the client see the link between events, thoughts, and feelings and to identify specific patterns of cognitive distortions (e.g., all-or-nothing thinking, mind reading, jumping to conclusions). Several versions of dysfunctional thought records often are used, ranging from three columns for early in therapy (e.g., event, automatic or unhelpful thoughts, and emotions) to five-column versions for later in the treatment process.

Does this work? The best known work on the effectiveness of brief, problem-focused individual psychotherapy was done by Thompson and Gallagher-Thompson. In their first outcome study (Thompson et al., 1987), they compared brief behavioral, cognitive, and dynamic therapies; all three were shown to be equally effective and superior to a waiting-list control group. Almost all patients who reached full remission of depression at the end of therapy maintained their gains throughout a 2-year follow-up period (Gallagher-Thompson, Hanley-Peterson, & Thompson, 1990). In their second study, they compared CBT with desipramine, showing a roughly equivalent impact of both interventions (Thompson et al., 1991).

The therapist also could decide to use bibliotherapy and encourage his or her client to read specific materials designed and tested to be effective in managing depression. Two excellent choices are *Control Your Depression* (Lewinsohn et al., 1986), for a behavioral approach, or *Feeling Good* (Burns, 1980), for a more cognitive approach. The client can be instructed to read and do the included assignments as a component of individual psychotherapy or as a stand-alone intervention in which the therapist contacts the participant weekly by telephone to determine progress and answer questions about the reading material. This approach has been demonstrated to be effective for mildly and moderately depressed older adults (Scogin,

Jamison, & Gochneaur, 1989); gains from bibliotherapy also were maintained at a 2-year follow-up (Scogin, Jamison, & Davis, 1990).

In contrast to individual therapy, the therapist has the option of conducting CBT in a group setting. Interventions are similar to those already described for individual therapy, but participants have the added benefit of hearing others describe their successes and responses to treatment. Yost et al. (1986) provided a detailed manual for group CBT with depressed older adults, and Beutler et al. (1987) demonstrated the positive results of cognitive–behavioral group therapy in contrast to pharmacological treatment alone or placebo. Using the approach developed by Yost et al. (1986), Kemp et al. (1992) demonstrated the efficacy of 12 weeks of group therapy for older adults with and without chronically disabling illnesses; these gains were maintained at a 6-month follow-up.

Anxiety Disorders

Sheikh (1996) commented on the surprising lack of psychological treatments for anxiety in the elderly given the rich literature on cognitive–behavioral treatments of anxiety in younger populations. In addition to case reports, there is a discussion by King and Barrowclough (1991) of a pilot study of CBT for anxiety disorders in the elderly. The average client was 73 years old and had shown no improvement from prior treatment with benzodiazepines or antidepressants. After an intervention averaging eight sessions, 9 of the 10 patients showed a decrease in symptoms after intervention. King and Barrowclough also provided two case illustrations and described the use of flash cards for patients to review anxious thoughts and counteracting reassuring thoughts outside the session. Using a different approach, Scogin et al. (1992) reported on the effectiveness of progressive muscle relaxation training and imagery for elders with anxiety problems. Progressive muscle relaxation and imagining muscle relaxation appear to be equally effective; results were maintained at a 1-year follow-up (Rickard, Scogin, & Keith, 1994).

Treating Depression and Anxiety: An In-Depth Case Example

So what might a combination of behavioral and cognitive approaches look like in clinical practice? We offer the following case example of A.T. to demonstrate some of the core features of a brief therapy for depression and anxiety using behavioral and cognitive approaches (e.g., self-monitoring, increasing pleasant events, relaxation training, and cognitive restructuring). We also emphasize some of the special problems of older adults and the way in which CBT needs to be adapted to be maximally beneficial to older clients.

A.T. was a 67-year-old woman with chronic obstructive pulmonary disease (emphysema) who was seen in her home by a psychologist working with a hospital-based home care team. The client initially presented with severe depression and suicidal ideation. SCL-90 scores were elevated on the Depression, Somatization, Obsessive–Compulsive, Anxiety, and Phobic Anxiety subscales. Beck Depression Inventory (BDI) and Geriatric Depression Scale (GDS) scores were comparably elevated. Her Folstein Mini-Mental Examination showed no cognitive impairment (30/30). She was using several bronchodilator medications, including one containing a corticosteroid, but she was not on direct oxygen.

A.T. was widowed and had two daughters and two sons; three of the children lived within an hour's drive. She had eight grandchildren, five of whom lived nearby. She had worked for a university extension program when she was in her late 40s and early 50s, helping to set up classes, manage enrollment, photocopy course materials, and so on. She left work at age 55, primarily because of worsening health. When she began CBT, she spent most of her days at home sitting in the living room; she read, watched TV, dozed, and occasionally made a telephone call. Her best days occurred when her children or grandchildren came to visit. At those times, she would fix special foods for them, play board games, and sit outside on her patio. However, most of the time she complained of shortness of breath at any exertion or just the thought of exertion. Her physician and nurse practitioner believed her illness to be real but that many of her symptoms represented excess disability (Roberts, 1986).

A.T. was receptive to the therapist, primarily because she appreciated the company. She expressed considerable skepticism that therapy could be of benefit to her. She had previously had an extended trial on tricyclic antidepressant medication, with no obvious benefit. Goals defined in the first phase of therapy were to (a) improve daily mood, (b) reduce episodes of breathing distress triggered by anxiety and depression, and (c) increase her sense of control and self-efficacy regarding her ability to be involved in meaningful activities.

Interventions involved both behavioral and cognitive components. A.T. filled out a Pleasant Events Schedule (Teri & Lewinsohn, 1986), which indicated an average amount of perceived possible pleasure for a wide range of activities but a low frequency of engagement for almost all of them. She also began consistently filling out a daily mood rating using the form shown in Figure 1. Her mood initially varied from 2 to 5, which is clearly in the depressed range. The client also developed a form for the daily tracking of pleasant activities, but she initially expressed grave doubts that this would be worthwhile. On her Daily Mood Records she strongly endorsed the opinion that her mood was determined by her physical condition, specifically her breathing difficulties. Furthermore, she argued that variability in her breathing difficulties was determined by variation in air quality; thus, she could have no control over her mood.

This opinion was accepted as potentially valid and worth testing. Therefore, in addition to tracking her daily moods, the therapist agreed to note the air quality index each day from the local paper. After 2 weeks, graphs comparing mood, activity, and air quality index were generated. These graphs showed little relationship between air quality and the client's mood but a strong relationship between mood and activity (see Figure 2). The client was encouraged to draw her own conclusions and to suggest what the data implied regarding the next steps to take. She was able to do this, which resulted in an enhanced therapeutic alliance and motivation on her part to use the therapy suggestions.

A.T.'s next concern was the belief that, although she felt better when good things happened, she had little control over making them happen. She also believed that she was so limited by her disease that there were few possible activities she could increase. Cognitive interventions were used to encourage her to challenge all-or-none thinking and selective attention to negatives. A five-column dysfunctional thought record was used to help A.T. clarify her negative thoughts and to learn to challenge them. This format is shown in Table 2 and contains examples from A.T. The dysfunctional thought record was helpful in reminding A.T. about the ideas

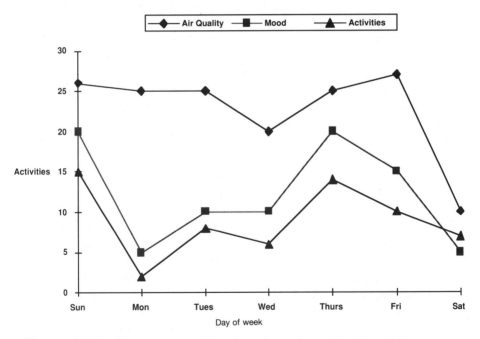

Figure 2. Relationships among activities, air quality, and mood for Client A.T.

TABLE 2
Daily Record of Dysfunctional Thoughts

Describe the event that led to your unpleasant emotions	What are your negative thoughts? Identify your unhelpful thought patterns. How strongly do you believe in these thoughts, from 0% to 100%?	What are you feeling? (sad, angry, anxious, etc.) How strong are these emotions, from 0% to 100%?	Challenge your negative thoughts and replace them with more helpful ones. How strongly do you believe in these thoughts?	Now, how strongly do you believe in your negative beliefs, from 0% to 100%? What emotions are you feeling now? Rate them from 0% to 100%
Date: Wednesday morning (6/8): Daughter called to say that she and grandkids couldn't make it over today	"My day is ruined. I might as well stay in bed because I don't feel up to doing anything on my own. They don't like to visit because I am a boring invalid." Belief: 80% Patterns: magnification, jumping to conclusions, emotional reasoning, mislabeling	Depressed, 75% Frustrated, 80% Irritated, 65%	"It is not their fault that their car needs to be fixed. We had a good time last weekend, so they are probably looking forward to coming soon. Just because my plans have changed doesn't mean that my day is ruined. I can work on the family tree on the computer."	Depressed, 30% Frustrated, 25% Irritated, 10% Determined, 80% Hopeful, 75%

Note. Ratings for intensity: 0% = *not at all*, 100% = *completely.*

discussed in the cognitive approach to therapy and how to repeat the process of identifying and challenging thoughts on her own.

A.T. was encouraged to think about ways to adapt formerly enjoyed activities in accordance with the realities of her health rather than abandoning activities altogether. For example, she was encouraged to set up a large planter box outside her living room window to hold her favorite flowers. She was able to do the gardening for this planter, although she could no longer keep up with her whole yard. She was encouraged to hire a gardener and accept offers of help from her family to keep the rest of the yard looking good so that she could still enjoy seeing it. Her family was delighted to be involved and set up a gardening day as her next mother's day present.

A.T. had used computers at work and was interested in continuing to use them, particularly as a way to record memories and write a family history. However, when she ran into any problem on her home computer, she became anxious and frustrated, which led to increased breathing difficulties and task abandonment. Relaxation training was used to provide a self-control skill for handling anxiety, enabling her to spend longer, more productive periods at the computer. After some time, she was able to work without stress, and she became a consultant to older friends who wanted to use the computer but were experiencing anxiety similar to her initial levels. She and her grandchildren also shared the role of family computer experts and enjoyed computer games together.

At the end of 20 sessions, A.T.'s depression and anxiety scores had significantly declined; these improvements were maintained at a 4-month follow-up. All subscales of the SCL-90 were in the normal range (see Figure 3). Beck Depression Inventory and Geriatric Depression Scale scores were similarly improved.

Discussion of Case Example

One can see in this vignette a number of behavioral and cognitive strategies for treating depression and anxiety. First and foremost was a careful assessment and conceptualization of the problem that was based heavily on the use of self-monitoring strategies. On the behavioral side, the client and therapist worked together to collect data on the relation between mood and key events and then developed goals and strategies for changing the client's range of pleasurable activities. This included relaxation training to reduce anxiety and frustration generated by computer-related problems. On the cognitive side of the approach, daily thought records were used to identify depression-producing thoughts. The client was then provided the skills needed to control and change these cognitions (e.g., identify the distortion, replace it with more adaptive thoughts, and then challenge beliefs about aging). The case example also demonstrates the tremendous

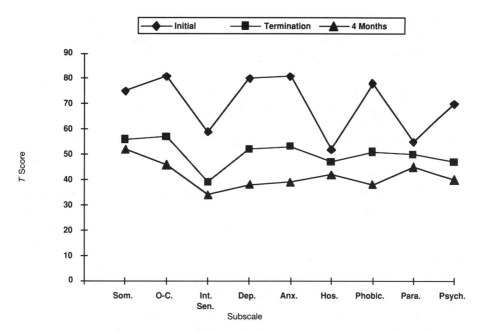

Figure 3. SCL-90-R scores for initial assessment, termination, and 4-month follow-up for Client A.T. Som. = Somatization; O-C = Obsessive–Compulsive; Int. Sen. = Interpersonal Sensitivity; Dep. = Depression; Anx. = Anxiety; Hos. = Hostility; Phobic = Phobic Anxiety; Para. = Paranoid Ideation; Psych. = Psychotism.

freedom that client and therapist have to creatively design a treatment strategy that takes advantage of the client's strengths and interests. We now discuss treatments for several other problems common in older adults.

Insomnia

Insomnia is a common problem for older adults, with sleep-maintenance insomnia being an age-related and debilitating condition (Bootzin, Engle-Friedman, & Hazelwood, 1983). In sleep-maintenance insomnia, affected individuals are typically awake for periods in the middle of the night. The next day, these insomniacs typically stay in bed in the morning to maximize hours of sleep or take naps during the day. This results in increasingly more time in bed in order to achieve a certain amount of sleep over a 24-hr period. Fortunately, the research literature on sleep-maintenance insomnia in older adults provides some excellent examples of empirically validated treatments.

On the basis of the research literature, we suggest a combination of education, sleep restrictions, and stimulus-control interventions. In sleep education, the therapist teaches the client about age-related changes in sleep; the effects of caffeine, nicotine, alcohol, sleeping aids, exercise, and nutrition; and the minimal effects of sleep deprivation for most people.

This latter information often serves to reduce the anxiety and catastrophising that accompanies insomnia. Clients also should be instructed to eliminate naps during the day and to use a specific bedtime and wake-up time (i.e., time-in-bed restrictions) on the basis of the number of hours of sleep they are currently getting. For example, a client typically goes to bed at 11:00 p.m. and has disrupted sleep during the night and then gets out of bed at 7:00 a.m. Using a daily sleep log for a week, the therapist and client determine that the client is actually sleeping an average of 5 hr a night. In the beginning of treatment, the therapist would suggest that the client go to bed at midnight and get out of bed at 5:00 a.m. As the client's sleep efficiency improves (i.e., less time awake during the night), her bedtime and wake-up time can be adjusted to permit more sleep. Stimulus-control procedures also are important; these include instructing the client to use the bed primarily for sleeping (e.g., no reading, relaxing, or watching TV in bed), leave the bed if awake for more than 30 min, and go to bed only when sleepy. For some clients, a cognitive therapy component adapted to insomnia also may be added. This would assist clients in (a) identifying their own dysfunctional thoughts; (b) challenging these maladaptive beliefs and attitudes about sleep and the impact of sleep loss on their daytime functioning; and (c) replacing these thoughts with more realistic alternatives.

Two research groups in particular have focused on sleep maintenance problems in older adults and have demonstrated the efficacy of the approaches just described: Hoelscher and colleagues (Edinger, Hoelscher, Marsh, Lipper, & Ionescu-Pioggia, 1992; Hoelscher & Edinger, 1988) and Morin and colleagues (Morin & Azrin, 1988; Morin, Kowatch, Barry, & Walton, 1993). Those investigators found that a combination of educational and stimulus-control procedures appears to work better than relaxation training or imagery training. Although some questions remain about the critical ingredients of the approach (i.e., Which components are essential for change?), we believe that these procedures have been proved effective and are ready for use in clinical settings.

Sexual Dysfunctions

The incidence of sexual dysfunction has been found to increase with age for both men and women (Mulligan, Retchin, Chinchilli, & Bettinger, 1988), mostly because of an increase in chronic health problems. Spence (1992) discussed the influences on sexual functioning that are relevant to older adults and outlined assessment and treatment options from a behavioral perspective.

For nondysfunctional adults, performance anxiety can be prevented through educating older adults about age-related changes in sexual behavior and anatomy (Masters & Johnson, 1970). As is true for other types of problems, therapeutic methods are similar for older and younger clients. It has been suggested that clinicians should use an individually tailored intervention that focuses on a combination of the following elements: increasing sexual knowledge, reducing sexual anxiety, changing maladaptive attitudes and beliefs about sexuality, enhancing the general quality of the relationship with the partner as well as improving communication skills during sexual encounters, and improving sexual techniques (Spence, 1991). This includes helping the couple expand the range of sexual activities that they find acceptable and pleasurable and that also meet physical limitations experienced by either partner.

However, there are few treatment–outcome studies in the area of sex therapy with older adults. The majority of the published accounts are case studies (Renshaw, 1988; Whitlach & Zarit, 1988) and descriptive research. For example, A. M. Zeiss, Zeiss, and Dornbrand (1992) examined outcomes in a sexual dysfunction clinic serving older adults, primarily older men with erection difficulties. In the clinic, an interdisciplinary approach was used that combined medical and psychosocial interventions. R. A. Zeiss et al. (1991) also presented data on the effectiveness of this approach for older men with psychiatric as well as medical problems related to sexual dysfunction.

In *Prime Time: Sexual Health for Men Over Fifty*, Schover (1984) provided an easy-to-follow discussion of common age-related changes in sexual functioning and treatment for sexual problems in men. Schover and Jensen (1988) also discussed a variety of training issues in an excellent book on sexuality and chronic illness. Key therapeutic skills in sex therapy with older adults include the ability to conduct a careful psychosexual assessment, work with the client to generate realistic therapy goals and acceptable treatment strategies, and respect therapist–client differences in attitudes toward specific sexual practices. Stone (1987) outlined possible difficulties and solutions in sex therapy with older clients, including problems in compliance with some between-sessions assignments (e.g., older women being uncomfortable with self-stimulation methods for treating female orgasmic dysfunction).

Dementia

Fisher and Carstensen (1990) reviewed the literature on behavioral assessment and treatment for dementia-related behavioral problems. They provided a good summary of stimulus-control techniques for wandering, inappropriate sexual behavior, incontinence, eating and self-feeding, grooming, and depression in patients with dementia. Less is known about the use of reinforcers with such patients. Teri (1990) created an excellent videotaped instructional series and handbook for formal and informal caregivers to use in managing behavioral problems in patients with dementia.

Titled "Managing and Understanding Behavior Problems in Alzheimer's Disease and Related Disorders," this program discusses the process of identifying the behavioral antecedents and consequences (ABCs) of specific difficult behaviors (e.g., wandering, depression, incontinence) in patients with dementia. Caregivers then are provided with the skills needed to modify the patients' environments in order to reduce the frequency of the problem behaviors. This series could be used by individual caregivers in their homes, within the context of individual or group therapy for caregiver distress and depression, or with paid caregivers (e.g., nurses, nursing assistants, and physical therapists) in long-term care settings. Pinkston, Linsk, and Young (1988) also outlined a program to train family members to use behavioral methods to manage behavior problems in patients with dementia.

Depression is a common problem in patients with dementia. Although we have already discussed brief psychotherapy for depression, we want to point out treatments that are specific to depressed patients with progressive memory loss. Teri and Gallagher-Thompson (1991) outlined cognitive and behavioral strategies for treating depression in patients with Alzheimer's disease. One approach uses a cognitive emphasis to treat patients with mild dementia, and a second approach uses a behavioral emphasis for adults with moderate and severe dementia. Especially helpful is a table in the text outlining the differences between cognitive and behavioral strategies for treating dysphoria, psychomotor retardation, agitation, complaints, concentration problems, loss of interest of pleasure, feelings of worthlessness, appetite and weight change, and sleep disturbances (Teri & Gallagher-Thompson, 1991). For example, a cognitive approach to addressing feelings of worthlessness is described in which negative thoughts are identified and challenged using daily thought records, with a focus on the patient's use of "should" rules. On the other hand, the behavioral approach to the same problem encourages the patient to reminisce about past and current pleasant activities.

In another article providing more clinical detail of the behavioral approach, Teri and Uomoto (1991) discussed training caregivers to manage depression in patients with dementia using behavioral strategies. Caregivers were instructed to track their relative's mood and the duration and frequency of pleasant activities. Caregivers then were taught how to increase pleasant activities for the patient and decrease the behavioral disturbances that interfered with the activities. This approach has been highly effective in treating patients with dementia and also seems to have an impact on caregivers' mood and well-being.

The issue of anger in family caregivers of patients with dementia has just recently been addressed. DeVries and Gallagher-Thompson (1993) described a brief group treatment of anger in caregivers that combines cognitive (identifying negative thoughts using daily thought records, challenging the thoughts and replacing them with more adaptive cognitions) and behavioral (relaxation and assertion training) strategies. This approach has been shown to decrease caregivers' anger and depression ratings and to increase their sense of self-efficacy as a caregiver (Steffen, Gallagher-Thompson, Willis-Shore, & Zeiss, 1994).

SUMMARY AND SUGGESTIONS FOR FURTHER TRAINING

In this chapter we have outlined the treatment of problems in older adults using a cognitive–behavioral perspective. This approach acknowledges a biopsychosocial model of mental health problems while emphasizing the role of learning in behavior change (including changes in affect, thoughts, and overt behaviors). Although there are many similarities in the application of these techniques with older adults and younger adults, some modifications for older clients were proposed in this chapter to respond to differences in learning styles, the rates of sensory deficits, and chronic health problems and to capitalize on the life experience and wisdom of older adults. We also noted that most older adults appear to be well suited to psychoeducational methods that emphasize the following: a collaborative relationship between client and therapist, explicit goal setting, and acknowledgment of the client's personal strengths.

In addition to offering a general introduction to CBT with older clients, we presented an overview of therapy methods and outcomes for a variety of problems (i.e., depression, anxiety, insomnia, sexual dysfunction, and dementia). This was not meant to be a comprehensive review. Rather, the overview was intended to stimulate interest in a variety of "packaged" applications while acknowledging the importance of individualized assessment and treatment.

Obviously, one book chapter cannot provide all of the training needed to acquire new skills as a therapist. How can therapists improve their ability to use a cognitive–behavioral approach with older clients? The Association for the Advancement of Behavior Therapy (AABT) is the professional association most closely aligned with the development and evaluation of cognitive–behavioral methods. The AABT's annual convention includes training workshops and other opportunities to meet professionals who are heavily involved in therapist training. In particular, the aging interest group of the AABT includes members who use CBTs to meet the needs of older adults. Some members of this interest group may be available in one's area; they may provide local training workshops or be willing to establish a supervisory relationship. Information on members is listed by geographic location in the association membership directory. In addition, there are often workshops held at the American Psychological

Association's annual convention on cognitive–behavioral approaches with the elderly, as well as training offered regionally by the American Psychological Association.

Regardless of the extent of one's current work with older people, we hope that this chapter will increase or renew excitement in the possibilities of clinical work with this population. The increased variability associated with aging means that older clients will all be interesting in some way and often much different from each other. It is this combination of varied experiences and attitudes that we love so much in our work with the elderly, and we hope that therapists have the opportunity to experience it for themselves.

REFERENCES

Baltes, P. B., & Staudinger, U. M. (1993). The search for a psychology of wisdom. *Current Directions in Psychological Science, 2*, 75–80.

Baltes, P. B., Staudinger, U. M., Maercker, A., & Smith, J. (1995). People nominated as wise: A comparative study of wisdom-related knowledge. *Psychology and Aging, 10*, 155–166.

Bandura, A. (1969). *Principles of behavior modification.* New York: Holt, Rinehart & Winston.

Beck, A. T., Rush, A. J., Shaw, B. F., & Emery, G. (1979). *Cognitive therapy of depression.* New York: Guilford Press.

Beutler, L. E., Scogin, F., Kirkish, P., Schretlen, D., Corbishley, A., Hamblin, D., Meredith, K., Potter, R., Bamford, C. R., & Levenson, A. I. (1987). Group cognitive therapy and alprazolam in the treatment of depression in older adults. *Journal of Consulting and Clinical Psychology, 55*, 550–556.

Blackman, D. K., Howe, M., & Pinkston, E. M. (1976). Increasing participation in social interactions of the institutionalized elderly. *The Gerontologist, 16*, 69–76.

Bootzin, R. R., Engle-Friedman, M., & Hazelwood, L. (1983). Insomnia. In P. M. Lewinsohn & L. Teri (Eds.), *Clinical geropsychology: New directions in assessment and treatment* (pp. 81–115). Elmsford, NY: Pergamon Press.

Burns, D. (1980). *Feeling good.* New York: Guilford Press.

Carstensen, L. L. (1988). The emerging field of behavioral gerontology. *Behavior Therapy, 19*, 259–281.

Carstensen, L. L., & Edelstein, B. A. (1987). *Handbook of clinical gerontology.* Elmsford, NY: Pergamon Press.

Craik, F. I. M. (1994). Memory changes in normal aging. *Current Directions in Psychological Science, 3*, 155–158.

DeVries, H., & Gallagher-Thompson, D. (1993). Cognitive–behavioral therapy and the aging caregiver. *Clinical Gerontologist, 13,* 53–57.

Edinger, J. D., Hoelscher, T. J., Marsh, G. R., Lipper, S., & Ionescu-Pioggia, M. (1992). A cognitive–behavioral therapy for sleep-maintenance insomnia in older adults. *Psychology and Aging, 7,* 282–289.

Fisher, J. E., & Carstensen, L. L. (1990). Behavior management of the dementias. *Clinical Psychology Review, 10,* 611–629.

Fries, J. F., & Crapo, L. M. (1981). *Vitality and aging.* New York: Freeman.

Gallagher, D., Thompson, L., Baffa, G., Piatt, C., Ringering, L., & Stone, V. (1981). *Depression in the elderly: A behavioral treatment manual.* Los Angeles: University of Southern California Press.

Gallagher-Thompson, D., Hanley-Peterson, P., & Thompson, L. W. (1990). Maintenance of gains versus relapse following brief psychotherapy for depression. *Journal of Consulting and Clinical Psychology, 58,* 371–374.

Gallagher-Thompson, D., Rose, J., Florsheim, M., Jacome, P., DelMaestro, S., Peters, L., Gantz, F., Arguello, D., Johnson, C., Moorehead, R. S., Polich, T. M., Chesney, M., & Thompson, L. W. (1992). *Controlling your frustration: A class for caregivers.* Palo Alto, CA: Department of Veterans Affairs Medical Center.

Glasgow, R. E., & Rosen, G. M. (1978). Behavioral bibliotherapy: A review of self-help behavior therapy manuals. *Psychological Bulletin, 85,* 1–23.

Goldfried, M. R., & Davison, G. C. (1994). *Clinical behavior therapy.* New York: Wiley.

Hoelscher, R. J., & Edinger, J. D. (1988). Treatment of sleep-maintenance insomnia in older adults: Sleep period reduction, sleep education, and modified stimulus control. *Psychology and Aging, 3,* 258–263.

Hussian, R. A. (1981). *Geriatric psychology: A behavioral perspective.* New York: Van Nostrand Reinhold.

Kemp, B., Corgiat, M., & Gill, C. (1992). Effects of brief cognitive–behavioral group psychotherapy on older persons with and without disabling illness. *Behavior, Health, and Aging, 2,* 21–28.

King, P., & Barrowclough, C. (1991). A clinical pilot study of cognitive–behavioural therapy for anxiety disorders in the elderly. *Behavioural Psychotherapy, 19,* 337–345.

Knight, B. (1986). *Psychotherapy with older adults.* Newbury Park, CA: Sage.

Lewinsohn, P. M., Antonuccio, D. O., Steinmetz, J. L., & Teri, L. (1984). *The coping with depression course: A psychoeducational intervention for unipolar depression.* Eugene, OR: Castalia.

Lewinsohn, P., Muñoz, R., Youngren, M., & Zeiss, A. (1986). *Control your depression.* Englewood Cliffs, NJ: Prentice Hall.

Lewinsohn, P. M., & Teri, L. (1984). *Clinical geropsychology: New directions in assessment and treatment.* Elmsford, NY: Pergamon Press.

Lichstein, K. L., & Johnson, R. S. (1993). Relaxation for insomnia and hypnotic medication use in older women. *Psychology and Aging, 8*, 103–111.

Masters, W. H., & Johnson, V. E. (1970). *Human sexual inadequacy*. Boston: Little, Brown.

McClanahan, L. E., & Risley, T. R. (1974). Design of living environments for nursing home residents: Recruiting attendance at activities. *The Gerontologist, 14*, 236–240.

Miller, W. R., & Munoz, R. F. (1982). *How to control your drinking*. Albuquerque: New Mexico Press.

Mischel, W. (1968). *Personality and assessment*. New York: Wiley.

Mischel, W. (1973). Towards a cognitive social learning reconceptualization of personality. *Psychological Review, 80*, 252–283.

Morin, C. M., & Azrin, N. H. (1988). Behavioral and cognitive treatments of geriatric insomnia. *Journal of Consulting and Clinical Psychology, 56*, 748–753.

Morin, C. M., Kowatch, R. A., Barry, T., & Walton, E. (1993). Cognitive–behavior therapy for late-life insomnia. *Journal of Consulting and Clinical Psychology, 61*, 137–146.

Mulligan, T., Retchin, S. M., Chinchilli, V. M., & Bettinger, C. B. (1988). The role of aging and chronic disease in sexual dysfunction. *Journal of the American Geriatrics Society, 36*, 520–524.

Pinkston, E. M., Linsk, N. L., & Young, R. N. (1988). Home-based behavioral family treatment of the impaired elderly. *Behavior Therapy, 19*, 331–344.

Renshaw, D. C. (1988). Sexual problems in later life: A case of impotence. *Clinical Gerontologist, 8*, 73–76.

Rickard, H., Scogin, F., & Keith, S. (1994). A one-year follow-up of relaxation training for elders with subjective anxiety. *Gerontologist, 34*, 121–122.

Roberts, A. H. (1986). Excess disability in the elderly: Exercise management. In L. Teri & P. M. Lewinsohn (Eds.), *Geropsychological assessment and treatment* (pp. 87–119). New York: Springer.

Saxon, S. V. (1991). *Pain management techniques for older adults*. Springfield, IL: Charles C Thomas.

Schover, L. (1984). *Prime time: Sexual health for men over fifty*. New York: Holt, Rinehart & Winston.

Schover, L., & Jensen, S. B. (1988). *Sexuality and chronic illness: A comprehensive approach*. New York: Guilford Press.

Scogin, F., Jamison, C., & Davis, N. (1990). Two-year follow-up of bibliotherapy for depression in older adults. *Journal of Consulting and Clinical Psychology, 58*, 665–667.

Scogin, F., Jamison, C., & Gochneaur, K. (1989). Comparative efficacy of cognitive and behavioral bibliotherapy for mildly and moderately depressed older adults. *Journal of Consulting and Clinical Psychology, 57*, 403–407.

Scogin, F., Rickard, H. C., Keith, S., Wilson, J., & McElreath, L. (1992). Progressive and imaginal relaxation training for elderly persons with subjective anxiety. *Psychology and Aging, 7*, 419–424.

Sheikh, J. (1996). Anxiety disorders. In J. Sheikh (Ed.), *Treating the elderly* (pp. 75–103). San Francisco: Jossey-Bass.

Spence, S. H. (1991). *Psychosexual therapy: A cognitive–behavioural approach.* London: Chapman & Hall.

Spence, S. H. (1992). Psychosexual dysfunction in the elderly. *Behavior Change, 9,* 55–64.

Steffen, A., Gallagher-Thompson, D., Willis-Shore, J., & Zeiss, A. (1994, August). *Self-efficacy for caregiving: Psychoeducational interventions with dementia family caregivers.* Poster presented at the 102nd Annual Convention of the American Psychological Association, Los Angeles.

Stone, J. D. (1987). Marital and sexual counseling of elderly couples. In G. R. Weeks & L. Hof (Eds.), *Integrating sex and marital therapy: A clinical guide* (pp. 221–244). New York: Brunner/Mazel.

Teri, L. (1990). *Managing and understanding behavior problems in Alzheimer's disease and related disorders.* Seattle: University of Washington Press.

Teri, L., & Gallagher-Thompson, D. (1991). Cognitive-behavioral interventions for treatment of depression in Alzheimer's patients. *The Gerontologist, 31,* 413–416.

Teri, L., & Lewinsohn, P. M. (1986). *Geropsychological assessment and treatment.* New York: Springer.

Teri, L., & Uomoto, J. M. (1991). Reducing excess disability in dementia patients: Training caregivers to manage patient depression. *Clinical Gerontologist, 10,* 49–63.

Thompson, L. W., Gallagher, D., & Breckenridge, J. S. (1987). Comparative effectiveness of psychotherapies for depressed elders. *Journal of Consulting and Clinical Psychology, 55,* 385–390.

Thompson, L. W., Gallagher, D., Hanser, S., Gantz, F., & Steffen, A. (1991, November). *Comparison of desipramine and cognitive/behavioral therapy in the treatment of late-life depression.* Paper presented at the meeting of Gerontological Society of America, San Francisco.

Verhaegen, P., Marcoen, A., & Goossens, L. (1993). Facts and fiction about memory aging: A quantitative integration of research findings. *Journal of Gerontology: Psychological Sciences, 48,* P157–P171.

Whitlach, C. J., & Zarit, S. H. (1988). Sexual dysfunction in an aged married couple: A case study of behavioural intervention. *Clinical Gerontologist, 8,* 43–62.

Yost, E. G., Beutler, L. E., Corbishley, A. M., & Allender, J. R. (1986). *Group cognitive therapy: A treatment approach for depressed older adults.* Elmsford, NY: Pergamon Press.

Zeiss, A. M., Lewinsohn, P. M., & Rohde, P. (in press). Functional impairment, physical disease, and depression in older adults. In P. Kato & T. Mann (Eds.), *Health psychology of special populations*. New York: Plenum.

Zeiss, A. M., & Steffen, A. M. (in press). Interdisciplinary health care teams: The basic unit of geriatric care. In L. L. Carstensen, B. A. Edelstein, & L. Dornbrand (Eds.), *The handbook of clinical gerontology*. Newbury Park, CA: Sage.

Zeiss, A. M., Zeiss, R. A., & Dornbrand, L. (1992, November). *Working with geriatric couples on sexual problems and concerns*. Paper presented at the meeting of the Gerontological Society of America, Washington, DC.

Zeiss, R. A., Delmonico, R. L., Zeiss, A. M., & Dornbrand, L. (1991). Psychological disorder and sexual dysfunction in elders. In L. K. Dial (Ed.), *Clinics in geriatric medicine: Sexuality and the elderly* (pp. 133–151). Philadelphia: W. B. Saunders.

3

APPLYING COGNITIVE–BEHAVIORAL THERAPY TO THE PSYCHOLOGICAL PROBLEMS OF LATER LIFE

DOLORES GALLAGHER-THOMPSON and LARRY W. THOMPSON

This chapter has two main goals: to provide an overview of cognitive–behavioral therapy (CBT) as it has been used successfully with a variety of elder outpatients having mental health problems, such as depression or anxiety disorders, and to review the research literature on psychotherapeutic intervention studies conducted with older adults.

To achieve the first goal, we provide background information. For example, we delineate several common issues that bring older adults to therapy and sketch out some basic similarities and differences in doing our preferred approach—CBT with older adults. We then review the overall treatment process, including some general points on assessment of cognitive and emotional functioning. We focus on the importance of socializing the elder patient into the unfamiliar role of being a client in CBT.

To accomplish the second goal, we review studies aimed at assessing the efficacy of CBT because that model (and its variants) makes up the bulk of current outcome research. We also briefly describe a variety of other applications of CBT, such as individual case reports and descriptions of group psychoeducational programs, to illustrate the many ways in which

This work was supported in part by Grant AG0-4572 from the National Institute on Aging and Grants MH-37196 and MH 43407 from the National Institute of Mental Health. Portions of this chapter were adapted from Dick, Gallagher-Thompson, and Thompson (1996).

CBT has been (and can be) used successfully with older adults. We conclude with suggestions for future research.

COMMON ISSUES THAT BRING OLDER PEOPLE TO THERAPY

Many of the normal events associated with aging are stressful, such as loss of significant others, changes in one's own physical health, or a decline in a loved one's health. Older adults seeking psychotherapy generally come in because of lifestyle changes resulting from these events. Although many individuals face these events without distress, some older adults respond by developing symptoms of depression or anxiety. Cognitively oriented theorists view these responses as being directly related to an individual's perceptions of the meaning of such major life events, which, for some individuals, triggers unhelpful thinking patterns. For example, individuals who believe that their life is meaningful only as long as they are earning money may respond to retirement with thoughts that they no longer have worth to themselves and to others; these individuals tend to become depressed.

Advancing age is typically accompanied by many deaths, including one's spouse, family members and friends, and, ultimately, the end of one's own life. Bereavement is thus common in the years after age 60. Common thoughts that may arise in individuals feeling overwhelming distress when faced with loss of others may be "I can't survive alone," "He had no right to leave me," and "I will never again be as close to anyone as the friends I've lost." Loss of friends and family also may result in narrowing of a person's opportunities for social interaction and involvement in activities that are pleasurable and self-enhancing. Another kind of loss is experienced by older adults who are caregivers for frail elders. The change in relationship that occurs when one party is cognitively or physically impaired and requires assistance can be experienced as a major loss of things that might have been. Similarly, facing the end of one's own life can lead to reflection on its meaning and quality. It also can mean facing missed opportunities, relationships that were never resolved, and life goals that were never achieved.

Relationship conflicts (with one's spouse or adult children) are another common antecedent to elders becoming depressed or anxious. For example, after one's spouse retires and is at home a great deal, certain beliefs may need to be questioned. A woman who has been a housewife may think, "The home is my territory. He's always interfering because he probably thinks I can't do anything right on my own." Other marital relationship problems occur when one or both of the partners become ill and increasing dependency occurs. Each may have to assume new responsibilities that he or she feels unprepared for; thoughts of failure and inadequacy are common.

In addition, many older adults have relationship conflicts with their adult children. Some elderly people disapprove of how their children or grandchildren "turned out" and may be harsh or critical of them; they may also feel like they "did a poor job" in raising them. Such thoughts interfere greatly with positive interaction and tend to cause much stress and tension when the parties are together or talk on the phone. Furthermore, disappointments can occur when older adults move to a new town or city to be with (or near) their adult children. Typically, expectations about the type and amount of contact that is "supposed" to occur are much different among the parties concerned; depression is a common outcome when the elders' expectations in this regard are not met consistently.

Finally, many older adults must adjust to chronic or acute illnesses, the frequency of which tends to increase with age. For example, an active elderly woman who breaks her hip or an older man with arthritis who can no longer play golf regularly may feel extremely isolated and depressed. This distress results, at least partly, from their maladaptive thoughts and their behavioral responses to the health changes that have occurred. Typical thoughts might be, "If I can't be as active as I once was, my life has little meaning" and "No one wants to be around someone who is sick. I'm only a burden to them." Behaviorally, physical disability can result in decreased involvement in pleasurable activities and a sense of reduced satisfaction with one's life. Additionally, elders facing physical limitations may find themselves having to rely on others for tasks they were once able to do on their own. Those who do not have adequate skills to communicate their special needs may feel distress when these needs are not met.

In summary, a variety of situations that occur in late life may result in serious depression, anxiety, or both. In our experience, the kinds of situations just detailed are the most common and represent the kinds of presenting problems most amenable to treatment with CBT.

SIMILARITIES AND DIFFERENCES IN CBT WITH OLDER AND YOUNGER ADULTS

In general, CBT with older people is similar to work done with younger people. Clients of any age enter treatment during various stages of the change process with biases, expectations, and different degrees of motivation to change. Although the content of presenting problems may differ (as noted earlier), an elder's emotional and behavioral reactions are not as distinct as might have been believed. Nevertheless, certain modifications in the implementation of treatment are helpful to keep in mind. These are based on our clinical experience and are offered as suggestions to the reader.

First, the therapist generally needs to be active during treatment sessions with an older client, keeping him or her focused on salient topics and maintaining the structure of the session. There is a tendency for older clients, who are often lonely, to digress from the task at hand and engage in "storytelling." Although some of this life review material may be clinically rich and relevant, the therapist must use his or her clinical judgment and often redirect the patient's focus to the "here-and-now" problem that initiated treatment.

Second, therapy with older people generally proceeds at a slower pace compared with CBT with younger people, partly because of the presence of common sensory problems, such as reduced visual or auditory acuity. For instance, significant hearing loss occurs in about 30% of the older population and can affect the rate and accuracy at which auditory information is processed (Cavanaugh, 1993). Therapists should speak more slowly than usual and enunciate clearly because unclear speech can further interfere with comprehension. A related issue is that most elders do not learn at the same rate or in the same manner as younger people and may be at a disadvantage in using inductive reasoning and abstract verbal processing (Cavanaugh, 1993). To compensate for this, material should be presented in manageable "chunks" with frequent repetition so that key points can be learned well.

Third, to compensate for cognitive slowing or sensory deficits, it is helpful to present important information in several different sensory modalities. For example, the therapist could present important themes and concepts both verbally and visually (e.g., using a blackboard) as well as have the patient take notes. The therapist often will want to provide a tape recording of the interview for review between sessions, particularly for patients exhibiting more severe sensory or cognitive impairment. Providing the client with handouts and soliciting written feedback also can facilitate the integration of important therapeutic concepts. Patience, persistence, and flexibility on the therapist's part are really critical to successful CBT with elders.

THE PROCESS OF COGNITIVE–BEHAVIORAL PSYCHOTHERAPY

The model of CBT that is described here was developed and used for the past 10 years at the Older Adult and Family Center at the Department of Veterans Affairs Health Care System in Palo Alto, California. We present a brief description of our 16- to 20-session protocol that was developed originally for use in psychotherapy outcome studies conducted at the center. The current version is now used both clinically and in research. This model is based on the work of Beck and colleagues (Beck, 1976; Beck,

Rush, Shaw, & Emery, 1979), who first described the cognitive theory of depression and then developed a series of techniques and interventions designed to help patients evaluate and challenge their negative thinking. According to Beck's view, depression results from consistent (and unrealistic) negative views of oneself, one's experiences, and the future. These views are supported and reinforced by the presence of multiple dysfunctional thinking patterns, such as the tendency to catastrophize when small things occur or the tendency to put the worst possible negative construction on the actions and words of others with whom one interacts. Because it is difficult for the client to recognize and label these dysfunctional thoughts as such, over time they take on a life of their own and are rarely questioned. They become fairly "automatic" and are not challenged spontaneously. A key goal of CBT therefore is to identify and challenge these negative thought patterns, so that more adaptive alternative viewpoints can be developed. Integral to the success of treatment is the inclusion of numerous "homework assignments" that the client is expected to do between sessions to increase the number of opportunities available for developing adaptive counterresponses. Some use also is made of behavioral assignments (e.g., to talk to one's spouse about a particular issue in a nonjudgmental manner and report on the results) to help the client obtain actual data to refute his or her negative beliefs about how the situation will turn out. Besides learning how to examine the evidence for and against specific negative thoughts, clients also learn such skills as how to do a cost–benefit analysis of the advantages and disadvantages of maintaining a particular set of negative beliefs and other related methods for gaining perspective on their beliefs. An excellent workbook was developed by one of Beck's students, David Burns, that explains these concepts in lay terms and contains many useful forms and questionnaires to assist in the therapeutic process (Burns, 1979, 1980). This may be recommended for the client to purchase as an adjunct to therapy sessions.

In our experience, it has proved helpful not to rely solely on cognitive techniques in therapy but to integrate behavioral methods and to use a variety of behavioral techniques with distressed older adults. These have been described by Lewinsohn, Biglan, and Zeiss (1979) and Lewinsohn, Muñoz, Youngren, and Zeiss (1978) and include such techniques as systematic relaxation training and the use of strategies to identify and increase everyday pleasurable activities. A more detailed clinical description of CBT as it relates to older adults can be found in Dick and Gallagher-Thompson (1995), Emery (1981), Thompson, Davies, Gallagher, and Krantz (1986), Thompson et al. (1991), and Zeiss and Lewinsohn (1986).

Assessment of Client Status

Assessment of the severity of the client's presenting complaints as well as the client's perception of his or her problems are critical pieces of information in CBT. They are needed partly to facilitate setting realistic treatment goals and partly to operationalize and evaluate change throughout the course of treatment regardless of the client's age. Baseline measures should be obtained at the start of treatment; we also ask clients to complete brief self-report measures before each session to assess change. For example, at intake, clients complete the long version of the Beck Depression Inventory (BDI; Beck, Ward, Mendelson, Mock, & Erbaugh, 1961), which has been shown to be a reliable measure of depressive symptoms in older adults (Gallagher, 1986), whereas the short form of the BDI is completed prior to each therapy session. A full description of the myriad of issues relating to assessment of affective disorders in older adults is beyond the scope of this chapter; other works, by Blazer (1993, 1994), Pachana, Thompson, and Gallagher-Thompson (1994), and Futterman, Thompson, Gallagher-Thompson, and Ferris (1995), and chapter 8 in this book contain that information. They should be consulted for a more in-depth view of the complexities involved, including the influence of physical health, medication usage, and cognitive functioning on the presentation of affective disorders. The choice of appropriate measures for pretreatment evaluation and ongoing assessment of the effectiveness of therapy can be a difficult one. Careful review of the most up-to-date information on these topics is essential so that informed choices can be made.

Besides knowing the older adult client's physical health status and medication regimen, it is also essential to evaluate directly his or her cognitive function. This information is crucial to designing an appropriate treatment plan because both the in-session work and homework rely heavily on the person's ability to comprehend, remember, and produce material in oral and written formats. We routinely administer the Mini-Mental State Examination (MMSE; Folstein, Folstein, & McHugh, 1975), which has been shown to be a valid and reliable screening measure to detect cognitive impairment in the elderly (Braekhus, Laake, & Engedal, 1992). In this way, clients can be referred for further neuropsychological testing if needed, and treatment planning can be done with knowledge about at least certain aspects of the older person's cognitive capabilities.

Treatment Phases

In our work, we have found it helpful to think in terms of tasks or phases to define the 16- to 20-session treatment process that we use. Of course, these phases are not rigidly adhered to, but they do provide a structure or framework within which to work. If a given facility has a maximum policy of 10 or 12 sessions, then the tasks of each phase will need to be collapsed in order to fit into the time available. A detailed description of these phases is found in our treatment manual for therapists, which is available from us. A client version also has been prepared for use as a handbook to accompany the actual therapy sessions. Although neither are yet available commercially, interested readers may contact us for advance copies. A brief description follows.

The initial therapeutic task is to establish a solid rapport with the client. It cannot be stated too frequently that CBT is not the application of a "bag of tricks" or the mechanical use of a set of techniques (Beck et al., 1979). Rather, as a form of psychotherapy, it relies heavily on the adequacy of the therapeutic relationship to establish a foundation for accomplishing its goals (Beck, 1976). The therapist also needs to "socialize" the client into treatment. In our experience, this is essential for older adults, who typically do not know what psychotherapy involves, how they are supposed to participate, and what will be asked of them. Because CBT is a relatively new form of treatment, most elders have had no prior knowledge of what it is and how it works. We use several sessions to socialize clients into treatment. A more detailed explanation of this particular process (which we regard as crucial) is given below.

We also explain the differences between CBT and prior forms of therapy experiences if needed (e.g., psychodynamic or supportive therapies, which are based on different theoretical models; see Horowitz & Kaltreider, 1979, for a discussion of the clinical application of these therapies and Silberschatz & Curtis, 1991, for an explanation of time-limited psychodynamic therapy with older adults). Once the basic CBT conceptual model and expectations for CBT have been discussed, the therapist and client must contract for a finite length of treatment. With older adults, it is important to set up the dates and times for all sessions at this point, so that the client sees the commitment involved and can discuss possible problems (e.g., conflicting medical appointments or transportation issues) that may interfere with keeping these appointments.

It is also necessary to determine target goals for treatment. This helps to keep the therapy focused on here-and-now issues. Examples of appropriate goals include being able to reduce conflict with one's adult daughter or learning to become more active and involved with other people (friends) in everyday life. By contrast, inappropriate goals would be more global, such as to feel better, to never become depressed again, or to have one's life back the way it used to be. Older adults tend to have difficulty setting realistic and attainable goals, so often this takes several sessions to concretize. Finally, the therapist shows how to begin to use the three-column dysfunctional thought record (DTR), which is one of the core cognitive tools used as therapy proceeds (Beck et al., 1979). Alternatively, the therapist may evaluate the client's current relationship between the frequency of various categories of pleasant events and the magnitude of pleasure experienced from each event. This can be done by asking the client to complete the Older Person's Pleasant Event Schedule (Gallagher et al., 1981). Using a more behavioral focus at the outset is particularly appropriate for highly depressed older people who may not be able to examine and evaluate their thoughts too well at the start of therapy. It also is helpful with people who have mild dementia and highly anxious individuals who may have difficulty monitoring specific thoughts and feelings. If this more behaviorally oriented approach is used, subsequent sessions would emphasize ways to increase pleasant activities and would put less emphasis on challenging dysfunctional thoughts. How to balance effectively the cognitive and behavioral elements of treatment is an individual matter and depends on the particular strengths and weaknesses of each client.

As treatment proceeds, the main work is to teach the client a variety of cognitive and behavioral skills that are applicable to the stated goals. These skills include the repetitive (sometimes daily) use of both the three- and five-column DTRs to (a) identify cognitive distortions, (b) examine the evidence to support or dispute particular beliefs, and (c) teach the client specific skills for challenging unhelpful thoughts and developing alternative views. Over time, this process will enable the client to learn how to develop more adaptive ways to think about and respond to stressful situations. For some clients (particularly those who are well educated and fairly "psychologically minded"), therapy also may include identification of core fundamental beliefs (or schemas) that the client has historically used to make sense of his or her environment.

In addition to this cognitive focus, clients may be asked to begin experiencing new pleasant events or to revisit pleasant activities that have been dropped because of depression or anxiety. Adding in this dimension enables the client to learn about the lawful relationship between activities and mood and how to improve mood by increasing daily pleasant events. Clients also learn about the interaction of cognitive and behavioral processes when, for example, their hesitation to increase pleasant events in their daily life can be addressed with the use of a DTR to identify the cognitions that stop them from trying these new behaviors.

As termination nears, goals shift to preparing the client to continue to use the skills learned in therapy independently. We generally create a written document with the client that summarizes what has been learned in treatment and anticipates how it could be used to reduce negative reactions to future events. Drawing on the extensive relapse prevention literature in the substance abuse field (see Marlatt & Gordon, 1985), we have named it a "maintenance guide," and we explain to clients that it is meant as a resource to use when stressful or depressogenic situations occur. We also discuss directly the feelings of the client about treatment termination. Older adults need time to explore both the feelings and thoughts involved because, for many, the therapy relationship fills a significant gap. In addition, we encourage the therapist to express what he or she has learned from the client. We have found this to be an important aspect of the termination process, in that it shows respect for the client and enables him or her to believe that something unique has been contributed. Finally, clients may be given referrals for other services (i.e., a support group) depending on their psychological status at termination.

SOCIALIZING THE OLDER CLIENT INTO TREATMENT

For the client to enter into the therapeutic contract, certain steps are advisable at the outset. First, it is necessary to elicit the client's expectations about treatment. Most elders are uninformed about therapy and do not know what to expect. Many have misconceptions about treatment: its length, the nature of the therapeutic contract, the amount of work involved, and so on. These need to be brought out into the open and discussed. We have found it effective to do this in the context of describing what CBT involves. We explain the rationale of CBT in some detail and inform clients that this type of treatment has been effectively used with both younger and older patients who have similar problems. We describe it as a skill-oriented treatment in which the client will be asked to learn a number of things about how to identify and cope with depressing thoughts and behaviors. Collaborative participation is expected: The cognitive–behavioral therapist is not the "expert" who sits back and waits for clients to reveal things, nor is the therapist passive. Rather, both client and therapist will be very active in a collaborative sense throughout therapy. Clients are told that CBT is time limited, with 10 to 20 sessions being the typical course. Because time is limited, it is important to make the most of each treatment hour. Thus, clients are advised that they will be expected to do homework between appointments and to bring that material in for discussion in the session. It is emphasized that only by mutual effort of this type will change be likely to occur. At this point, clients are asked for their reaction to what has been said, and further discussion occurs, if necessary, until the client understands what he or she is getting into. This matter of clarifying expectations is returned to again in the early treatment sessions, because we have found that this type of discussion in the first meeting often stimulates more ideas on the client's part than can be addressed right at that time.

Second, we discuss the fact that in CBT client and therapist will set concrete goals for change. The aim is not, for example, to "improve the client's personality" or to "turn back the clock to the way things used to be"; rather, specific, observable goals need to be set. In the first session, we do not attempt to fully delineate goals, because that process takes more time and mutual exploration of the problem by therapist and client; however, we do tell the client that this is what is in store and indicate that this will become clearer in the next few sessions. We then ask for feedback, to get the client's perspective as to whether they understand what is being said and want to proceed.

Third, we recognize that most clients are not that sure of what they want and need and may be a bit overwhelmed at the outset by all of this new information, so we indicate that these points will be reiterated frequently in the course of treatment. What we ask for in the first session is the client's cooperation and willingness to experiment with this approach. In our setting, we reevaluate the progress of all therapy cases after about 10 sessions. We let the client know that an independent staff member will meet with them at that time to discuss their satisfaction with treatment and perception of progress. Thus, if there are problems, adjustments can be made. This usually is very reassuring to older clients and allows them to make at least some level of commitment to CBT in the first few sessions. Clients are also told that feedback is not only encouraged but is really necessary for the therapist to gauge what is happening. This too is appealing to older individuals. They feel it is respectful of their years of experience, and they have social permission to comment (both positively and negatively) about therapy and the therapist. As with the other points noted earlier, this one needs frequent repetition, until the habit has been comfortably established.

Of course, it goes without saying that another important goal of early CBT sessions is to gather information about the client's presenting problems. Depending on the extent of information already available (e.g., from an intake interview), a greater or lesser amount of time in the first few therapy hours will need to be spent on this. Assuming that a pretty full description of symptoms and history is available, it is still important to have clients describe in their own words what brought them into therapy. We have found that, for many older adults, it is difficult to respond to this question without considerable extraneous detail (e.g., facts about other family members and digression into remote personal history). The cognitive–behavioral therapist should be well informed about any intake data previously collected so that he or she can recognize and discourage digressions. Considering that there are so many topics on the agenda for the first few sessions, it is important that therapists do their homework in this regard. But what if there are little background data available? Then out of necessity the therapist will spend the first one or two sessions on history gathering and review of symptoms, with a clear intent to begin covering the other points mentioned at subsequent meetings.

Finally, how the first few sessions end is very important in setting the tone for future meetings. Typically, the cognitive–behavioral therapist will give the client a handout of some kind describing the CBT model. The client will be asked to read this and underline salient points before the next session. Also, a request for both positive and negative feedback will be made. These two behaviors reinforce what has been said about the nature of CBT and help the client learn what is expected in treatment.

In the next few sessions (ideally, the third and fourth meetings), continued work is done on clients' expectations for therapy and on delineation of concrete treatment goals. Regarding expectations: Older clients often come back with their homework assignments not completed, or, if they have read the handout, they usually have questions about how this approach applies to them. Many will say that they are "too old to change" or that it is too complex; they just want someone to listen to their problems. The cognitive–behavioral therapist will point out that the client probably has other people in the environment who "just listen" but that this in itself does not seem to have helped. Also, clients will be asked if they are too old to learn, reemphasizing that CBT is a learning situation. Most clients can generate examples of recent successful learning experiences; this seems to help demystify the approach and make it more understandable to the average older person.

Sometimes clients will come back saying that unless a specific external situation can be changed, they will not be happy again. They are saying, in effect, that CBT will not be helpful because its goals are to modify dysfunctional thoughts and attitudes (not to change the environment). Many bereaved elders, for example, say that "unless life can be the way it was before, I'll always be depressed." Those with serious physical health problems and those far away from their adult children or other sources of support also tend to report that CBT is unlikely to be very helpful to them. The therapist will then ask if the person has been through transition periods before in life, when things changed and the changes were not necessarily positive. Elders usually have a vast store of experience in this regard and can think back to other times when they were able to adapt to negative situations. By drawing on previous positive coping experiences, the therapist begins to reduce the client's sense of helplessness about the current situation. This reinforces the notion that changing perceptions, looking at things from different points of view, and examining the meaning of various events and situations can be very adaptive and often has led to reduction in distress. Once the client really understands this point, CBT is about ready to begin in earnest.

The final aspect of the CBT socialization process is the mutual determination of treatment goals. The therapist explains to the client that unless it is clear where the therapy is headed, it is difficult to determine if it has gotten there; the roadmap analogy is helpful to use in this regard. Of course, goals are not "set in concrete"; sometimes things will come up during the course of therapy that are very important. In that case, new goals are set. But the point is that a mutually agreed upon focus is necessary for CBT to be effective. This process tends to be difficult for older adults, who often report their complaints globally (e.g., "I'm so unhappy I can't stand it" or "everything is wrong"). What is needed is for the global to become specific: This is accomplished by the therapist asking many questions about the complaint and about what the client wants in the way of change. For example, the therapist would begin by asking, "Under what circumstances are you unhappy? Is there anything in your life that is going well?" and the client might respond that some things are going all right but "family matters are troublesome." The therapist needs to narrow this down and, perhaps on the basis of prior information, may know that a daughter living nearby is not visiting or calling often. So the therapist might then ask: "Is it your relationship with all members of the family that is giving you grief or primarily your relationship with your daughter?" If the client identifies an issue with the daughter, then the next series of questions might be as follows: "How do you want to see that changed? Does the relationship with your daughter have to be perfect in order for you to be happy? What if we worked on your thoughts about why your daughter is so difficult and how you think she thinks about you? That way we can isolate specific thoughts that are particularly troublesome, and then work out ways for you to test out and evaluate these beliefs." Assuming the client agrees with this general thrust, the therapist would know how to proceed.

On the other hand, if the client brings in other matters in response to these kinds of questions, then it is generally good to pick up on the new topics until a specific problem is defined. Generally, at least one goal can be set through the process of inquiry just described, and that is enough to get started. Some clients have multiple goals at the outset; with them the issue is how to prioritize so that initial goals are set that are salient and also attainable. Others want to tackle a very difficult goal right at the outset—for example, reconciliation with a family member after many years of estrangement. Generally, the cognitive–behavioral therapist will try to select an initial goal that is more within the client's grasp and that will provide a "success experience" to build on over time. Going through the process of goal setting helps the client understand that very specific, everyday situations will be the main "grist" for the therapy mill. This is usually reassuring and suggests that improvements in daily life will lead to improvement in distressing symptoms.

We have described several specific socialization tasks that face the cognitive–behavioral therapist in early treatment sessions. These include describing the rationale and methods of CBT; emphasizing its collaborative nature; examining client expectations about treatment; and establishing concrete, realistic goals for change. We have also provided suggestions for how these tasks can be accomplished with older clients. We believe strongly in the importance of these points: When these tasks are neglected or hurried through clients tend to become dissatisfied with CBT and may drop out before having had the opportunity to experience its helpfulness.

CHANGING CORE BELIEFS

For many older adults, negative core beliefs about themselves and their self-worth underlie their depression (or other affective disorder). These beliefs typically developed in childhood or adolescence and are often firmly entrenched. Challenging them and revising them is beyond the scope of standard CBT. However, some clients are motivated to remain in treatment after their 20 sessions are completed and wish to explore and challenge deeply held dysfunctional beliefs that they may have become aware of during therapy. In that case, the therapist and client can renegotiate for additional treatment, which will focus on identification and modification of these core beliefs. In our experience, most older adults attain sufficient benefit from short-term CBT and do not require (or request) this additional treatment. However, some do (e.g., those with dependent or avoidant personality features tend to be interested in going on in treatment at our center). For them, schema therapy would be the next step.

Various approaches for changing dysfunctional schemas have been developed for working with clients who have personality disorders or strong dysfunctional personality features (Beck, Freeman, & Associates, 1990; Young, 1990, 1994). Beck et al. (1990) described those with personality disorders as people who maintain a rigid, long-standing belief system that functions as the person's interpretive model. Young (1990, 1994) described this process as the development of a set of stable negative themes that are seen as early as childhood as a result of negative interactions with peers or family. This set is referred to as *early maladaptive schemas*. Schemas are thus deeply ingrained maladaptive beliefs that are seldom questioned but that interfere significantly with normal life, such as "I am no good," "I am a failure in life," "No one loves me or can love me," and "I am and will always continue to be inadequate." These beliefs tend to be highly resistant to change.

The process of schema change therapy differs from standard CBT on several counts. First, this part of therapy is longer and more affectively driven. It generally does not begin until after standard CBT is completed, with more focus on the relationship between client and therapist. The therapeutic relationship itself becomes a core vehicle for changing the dysfunctional schema, as clients usually enact the schema within the context of the relationship. There they also can experiment with a new set of more adaptive schemas. Schema change therapy is usually longer than the standard course of CBT (e.g., an additional 20 or more sessions may be required), and change occurs at a slower rate. A key element is the introduction and development of new schemas that are more adaptive and that can gradually replace the dysfunctional beliefs. Therapy is ended when progress has been made in this regard, with full recognition that the job is not "over" at the end of the formal treatment. Rather, a process has begun that the client needs to continue on his or her own, so that the more functional schemas become operative in the client's daily life. It is only by the continued challenging of dysfunctional beliefs and their replacement with more moderate and adaptive ones that the client will solidify the gains made.

One of the schema change methods that we frequently use is called the "historical test of schemas." It was first described by Young (1990, 1994) and Young, Beck, and Weinberger (1993). We have modified their basic method to include a focus on every important era in the person's life, with considerable time spent reviewing key life events and doing a sort of "life review" with the client. The goal of this technique is to help the client understand the development and the maintenance of the schema during significant periods in his or her life. The steps in this process include the following: (a) the client's creation of a time line of his or her life marked by pivotal events (i.e., birth of siblings, school graduations, marriages, children, or any other emotionally laden event); (b) the therapist and the client discussing each time period, charting events and memories that either contradict or support the schema, with careful attention given to formulating conclusions about the veridicality of the schema at each time period; and (c) the formulation of a new schema based on the consolidation of evidence from the details of the client's history. A more complete description of this method, including a detailed case study, can be found in the article by Dick and Gallagher-Thompson (1995), who used this approach with an older depressed person who had a dependent personality style.

THE EFFICACY OF CBT WITH OLDER ADULTS

We recently wrote a comprehensive review chapter on the efficacy of psychotherapy (in general) with older adults (Gallagher-Thompson & Thompson, 1995). In addition, a detailed summary of the efficacy of cognitive and behavioral therapies with clinically depressed elders can be found in Teri, Curtis, Gallagher-Thompson, and Thompson (1994). The first review indicates that there are several varieties of psychotherapy that have been empirically demonstrated to be effective with older adults, including brief forms of cognitive, behavioral, psychodynamic, personal construct, and control mastery therapies. Various group treatments, such as cognitive–behavioral or psychodynamically oriented group therapies and several types of psychoeducational approaches, also have been studied, and the authors concluded that the results generally have been promising and positive. Findings of 20 outcome studies reported by Teri et al. (1994), which included data from controlled clinical trials, case reports, and individual, group, and psychoeducational interventions, clearly supported the utility of cognitive–behavioral therapies in the treatment of late-life depression. Despite these data, the recommendation from a recent National Institutes of Health (1992) consensus conference was for initial treatment of depressed elders with antidepressant medication. New findings from meta-analyses of 17 carefully controlled empirical studies of psychotherapy with depressed older adults, however, continue to challenge such endorsements. These data suggest that individual therapy, psychoeducational programs, and group or self-administered treatments are reliably more effective than no treatment conditions (Scogin & McElreath, 1994). The obtained mean effect size of .78 was comparable to the .85 effect size reported in Smith, Glass, and Miller's (1980) meta-analysis of psychotherapy studies. The effect size for studies using CBT was .85, which was considerably stronger than the effect size when other treatments were used (Scogin & McElreath, 1994).

With our associates, we have compared various forms of individual therapy for outpatients older than 60 who were experiencing a current episode of major depressive disorder. One study compared cognitive therapy, behavioral therapy, and relationship-oriented therapy in a small sample of depressed elders. Significant change resulted from all three forms of therapy. However, recipients of cognitive or behavioral therapy maintained their improvements best at the 1-year follow-up (Gallagher & Thompson, 1982, 1983; Thompson & Gallagher, 1984). A second study comparing the efficacy of cognitive, behavioral, and brief psychodynamic therapies revealed significant improvements from all three forms. One and 2-year follow-ups showed a comparable extent of maintenance of treatment gains in all three groups (Gallagher-Thompson, Hanley-Peterson, & Thompson, 1990; Thompson, Gallagher, & Breckenridge, 1987). A third study of older adults serving as the primary caregivers of impaired relatives compared brief psychodynamic therapy with CBT. Results revealed that the efficacy of each method depended on the length of time the client had served as a caregiver. Clients who had been caregivers for 44 months or less responded better to psychodynamic therapy, whereas those who had served longer improved more with CBT (Gallagher-Thompson & Steffen, 1994).

Many believe that the combination of pharmacotherapy and psychotherapy should be maximally effective in the treatment of late-life depression. Results of a study in our laboratory are presented here, although they have not yet been published (Thompson & Gallagher-Thompson, 1994). We compared use of the tricyclic antidepressant drug desipramine alone with use of CBT alone, versus the two in combination, in a randomized design for a period of 16–20 sessions. Endpoint analysis (including dropouts) showed no difference in change in diagnoses of depression between CBT and the combined condition, but both of these showed significant improvement when compared with the desipramine-alone condition. Comparisons of pre- and postchanges in depression diagnoses (done only with completers) showed no difference between CBT alone and desipramine alone and no difference between CBT and the combination of the two. However, patients receiving the combination showed greater improvement than those in the desipramine-alone condition. One-year follow-up showed no differences among the three conditions in terms of rates of prevalence of depressive diagnoses. Approximately 65% showed substantial clinical improvement from their initial diagnosis. Thus, these results, along with those reported in other studies, suggest that CBT is an effective treatment for some well-defined depressive disorders in the elderly. Furthermore, what little evidence is currently available suggests that this modality compares favorably with pharmacotherapy generally and desipramine specifically. It is possible that the combination of medication and CBT should be reserved for the most refractory patients, who typically do not respond to CBT alone.

With regard to the use of CBT in a group therapy mode (see, e.g., Ellis, 1992; Rose, 1989; Wessler & Hankin-Wessler, 1989), fewer empirical studies have been conducted on this type of intervention than on individual therapy. Investigators have identified several methodological challenges associated with such research, including issues such as the need for diagnostic homogeneity and comparable levels of distress at the outset, along with potential difficulties caused by dominant or submissive participants. Despite these obstacles, Beutler et al. (1987) conducted a controlled clinical trial with 56 elderly people with major depression who were randomly assigned to receive cognitive therapy with either placebo or alprazolam, placebo alone, or alprazolam alone. Significantly more change on measures of self-reported depression and sleep efficiency were reported by participants who received cognitive therapy than by non-group-therapy participants in both pre- and postcomparisons and at 3-month follow-up. The authors concluded that cognitive group therapy was effective in reducing subjective depressive symptomatology (Beutler et al., 1987).

Various psychoeducational interventions also have used a CBT conceptual framework and have been implemented in a group format. Lewinsohn, Antonuccio, Steinmetz, and Teri (1984) developed and empirically evaluated a coping with depression course that was well received by consumers. It focused on adults in general, and not specifically on older adults. To adapt these principles for older adults, Thompson and colleagues modified the content and some of the methodology and called the new program the Increasing Life Satisfaction class (Gallagher, Lovett, & Thompson, 1988; Thompson & Gallagher, 1983; Thompson, Gallagher, Nies, & Epstein, 1983). Studies comparing its effectiveness with a waiting-list condition have shown improvement in self-reported depressive symptoms (Breckenridge, Thompson, Breckenridge, & Gallagher, 1985). This approach also has been effectively modified and used with psychologically distressed family caregivers (Gallagher-Thompson, Lovett, Rose, Futterman, Coon, & Thompson, 1996; Lovett & Gallagher, 1988) and has led to the development of classes specifically for the management of anger and frustration that so often are experienced by caregivers (Gallagher-Thompson et al., 1992). Most recently, modifications to the anger management class have made the intervention more culturally sensitive and relevant to Spanish-speaking caregivers of Hispanic descent. Preliminary analyses of pre- to postchange for 50 Hispanic caregivers in the state of California revealed several measureable changes, including reduced levels of depression and frustration and increased social support from family members. More research is needed, however, to determine whether this type of intervention is more or less effective than traditional support group services used by distressed Hispanic caregivers.

ADDITIONAL APPLICATIONS OF CBT

Besides using CBT to treat late-life depression and other problems centering on negative affect, variants of CBT have been used by individuals affiliated with our center to treat many other common psychological problems of later life. Detailed description of all of these applications is beyond the scope of this chapter; however, we refer interested readers to the following publications for more information. Some are case reports dealing with, for example, the facilitation of inhibited grief (Florsheim & Gallagher-Thompson, 1990; Gantz, Gallagher-Thompson, & Rodman, 1992) and the use of crisis intervention with suicidal elders (DeVries & Gallagher-Thompson, 1994). Others focus on topics such as increasing the use of interpersonal data to challenge negative thoughts (Florsheim, Leavesley, Hanley-Peterson, & Gallagher-Thompson, 1991). Still others focus on specific subgroups of elders, such as family caregivers (DeVries & Gallagher-Thompson, 1993; Gallagher-Thompson, 1994; Gallagher-Thompson & Thompson, 1995; Kaplan & Gallagher-Thompson, 1995) and the medically ill or frail elderly (Rybarczyk et al., 1992; Thompson & Gallagher-Thompson, in press). Reviewing these articles will give readers an even clearer sense of the range of problems that can be successfully treated with CBT, as well as other modifications that can be made to "tailor" the basic treatment approach to the needs of the individual elderly client.

SUMMARY

In closing, we review some of the main points made in this chapter. First, we delineated the general outline of how we conduct CBT with elders having a variety of presenting problems. Second, we indicated several special issues that need to be considered in the application of CBT with older adults. Finally, we reviewed the growing body of outcome data supporting the efficacy of CBT for treatment of many kinds of late-life distress. However, although much progress has been made in the development and use of this modality with older adults, there is still much work to be done. For example, to our knowledge, there are no controlled outcome studies indicating the efficacy of CBT with elders who have significant personality disorders, nor are there any controlled studies about the kinds of modifications that may be needed to make this approach optimally effective with those who have chronic dysthymic disorders. Additional research is needed with less highly functional elders (e.g., with the frail elderly and those with significant cognitive impairments) to specify more clearly what client characteristics are associated with better therapeutic outcomes. These and similar studies would represent the next generation of outcome research needed to expand knowledge and to increase creative thinking about the applicability of CBT with older adults.

REFERENCES

Beck, A. T. (1976). *Cognitive therapy and the emotional disorders*. New York: International Universities Press.

Beck, A. T., Freeman, A., & Associates (1990). *Cognitive therapy of personality disorders*. New York: Guilford Press.

Beck, A. T., Rush, J., Shaw, B., & Emery, G. (1979). *Cognitive therapy of depression*. New York: Guilford Press.

Beck, A. T., Ward, C. H., Mendelson, M., Mock, J., & Erbaugh, J. (1961). An inventory for measuring depression. *Archives of General Psychiatry, 4*, 561–571.

Beutler, L. E., Scogin, F., Kirkish, P., Schretlen, D., Corbishley, A., Hamblin, D., Meredith, K., Potter, R., Bamford, C. R., & Levenson, A. I. (1987). Group cognitive therapy and alprazolam in the treatment of depression in older adults. *Journal of Consulting and Clinical Psychology, 55*, 550–556.

Blazer, D. G. (1993). *Depression in late life* (2nd ed.). St. Louis, MO: Mosby-Yearbook.

Blazer, D. G. (1994). Epidemiology of late-life depression. In L. Schneider, C. F. Reynolds, B. Lebowitz, & A. Fiedhoff (Eds.), *Diagnosis and treatment of depression in late life* (pp. 9–19). Washington, DC: American Psychiatric Press.

Braekhus, A., Laake, K., & Engedal, K. (1992). The Mini-Mental State Examination: Identifying the most efficient variables for detecting cognitive impairment in the elderly. *Journal of the American Geriatrics Society, 40*, 1139–1145.

Breckenridge, J. S., Thompson, L. W., Breckenridge, J. N., & Gallagher, D. (1985). Behavioral group therapy with the elderly. In S. Upper & S. Ross (Eds.), *Handbook of behavioral group therapy* (pp. 275–299). New York: Plenum.

Burns, D. D. (1979). *Feeling good: The new mood therapy*. New York: Signet Books.

Burns, D. D. (1980). *The feeling good handbook: Using the new mood therapy in everyday life*. New York: William Morrow.

Cavanaugh, J. (1993). *Adult development and aging* (2nd ed.). Pacific Grove, CA: Brooks/Cole.

DeVries, H., & Gallagher-Thompson, D. (1993). Cognitive/behavioral therapy and the angry caregiver. *Clinical Gerontologist, 13*(4), 53–57.

DeVries, H., & Gallagher-Thompson, D. (1994). Crises with geriatric patients. In F. Dattilio & A. Freeman (Eds.), *Cognitive–behavior therapy and crisis intervention* (pp. 200–218). New York: Guilford Press.

Dick, L. P., & Gallagher-Thompson, D. (1995). Cognitive therapy with the core beliefs of a distressed, lonely caregiver. *Journal of Cognitive Psychotherapy: An International Quarterly, 9*, 215–227.

Dick, L. P., Gallagher-Thompson, D. & Thompson, L. W. (1996). Cognitive–behavioral therapy. In R. T. Woods (Ed.), *Handbook of the clinical psychology of ageing* (pp. 509–544). New York: Wiley.

Ellis, A. (1992). Group rational-emotive and cognitive-behavioral therapy. *International Journal of Group Psychotherapy, 42*, 63–80.

Emery, G. (1981). Cognitive therapy with the elderly. In G. Emery, S. D. Holton, & R. C. Bedrosian (Eds.), *New directions in cognitive therapy* (pp. 84–98). New York: Guilford Press.

Florsheim, M. J., & Gallagher-Thompson, D. (1990). Cognitive/behavioral treatment of atypical bereavement: A case study. *Clinical Gerontologist, 10*(2), 73–76.

Florsheim, M. J., Leavesley, G., Hanley-Peterson, P., & Gallagher-Thompson, D. (1991). An expansion of the A-B-C approach to cognitive/behavioral therapy. *Clinical Gerontologist, 10*(4), 65–69.

Folstein, M., Folstein, S., & McHugh, P. (1975). "Mini-Mental State": A practical method for grading the cognitive status of patients for the clinician. *Journal of Psychiatric Research, 12*, 189–198.

Futterman, A., Thompson, L. W., Gallagher-Thompson, D., & Ferris, R. (1995). Depression in later life: Epidemiology, assessment, etiology and treatment. In E. Beckham & R. Leber (Eds.), *Handbook of depression* (2nd ed., pp. 494–525). New York: Guilford Press.

Gallagher, D. (1986). The Beck Depression Inventory and older adults: Review of its development and utility. *Clinical Gerontologist, 5*(2), 149–163.

Gallagher, D., Lovett, S., & Thompson, L. W. (1988). *"Increasing Life Satisfaction" class for caregivers: Class leaders' manual*. Palo Alto, CA: Department of Veterans Affairs Medical Center.

Gallagher, D., & Thompson, L. W. (1982). Treatment of Major Depressive Disorder in older adult outpatients with brief psychotherapies. *Psychotherapy: Theory, Research, and Practice, 19,* 482–490.

Gallagher, D., & Thompson, L. W. (1983). Effectiveness of psychotherapy for both endogenous and nonendogenous depression in older adult outpatients. *Journal of Gerontology, 38,* 707–712.

Gallagher, D., Thompson, L. W., Baffa, G., Piatt, C., Ringering, L., & Stone, V. (1981). *Depression in the elderly: A behavioral treatment manual.* Los Angeles: University of Southern California Press.

Gallagher-Thompson, D. (1994). Clinical intervention strategies for distressed family caregivers: Rationale and development of psychoeducational approaches. In E. Light, G. Niederehe, & B. Lebowitz (Eds.), *Stress effects on family caregivers of Alzheimer's patients* (pp. 260–277). New York: Springer.

Gallagher-Thompson, D., Hanley-Peterson, P., & Thompson, L.W. (1990). Maintenance of gains versus relapse following brief psychotherapy for depression. *Journal of Counseling and Clinical Psychology, 58,* 371–374.

Gallagher-Thompson, D., Lovett, S., Rose, J., Futterman, A., Coon, D., & Thompson, L. W. (1996). The impact of psychoeducational interventions on distressed family caregivers. Manuscript submitted for publication.

Gallagher-Thompson, D., Rose, J., Florsheim, M., Jacome, P., DelMaestro, S., Peters, L., Gantz, F., Arguello, D., Johnson, C., Moorehead, R. S., Polich, T. M., Chesney, M., & Thompson, L. W. (1992). *Controlling your frustration: A class for caregivers.* Palo Alto, CA: Department of Veterans Affairs Medical Center.

Gallagher-Thompson, D., & Steffen, A. M. (1994). Comparative effects of cognitive-behavioral and brief psychodynamic psychotherapies for depressed family caregivers. *Journal of Consulting and Clinical Psychology, 62,* 543–549.

Gallagher-Thompson, D., & Thompson, L. W. (1995). Psychotherapy with older adults in theory and practice. In B. Bonger & L. Beutler (Eds.), *Comprehensive textbook of psychotherapy* (pp. 357–379). New York: Oxford University Press.

Gantz, F., Gallagher-Thompson, D., & Rodman, J. (1992). Cognitive/behavioral facilitation of inhibited grief. In A. Freeman & F. Dattilio (Eds.), *Comprehensive casebook of cognitive–behavioral therapy* (pp. 359–379). London: Oxford University Press.

Horowitz, M., & Kaltreider, N. (1979). Brief therapy of the stress response syndrome. *Psychiatric Clinics of North America, 2,* 365–377.

Kaplan, C., & Gallagher-Thompson, D. (1995). The treatment of clinical depression in caregivers of spouses with dementia. *Journal of Cognitive Psychotherapy: An International Quarterly, 9,* 35–44.

Lewinsohn, P. M., Antonuccio, D. O., Steinmetz, J. L., & Teri, L. (1984). *The coping with depression course: A psychoeducational intervention for unipolar depression.* Eugene, OR: Castalia.

Lewinsohn, P. M., Biglan, A., & Zeiss, A. (1979). Behavioral treatment of depression. In P. Davidson (Ed.), *Behavioral management of anxiety, depression, and pain* (pp. 91–146). New York: Brunner/Mazel.

Lewinsohn, P. M., Muñoz, R. F., Youngren, M. A., & Zeiss, A. M. (1978). *Control your depression*. Englewood Cliffs, NJ: Prentice Hall.

Lovett, S., & Gallagher, D. (1988). Psychoeducational interventions for family caregivers: Preliminary efficacy data. *Behavior Therapy, 19,* 321–330.

Marlatt, G. A., & Gordon, J. R. (Eds.). (1985). *Relapse prevention: Maintenance strategies in the treatment of addictive behaviors.* New York: Guilford Press.

National Institutes of Health. (1992). National Institutes of Health consensus conference statement: Diagnosis and treatment of depression in late life. *Journal of the American Medical Association, 268,* 1018–1024.

Pachana, N., Thompson, L. W., & Gallagher-Thompson, D. (1994). Measurement of depression. In M. P. Lawton & J. Teresi (Eds.), *Annual review of gerontology and geriatrics* (Vol. 14, pp. 234–256). New York: Springer.

Rose, S. D. (1989). Coping skill training in groups. *International Journal of Group Psychotherapy, 39,* 59–78.

Rybarczyk, B., Gallagher-Thompson, D., Rodman, J., Zeiss, A., Gantz, F., & Yesavage, J. (1992). Applying cognitive–behavioral psychotherapy to the chronically ill elderly: Treatment issues and case illustration. *International Psychogeriatrics, 4,* 127–140.

Scogin, F., & McElreath, L. (1994). Efficacy of psychosocial treatments for geriatric depression: A quantitative review. *Journal of Counseling and Clinical Psychology, 62,* 69–74.

Silberschatz, G., & Curtis, J. T. (1991). Time-limited psychodynamic therapy with older adults. In W. Myers (Ed.), *New techniques in the psychotherapy of older patients* (pp. 95–108). Washington, DC: American Psychiatric Press.

Smith, M. L., Glass, G. V., & Miller, T. I. (1980). *The benefits of psychotherapy.* Baltimore: Johns Hopkins University Press.

Teri, L., Curtis, J., Gallagher-Thompson, D., & Thompson, L. (1994). Cognitive–behavioral therapy with depressed older adults. In L. S. Schneider, C. F. Reynolds, B. D. Lebowitz, & A. J. Friedhoff (Eds.), *Diagnosis and treatment of depression in late life: Results of the NIH consensus development conference* (pp. 279–291). Washington, DC: American Psychiatric Press.

Thompson, L. W., Davies, R., Gallagher, D., & Krantz, S. E. (1986). Cognitive therapy with older adults. *Clinical Gerontologist, 5*(3/4), 245–279.

Thompson, L. W., & Gallagher, D. (1983). A psychoeducational approach for the treatment of depression in elders. *Psychotherapy in Private Practice, 1,* 25–28.

Thompson, L. W., & Gallagher, D. (1984). Efficacy of psychotherapy in the treatment of late-life depression. *Advances in Behavior Research and Therapy, 6,* 127–139.

Thompson, L. W., Gallagher, D., & Breckenridge, J. S. (1987). Comparative effectiveness of psychotherapies for depressed elders. *Journal of Consulting and Clinical Psychology, 55,* 385–390.

Thompson, L. W., Gallagher, D., Nies, G., & Epstein, D. (1983). Evaluation of the effectiveness of professionals and nonprofessionals as instructors of "Coping with Depression" classes for elders. *The Gerontologist, 23,* 390–396.

Thompson, L. W., & Gallagher-Thompson, D. (1994, August). *Comparison of desipramine and cognitive/behavioral therapy for the treatment of late-life depression: A progress report*. Paper presented at the 102nd Annual Convention of the American Psychological Association, Los Angeles.

Thompson, L. W., & Gallagher-Thompson, D. (in press). Psychotherapeutic interventions with older adults in outpatient and extended care settings. In R. L. Rubenstein & M. P. Lawton (Eds.), *Aging and depression in long term and residential care*. New York: Springer.

Thompson, L. W., Gantz, F., Florsheim, M., Del Maestro, S., Rodman, J., Gallagher-Thompson, D., & Bryan, H. (1991). Cognitive/behavioral therapy for affective disorders in the elderly. In W. Myers (Ed.), *New techniques in the psychotherapy of older patients* (pp. 3–19). Washington, DC: American Psychiatric Press.

Wessler, R. L., & Hankin-Wessler, S. W. (1989). Nonconscious algorithms in cognitive and affective processes. *Journal of Cognitive Psychotherapy, 3*, 243–254.

Young, J. E. (1990). *Cognitive therapy for personality disorders: A schema focused approach*. Sarasota, FL: Professional Resource Exchange.

Young, J. E. (1994). *Cognitive therapy for personality disorders: A schema-focused approach* (Rev. ed.). Sarasota, FL: Professional Resource Exchange.

Young, J. E., Beck, A. T., & Weinberger, A. (1993). Depression. In D. Barlow (Ed.), *Clinical handbook of psychological disorders* (pp. 240–277). New York: Guilford Press.

Zeiss, A. M., & Lewinsohn, P. M. (1986). Adapting behavioral treatment for depression to meet the needs of the elderly. *The Clinical Psychologist, 39*, 98–100.

4

USING INTERPERSONAL PSYCHOTHERAPY WITH DEPRESSED ELDERS

MARK D. MILLER and REBECCA L. SILBERMAN

Although many of its principles derive from the broader school of interpersonal psychiatry,

> interpersonal psychotherapy of depression is a psychological treatment designed specifically for the needs of depressed patients. It is a focused, short-term time-limited therapy that emphasizes the current interpersonal relations of the depressed patient while recognizing the role of genetic, biochemical, developmental, and personality factors in causation and vulnerability to depression. We are convinced from clinical experience and research evidence that clinical depression occurs in an interpersonal context and that psychotherapeutic intervention directed at this interpersonal context will facilitate the patient's recovery from the acute episode and possibly have preventative effects against relapse and recurrence. (Klerman, Weissman, Rounsaville, & Chevron, 1984, p. 5)

In this chapter, we discuss our experiences using interpersonal psychotherapy (IPT) with an elderly depressed population. We elucidate the

We wish to acknowledge the other interpersonal psychotherapy therapists—Lin Ehrenpreis, Lee Wolfson, Jean Zaltman, and Julie Malloy; the principal investigator of the National Institute of Mental Health-funded (MH43832) Maintenance Therapies in Late Life Depression Study—Charles F. Reynolds III; other mentors and supervisors—Ellen Frank, Cleon Cornes, and Stanley Imber; the program coordinator—Jacqueline Stack; and the administrative assistants—Donna M. Ulrich and Diana Donnelly.

83

background of the theory of IPT and provide an overview of the therapy's mechanics and structure and then show how IPT is used successfully with older patients. The problem areas addressed by IPT fit well with those issues confronted by older patients who are experiencing depression. We describe which IPT problem areas occur most frequently and how they manifest specifically in older patients' lives. We illustrate these points using case vignettes from our work.

FOUNDATIONS OF IPT

Klerman et al. (1984), in a New Haven–Boston collaboration, developed and refined the tenets of IPT and codified them into a manual of treatment guidelines that are currently available in book form. This document serves the novice IPT therapist as the standard introductory text for IPT. Many predecessors of that research group also contributed to the precursors of IPT and are briefly mentioned here.

J. D. Frank (1969; J. D. Frank & Frank, 1991) noted that many psychotherapies have common goals: They give the patient a sense of mastery, they combat social isolation, they restore a sense of group belonging, and they help patients to find meaning in their lives. The theories of interpersonal psychology are best represented by the writings of Harry Stack Sullivan (1953), who taught that psychiatry involved the scientific study of people and the processes between them, not just the study of the brain, mind, or society. The psychobiological approach of Meyer (1957) greatly emphasized the patient's current experience in social relationships. Bowlby (1969, 1977) and Parker, Barrett, and Hickie (1992) contributed their views on attachment theory as a strong theoretical basis for understanding the interpersonal context of depression and for the development of therapeutic strategies to correct the distortions produced by faulty attachments in childhood. Fromm-Reichmann (1960) and Cohen, Baker, Cohen, Fromm-Reichmann, and Weigert (1954) applied IPT to schizophrenic patients and manic–depressive patients, respectively. For an indepth discussion of the individuals who shaped IPT's development, see Cornes (1990) or Klerman et al. (1984).

THE INTERPERSONAL THERAPEUTIC MODEL

Having reviewed the major contributors to the development of IPT, we now turn our attention to the methods used in IPT and their particular relevance for the elderly patient. During the initial phases of IPT, a thorough diagnostic assessment is obtained to establish the symptoms of depression and to provide ample psychoeducation for the patient about the nature of depression and how the mechanics of IPT will treat the patient's own depressive symptoms. During this time, rapport is established and the patient is given the "sick role." Being in the sick role means having permission to feel the full weight of one's depression and to acknowledge that one is suffering from an illness that may curtail one's ability to perform usual tasks and responsibilities. These general principles promote a gentle introduction to IPT, which improves its acceptance, particularly for older patients, who may have trepidations about entering a treatment that is unfamiliar or poorly understood.

Next, a complete inventory is obtained of the patient's past and current relationships to establish who has been and who are the important players in the patient's life. Although the main emphasis of IPT is on the present, when dealing with the elderly particular attention must be paid to contrasts between present and past relationships and milieus. Many elderly people face a shrinking support base as parents, spouses, siblings, and friends die and children move away. A series of questions to ascertain by whom the patient feels most supported and, alternatively, most in conflict, is often perceived by the elderly patient as support-building concern on the part of the IPT therapist. It is crucial that this lifelong interpersonal inventory include all aspects of the patient's life, such as relationships with family, coworkers, friends, love relationships, and community contacts. Particular attention should be paid to patterns of interpersonal interactions that are problematic and may have been associated with past depressions.

Through this initial process, the therapist and patient begin to identify the major problem area that will be the focus of treatment. The developers of IPT recognized that the interpersonal problems in depressed patients' lives that are most critical in the development and maintenance of their depressive symptoms fall into four general areas: grief, interpersonal disputes, role transitions, and interpersonal deficit. It is the articulation of these four specific problem areas that is the hallmark and center of IPT. For the bulk of the therapeutic work, the therapist and patient keep their attentions on one or two mutually agreed-on focus areas. Why focus on these four areas? Klerman et al. (1984) explained that

> this classification of problem areas conceptualizes interpersonal problems according to a system that focuses on potential areas of change in treatment. The classifications are not exhaustive and they do not represent in-depth formulations, nor do they attempt to explain the dynamics of the depressive disorder. Instead, this classification system is intended to help the therapist outline realistic goals and follow appropriate treatment strategies. These areas are not necessarily mutually exclusive. Patients may come for treatment with a combination of problems in several areas, or there may be no clear-cut, significant

difficulties in any one area. For each person the psychotherapist assesses individual needs and what the patient considers the factors that have contributed to the depression. For patients with wide-ranging problems, the therapist may be guided in the choice of focus by the precipitating events of the current depressive episode. (p. 88)

Detailed treatment strategies are discussed in *Interpersonal Psychotherapy of Depression* (Klerman et al., 1984) for each problem area and are outlined briefly here. In grief work, for example, the goal is to facilitate the completion of the mourning process and ultimately to help the patient explore appropriate substitutes for the loss. In interpersonal disputes, IPT explores possible alternate coping strategies for unsatisfying relationships. In role transitions, the goal of IPT is to mourn the loss of the old role, to see the new role more positively, and to restore self-esteem through mastery of that new role. Finally, the IPT goal for the problem area of interpersonal deficits is to encourage meaningful socialization. The therapist's role is that of an active patient advocate.

IPT is time limited, usually 12–20 weekly 45- to 60-min sessions. The number of sessions will vary depending on the complexity of the problems and the patient's level of motivation for change. Prior research has shown this length of treatment to be efficacious for most patients (Klerman et al., 1984). The time-limited nature of IPT avoids the potential disadvantages of reinforcing avoidance behavior and fostering dependence on the therapist. Because IPT is focused on one or two main problem areas, it is possible to work through the issues relevant to the patient's depression within a short-term model.

In IPT, no assumption is made about the cause of depression. The premise of IPT is that all depressions occur in an interpersonal context regardless of severity, biological vulnerability, or predisposing personality traits. The hallmark components of IPT are to seek relief from depressive symptoms and to seek more effective coping strategies for interpersonal difficulties.

IPT uses well-established techniques such as reassurance, clarification of emotional states, improved interpersonal communication, and the testing of perceptions and performance. IPT is focused on interpersonal, not intrapsychic, themes. The therapist works with the patient's current problems at the conscious and preconscious levels. Unconscious material is recognized by the therapist, but it is not a direct focus of attention. The IPT therapist might observe intrapsychic defenses at work in patients, such as projection, denial, isolation, undoing, or repression, but he or she does not encourage the patient to search for internal conflict. Rather, patients are encouraged to explore conflicts in an interpersonal context. Emphasis is placed on current interpersonal problems and their accompanying frustrations, anxieties, and wishes. IPT is focused on current, not past, relationships. Early childhood influences are recognized but are not an emphasis of treatment. Similarly, past problems or traumas are acknowledged, but every attempt is made to focus therapy on residual elements in the here and now, particularly current problems. IPT can be used individually or in combination with antidepressant medication. IPT is different from cognitive–behavioral therapy in that unpleasant events or negative cognitions are a focus of treatment only to the extent that they impinge on interpersonal relationships.

It is well recognized that personality traits or disorders can be risk factors for depression (Shea, Glass, Pilkonis, Watkins & Docherty, 1987) and can affect the process of psychotherapy. Similarly, personality traits play a role in recurrent interpersonal problems. IPT points out maladaptive patterns in the patient's dealings with others and helps him or her to practice alternative strategies, but no attempt is made to change personality structure.

In summary, IPT has multiple features that make it thoroughly relevant for geriatric depression. IPT is short term and goal oriented rather than open ended, a feature that appeals to many elders. A focus on the here and now and the integrated psychoeducational component make IPT graspable, even for those with little prior experience with psychotherapy. Finally, the simple but encompassing major foci of IPT are both practical and pertinent to the needs of the elderly, who are confronted with a high prevalence of grief after loss and of role transitions that accompany the many adjustments necessitated by the changing circumstances of later life.

The efficacy of IPT in the treatment of depression has been established in several studies using adult patients who ranged in age up to 60 (Elkin et al., 1989; E. Frank et al., 1990). In reviewing the literature on the use of IPT in the elderly, we found one series of case reports and discussion by Sholomskas, Chevron, Prusoff, and Berry (1983). In the only published research that we are aware of using IPT and the elderly, Sloane, Staples, and Schneider (1985) randomly assigned 29 depressed elderly patients to either nortriptyline, placebo, or IPT and found that all three groups improved significantly at 6 weeks but that the IPT group had the fewest dropouts. No description was given of the types of patient problems encountered.

USING IPT WITH DEPRESSED ELDERS IN A RESEARCH SETTING: THE MAINTENANCE THERAPIES IN LATE-LIFE DEPRESSION STUDY

As geriatric depression became recognized as an important public health concern in the late 1970s, research into more effective treatments were sought. It was in this context that IPT was developed as a treatment for depression that could be used in a research setting. Increasingly, it became clear that depression also was a major health concern in the geriatric population, and interest developed in studying psychotherapy as well as antidepressant medications in the groups.

Our experience using IPT in the elderly came about through one study of geriatric depression that began in 1989 at the University of Pittsburgh's Western Psychiatric Institute and Clinic. The Maintenance Therapies in Late-Life Depression (MTLLD) Study is a prospective double-blind, placebo-controlled maintenance study designed to test the efficacy of IPT, antidepressant medication (nortriptyline), and their combination in maintaining wellness among elders with recurrent depression. A brief description of the study is included here to allow the reader to understand the context within which we have gained our experience using IPT with elderly depressed patients.

IPT was chosen as the designated psychotherapy for several reasons: (a) Considerable experience had been accrued in our department using IPT in the National Institute of Mental Health Collaborative Study and the Maintenance Therapies in Recurrent Depression Study (E. Frank et al., 1990); (b) it was anticipated that IPT would be readily adaptable to the types of problems we expected to find in elderly depressed patients (e.g., grief issues and role transitions); and (c) IPT is manual based and can be taught reliably to therapists. Its consistent application by different therapists can be certified by review of audiotaped sessions.

Because the first task of the MTLLD Study is to help the patients recover from their current depression, all participants receive combined treatment with IPT and nortriptyline. All participants receive a minimum of 12 weekly IPT sessions with an experienced therapist. Those who sustain a recovery become eligible for the experimental phase of the study, which we call the "maintenance phase." It is in this phase that we want to see how treatments compare in maintaining a patient's wellness by randomly assigning patients to one of four treatment cells for double-blind, monthly maintenance follow-up: nortriptyline and IPT, placebo and IPT, nortriptyline and medication clinic, and placebo and medication clinic. The medication clinic visit consists of a 15-min visit focusing on any change in symptoms since the patient's last visit (this is not an active psychotherapy condition). (For a more in-depth view of the MTLLD Study, see Reynolds et al., 1992, 1994). Recurrence rates among randomly assigned participants to the four experimental maintenance conditions are catalogued.

Because the MTLLD Study is ongoing, no conclusions yet can be drawn about the efficacy of IPT compared with medication or their combination as a maintenance treatment. We also cannot conclude from our data that IPT alone is an effective therapy for acute depression because all MTLLD participants received a combination of IPT and nortriptyline in the acute phase of the study. Rather, our intent here is to describe our experiences in applying IPT with elderly depressed participants enrolled in a well-controlled research protocol and to comment on the types of problems we encountered in the lives of our depressed elderly patients. Because dementia was an exclusion for the MTLLD Study, we have not attempted to apply IPT with patients with cognitive impairments.

ADAPTING IPT FOR THE ELDERLY

In planning to use IPT with elderly patients in the MTLLD Study, much discussion ensued about the possibility that IPT would require an adaptation for special needs the elderly might present. A review of the literature provided some recommendations to test, such as the pilot work of Sholomskas et al. (1983), who recommended more flexibility in applying IPT to older patients to accommodate more frequent intolerance of full-length sessions. They also suggested anticipating increased dependency needs such as the need for practical help with financial matters and transportation. Finally, Sholomskas et al. warned that the IPT therapist's role might be to encourage toleration of conflictual relationships in elders more so than with younger patients who might, for example, choose to terminate a chronically conflictual relationship. Older patients might see themselves as having fewer options. In summary, Sholomskas et al. recommended three general strategies: (a) emphasize the active, nonneutral stance of IPT; (b) be prepared to help the patient in practical ways; and (c) be aware of limited options a patient may have for changing difficult problems, particularly regarding themes of functional limitation, lifelong psychopathology, interpersonal conflict, or existential issues such as the effects of aging or impending death. E. Frank and colleagues further cautioned therapists to avoid excessive dependency by maintaining the IPT tenet of avoiding interpretation of positive transference. For example, some elderly patients commonly show appreciation by bringing small gifts or baked goods (E. Frank & Frank, 1988a, 1988b; E. Frank et al., 1993).

However, after 6 years of experience, the overwhelming consensus among the MTLLD psychotherapists is that IPT with elders has far more similarities to than differences with IPT with younger patients. To be sure, therapists could recall selected patients who could not tolerate a full session of IPT in the beginning phases of therapy, but in general our elderly patients tolerated 45- to 50-min sessions well. In fact, once rapport was established, many of our elderly patients described looking forward to their IPT session as the high point of their week, and many were greatly appreciative for the chance to express themselves because they had no other confidant or family in proximity with which to share intimate or difficult feelings. Gift giving, in general, was handled easily in our experience with good-natured nonchalance and appreciativeness, and at no time was gift giving excessive, inappropriate, or refused.

Practical problems such as financial distress or the need for community services for the patient or a family member did arise, although rarely. Occasional referrals to social services or legal aid were recommended; however, there did not seem to be a grossly disproportionate number of such instances compared with therapeutic work with younger patients. In summary, little adaptation was required to apply IPT to the elderly compared with younger age groups.

Thus far, it has been our experience that the gains made in the acute therapy generally have been sustained during the maintenance period. Whether these adaptive gains or skills will offer protection from a recurrence of depression remains to be evaluated on completion of the MTLLD Study.

Some of our patients had little formal schooling and some had little psychological sophistication. Furthermore, many patients who agreed to participate in the MTLLD Study just wanted to feel better. They did not come looking for psychotherapy in particular. Because combined therapy with nortriptyline and IPT was a protocol requirement, therapists sometimes found themselves face to face with patients who had no idea what psychotherapy was or who had little interest in self-reflection. Despite not having sought out therapy, we were impressed with the ability of the great majority of our patients to learn from the psychoeducational aspect of the early sessions, to review sessions on their own, and to become viable working partners in psychotherapy. Ultimately, most patients made significant gains over the course of 6–9 months of acute and continuation therapy. There were some patients (approximately 24%) who never fully engaged in psychotherapy. However, the number of patients who were poor psychotherapy candidates did not seem of any greater proportion in our elderly patients than in psychotherapy work with younger patients. Many factors may contribute to a patient's suitability for psychotherapy, but age alone does not seem to be one of them.

CLINICAL DATA AND CASE VIGNETTES

After 6 years of experience using IPT with elderly clients, we were interested to learn which of the IPT problem areas occurred most often and what the relevant therapeutic life issues were for our research patients. We found no association between a particular IPT problem area and successful recovery from the index episode of depression. Of 113 elderly patients recruited thus far, 49 (43.4%) had a primary focus of role transition,

42 (37.2%) on role dispute, 21 (18.6%) on grief, and 1 (0.9%) on interpersonal deficits. Thus, the most common primary foci were role transition and role dispute.

Adaptation to Life Change

In general, the MTLLD IPT therapists were impressed with their patients' abilities to adapt to many life changes beyond their control. When changes or the role transitions required of patients became too stressful, however, depression sometimes resulted. The following case vignette illustrates the extreme stresses associated with the burden of caregiving for an ill spouse, particularly one suffering from a cognitive disability.

Case Vignette: Role Transition

Mr. R. became acutely depressed when he had to place his second wife (suffering from Alzheimer's disease) in a nursing home. He was experiencing two major role transition crises to which he could not easily adjust. First, in having his wife in an alternative living situation for care, Mr. R. felt he was failing in his role as her husband. On retiring several years previously, he had devoted his life to his marriage, particularly his wife's care. He was now experiencing a simultaneous loss of job and purpose. Second, he could not easily adjust to being married to someone who was incapacitated, disoriented, and who, most of the time, did not know who he was. His wife could no longer be a partner to him. Mr. R. described feeling like a married single person or a widower whose wife was still living, roles for which there seemed to be no adequate standards.

In IPT, Mr. R. was provided ample opportunity to express his varying feelings of sadness, resentment, guilt, and feeling "on hold," as if he could not move on with his life as long as his wife was not moving on. Mr. R. was someone who had always put his own needs last. His IPT therapist felt that he needed some confrontation and gentle encouragement to learn how to pursue his own life and interests simultaneously. When challenged, he found, to his surprise, that he was able to keep up with his wife's care without spending endless hours at the nursing home, and he began to pursue activities he had always wanted to pursue but had not done so because he had felt that the needs of his wife and family should come first. Mr. R. continued to grieve the loss of his wife's former self and the marriage they shared, but he was able to learn to start living again for himself.

Because role transition was such a common focus of therapy, we also were interested to learn what kinds of role transitions (i.e., what kinds of changes in our patients' lives) had been involved in patients' depressive episodes. The three most frequent role transitions, in descending order, were aging issues ($n = 12$), retirement ($n = 9$), and changes in health ($n = 7$). All three of these issues are specifically related to the developmental stage of late life. They are common geriatric issues.

Our participants who found aging to be a difficult role transition were often confronted with a loss of their former selves. They could not adjust smoothly to a new identity as an older person and instead focused on losses of family and friends, abilities, looks, and energy. Often, our patients were preoccupied with illnesses and deaths around them, not wanting to think of themselves as "old people." By and large, they felt vulnerable physically and emotionally. They may have been healthy, but they often made extra visits to their doctors, worrying about their health in the future.

Retirement often brought a threatened loss of identity, with the patient frequently feeling lost and out of place. Patients described missing the prestige, appreciation, and camaraderie of being in the workforce. They had difficulty structuring their time and finding meaning in their activities.

When our participants had health problems related to their depressions, the issue was one of adjusting to disabilities and limitations. The most common medical problems that occurred in our group included loss of eyesight, crippling arthritis, chronic obstructive pulmonary disease (emphysema), cancer, and heart disease. These participants needed to learn what kind of people they could become with their disabilities. This process often involved accepting their new selves rather than rejecting the disabled or diseased parts of themselves.

Interestingly, when role transitions became the secondary, rather than the primary, focus of psychotherapy, aging and health issues were almost never the area of concern. Only one participant dealt with aging issues as a secondary focus and none dealt with health problems. What this seems to suggest is that when aging or health is an issue for an elderly depressed person, it overrides other concerns in a way that other issues, such as retirement, do not. Retirement was by far the most common role transition to be discussed as a secondary focus of therapy.

Besides aging, retirement, and health problems, the other most frequent role transitions that were relevant for our participants were widowhood, relocation, and the "empty-nest" syndrome (i.e., children moving out of the house). All three represent a significant change in the composition or location of one's home life.

Other role transitions that occurred as foci for IPT included romantic breakups, dating, divorce, unemployment, and new jobs. These life changes are noteworthy because they appear to represent more middle and younger adult issues rather than the traditional geriatric issues. It is important to recognize that the elderly are not a homogenous group and that the issues of relevance in their lives that can cause stress, difficulty, and depression span the human condition.

A Focus on Interpersonal Disputes

After role transitions, interpersonal disputes were the next most common primary focus for IPT in our population. Forty-two percent of our elderly participants felt that in order to recover from their depressive episodes, they needed to resolve interpersonal conflicts, tensions, disagreements, or impasses. As a primary focus, 21 of our participants focused on disputes with their spouses, 13 with children, and five with multiple relationships, both within the family and with others. As a secondary focus, the most frequent role disputes were with children ($n = 9$), followed by spouses ($n = 6$), and siblings ($n = 3$).

The frequency of conflictual interpersonal relationships was surprising. Focusing on marital issues, no patient elected to divorce his or her spouse during therapy; however, not surprisingly, many long-standing conflicted relationships remained so. A conflicted relationship would be expected to be more difficult when one partner is suffering from major depression. Although we witnessed improved coping skills in many patients, we do not know whether IPT accounted for the changes because we used a combination of medication and psychotherapy in the acute phase of the study.

In keeping with the goals of IPT, when interpersonal conflict is the focus of therapy, the following case vignette illustrates the therapist's success in helping the patient to seek alternative coping strategies that gave her renewed hope for a more meaningful give-and-take relationship with her husband.

Case Vignette: Interpersonal Dispute

Mrs. F. presented for treatment complaining of financial problems, concerns about poor health due to a long-standing disability with arthritis, and, most significant, marital conflict. She felt that long-standing tensions and disagreements with her husband of 40 years had become more uncomfortable since his recent retirement. Mrs. F. was already aware that these conflicts were contributing to her current depression when she presented for treatment.

In examining their relationship, it quickly became clear that Mr. and Mrs. F. largely avoided each other. Communication was rare or ineffective. Mrs. F. viewed her husband as controlling, negative, and complaining. When she would encounter an area of tension with him, because she assumed that he was impossible to deal with, Mrs. F. would typically avoid him or placate him. Sometimes, due to her accumulated anger and resentment, she would actually escalate a disagreement by pushing him to defend his position.

In her IPT sessions, Mrs. F. learned that neither giving in to her husband nor taking an unyielding stand left room for meaningful negotiation or communication. Through repeated clarification and gentle confrontation, Mrs. F. began to practice trying to work with her husband, trying to be more open to his point of view. When Mrs. F. stopped typecasting him as the troublemaker, she found that sometimes he actually was being more considerate than she would have otherwise expected. Mrs. F. acknowledged that since his retirement, Mr. F. now participated in household chores, an area that had been entirely her domain in the past. As Mrs. F. became more engaged with her husband, her depressive symptoms began to remit, and she felt like she had more power in the relationship.

In this case, the therapist also was able to point out the success of the new strategies by underscoring the behavioral changes made by her husband (doing more chores) that occurred as a response to her decision to change her usual way of relating to him.

A Focus on Grief

Leick and Davidsen-Nielsen (1987/1991), in response to Engel's (1961) article, stated, "grief is not a disease, but it can develop into one" (pp. 12–13). The ubiquitous necessity of mourning, the process by which people struggle to cope with the acute pain of loss, work through its many meanings, and survive to reinvest themselves anew, is not an orderly process. Mourning can be delayed, denied, chronic, or arrested when conflicting emotions seem to have no meaningful resolution. Psychotherapy can help the patient return to the unfinished business of mourning and provide a forum for working through its various elements.

IPT posits that inadequate grieving after a loss can lead to depression. IPT seeks to assess what is blocking the grieving process, work through the block, and then help the patient to establish new interests and relationships that can substitute for the loss. The first task usually entails reconstructing the lost relationship in all of its complexities, assessing both its positive and negative aspects for the patient. There may be some unresolved aspect of the relationship that the patient is avoiding working through, often because of guilt around negative feelings. The second task, establishing a new life with full interests and other relationships, often entails the reshaping of one's identity. For example, after numerous years of marriage, it may be a challenge to discover what one's identity as a single person might be. Moving on means letting the deceased go, something many depressed grievers do not feel prepared to do. For an in-depth review of the accumulated efforts of our group in applying the principles of IPT to grief work among the elderly, see Miller et al. (1994).

The following vignette illustrates the patient's ability to successfully work through ambivalent feelings in IPT after the death of her husband.

Case Vignette: Grief

Mrs. W., a 72-year-old widow, related the onset of her depressive symptoms to a recent romantic breakup. She described herself as always having been "dependent on a man," not feeling "whole" outside of a relationship, and feeling badly about the loss of her boyfriend. However, in exploring this relationship further, it was revealed that Mrs. W. had become romantically involved shortly after her husband's death. Involvement in this new relationship had cushioned Mrs. W. from the pain of grieving for her husband. Now that this cushion was gone, she was reexperiencing painful thoughts and emotions regarding her husband's death and the relationship they shared together. Thus, the initial appearance of a role transition was actually disguising significant unresolved grief, which eventually became the primary focus for IPT.

Mrs. W. described feeling considerable guilt about her marriage. She idealized her late husband as having been perfect, describing him as "good, loving, generous, and devoted." By contrast, she saw herself as having mistreated him and as having "walked all over him." Through IPT, Mrs. W. came to learn about her ambivalent feelings toward her husband and the guilt associated with her negative feelings that she had successfully avoided by immersing herself in another relationship. Mrs. W. felt annoyed and angry at her late husband for being a "doormat," for always laying himself at her feet to be stepped on. In fact, she often felt as if she were tripping over him as he tried to do more and more for her. However, she also depended on him to do things for her and at times felt helpless in caring for herself. Through IPT, Mrs. W. was given ample opportunity to discuss the good and the bad in her late marriage and was able to reenter and complete the mourning process.

A Focus on Interpersonal Deficit

We have had only one participant thus far whose primary focus for IPT was interpersonal deficit. The reasons for this are unclear. Perhaps the IPT therapists in our study avoided choosing interpersonal deficit as a primary problem area in an effort to find a more circumscribed focus for therapy whenever possible. It is also possible that patients with severely limited interpersonal resources did not approach us as a result of the structure of our research protocol.

Klerman et al. (1984) pointed out that patients with a severely limited social sphere are often those who are most severely disturbed, those with the least internal and interpersonal resources on which to draw. Because IPT is designed as a short-term therapy, the goal for these more isolated patients is usually to begin working on issues rather than to bring them to resolution. The focus of IPT in these cases is to decrease social isolation. This is accomplished by reviewing the ups and downs of any past relationships and exploring the patient's current relationship with the IPT therapist in order to seek improved strategies for relating to others. Because these patients have less experience in intimacy, whatever relationships they have had, including the one developed in the therapy, can be used to do this work. One of IPT's general rules is to avoid addressing transference issues unless the therapy is threatened. However, in treating patients with interpersonal deficits, the transference is the main and sometimes only interpersonal relationship with which to work. The following case illustrates a successful outcome in a patient with a restricted social sphere.

Case Vignette: Interpersonal Deficit

Mr. C., a 70-year-old bachelor, had been diagnosed as having both recurrent major depression and lifelong dysthymia. He had a degree in accounting but had not been able to sustain a job for more than a year or two. On entering treatment, he had not worked in many years. Throughout his life, Mr. C. had been unable to establish even superficial relationships with anyone and had never dated. Up until his 30s or 40s, he had sparse contact with a few relatives, but none since that time. Mr. C. spent his days alone in his house, having absolutely no contact with anyone. He made only perfunctory telephone calls. He had no group social activities. On entering treatment, he was severely depressed, anergic, and suicidal. He did, however, report that life would be better for him if there were someone in his life who cared for him.

Because of the degree of Mr. C.'s isolation, it was somewhat surprising that he could tolerate committing to his clinic appointments. Yet, he was extremely reliable. It seemed important to him to have someone with whom to talk. Given the opportunity, he was able to discuss issues that were on his mind, such as past familial relationships and old hurts and disappointments. He was not particularly interested in hearing anything from his therapist, and there was no real engagement or discussion. However, these monologues seemed to help him process some issues and feel some contact with someone else.

Gradually, he began to undertake some group activities outside of the home, participating in two classes offered by his neighborhood's senior center. He did not establish any relationships, but his major depressive symptoms did remit back to his dysthymic baseline.

It remains unclear exactly how the psychotherapy helped to bring about these changes for Mr. C. and the improvement in his depressive symptomatology, particularly given the unilaterality of the interaction and the schizoid presentation of the patient. It may be that the process of establishing a relationship with the therapist unlocked his capacity for more engagement in the world and decreased his sense of despairing isolation. In reviewing relationships from his younger years, Mr. C. described numerous instances of experienced rejection and lack of perceived commitment from others. In the psychotherapeutic relationship, the therapist was both accepting and committed.

SUMMARY

Our collective clinical experience suggests that IPT is a viable approach for treating depressed elders. We hope that the reader has gleaned a working familiarity with the principles of IPT as we have applied them to the elderly within a research protocol.

Overall, we experienced IPT to be readily applicable for use with the elderly without any substantial adaptation. Many elderly patients responded positively to the psychoeducational component of IPT and became excellent working partners even though they had no prior experience with therapy or even the abstract concept of depression as a constellation of symptoms.

A striking finding was the high frequency of interpersonal disputes with spouses. We learned not to assume anything about the current state of marriage solely on the basis of the number of years of marriage. Changing circumstances often through illness or increasing disability frequently caused decompensation within marriages.

Given the serious public health problem of undertreated geriatric depression and the frequent coexistence of significant medical problems that complicate pharmacological treatments, advances in practical short-term psychotherapies are a welcome addition to the armamentarium of the clinician treating geriatric depression. In our experience, the tenets of interpersonal psychotherapy are readily taught with proper supervision. IPT addresses problems commonly found in depressed elders, and its short-term orientation is appreciated by patients. Finally, IPT has proved efficacious in rigorously controlled studies (thus far limited to nongeriatric adults and adolescents). On its completion, the MTLLD Study will report on the comparative efficacy of IPT, nortriptyline, and their combination as maintenance treatments for recurrent geriatric depression. In the meantime, we have found IPT to be "user-friendly" for the great majority of depressed elders we encountered. Our elderly patients grasped the IPT approach and were eager to learn all they could about depression. As IPT therapists working with depressed elderly people, we found the work both rich and rewarding.

REFERENCES

Bowlby, J. (1969). *Attachment*. New York: Basic Books.

Bowlby, J. (1977). The making and breaking of affectional bonds: II. Some principles of psychotherapy. *British Journal of Psychiatry, 130,* 421–431.

Cohen, M. B., Baker, G., Cohen, R. A., Fromm-Reichmann, F., & Weigert E. A. (1954). An intensive study of twelve cases of manic depressive psychoses. *Psychiatry*, *17*, 103–137.

Cornes, C. (1990). Interpersonal psychotherapy of depression (IPT). In R. A. Wells & V. J. Giannetti (Eds.), *Handbook of the brief psychotherapies* (pp. 261–276). New York: Plenum.

Elkin, J., Shea, M. T., Watkins, J. T., Imber, S. D., Sotsky, S. M., Collins, J. F., Glass, D. R., Pilkonis, P. A., Leber, W. R., Docherty, J. P., Fiester, S. J., & Parloff, M. B. (1989). National Institute of Mental Health Treatment of Depression Collaborative Research Program: General effectiveness of treatment. *Archives of General Psychiatry*, *46*, 971–983.

Engel, G. L. (1961). Is grief a disease? A challenge for medical research. *Psychosomatic Medicine*, *23*, 18–22.

Frank, E., & Frank, N. (1988a). *Manual for the adaptation of interpersonal psychotherapy to acute treatment of recurrent depression in late life (IPT-LL; Maintenance Therapies in Late-Life Depression Study; MH43832)*. Unpublished manuscript.

Frank, E., & Frank, N. (1988b). *Manual for the adaptation of interpersonal psychotherapy to maintenance treatment of recurrent depression in late life (IPT-LLM; Maintenance Therapies in Late-Life Depression Study; MH43832)*. Unpublished manuscript.

Frank, E., Frank, N., Cornes, C., Imber, S. D., Miller, M. D., Morris, S. M., & Reynolds, C. F. (1993). Interpersonal psychotherapy in the treatment of late-life depression. In G. L. Klerman & M. M. Weissman (Eds.), *New applications of interpersonal psychotherapy* (pp. 167–198). Washington, DC: American Psychiatric Press.

Frank, E., Kupfer, D. J., Perel, J. M., Cornes, C., Jarrett, D. B., Mallinger, A. G., Thase, M. E., McEachran, A. B., & Grochocinski, V. J. (1990). Three-year outcomes for maintenance therapies in recurrent depression. *Archives of General Psychiatry*, *47*, 1093–1099.

Frank, J. D. (1969). Common features account for effectiveness. *International Journal of Psychiatry*, *7*, 122–127.

Frank, J. D., & Frank, J. B. (1991). *Persuasion and healing: A comparative study of psychotherapy* (3rd ed.). Baltimore: Johns Hopkins University Press.

Fromm-Reichmann, F. (1960). *Principles of intensive psychotherapy*. Chicago: Phoenix Books.

Klerman, G. L., Weissman, M. M., Rounsaville, B. J., & Chevron, E. (1984). *Interpersonal psychotherapy of depression*. New York: Basic Books.

Leick, N., & Davidsen-Nielsen, M. (1991). *Healing pain: Attachment, loss and grief therapy* (D. Stoner, Trans.). New York: Tavistock/Routledge. (Original work published 1987)

Meyer, A. (1957). *Psychobiology: A science of man*. Springfield, IL: Charles C Thomas.

Miller, M. D., Frank, E., Cornes, C., Imber, S. D., Anderson, B., Ehrenpreis, L., Malloy, J., Silberman, R., Wolfson, L., Zaltman, J., & Reynolds, C. F. (1994).

Applying interpersonal psychotherapy to bereavement-related depression following loss of a spouse in late life. *Journal of Psychotherapy Practice and Research, 3*, 149–162.

Parker, G. B., Barrett, E. A., & Hickie, I. B. (1992). From nurture to network: Examining links between perceptions of parenting received in childhood and social bonds in adulthood. *American Journal of Psychiatry, 149*, 877–885.

Reynolds, C. F., Frank, E., Perel, J. M., Imber, S. D., Cornes, C., Morycz, R. K., Mazumdar, S., Miller, M. D., Pollock, B. G., Rifai, A. H., Stack, J. A., George, C. J., Houck, P. R., & Kupfer, D. J. (1992). Combined pharmacotherapy and psychotherapy in the acute and continuation treatment of elderly patients with recurrent major depression: A preliminary report. *American Journal of Psychiatry, 149*, 1687–1692.

Reynolds, C. F., Frank, E., Perel, J. M., Miller, M. D., Cornes, C., Rifai, A. H., Pollock, B. G., Mazumdar, S., George, C. J., Houck, P. R., & Kupfer, D. J. (1994). Treatment of consecutive episodes of major depression in the elderly. *American Journal of Psychiatry, 151*, 1740–1743.

Shea, T., Glass, D., Pilkonis, P. A., Watkins, J., & Docherty, J. (1987). Frequency and implications of personality disorders in a sample of depressed outpatients. *Journal of Personality Disorders, 1*, 27–42.

Sholomskas, A. J., Chevron, E. S., Prusoff, B. A., & Berry, C. (1983). Short-term interpersonal psychotherapy (IPT) with the depressed elderly: Case reports and discussion. *American Journal of Psychotherapy, 37*, 552–566.

Sloane, R. B., Staples, F. R., Schneider, L. S. (1985). Interpersonal therapy versus nortriptyline for depression in the elderly. In G. Burrows, T. R. Norman, & L. Dennerstein (Eds.), *Clinical and pharmacological studies in psychiatric disorders* (pp. 344–346). London: John Libbey.

Sullivan, H. S. (1953). *The interpersonal theory of psychiatry.* New York: Norton.

5

MODERN PSYCHOANALYTIC TREATMENT OF THE OLDER PATIENT

VICKI GRANET SEMEL

More than 15 years ago, I began work with older patients in a nursing home unit in a medical center. Because these elderly patients were physically impaired and often had dementia, I expected that they would be much different from the younger patients with whom I had had more experience. Initially, I was put off by their appearance. In my other work with patients with schizophrenia in locked wards, my initial reaction was similar—a response therapists often experience to the physical effects of institutionalization. At the core of my psychoanalytic practice, however, is the belief that all patients, whatever their diagnoses, can be helped to develop more mature coping styles. So I began to look at similarities and to discover the ways in which these elderly patients were similar to patients of all ages.

I began to use the same method of treatment, modern psychoanalysis, which involves the patient as a consultant in the therapy and enables the patient to decide the issues on which to work. The patients responded in fashion similar to patients of all ages, talking more openly and relating better in their lives. This approach, as a theory and technique, resolves self-attacking patterns by protecting the patient's defenses and strengthening the ego. The interventions proved to be highly effective with the aging patient, who has often sustained blows to his or her self-esteem.

I discovered that if I kept this technique unrevised in the beginning of my work with the older patient and listened to the individual story being told, the patient would guide me toward understanding where and how, if at all, the issues of aging were relevant to that particular therapy. The approach involves following the lead of the patient, almost "becoming the patient," and joining in his or her state of mind (Meadow, 1990, 1991). A major benefit in this approach is that it enables the practitioner to keep an open mind about the issues and helps to avoid the bias and prejudice associated with ageism. If a therapist assumes that the older person is inherently different and selects the patient's issues and problems on the basis of age, the therapist is in danger of mistreating the patient.

Concerns about ageism are certainly relevant and are supported by an observation of the health system. It is empowering for the patient to be considered helpful in his or her treatment. However, having one's opinions respected is negated by the picture one sees of how the aged are infantalized when they do seek medical or mental health services. The belief of the mental health practitioner that the patient is "too old" and that different measures need to be used than the therapist's usual armamentarium is the ultimate undermining attack on the patient.

Thus, when medical and mental health professionals treat the older patient as if the professionals know what is best, disregarding the patient's wishes and information about the self, they are falling into the prejudice of ageism. For treatment to promote the further maturation of the older patient, a relationship may need to be developed in which the patient can advise the therapist about both how to treat or not to treat. This approach is especially useful in a private-practice setting, but it also is valuable in other arenas.

One advantage of this particular technique of modern psychoanalysis, which I discuss in more detail later, is that it helps the therapist begin treatment with an open mind to the patient's messages. Over the years, with this attitude toward my work with older patients, I have successfully applied the modern psychoanalytic approach in nursing homes, with individual patients in my office, with couples, and with groups.

I find that my work with the elderly lies along two continua: either the acute or the chronic seriously disturbed patient. I have rarely treated older patients who are doing relatively well but who want to improve their functioning, a population one might find attracted to therapy in a younger age group. I think this pattern may change as a more psychologically minded generation approaches older age.

In this chapter I explore the clinical application of modern psychoanalytic treatment using two cases of elderly patients to illustrate how similar the aged can be to every patient if the therapist operates from a nonageist position. First, I compare treatment of the child with treatment of the elderly to clarify some salient factors that may influence the therapist in working with the older patient. I then review the psychoanalytic literature on work with aging patients, proposing the study of case material that describes such work. I describe the modern psychoanalytic approach and its relevance for treating the older patient. Finally, the cases of Mr. F. and Mrs. T. are presented to illustrate that office treatment of the older patient does not have to differ from that of young adults in the therapist's private practice.

DISTINCTIONS IN TREATMENT OF THE OLDER PATIENT

In thinking about whether the older patient who comes for therapy is distinctly different from other patient groups, I first looked to see whether there would be some important ways that therapy for the child at the beginning of life is similar to the therapy of those approaching the end of life. In attempting to highlight the distinctions, I kept returning to the experience of treating children, in which the therapist helps unleash their potential so that development can proceed. It is the child's developmental thrust that, once unfettered by therapy, leads to a continuation of natural developmental processes. To some degree, this result also is possible with the older patient as blocks are resolved.

An important distinction concerns independence or self-reliance. As the child matures, he or she becomes more independent and more able to cope without the involvement of others. With the older patient, however, the progression is to need increasing amounts of external help when advancing in years. Although this pattern is not true of all, it is the most likely process that occurs with aging. The young-old (up to age 70) may have far fewer of these needs. However, the middle-old (in the 70s) begin to be aware of physical and physiological shifts. Then, by the 80s, it is the rare individual who has not had to deal with some decrease in physical capacities. It is almost as if the patient has to learn ways to cope with not coping. Sometimes, in fact, therapy helps the older patient figure out ways to receive support and help in a nondemeaning fashion.

Another distinction lies in the role of verbalization. The child needs the therapist to be intuitive. The baby and small child cannot articulate their needs directly, so the therapist needs to recognize this less developed facility. Symbolic communication through play is usually necessary at first. The older patient can verbally work with the therapist about resolving conflicts that brought the patient to therapy.

Sensitivity to levels of functioning is necessary in the treatment of both the child and the aging person. The small boy needs to feel helpful as he pushes the vacuum cleaner along with his mother. The older patient has to learn how to let someone else push the vacuum cleaner and yet not feel demeaned by being helped. Issues of helping, being productive, and having one's opinions accepted appear to be essential for the aging patient.

Although the child can be taught to cope and be independent, the older adult is less and less able to cope in the outside world and other people become increasingly important in the elder's day-to-day functioning. The need of the older adult may not be how to think for himself or herself and become independent but to learn how to accept help from others without feeling humiliated or insulted because of growing fragility.

For the child the therapist has the hopeful attitude of a teacher with a beginning pupil, whereas with the elderly patient the therapist is more likely to sense hopelessness about the future learning of skills to function independently. In both situations, it is the therapist's underlying respect for the individuality of each patient that helps provide the foundation for forward movement in therapy.

The therapist's thoughts and attitudes about therapy do not mean that these are the articulated issues of the older patient. Although the patient may need help in resolving resistance to expressing certain thoughts, patients treated in the office have the potential to verbalize everything. The goal of analytic therapy with the child and the adult is to help the individual get more and more thoughts and feelings into words and to resolve the blocks that impede mature functioning.

PSYCHODYNAMIC LITERATURE ON ELDERLY PEOPLE

It seems ironic that early treatment of the elderly from a psychodynamic perspective was rejected on the grounds that older patients probably could not be helped. Clinicians have moved far in the psychodynamic and psychoanalytic literature from the early admonitions of Freud (1905/1953) against even treating the older patient (i.e., someone over 50). King (1974) pointed out the irony of his view, as Freud was approximately 50 years old when he wrote this warning and still had much productivity ahead of him. In fact, this viewpoint seems oddly self-attacking.

Freud was concerned about the amount of material for the patient to cover, which might become too voluminous with long years to report. Also, there was a concern about the growing inflexibility of the character as age progressed. Because modern psychoanalysts are less interested in detailed historical reporting and are focused more on the current relationship with the therapist, this particular issue is less relevant today. Abraham (1919/1927) believed that the length of time of the neurosis was more relevant to the treatment than the age of the patient, but he followed with little clinical commentary on this viewpoint. Although sprinklings of psychoanalytic interest in the older patient did occur (Grotjahn, 1955; Kaufman, 1940; Segal, 1958), it is more within the past two decades that there has developed a greater interest in treating psychodynamically the older patient.

The clinical literature is highly diverse and reflects much interest in the developmental periods in order to study whether the developmental approach illuminates this complex period. Erikson (1959), in a theory of life span development, traced his developmental stages, issues, conflicts, and resolutions in old age. Nemiroff and Colarusso (1985) concentrated on the "race against time" and its effect on the older person who may be somewhat propelled toward cure by the awareness that time is slipping away. There is a concern with the continuing periods of development that are unique throughout life.

Other clinicians, rather than finding new theoretical constructs to understand late-life development, have discovered replays of earlier stages in this older period. King (1974, 1980) and Sandler (1978, 1982) found that this period revived earlier childhood and especially adolescent issues. Those clinicians noted the earlier unresolved issues that replay in later life.

Although some clinicians express an interest in developmental constructs, others are more focused on particular issues in the aging process. For these clinicians, content issues are important in their study of the older patient. Powerful reactions to loss, especially loss of functions or roles, pervade this literature (Myers, 1984). Whether these losses are attributable to role loss through retirement (Brody & Semel, 1993; Kahana, 1985; Semel, 1986; Wasylenki, 1982), through illness or death (Solis & Brink, 1989), or simply the loss of youth (Pollock, 1987), the importance of losses shapes their work.

Although these theoretical positions can be useful, I recommend the individual study of particular cases that are as close to the clinical description as possible to discover one's own understanding of these patients, their interactions with their therapists, and the effects of the aging processes. Some of the more recent literature provides case examples of the diverse kinds of psychodynamic treatment or conceptualization (Coltart, 1991; Crusey, 1985; Knight, 1993; Miller, 1987; Muslin & Clarke, 1988; Myers, 1984; Sandler, 1978, 1982; Simburg, 1985; Solis & Brink, 1989; Wasylenki, 1982; Wylie & Wylie, 1987). My own work also emphasizes case examples (Semel, 1986, 1993b).

THE MODERN PSYCHOANALYTIC APPROACH

The method I use to treat patients is useful in studying dynamics. It is based on the underlying assumption that a patient cannot hear an idea or information for which he or she is not ready. Such information about the patient, in fact, usually hardens the defenses and makes them more difficult to resolve during the later course of therapy. Therefore, with this basic assumption in mind, I approach the patient with a modern psychoanalytic perspective. No ideas, projections, or delusions are questioned. The therapist creates a nonstimulating environment for the patient to relax and talk freely. I am able to study the patient's issues and character traits with this method, which is relatively nonintrusive in the initial stages and permits me to develop an understanding of how and if the patient's aging processes are interfering with effective coping styles or whether other issues are involved.

Modern psychoanalysis provides the therapist with concrete tools for understanding and treating patients, especially those with narcissistic or preoedipal problems. These are patients who have difficulty relating to others or who have borderline, serious depressive, schizophrenic, impulse-disordered, or character-disordered problems. In more traditional psychoanalytic work, such patients might be considered not treatable because the essential technique of exploring interpretations and insight with such patients frequently causes them to regress and become more symptomatic.

This approach was developed originally by Spotnitz (1976, 1985) and has been expanded by his colleagues (Margolis, 1986, 1994; Meadow, 1990, 1991; Spotnitz & Meadow, 1995). The treatment method is goal directed: to strengthen the ego of the preoedipal patient through helping the patient talk and by developing a relationship in the here and now with the therapist. Although no particular methods have been adapted to be used with the older patient, the work is easily applicable to those of all ages who have unresolved personality issues.

These patients are conceptualized as displaying a narcissistic defense in which they attack themselves in various ways to shield others from their hostile or aggressive impulses. Thus, the patient with a serious disorder sacrifices functioning and turns aggressive impulsivity against the self or mind or body. Such acts of aggression against the self are understood as the narcissistic defense. This concept of the patient as self-involved, or narcissistic, places this pattern as a defensive mode to protect the important people in the patient's life. From this theoretical position, the therapist sees the patient as being devoted to the objects in his or her life and withdrawn more as a way to protect the objects rather than being protective out of self-love.

This shift in perspective reorients the relationship between the therapist and the patient in that the patient's need for the narcissistic defense is respected. The early stage of treatment protects the patient's ego by creating a nonstimulating environment so that he or she sets the tone of the sessions. Modern psychoanalysis, with its roots in the treatment of the patient with a weaker ego and more primitive defenses, may be especially ideal for the older person who is beginning to deal with the stresses of the aging process and who may become physically and psychically vulnerable. The protection of defenses in treatment is at the center of this approach.

The patient chooses the amount of stimulation through verbal contacts with the therapist. Thus, the therapist talks no more than the patient seeks. The patient's silence begets analyst's silence, and questions beget questions. If a silence continues for a period and the patient seems uncomfortable, the therapist might ask an object-oriented question, "How is the silence?" "Should I be talking?" "Is this a comfortable silence?" This technical device is termed *following the contact function* and can be used widely in the early period of treatment to study and diagnose any patient. In such a situation, the patient's "contacts" (i.e., verbal attempts to reach out to the therapist) are studied as demonstrations of particular symptom pictures and character styles.

When speaking during this period, the therapist avoids introducing information that the patient does not want. In such an environment, the therapist does not interfere with the patient perceiving the therapist as being similar to the self, and the narcissistic transference begins to develop. Interventions enable the patient to experience the therapist as one with the self (Margolis, 1986), almost like the small baby and mother, who are at one with each other. This period in the therapy creates the narcissistic transference.

During this early stage, the narcissistic transference begins its curative effect and the patient becomes involved with the therapist in his or her own unique fashion. The patient's defenses are respected, but after a while the defenses become less necessary. In other words, when this indirect method of treatment is used, the symptoms and maladaptive character traits diminish as they become less needed.

A natural development of the relationship occurs wherein the patient frequently idealizes and then hates the therapist. Often, when the patient experiences the therapist as a distinct and disappointing being, much anger and hostility accompany this disillusionment, perhaps as the small child, too, begins to express anger at the less-than-perfect parent.

The true contribution of modern psychoanalysis is in the orientation toward protecting the defenses of the patient and working with, and welcoming, the development of direct verbal hostility toward the therapist as the ego strengthens and the patient becomes more object oriented. Once the patient is able to distinguish the self from others, a relationship with people who think and feel differently can begin.

Although this approach is applicable to a wide range of diagnostic problems, it does make the therapist self-aware and willing to accept the patient's perceptions and views of the therapist and the world without rushing to correct them. Some supervision of and further training to develop one's therapeutic skills are recommended in this work.

This theoretical stance, however, is a far cry from the trials and tribulations of actually working with a rageful patient who directs personal expressions of anger toward the analyst. It is because these patients are often preverbal in their reactions that the feelings and reactions of the therapist are essential to understanding the patient. The unexpressed reactions of the patient frequently are passed on to the therapist and are useful information in learning more about the patient and his or her unexpressed feelings. How to use these feelings productively in the therapy to help each patient mature is the goal.

The use of feelings, which is widespread in therapy today, was an important early contribution of modern psychoanalysis. This acceptance of countertransference as a form of therapeutic information available in the session to the attuned therapist is a useful addition to the theory of technique of the modern therapist (Spotnitz, 1985; Spotnitz & Meadow, 1995; Winnicott, 1958). Those interested in aging also have been expanding on the issues of countertransference with the elderly (Hinze, 1987; Myers, 1984; Semel, 1993a; Wylie & Wylie, 1987).

I now describe two cases that illustrate the modern psychoanalytic approach to treating the older patient. The first case involves brief psychodynamic treatment of an 82-year-old, frail, retired businessman; the second case involves long-term modern psychoanalytic treatment of a 69-year-old woman who taught school. The businessman was in acute distress, and the schoolteacher was a chronic and seriously disturbed patient who had fought mental illness her whole life.

In the first case, I used my technique to understand the dynamics of the patient and help him resolve a painful symptom. In the second, the patient's unresolved character issues made a longer term relationship with me the mechanism for helping her develop more mature coping styles in which we replayed her life's issues in the transference.

In Case 1, the aspects of modern analytic techniques used were following the contact function and protecting defenses.[1] The client and I did not develop a relationship in which to work through his personality issues. In fact, he did not want to be in treatment, and I honored his wish as I might do with any patient. In the first brief case study, Mr. F. experienced an acute onslaught of symptoms. He could not stop crying. I worked with him in a short-term dynamically oriented fashion only in two individual sessions and four that he came to with his wife.

The Case of Mr. F.

My relationship with Mr. F. began after he had a serious stroke, which led him to fixate on the belief that his wife was going to die. He sobbed and was inconsolable about her possible death, yet it was he who was ill and wheelchair bound and more likely to die.

---

[1]Part of this case was presented in *Strategies for Therapy With the Elderly: Living With Hope and Meaning* (pp. 123–124), edited by C. M. Brody and V. G. Semel, 1993, New York: Springer. Copyright 1993 by Springer Publishing Company, Inc. Reprinted with permission.

Mr. F. was referred by his internist and brought to see me by his irritated and upset wife of 56 years. He would accept no reassurance from either his physician or his wife that could stop his tears. He came to therapy unwillingly, but he quickly and eagerly told me his story.

Mr. F. had been raised in an Irish immigrant family and became wealthy through his own efforts. Mrs. F. was committed totally to raising their five children and had remained home to care for them and for both sets of in-laws.

Through his business Mr. F had entered a more cosmopolitan world, marketing his product and, in the process, becoming a "man about town." He also became a womanizer and enjoyed this aspect of his life.

As the years went on and he became physically ill, his freedom to wander became limited. He had thought that a retirement community with a superabundance of widows would solve his urge for wanderlust, because even if he were not as mobile, the female residents would be there and could find him. As his health worsened, however, he realized that his wife might well outlive him and that she was in total control of his life. He said, quite revealingly, that there would be no way to escape her clutches. So he cried, unconsciously wishing to mourn his wife's death, his fantasized way to freedom.

In therapy, I simply asked a few questions and helped him to talk. I did not give him any interpretations of his hostile impulses toward his wife, but waited for him to describe how she had him right where she wanted him: under her thumb. Once he was able to express anger at her in the treatment alone with me, his crying stopped.

What part did aging play in Mr. F.'s conflict? Physical frailty prevented his decades-long defense of philandering, which he had used to block his frustration with his wife. Now that infirmity left him unable to use this defense, he first developed wishes for her death and, unable to acknowledge his frustration and rage at her, developed the indirect symptom of crying.

These issues are an example of how age influenced the symptom picture of an older patient. The content of Mr. F.'s sessions was related to his age but, as a therapist, did I function any differently because of his age? I do not believe so. He was a somewhat unwilling patient; he presented with the issue of crying; when he stopped crying, he stopped therapy. I did ask him and his wife about working on their relationship, but they were not interested. I left the door open for them to return.

I helped him with an acute problem, and we parted after a brief interaction. I did not discuss with him his unconscious processes. He disclosed his hostility toward his wife independently in the session. It was his work that eliminated his symptom. Although his issue was related to age infirmity, his treatment necessitated no adaptation in my approach, except perhaps for having a wheelchair-accessible office.

I now discuss the long-term work with a more disturbed patient with chronic problems.

The Case of Mrs. T.

When looking back on my relationship with Mrs. T.,[2] I realized that she had been trying to help me with her treatment since its inception. As I reviewed her file, I noted that it was replete with informational pamphlets on various topics she felt would help me treat her in a better fashion. Yet, my previous awareness of such a goal on her part was nonexistent. Her ability to express this need directly was limited in the initial stages of treatment. This clinical study guided me to become aware of how important the need to help the therapist can be, especially for the older patient.

So what happens when the patient seeks to be helpful, but her character patterns lead others to feel simply controlled, put down, or inadequate? How does the therapist become aware that this method is a maladaptive attempt to be helpful that comes off as the reverse because of the individual's psychopathology? To be called "whippersnapper, too young, and unseasoned in life" compared with her does not promote an understanding that the patient wants to be a valuable consultant in the work. It feels more like a deprecation of the therapist. Patients who reach old age with this critical pattern need first to grow in therapy in order to become truly helpful in their own treatment and also to guide their therapist in how to be more helpful to them.

Recall the idea of this older patient as a consultant who will help in her own therapy. It is more likely that the patient has a maladaptive way of giving and receiving help, or else she might never have come to my office; she would simply cope with difficult life issues. This case is about how Mrs. T. made use of therapy to become both helpful in therapy and a more helpful participant in her own world.

There are two beginnings in this story. One is Mrs. T.'s actual beginnings of life. The second is her beginning with me. Both are essential for the story of therapy and how she finally began to be a helpful therapy consultant. First, the beginning with me consisted of every other week for 3 years, then weekly treatment for 3 years, then every other week again in the last 3 years.

About 9 years ago, Mrs. T. approached me for supervision in her work as a teacher of people with emotional problems. At 60 years of age she had spent a lifetime working to be freed from the residual effects of a schizophrenic break and hospitalization when she had tried to leave home

---

[2]Part of this case was presented in *Strategies for Therapy With the Elderly: Living With Hope and Meaning* (pp. 135–137), edited by C. M. Brody and V. G. Semel, 1993, New York: Springer. Copyright 1993 by Springer Publishing Company, Inc. Reprinted with permission.

at the age of 20. What seemingly brought her for professional help with her difficult students eventually appeared as a cry for help for her tormented thought-disordered self and for her son suffering from a similar disorder. She was isolated and unable to relate to her family and students.

Mrs. T. came into therapy with the issue of help in the foreground. She began by trying to help her students but quickly shifted into a therapy relationship with me in which she talked of her wish to save her acutely psychotic son. In addition to this omnipresent issue with her son, there also was a new issue with her husband.

A crisis in her life was approaching as her husband prepared for retirement, pressuring her to join him. Her spouse, moderately successful, also in the field of education, perceived Mrs. T. as an inadequate human being that he accepted as his lot in life, according to his wife's description. He wanted companionship in his retirement and opportunities to visit family members in states around the country. Her part-time work, useless as it seemed to him, interfered with his plan, developed without any discussion with her. The issue of retirement was central to her life and appeared as a conflict with the spouse.

As to Mrs. T.'s beginnings, the earliest stories of her life began to unfold during alleged supervision of difficult children in her classes. She was indirectly asking for therapy, rather than supervision, and soon did ask for analysis. She was born into a mixed Jewish and Protestant home in Upstate New York. Her father died when she was around 5 years old, and she may have actually witnessed something about his death or had a "screen" memory of him either drunk or ill and lying on the floor. The patient had injured her finger, and she recalled running out of her room in great pain seeking her mother but finding her father on the floor and no mother around. This was her first memory, and it certainly involved a trauma around being helped.

After her father's death, her mother, overburdened and poverty stricken, began to work in a grocery store and had no time for a small daughter and her son (older by 3 years). Thus, life's circumstances forced her into a neglected life because there was no local extended family to give her attention. She and her brother often played in the streets.

Mrs. T.'s second memory of helping another was equally tragic. Someone gave her a puppy when she was about 8 years old. She was ecstatic. While standing on the corner with her dog, a man asked her to get a newspaper for him. The gentleman then gave her some coins as a thank you, but he dropped them. She let go of the dog's leash to retrieve the money, and the dog ran into the street and was killed. Her earliest memories involve helping and needing help but being tragically used and harmed when she helped others and trusted them.

Mrs. T. said that she was considered an "odd" child, terrified by most things. Her mother used this as a reason to sleep with her after the father's death and did not stop sharing a bed with her daughter until Mrs. T. herself insisted on her own bed at the age of 15.

Unsupervised children, wandering the streets, will get into trouble, even quiet, nearly schizoid ones. Mrs. T. was involved in sexual play and abused by neighborhood children. She reported that her family always thought there was something wrong with her and advised the mother that she seemed strange and quiet. Mrs. T. also had no friends and had difficulty concentrating in school. Her older brother was somewhat more gregarious and successful with friends, although he made no attempt to protect her.

She stayed around home after high school and began a clerical job. When someone at work encouraged her to take another position in a nearby state, she impulsively agreed and set out to leave home. The act of getting on the train and moving led to massive confusion and delusions. She panicked, thought people were following her, and believed that women wanted to have sex with her. She developed a full-blown psychosis with an obvious thought disorder and was hospitalized for about a year. At that time, Mrs. T. was administered shock therapy, insulin therapy, and some psychotherapy and was subsequently released in fragile condition, having been diagnosed with a paranoid schizophrenic episode.

A caring psychiatrist who treated her in the hospital continued to work with her as an outpatient, helping her attend college and encouraging her to find a boyfriend. Unable to do so, Mrs. T. believed she had disappointed the therapist and stopped seeing him.

In the ensuing years, Mrs. T. did indeed become a teacher and eventually married another teacher, who was a devout Jew. After her conversion, he brought this isolated woman into an important network of family and a religious community. They moved to New York City, where she had a son and daughter; the son developed problems similar to hers in late adolescence. She also continued attempts to be cured during the middle adult years of her life, switching from therapist to therapist.

This information is much clearer in my presentation than it was in her confused and disorganized account. It took me years to understand her confused statements. Her sessions were composed of silence, much blocking, little verbal contact (i.e., few questions asked), and thought-disordered talk. Looking back at my initial work with Mrs. T., I realize now that she had a need to help me.

She would flood me with articles and videotapes about work with children with handicaps and the particular religious sect to which she belonged, yet her talk was confused. I would thank her politely for the material, which we never discussed. I am not sure I could have discussed them because the therapy sessions were highly disorganized because of her thought disorder.

Mrs. T. was eager to help her son, whose schizophrenic break left him with acute episodes during which he would be in and out of hospitals. She was trying to help him by telling him what to do and pointing out the inadequacies of his decision-making abilities. Her approach attacked this young man's fragile ego and left him more prone to psychotic breaks.

When Mrs. T. invited her son to a few sessions, I took his side and told her she was being authoritarian. Although furious at me for this, she began to sound more supportive of her son. His more blatant psychotic symptoms diminished, and he decided to go back to finish college. Mrs. T. and I then began a period of total idealization.

I was wonderful and would "remove the cobwebs" from her "confused head" and also "cure" her son. In this period the idealization led her to educate me and inform me further. She was a peer and a passionately involved patient. Her love for me developed, and she allowed herself this powerful emotional response.

Then she began to call me at home with helpful information about certain TV programs she thought I should watch. Our relationship, of course, belonged in the treatment room. In a fairly heavy-handed fashion, I talked with her about our relationship and the reasons for her telephone calls. The calls stopped immediately, but then I had a rejected suitor on my hands.

Mrs. T. believed that she had tried to be helpful and that I had overreacted. So, in some sense, I was repeating her earlier negative experiences with helping and receiving help. I, as the helper, was hurtful. She as the helper was injured.

After this intervention about her calls, she developed a series of physical symptoms (e.g., a blood clot) that put her in the hospital. She also rapidly gained nearly 30 lb (13.60 kg). Her anger at me seemed to be coming out against her soma, as she protected me from direct expression of her feelings about my rejection. Now, I also was "neglectful," for somehow the therapy was failing her and leading to illnesses.

By the 4th year of treatment, the feelings in the sessions shifted. Mrs. T.'s health improved, and indirect but obvious attacks on me began to become the mainstay of the therapy sessions. Although these were off-kilter and sarcastic, they also were much clearer. In a sarcastic and challenging fashion, Mrs. T. would denigrate what she believed was my brand of Judaism and found criticisms of modern psychoanalysis and reported them with great delight. Indirect hostility had replaced a confused thought-disordered presentation.

During this period, there were two general issues that were discussed in the sessions apart from our hostile relationship. One involved the patient's increasing awareness of her pattern of drifting off and falling asleep in the classroom while she was involved with a particular child. The other involved her hygiene. The children would report her sleeping to their parents. Mrs. T. was under strict supervision at work, and the administrator wanted to fire her.

This pattern was evident in our sessions, during which she would often lapse into silence and seem to be blocking and drifting off. She appeared odd, confused, and withdrawn. In an idiosyncratic theory, she related this withdrawal to the injury she had experienced when her father was dying. She even thought she might have had a strokelike episode at that time of stress and subsequent confusion and neglect. Mrs. T. went for an electroencephalogram to confirm her suspicions and the doctor thought there might indeed have been some previous minor insult.

She also described a tic, which seemed to be internally experienced, although she believed it was visible in the office and would feel a tightening around her head. Although she went to a neurologist, no one discovered the source of this tic, which did resolve to some degree during our treatment, along with the drifting off and sleeping issues. So, interspersed with her critical comments, laced with ridicule and sarcasm, was discussion of work and somatic complaints.

The second issue that came to the forefront during this period was that of hygiene. For years Mrs. T. had body odor. At times I would even spray the office after her appointments. In her narcissistic state she was unaware of it, and I did not feel ready to address the issue. I could see how her behavior at work and her appearance would make her a prime target for dismissal, but she was not interested in this issue and for a time I, too, followed the contact and did not intervene. I did not help her; I just listened.

One day she began to complain about how this person "is rotten," that school "stinks," and this and that authority "stink." Then she said with real feeling, "You stink, too!" Her direct verbal expression of feeling toward me seemed genuine and appropriate. Although Mrs. T. was not stating she was furious with me, it was more direct than critical. So I asked her, "Do you stink?" She heard the question on two levels, about being both rotten and smelling. We had a discussion about hygiene in which we talked pragmatically about clean underwear, dry-cleaning clothes, bathing, and deodorant.

The next session she came in and told me how furious she was that I did not tell her before that she smelled. I told her I would be glad to do so in the future. After that point, whenever she came in smelling, which was much less frequently, I would raise the issue of hygiene.

Mrs. T. continued to be curious about the "glitch" in her brain (her cognitive confusion and drifting off), believing that such thoughts were peculiar but that they were from the injury to her thumb. She noted feeling somewhat more relaxed and for the first time sleeping more easily at night. She recalled an entirely different version of her dog being killed. Now, she reported that the puppy was with her mother, being watched while she went to get the newspaper for the man. Mrs. T. needed her mother to help her and she did not. In fact, help was related to danger and harm if one depends on another person. "Maybe she used me. I was too close to her." I heard the message about me loud and clear.

Mrs. T. continuously talked about how she was going to be fired and yet how important it was for her to be able to help her students. I would not guide her directly but simply ask questions in keeping with her stated goals. When asked about how she could maintain her job and what would she have to do, Mrs. T. made it clear she would have to cooperate with the administrator, whom she thought of as inadequate to supervise her. Her arrogance continued to get her in trouble: As she became clearer, she became more grandiose and hostile.

She left that school and found another in which a similar pattern presented itself. Despising authority figures made it impossible for her to cooperate with others and to protect herself and advance in her profession. I was aware of the transference similarity because I had thoughts of firing her too and began to be clearly aware of her age, possibly "too old" for analysis.

Getting and giving help were fraught not only with frustration but danger. Mrs. T. began to complain about how I did not tell her anything in the sessions. I, however, could not tell she was asking for anything. One day she remarked with feeling, "Maybe if you tell me something I can respond to then I'll answer, 'So what? Who doesn't know that!'" She talked about experiencing a film over her brain when she was with people, and she expressed anger at me because she both loved and hated me. The litany of criticism and complaints continued, and accepting them, when I really felt like terminating the treatment, was difficult. I continued to think of her increased age.

Mrs. T. then decided to consult a wide variety of therapists, letting them know how terrible I was. She was sent back to discuss our relationship each time. I told her about the different theories we were using in the treatment. She was operating as if hate begot love, but in reality hate begets hate: If she wanted to have a more loving relationship with me, then she had to be more loving.

Mrs. T. then began to have sexual fantasies. I believed the continuing hostility also was a way to shield her from a more emotionally intimate relationship with me. We began to talk about getting rid of each other. Then one day I told her, with a lot of feeling, "Look, I'm not going to get rid of you and you aren't going to get rid of me, so you might as well settle down to your therapy!" She became clear that there would be no action between us: I would not terminate with her, although at times I was tempted to.

She then spoke of her sexual humiliations and seductions as a child. She became sad and reported that she had hoped I might learn from her. Mrs. T. did not expect me to know so much but to let her know more and teach me. She thought she could help me learn how to treat a patient with schizophrenia, that I would learn through her how to cure the serious disorders. Mrs. T. was gloomy about this possibility. Her need to be helpful was clear. I was moved for the first time with her and realized I was feeling more hopeful.

In a letter she wrote to me during this period, she complained and described all my failures. I was somehow able to thank her for her letter and tell her I appreciated her wish to help me be a better therapist. Could she suggest further ways for me to improve the treatment? She told me that I talked too much and that I did not give her enough interpretations. I tried to follow her recommendations. These interactions had a profound effect on our relationship.

Soon after beginning to be helpful as a consultant in her therapy, Mrs. T. startled me by describing some actual awareness of another person and the pain that others might feel in her workplace. I noticed that my feelings had truly changed and that I now thought of her with respect.

In the latest session with Mrs. T., I noted how she seemed to be relating to and in contact with a fellow teacher who was agonizing about kicking a ne'er-do-well brother out of her tiny apartment. Everyone was encouraging her to do what she could not bring herself to do. Only Mrs. T., after careful listening, was able to say, "Look, when you get ready to make a decision, you will. It doesn't matter if he stays a little longer until you are sure. When it's right for you, it will fall into place." The woman began to relax, told a joke about her situation, and the other teachers became more supportive.

After my 8 years of contact with Mrs. T., I felt like cheering. She was indeed helpful, and that came about because she was able to simply sit and listen to the other woman without imposing her own judgments and pressures. She heard her colleague's impossible struggle and was able to empathize because her cognitive confusion had dissipated and her ability to hear another person grew. She then told me of great pain she was feeling and that it was because she was not insulting me anymore. The cognitive confusion and isolation were diminishing. She became more related in an emotionally relevant way in the sessions.

I have described my ongoing treatment of this seriously disturbed woman and her movement in the relationship with me into a more helpful participant in the world—her lifelong goal. This work is slow, and more remains to be done. Yet, whenever I found Mrs. T. difficult to be with and I would think of her age, I believe I was using age to hide my counter-transference frustrations. The patient was merely being herself, and she brought into my office her repetitive patterns. These repetitions are the necessary bedrock of any psychoanalytically oriented work. The modern psychoanalytic approach accepts the narcissistic state of the patient and draws it into the relationship in the therapy room with all the boredom, love, and hate that it entails. Mrs. T. was a cooperative patient as she revealed her repetitious patterns so clearly and passionately, and brought them into the relationship with me willingly.

For a while, I was unable to hear her need to be helpful in the treatment. At first, it was because of her psychopathology, but I also have to consider whether it was my own bias about her age. Clearly, my countertransference issues hid my negative feelings about working with her. As I was able to resolve them, the therapy moved forward.

CONCLUSION

I believe that the content issues presented in these two cases of older patients, one short-term crisis treatment and the other long-term analytic work with a woman with schizophrenia, reflect the issues of aging, such as how one deals with illness (both physical and psychological), and the issues around retirement, especially for those older individuals who have not yet felt successful in life. Yet, I think the work of the therapist remains relatively unchanged in terms of approach. The content may change as the individual ages, yet the therapist's techniques can remain much the same. In fact, the approach, which uses the patient as consultant, as was demonstrated with Mrs. T. in helping her select her own goals and strategies for treatment as one would with younger patients, helps the therapist avoid an age bias in the treatment.

In my work with Mr. F., he resolved a symptom related to his anger and mourning for his loss of independence and freedom from his wife's control. The long-term therapy with Mrs. T. helped her to considerably clear up thought-disordered thinking and to begin to interact with people rather than exist in a narcissistic haze.

When my concerns about the fragility of the patient for such consultative work surfaced, I was more likely to be in a state in which I remained unaware of my frustrated reactions to the patient. This might be described as a state in which my countertransference interfered with my therapeutic stance. Because these reactions also can be useful information about the patient's unexpressed feelings, understanding the therapist's reactions is essential to this work. When understanding myself and resolving my blocks, my treatment of the older patient proceeded simply and age became irrelevant to my therapeutic position.

REFERENCES

Abraham, K. (1927). The applicability of psycho-analytic treatment to patients at an advanced age. In D. Bryan & A. Strachey (Trans.), *Selected papers on psycho-analysis* (pp. 312–317). London: Hogarth Press. (Original work published 1919)

Brody, C. M., & Semel, V. G. (1993). *Strategies for therapy with the elderly: Living with hope and meaning.* New York: Springer.

Coltart, N. E. (1991). The analysis of an elderly patient. *International Journal of Psycho-Analysis, 72,* 209–219.

Crusey, J. (1985). Short-term psychodynamic psychotherapy with a sixty-two-year-old man. In R. A. Nemiroff & C. A. Colarusso (Eds.), *The race against time: Psychotherapy and psychoanalysis in the second half of life* (pp. 147–166). New York: Plenum.

Erikson, E. (1959). Identity and the life cycle [Monograph]. *Psychological Issues, 1.*

Freud, S. (1953). On psychotherapy. In J. Strachey (Ed. and Trans.), *The standard edition of the complete psychological works of Sigmund Freud* (Vol. 7, pp. 257–268). London: Hogarth Press. (Original work published 1905)

Grotjahn, M. (1955). Analytic psychotherapy with the elderly. *Psychoanalytic Review, 42,* 419–427.

Hinze, E. (1987). Transference and countertransference in the psychoanalytic treatment of older patients. *International Review of Psycho-Analysis, 14,* 465–473.

Kahana, R. J. (1985). The ant and the grasshopper in later life: Aging in relation to work and gratification. In R. A. Nemiroff & C. A. Colarusso (Eds.), *The race against time: Psychotherapy and psychoanalysis in the second half of life* (pp. 263–329). New York: Plenum.

Kaufman, M. R. (1940). Old age and aging: The psychoanalytic point of view. *American Journal of Orthopsychiatry, 10,* 73–79.

King, P. H. M. (1974). Notes on the psychoanalysis of older patients: Reappraisal of the potentialities for change during the second half of life. *Journal of Analytic Psychology, 19,* 22–37.

King, P. H. M. (1980). The life cycle as indicated by the nature of the transference in the psychoanalysis of middle-aged and elderly. *International Journal of Psycho-Analysis, 61,* 153–160.

Knight, B. G. (1993). *Older adults in psychotherapy: Case histories.* Newbury Park, CA: Sage.

Margolis, B. (1986). Joining, mirroring, psychological reflection: Terminology, definitions, and theoretical considerations. *Modern Psychoanalysis, 11,* 19–35.

Margolis, B. D. (1994). Selected papers on modern psychoanalysis with an introduction by Robert J. Marshall. *Modern Psychoanalysis, 19,* 139–254.

Meadow, P. W. (1990, April). *On becoming the patient.* Paper presented at the meeting of the Boston Center for Modern Psychoanalytic Studies, Brookline, MA.

Meadow, P. W. (1991). Resonating with the psychotic patient. *Modern Psychoanalysis, 16,* 87–103.

Miller, E. (1987). The Oedipus complex and rejuvenation fantasies in the analysis of a seventy-year old woman. *Journal of Geriatric Psychiatry, 20,* 29–51.

Muslin, H., & Clarke, S. (1988). The transference of the therapist of the elderly. *Journal of American Academy of Psychoanalysis, 16,* 295–315.

Myers, W. A. (1984). *Dynamic therapy of the older patient.* Northvale, NJ: Jason Aronson.

Nemiroff, R. A., & Colarusso, C. A. (1985). *The race against time: Psychotherapy and psychoanalysis in the second half of life.* New York: Plenum.

Pollock, G. H. (1987). The mourning-liberation process: Ideas on the inner life of the older adult. In J. Sadovoy & M. Leszcz (Eds.), *Treating the elderly with psychotherapy: The scope for change in later life* (pp. 3–29). Madison, CT: International Universities Press.

Sandler, A. (1978). Psychoanalysis in later life: Problems in the psychoanalysis of an aging narcissistic patient. *Journal of Geriatric Psychiatry, 11,* 5–36.

Sandler, A. (1982). Psychoanalysis and psychoanalytic psychotherapy of the older patient: A developmental crisis in an aging patient. Comments on development adaptation. *Journal of Geriatric Psychiatry, 15,* 11–32.

Segal, H. (1958). Fear of death: Notes on the analysis of an old man. *International Journal of Psycho-Analysis, 39,* 178–191.

Semel, V. G. (1986). The aging woman: Confrontations with hopelessness. In T. Bernay & D. W. Cantor (Eds.), *The psychology of today's woman: New psychoanalytic visions* (pp. 253–269). Hillsdale, NJ: Analytic Press.

Semel, V. G. (1993a). Countertransference and ageism: Therapist reactions to the older patient. In C. M. Brody & V. G. Semel (Eds.), *Strategies for therapy with the elderly: Living with hope and meaning* (pp. 130–138). New York: Springer.

Semel, V. G. (1993b). Individual treatment of a rageful, borderline, older woman: The case of Mrs. Z. In C. M. Brody & V. G. Semel (Eds.), *Strategies for therapy with the elderly: Living with hope and meaning* (pp. 93–106). New York: Springer.

Simburg, E. J. (1985). Psychoanalysis of the older patient. *Journal of the American Psychoanalytic Association, 33,* 117–132.

Solis, J., & Brink, T. L. (1989). Adlerian approaches in geriatric psychotherapy: Case of an American widow. *Individual Psychology, 45,* 178–185.

Spotnitz, H. (1976). *Psychotherapy of pre-oedipal conditions.* New York: Human Sciences Press.

Spotnitz, H. (1985). *Modern psychoanalysis of the schizophrenic patient* (2nd ed.). Northvale, NJ: Jason Aronson.

Spotnitz, H., & Meadow, P. W. (1995). *Treatment of the narcissistic neuroses* (Rev. ed.). Northvale, NJ: Jason Aronson.

Wasylenki, D. A. (1982). Psychodynamics and aging. *Canadian Journal of Psychiatry, 27,* 11–17.

Winnicott, D. W. (1958). Hate in the countertransference. In D. W. Winnicott (Ed.), *Through paediatrics to psycho-analysis* (pp. 194–203). New York: Basic Books. (Original work published 1949)

Wylie, H. W., & Wylie, M. L. (1987). The older analysand: Countertransference issues in psychoanalysis. *International Journal of Psycho-Analysis, 68,* 343–352.

6

FAMILY THERAPY WITH AGING FAMILIES

SARA HONN QUALLS

Family therapy addresses the mental disorders and behavior problems of older adults within their primary interpersonal context, the family. Recent changes in family structure and functioning often place families in unfamiliar and challenging interpersonal contexts. Therapists who are called on to assist families through the normative and nonnormative events of later life can draw on a fledgling literature on the applications of family therapy theory and technique to later-life families. In this chapter I provide a rationale for conducting family therapy with later-life families, examine the history of family therapy with later-life families, suggest benefits and disadvantages of this particular therapeutic approach, and describe the theory and basic techniques used in family therapy with aging families.

DEFINING THE FAMILY THERAPY APPROACH

What Is a Later-Life Family?

The later-life families referred to in this chapter are those in which concerns about aging are central to the distress of adult family members. The aging process itself may be the focus of concern, or aging may be directly or indirectly affecting the ability of the family to meet its members' needs. For example, a family may seek assistance while planning for grandma's placement in a nursing home, or grandma may seek help arranging for the care of her daughter with developmental disabilities in anticipation of her health decline and death. In both cases, it is the aging process that provokes a shift in the family structure or function.

What Is Family Therapy?

Family therapies intentionally attempt to alter the structure or function of the family in order to benefit one or more members. Interventions are defined as family therapy when either the locus of intervention is family interaction or when the framework for conceptualizing the client problem involves the family's structure or functioning. Many interventions with older adults require some involvement of family members, but only when the intervention is targeted at the structure or functioning of the family is the term *family therapy* appropriate.

Rationale for Family Therapy With Later-Life Families

Why consider family therapy for issues related to aging? The first reason is that older adults' lives are deeply embedded within families. Older adults live in close contact with families and rely on families for significant amounts of emotional and instrumental support (Shanas, 1979). Thus, families are key to the well-being of many older individuals. Families often are challenged, however, to address the needs of aging family members because they are learning to function within rapidly changing structures that often render family traditions useless or counterproductive.

Families are caught in the midst of profound cultural shifts that alter the structure and function of families. Changes in the population structure create one source of pressure on families (Kinsella, 1995). Demographic shifts that affect the family include increased life expectancy, decreased rates of fertility, increased rate of divorce and remarriage, increased rate of women in the workforce, increasingly imbalanced gender ratios, and increased ethnic diversification. These population patterns have direct effects on aging families that clinicians need to recognize.

The increased life expectancy makes three-, four-, and five-generation families a common occurrence. With fewer members born into each generation, family trees are increasingly thin in intragenerational linkages. The combination of these two patterns produces what Hagestad (1988) referred to as "beanpole families"—tall, skinny family trees.

The increased rate of divorce and remarriage has produced increasingly complex relationships. Even the labels for such relationships may be cumbersome (e.g., ex-granddaughter-in-law). The impact of divorce and remarriage among young and midlife adults also extends to elderly families

(Johnson, 1988). Consider the relationship between a 55-year-old recent divorcée and her ex-in-laws of 35 years. Their predivorce close relationship no longer has a familial sanction. If the aging ex-parents-in-law need assistance, should she be involved in the caregiving plan as she would have before the divorce? Should nursing home staff exclude her from a case conference for treatment planning even if she visits weekly just because she is no longer part of the family? The rules for navigating the often-turbulent waters of complex relationships are ambiguous at best and more often have simply not been articulated even in vague or ambiguous terms.

In adulthood, women outnumber men in an imbalanced gender ratio that increases with age. By age 65, there are 4 women for every 3 men, and by age 85, there are approximately 2 women for every man. Women are simply more prevalent in families. Combined with the social and legal custom of awarding custody of children more often to women than to men after divorce, the matrilineal linkages in families become more important. Although women are less available for full-time caregiving of aging parents because they work, they retain their roles as family "kin-keepers" and primary caregivers (Rosenthal, 1985). In particular, women in the middle generations are pressured by their familial responsibilities to the generations above and below them in the family tree. Men also are affected by the "sandwich generation" phenomenon, but seldom with as many familial linkages or responsibilities.

One effect of the beanpole family structure is the increased number of years that people now live within each family relationship. Sibling relationships often last 70 or 80 years. Parent–child relationships often last 50 years, including far more time spent in an adult–adult relationship than is spent in an adult parent–dependent child relationship. Another consequence of beanpole structures is the limited set of choices available within each relational structure. In a generation with only two siblings, it is hard to have a "favorite" sister or aunt. Children have far fewer familial models of adulthood in the preceding generation and noticeably fewer familial alternatives to parents when adolescent pressures provoke distance from parents.

A family stretched across the full range of the life cycle finds members of different generations struggling with distinctly different forms of similar developmental tasks. For example, a 70-year-old recently retired workaholic struggling to create a new identity may be less than sympathetic with his 23-year-old grandson whose recent graduation from college has left him floundering to find his niche (i.e., identity). If the grandfather lacks insight into his own developmental task, he may impatiently criticize his grandson for being too lazy to work. Similarly, a 74-year-old recent widow who is trying to create a new social milieu may have much in common with her 47-year-old daughter who has recently experienced both divorce and the "empty nest."

The complex, unprecedented family structures are likely to produce some difficulties accomplishing many developmental tasks, including the major events of later life. Life events affect the entire "web" of interpersonal relationships surrounding the aging individual (Pruchno, Blow, & Smyer, 1984). Primary among those events are retirement, onset of chronic illness, relocation, and deaths of family and friends. Adaptation to each event is likely to create behavior change that will reverberate throughout the family system. For example, retirement may increase frequency of contact between spouses or with children, thus decreasing the time others have available for other activities.

Each significant event tends to generate the anxiety of the unfamiliar, whether the event is positive or negative. During periods of uncertainty, families rely on familiar themes and strategies, regardless of their historical effectiveness. For example, some families approach their parents' aging with decades of experience enacting the theme, "Mom is strong; she will take care of us," whereas others carry out the theme, "What we don't talk about won't hurt us." The multitude of family themes that can be identified helps therapists organize the unspoken rules by which families approach interaction. Themes enacted throughout the life span will be carried into old age as well.

The functions of the family go beyond simply assisting members with adaptation to events. Families are the primary social group within which basic individual developmental processes take place. Several normal psychological processes that are basic to humans' social existence are enacted initially and most powerfully within the family. Bengtson and Kuypers (1984) identified three polarities that represent continua along which social and familial experiences fluctuate: autonomy–dependency, connectedness–separateness, and continuity–dislocation of the family over time. The infant's experience is characterized by nearly total dependency, connectedness, and continuity of experience. Early child development introduces the range of experiences along the continua. Throughout the life span, individuals slide between the ends of each continuum several times. For example, in the domains of health and finances, adults slide back and forth between near full autonomy (or the belief in it) to near dependency (when recuperating from an operation or recovering from financial loss in divorce or bankruptcy). Similarly, on the other two continua, adults experience shifts in the balance of degree of closeness and continuity. Although not experienced exclusively within the family, many of the most powerful experiences shaping psychological development occur within the context of their family relationships. To these three, I would add a fourth dimension: idealization–disappointment. This narcissistic process (Horney, 1945) operates in family members' self-perceptions as well as in their interactions with others. Idealization, the fantasy of perfection, sets up disappointment that can destroy relationships or can reorient families to realistic expectations of each other. Each of these four continua can be used to describe and track the interactions of families in later life. Many of the challenges faced by later-life families can be linked to a shift in family members' functioning on one or more of the continua.

Particularly salient among the interpersonal themes threaded through the life span is the issue of individual autonomy. One paradox faced by families in the life cycle stages after child rearing is that the adults are mutually autonomous, yet they remain identified in their generational roles as siblings, parents, daughters, or sons. I am my mother's peer in the sense that we are mutually autonomous adults responsible for ourselves legally and morally. Nonetheless, I am, and will always be, my mother's daughter. My mother and I can never fully cross generational boundaries regardless of our functional roles. The historical experience of rearing and being reared by another forever has an impact on the dynamics of the relationship: The process of taking full responsibility for another, constraining, supporting, and shaping the other's capacity to function independently, and then launching the other into autonomous adulthood, creates a permanent hierarchy that has meaning. At the same time, an adult child's maturation process is profoundly affected by the recognition, acceptance, and ownership of adult peer status with his or her parents (Williamson, 1982). Thus, the paradoxical experience of being one's parents' peers is one of life's profound puzzles.

Disruptions in family functioning that occur in later life often reflect ongoing challenges experienced across the life span. The content of old conflicts may be reawakened (e.g., "You always have had to have control" and "You never believed I would amount to anything") as families attempt to adjust to the events of later life. In the process of becoming autonomous, many adults initially created separation or enmeshment to avoid engaging in the real conflict (or fear of conflict) inevitable in adult–adult interactions. The separation or enmeshment may have remained fairly static throughout the course of middle adulthood. When elder care issues bring those family members together to engage in decision making, the pseudo-solution to their differences breaks down. Phantoms of the past appear in the middle of family discussions. Family members' images of each other as 8-, 12-, and 16-year-olds influence the interaction patterns because the powerful emotional exchanges from that period of constant interaction are often neither forgotten nor sometimes forgiven. Development achieved in adulthood may be unknown or unrecognized by midlife adult siblings or aging parents if their contact has been limited in recent decades. Thus, 52- and 57-year-old siblings may respond to their recalled images as much as they do to the real thoughts, feelings, and behaviors of the current sibling.

Most families appear to negotiate the transitions of later life well. What gets a family in sufficient difficulty that family therapy is warranted?

The traditional family therapy guidelines seem as applicable with later-life families as with child rearing families: When the strategies used to address life challenges are repetitive but ineffective at solving the problems or decreasing family members' anxiety and stress, therapy is appropriate (Minuchin, 1981). In other words, the family is not generating new approaches, but the old ones do not work to either resolve the problems generated by the transition or to assist members in dealing with their anxiety about change. In healthy families, the anxiety created by a demand for change that accompanies life events is used to generate novel solutions until one works. Healthy families have sufficient flexibility in roles and rules to allow members to flexibly structure themselves in various subsystems to tackle the problems for which they have skill and courage. Families who can benefit from therapy are those who have become stuck in redundant, non-useful approaches to managing both their anxiety about the problem and the problem itself.

History of Family Therapy With Later-Life Families

Most theories and techniques in family therapy were developed initially to address the problems of child rearing or child-launching families (in the case of families of young adults with schizophrenia). The typical family therapy scenario involved parents bringing a child whose behavior problems had earned him or her the focus as the "identified patient." Therapists worked to strengthen the parenting alliance and the skills of the parents with the goal of reestablishing generational hierarchies. Stronger marital bonds were believed to lead to better consensus and more consistency in parenting strategies. The positive consequences of this approach were that parents worked to improve their marriage, thus removing the child from the stress point of a triangle while defusing the child's ability to undermine the shared power of the parental position.

Several theoretical models emerged nearly simultaneously in the 1960s and 1970s to guide the basic task of restructuring the family. Psychodynamic approaches to families emphasized the complex intrapsychic representations of families (Ackerman, 1966). Theorists in some schools focused primarily on family structure: the hierarchies, triangles, roles, boundaries (e.g., Minuchin, 1974). Watzlawick, Beavin, and Jackson (1967) laid the foundation for both communication and strategic approaches to intervention in their seminal book describing behavior as the primary communication modality in interpersonal systems.

Three family therapy leaders drew attention to the importance and power of intergenerational relationships. Bowen (1978) described the transmission of family dysfunction from generation to generation. Boszormenyi-Nagy and colleagues (Boszormenyi-Nagy & Krasner, 1986; Boszormenyi-Nagy & Spark, 1984) explored the balances of family obligations that are transmitted across generations and across the life span of multigenerational relationships (e.g., mother–daughter). Framo (1991) developed an approach to working with the family of origin of adult clients to help individual clients achieve some leverage in their relationships within the family. Although the focus of Framo's work is not identical to that described in this chapter because the concerns are not initiated by aging-related problems, the practical benefits of his approach can extend beyond the adult child's well-being to have a positive impact on the broader family system.

None of these models initially explicitly examined the differential impact of their theory or techniques for families in different phases of the family life cycle. Once family diversity attributable to life cycle and cultural factors was recognized (Carter & McGoldrick, 1980), later life gained an identity as a distinct period with its own challenges to family structure and function. Walsh (1988) described the key family events of the later-life stage and explored the dynamics that might challenge families in that stage. Williamson's (1982) postulate that adults terminate parental authority during the early midlife stage is exemplary of theoretical work to articulate specific processes in adult family development. In the post-child-rearing phases of the family life cycle, the key developmental issues are negotiating structures among generations that respect adult autonomy while being able to negotiate the shifts in family structure that are needed to accommodate increasing dependency in older members.

During the past two decades, family therapists with cross-training in gerontology have begun to apply traditional models of intervention to families dealing with aging issues. Seminal in that movement were Herr and Weakland (1979), whose book applied the problem-focused brief therapy model to older families. More recently, Hargrave and Anderson (1992) applied Boszormenyi-Nagy's model to older family issues, and Neidhardt and Allen (1993) developed a broad systems-based framework for family therapy.

Within the domain of family therapy scholarship, research has lagged far behind the development of theory, concepts, and technique. The complexities inherent in studying the dynamic, ongoing nature of human relationships have gained respect and often have constrained scientific investigations. The systems model sparked lively discussions in journals such as *Family Process* regarding the basic theoretical and metatheoretical assumptions in family therapy models, the scientific paradigms appropriate to study family therapy, epistemologies consistent with systems theory, and research methods' appropriate use in studying family interventions. Research describing family structures and dynamics in dysfunctional or symptomatic families is sparse. Notable contributions have been made by Shields (1992), whose observations of depressed caregivers interacting with family members mapped relationship dynamics. Mittleman et al. (1993) conducted one of the few studies of a family intervention, finding the family intervention to be effective at decreasing caregiver symptoms, increasing assistance from family to caregivers, and reducing institutionalization. Other intervention studies have tended to focus on a single family caregiver and have demonstrated client satisfaction but inconsistent outcomes (Zarit & Teri, 1991).

Despite the dearth of research describing troubled families and interventions with families, a substantial body of descriptive research on later-life families has emerged (see the recent handbook by Blieszner & Bedford, 1995). Family sociologists and gerontologists have described the structures of later-life families, contact patterns, perceptions, sources of stress, relationship specific functions, and effects of cultural diversity. Therapists can draw on this body of knowledge to guide their conceptualizations of families in the last stages of the family life cycle. Reciprocally, the constructs that therapists have found useful for describing family dynamics may generate new research paradigms in family gerontology. The beginnings of dialogue between family therapy researchers and family gerontologists are likely to strengthen the research in both fields (Qualls, 1995).

Benefits of Family Therapy With Older Clients

Given the rationale offered earlier that older adults are intimately connected to their families and that family members are frequently affected by, and contributing to, events occurring in an elderly person's life, it seems apparent that the family is often an appropriate locus of intervention. The systems model takes the rationale one step further to suggest that many problems identified with elderly individuals really reside in the inability of the family systems to adapt in ways that meet the elderly person's needs.

Systems approaches also are useful with the many social systems within which aging individuals and families are embedded. The health care, housing, and social services industries are frequently confronted with situations in which their efforts to help an elderly client appear to be sabotaged by family members. On the other hand, families do not always find it easy to meet the needs of their elderly members in complex systems that are not functioning efficiently or consistently with their stated mandate or purpose. Conflict among family members, or between family and formal support network staff, requires an interpersonal approach that extends beyond the needs of the individual client. Systems interventions may be needed to resolve family–staff conflict or family distress in the nursing home setting (Cohn, 1988).

Therapists working with midlife or young-old adults may find that their clients' concerns focus on family concerns. Aging issues are among the family process concerns that may be restricting the adult child's development. Family therapy models such as those of Framo (1991), Bowen

(1978), and Boszormenyi-Nagy and Krasner (1986) appear to be highly useful to adults in individual therapy who are working on their family issues.

Disadvantages of Family Therapy With Later-Life Families

A primary disadvantage of family therapy is the lack of empirical data to document whether, when, or why this approach works. In the absence of such data, therapists must rely on their own evaluation tools to determine when the approach is useful and when a different approach is needed. Limited case descriptions are available to spur interest and experimentation by clinicians, as described and referenced in this chapter.

The family therapy literature is replete with descriptions of therapists' struggle to gain enough power to resist the homeostatic mechanisms of families. The flexibilities in therapy that are necessary with later-life families (e.g., inconsistent participation of geographically distant members) offer the families even more opportunities to defend against the anxiety needed for change. A revolving door of family members leaves the therapist unsure when one member has left appropriately and when he or she is undermining change. The measurement of change is difficult when the therapist may never have the opportunity to watch a direct face-to-face interaction with the key players. When the liabilities of this approach are great enough with a particular family, a therapist may choose to focus on the needs of one individual, serving as more of an advocate within the family system than a therapist for the entire system, thus leaving the family approach behind in favor of an individually focused therapy.

How Is Therapy Accomplished?

In a manner similar to child rearing families, later-life families often bring to therapy their concerns about an identified patient. The therapist and family must work from accurate, reality-based information about the actual functioning of the identified patient, particularly when he or she is an older adult who may indeed be experiencing a significant health-related or pharmacologically induced compromise in functioning. The process by which the family obtains accurate information about the identified patient tells the therapist a lot about the structure and function of the family. Once accurate information about the identified patient is obtained, the family may adapt by reconfiguring itself to meet the challenges that have been redefined. Families may not figure out how to proceed with the information, however, because of the same family dysfunction that initially made it hard for them to obtain accurate information.

Assessment is a continuous process that begins with the first contact to make an appointment and continues through termination. The evaluation may include a simple description of basic family structure and current developmental tasks, or it may require in-depth probing into the family's history of handling significant psychological events of the past several generations. Beginning with the simpler evaluation, therapists and families proceed to greater depth as it becomes apparent that straightforward information is not being used well by the families.

Therapists want to focus their family assessment on two areas: determining the capacity of the family to meet members' needs and its capacity to manage anxiety. To meet members' needs, the family must have subsystems that can function to accomplish family maintenance tasks, must have adequate knowledge of developmental needs of members, and must have sufficient flexibility in roles to meet the evolving needs of family members. For example, a primary caregiver of a person with dementia may need to renegotiate with other family members the caregiving responsibilities if he or she becomes sick, takes on other responsibilities, or gets burned out. Later-life families may be poorly organized because they previously have not shared tasks as an extended family. The simple lack of organizational structure to handle family tasks can generate a chaotic response to a later-life crisis (e.g., parent illness). Problems are likely to be resolved effectively if all the relevant family members understand the care demands of the person with dementia, share rules about how to communicate with other family members, and can be flexible about the roles they adopt within the family. Many families lack such interpersonal structures and are vulnerable to family conflict, anxiety, and ineffective problem-solving strategies.

Managing anxiety is particularly important in later-life families because so many of the key events of later life generate anxiety because of their inherent psychological meaning. Death, dying, and chronic illness generate anxiety nearly universally (Becker, 1973). The many losses associated with the end of life require psychological adaptation in the form of grief, an inherently anxiety-provoking process. Later-life families must manage the anxiety of interacting in new configurations while facing novel problems for which they often lack culturally transmitted rules, and the content of those problems is often inherently anxiety provoking. The stress associated with these transitions, then, sets families up to respond in defensive ways that may not enhance problem-solving ability or the capacity to nurture family members. In times of great stress, families often revert to familiar family myths (Ferreira, 1963) that not only fail to offer problem-solving help but also constrain the family from seeking novel solutions. Individual members' psychological and behavioral symptoms may be rooted in the family's inability to adapt to stressful events. The importance of respecting individuals' anxieties is emphasized in the suggestion that the therapist engage in multidirectional partiality by shifting support and empathy from one member to another, as needed, to retain the family's trust that each member's needs are understood and respected (Boszormenyi-Nagy & Krasner, 1986; Hargrave & Anderson, 1992).

The process of understanding the family structure and functioning can be enhanced by using a combination of traditional and nontraditional assessment approaches. Tools created for child rearing families are often helpful with aging families. A simple genogram (McGoldrick & Gerson, 1985) describing the basic structure of the family is almost always useful. More detailed genograms can map the alliances, bonds, and coalitions of the multigenerational family to assist them in identifying the structure and flexibility of its subsystems. Labels for myths, roles, and family rules offer families the option of altering them. Detailed observation of interaction sequences have yielded meaningful results in laboratory studies (e.g., Shields, 1992). Close attention to interaction during therapy requires the family to slow down their interpretations of interactions long enough to clarify the reinforcement contingencies shaping family interactions. Problem-solving skill can be evaluated by observing the strategies used to accomplish practical family tasks (e.g., accomplishing the evaluation of the identified patient or arranging for respite care for the primary caregiver). Herr and Weakland (1979) encouraged the assessment of how the family has already attempted to solve its problem. The importance of assessing failed attempts at solutions is predicated on the assumption that some of the family's failed solutions may now be perpetuating or exacerbating the problem. For example, a daughter's efforts to support her father's return to independence after a hip fracture may actually reinforce his dependency behaviors (see the description of such a case by Herr & Weakland, 1979, pp. 103–112). Finally, information about how the family system is linked with other community and cultural systems should be gathered. Health care providers, school systems, senior housing staff, and social service workers are among those whose presence and impact should be evaluated. For example, Cohn (1988) described the systemic relations between families and nursing home staff that may warrant intervention.

With some families, the therapist may move beyond a problem-focused assessment of current family structure and function to explore the history of the family's structure and its functioning during previous transitions. In particular, a description of previous adaptations may help the family identify either a familiar but ineffective adaptation strategy that could be changed or some previously successful strategies that could be used in the current situation. The long family history can be a useful resource as well as a constraint.

Family therapy theory presumes that family systems are powerful constraining forces because the interaction patterns that create the structure of the family operate with a homeostatic mechanism. Family patterns are in place because they worked at some point and in some context. Thus, it is adaptive for the family to attempt to maintain equilibrium by retaining familiar patterns. However, when stress is placed on the family or the family is required to adapt, familiar patterns appropriate for former contexts may not function well.

Therapists begin their interactions with a family by attempting to join the family. Family structures have no inherent space, roles, or rules for incorporating the therapist, so the joining process is an intervention in and of itself. Later-life families seeking assistance with a physically frail older member may establish a role for the therapist as "expert consultant." This role allows the therapist to educate members about the impact of the illness on the older member's functioning. Families that distribute information well make it possible for members to enact their roles flexibly because they have a reasonably common perception of the problem. Different perceptions and attributions for the problem can generate conflict. An example would be a situation in which a daughter on the East Coast who is burdened by the medical care of her father, who has dementia, feels insulted when her sister on the West Coast questions whether the problem with the father is that he does not have enough fun things to do. Differing perceptions of the problem, which are likely based on different amounts of information, set up interpersonal conflict.

Educating families about the events of later life generally, and specifically about the demands of the transition they are experiencing, may not be enough if the family cannot adapt itself to manage anxiety and meet members' needs. In addition to the need for information, families also may need help reframing the problem from a trait-based framework in which the problem exists within the personality or physical functioning of one member to a behaviorally defined, problem-focused framework that points to communication and role shifts that can solve problems. Reframing takes the identified patient off the immediate hook and shifts focus onto the family's response to the demands on it that may or may not relate closely to the identified patient. In the previous example, the West Coast sister may benefit from learning the test results about her father's cognitive decline, but the conflict between the sisters also may require that they work on their communication patterns. The West Coast sister could learn to make her inquiries more tentative, taking care to state her respect for her sister's dedication to excellent care, whereas the East Coast sister could learn to respect the anxiety her distant sister must manage in the absence of daily information, without taking inquiries personally. The sisters might set up an information-sharing system in which the West Coast sister is kept informed about care and perhaps is even involved in care decisions. The new communication pattern allows them to negotiate more directly their roles in parent care and their strategies for managing the anxiety of observing their father's decline while enhancing mutual support.

Therapeutic interventions often target the structures of families when the boundaries and subsystems in the family need to be loosened or altered in order to free the family to create more useful structures. A common later-life problem is the structuring of generational boundaries. As described earlier, the paradox of being one's parents' peer generates some confusion about who is to be involved in what decisions. For example, the compromised decision-making ability of one parent may bring the other parent together with adult children to share decision making about the care of the ill parent. Adult children are crossing the long-held boundary between generations about deciding with or for one's parent. Some family members may find it awkward to have their parent seeking the adult child's advice, whereas other family members may believe the generational boundaries should be given no credence at all, placing all decision-making roles in the hands of the most capable family member. Other structural problems include those that constrain one family member in a role that overburdens him or her when other responsibilities of life increase. For example, a caregiving daughter may function well until her young adult child moves back home with two small grandchildren. Families must be flexible enough to allow for ongoing negotiation of roles.

Finally, a major role of a therapist is to disempower family myths and rules to free the individuals and the entire family to create new self-images. Individual maturity requires increased emotional differentiation from the group (Bowen, 1978), a process that is highly threatening to some families. The anxiety evoked by having family members change, or even recognizing the inherent differences among members, can prompt an enmeshment or withdrawal response. The process of intervention frequently requires that the family tolerate an added level of anxiety while old self-images (myths) are debunked and new images are still forming. The ambiguity involved in functioning within an unclear family structure during a transition necessarily generates anxiety.

Therapists are encouraged to view their role as a provocateur of change. The family's self-regulatory capability is trusted to generate new structures that will meet needs and manage anxiety. The therapist's primary role is to restrict the family from relying on familiar strategies, a process that inevitably increases the anxiety level enough to generate the potential for change. The family may or may not be able to articulate the details of the old or new structures. Insight is neither necessary nor sufficient. Shifting the patterns of interpersonal behavior is the focus of the intervention and the criterion of success.

A general guideline for family interventions is to consider progressing from the least intrusive to more intrusive interventions only if the family cannot use effectively the milder form. Annon (1975) recommended implementing the principle of least intrusion in the following sequence: permission, limited information, specific suggestion, and intensive therapy. This model is consistent with behavioral approaches to assisting caregiving families (Zarit, Anthony, & Boutselis, 1987). Zarit et al. suggested that support, information, and problem solving are the key components to caregiver intervention, implying that intensive family therapy is relatively rarely needed. If family struggles indeed reflect efforts to manage normative challenges of later life, permission to respect the impact of the event and information about the challenges and available resources may be sufficient. Other families will need assistance solving specific problems (e.g., managing problem behaviors). The families for whom the validation and information are insufficient may require more intensive intervention with the dysfunctional patterns or structures that impair their adaptation.

Therapeutic work with later-life families often requires flexibility in therapeutic procedures and techniques (Duffy, 1986). The key players in family decision making are likely dispersed geographically over thousands of miles. It is not practical to presume that all families must demonstrate their commitment to change by gathering biweekly or monthly for therapy sessions. Members may participate in the therapy through telephone contacts with the therapist, speaker phone connections during a family meeting, or letters. Sessions may need to be scheduled at holiday time when members gather in one place.

Therapists must be flexible about who is considered "in the family." Traditional family therapy literature calls for inclusion of all those who live under one roof, regardless of exact blood relationship. Later-life family therapy requires an even broader definition of family—all those involved in the problem. Geographically or emotionally distant children or siblings also may be relevant for the role they play in the system despite their apparent absence. Likely, the key players include people who do not live with the identified patient, and may not even be related genetically (e.g., neighbors).

Later-life families tend to be problem focused and thus prefer the therapist to balance carefully any focus on past relationships with a clear application to the present problem. Families may struggle with the balance among the varied individual preferences and needs, struggling to integrate the needs of individuals with the benefit to the entire family system. Focusing on the problem allows the therapist to support the family's efforts to create new structures and balance its needs while meeting the immediate demands of the current developmental task.

SUMMARY

Family therapy is a relatively late addition to the clinical geropsychology literature. The last stages of the family life cycle are challenging times for many families, and evidence of the importance of aging-related issues in families abounds. A clinical literature has emerged that extends traditional family therapy models to include later-life family structures and dynamics. Despite the apparent promise of the clinical literature, little empirical work supports the efficacy of family therapy constructs or interventions. A growing dialogue between family gerontologists and family therapists indicates that this is likely to be a productive research area in the near future.

REFERENCES

Ackerman, N. (1966). *Treating the troubled family.* New York: Basic Books.

Annon, J. F. (1975). *The behavioral treatment of sexual problems.* Honolulu, HI: Enabling Systems.

Becker, E. (1973). *The denial of death.* New York: Free Press.

Bengtson, V. L., & Kuypers, J. A. (1984). The family support cycle: Psychosocial issues in the aging family. In J. M A. Munnichs, P. Mussen, E. Olbrich, & P. G. Coleman (Eds.), *Life-span and change in a gerontological perspective* (pp. 257–273). San Diego, CA: Academic Press.

Blieszner, R., & Bedford, V. H. (Eds.). (1995). *Handbook of aging and the family.* Westport, CT: Greenwood Press.

Boszormenyi-Nagy, I., & Krasner, B. (1986). *Between give and take: A clinical guide to contextual therapy.* New York: Brunner/Mazel.

Boszormenyi-Nagy, I., & Spark, G. M. (1984). *Invisible loyalties.* New York: Brunner/Mazel.

Bowen, M. (1978). *Family therapy in clinical practice.* Northvale, NJ: Jason Aronson.

Carter, E., & McGoldrick, M. (1980). *The family life cycle: A framework for family therapy* (2nd ed.). New York: Gardner Press.

Cohn, M. D. (1988). Consultation strategies with families. In M. A. Smyer, M. D. Cohn, & D. Brannon (Eds.), *Mental health consultation in nursing homes* (pp. 169–191). New York: New York University Press.

Duffy, M. (1986). The techniques and contexts of multigenerational therapy. In T. L. Brink (Ed.), *Clinical gerontology* (pp. 347–362). New York: Haworth Press.

Ferreira, A. (1963). Family myth and homeostasis. *Archives of General Psychiatry, 9,* 457–463.

Framo, J. (1991). *Family of origin therapy: An intergenerational approach.* New York: Brunner/Mazel.

Hagestad, G. O. (1988). Demographic change and the life course: Some emerging trends in the family realm. *Family Relations, 37,* 405–410.

Hargrave, T. D., & Anderson, W. T. (1992). *Finishing well: Aging and reparation in the intergenerational family.* New York: Brunner/Mazel.

Herr, J. J., & Weakland, J. H. (1979). *Counseling elders and their families*. New York: Springer.

Horney, K. (1945). *Our inner conflicts*. New York: Norton.

Johnson, C. L. (1988). Postdivorce reorganization of relationships between divorcing children and their parents. *Journal of Marriage and the Family, 50*, 221–231.

Kinsella, K. (1995). Aging and the family: Present and future demographic issues. In R. Blieszner & V. H. Bedford (Eds.), *Handbook on aging and the family* (pp. 32–56). Westport, CT: Greenwood Press.

McGoldrick, M., & Gerson, R. (1985). *Genograms in family assessment*. New York: Norton.

Minuchin, S. (1974). *Families and family therapy*. Cambridge, MA: Harvard University Press.

Minuchin, S. (1981). Structural family therapy. In R. J. Green & J. L. Framo (Eds.), *Family therapy: Major contributions* (pp. 445–473). Madison, CT: International Universities Press.

Mittelman, M. S., Ferris, S, H., Steinberg, G., Shulman, E., Mackell, J. A., Ambinder, A., & Cohen, J. (1993). An intervention that delays institutionalization of Alzheimer's disease patients. *The Gerontologist, 33*, 730–740.

Neidhardt, E. R., & Allen, J. A. (1993). *Family therapy with the elderly*. Newbury Park, CA: Sage.

Pruchno, R. A., Blow, F. C., & Smyer, M. A. (1984). Life events and interdependent lives: Implications for research and intervention. *Human Development, 27*, 31–41.

Qualls, S. H. (1995). Clinical interventions with later life families. In R. Blieszner & V. H. Bedford (Eds.), *Handbook on aging and the family* (pp. 474–494). Westport, CT: Greenwood Press.

Rosenthal, C. (1985). Kinkeeping in the familial division of labor. *Journal of Marriage and the Family, 47*, 965–974.

Shanas, E. (1979). Social myth as hypothesis: The case of the family relations of old people. *The Gerontologist, 19*, 3–9.

Shields, C. G. (1992). Family interaction and caregivers of Alzheimer's disease patients: Correlates of depression. *Family Process, 31*, 19–33.

Walsh, F. (1988). The family in later life. In B. Carter & M. McGoldrick (Eds.), *The changing family life cycle* (2nd ed., pp. 311–332). New York: Gardner Press.

Watzlawick, P., Beavin, J. H., & Jackson, D. D. (1967). *Pragmatics of human communication: A study of interactional patterns, pathologies, and paradoxes*. New York: Norton.

Williamson, D. S. (1982). Personal authority via termination of the intergenerational hierarchical boundary: 2. The consultation process and the therapeutic method. *Journal of Marriage and Family Therapy, 8*, 23–37.

Zarit, S. H., Anthony, C. R., & Boutselis, M. (1987). Interventions with care givers of dementia patients: Comparison of two approaches. *Psychology and Aging, 2,* 225–232.

Zarit, S. H., & Teri, L. (1991). Interventions and services for family caregivers. *Annual Review of Gerontology and Geriatrics, 11,* 287–310.

7

INTERVENTIONS WITH FAMILY CAREGIVERS

STEVEN H. ZARIT

A woman is torn by the competing demands of caring for aged parents and her own teenage children while sustaining a career. A man in his 70s, despondent over his wife's dementia and growing incapacity, contemplates ending his wife's life and then his own. An only child living several hundred miles from her parents must decide whether to move them into her house or whether they can still remain safely in their own home. In these examples, and in many similar situations, caring for an elderly relative touches people's lives and presents many unforeseen challenges and demands.

Caring for elderly relatives always has been a concern of families and society, but caregiving in the past was a relatively rare and short-term occurrence. Because of the dramatic increase in life expectancy seen in this century, more and more people survive to old age, including to age 80 and older. This trend reflects a shift in the most common causes of death. Acute, infectious disease has decreased as a cause of mortality, whereas chronic illness has become increasingly important. The result is that more and more people are living to ages at which they have a risk of becoming disabled before the end of life, and, because of the slow, progressive nature of many chronic illnesses, they often require care for several years or more. These trends have created an unprecedented situation: large numbers of older people needing regular and sustained assistance for long periods of time. Although many elderly are cared for in formal settings such as nursing homes or assisted-living facilities, the majority of disabled family members are assisted by family members at home (Stone, Cafferata, & Sangl, 1987). Decisions about when, how, and how long to provide care are among the most difficult faced by families. Providing care for a sustained period of time can be physically and emotionally exhausting and can adversely affect the caregiver's own health and well-being (Zarit, 1994).

The following sections provide an introduction to clinical issues in caregiving. I begin by providing background on demographic changes that have established the contemporary context in which caregiving occurs. I then review briefly the theoretical and empirical issues concerning family caregiving. Following that is a discussion of clinical approaches to caregiving. The emphasis is on the care of people with dementia, which is the most common and most demanding situation. However, the relevance to other types of caregiving should be apparent.

DEMOGRAPHIC IMPERATIVES OF AN AGING SOCIETY

The aging of the population and increased survival of people to advanced ages is a well-known phenomenon, which makes it likely that people will need help in later life. Several related social trends also have had an important effect in setting the context for caregiving. To understand how caregiving is provided, one should first consider who becomes the caregiver to a disabled elder. Although one often thinks about daughters as caregivers of their aging parents, the most likely person to assume caregiving responsibilities is the husband or wife of a disabled elder (Soldo & Myllyuoma, 1983; Stone et al., 1987). When both parents are living, daughters will provide some help to a disabled parent, but the main responsibility for care will fall on their other parent. When one parent is deceased or both are incapacitated, daughters then are most likely to assume the responsibility for care. Brothers often will help their sisters with some caregiving tasks, but they are not likely to take on the main caregiving role, except when they do not have a sister. In some instances, daughters-in-law will actually perform many of the care-related activities. Finally, for people without children, a variety of other caregivers may emerge, including siblings, grandchildren, and occasionally friends.

Because the most likely caregiver is a spouse, it follows that caregivers themselves are older and may be suffering from limitations attributable to chronic problems of their own. On the basis of data from a national survey drawn from Medicare rolls, the mean ages of husbands and wives who function as primary caregivers of their spouse are 73 and 69 years, respectively (Stone et al., 1987). Daughters who are assisting a parent also may be older. The mean age of daughters caring for a parent was 52 years, whereas 13% were older than 65 (Stone et al., 1987).

A second consideration is that daughters assisting their parents are increasingly balancing multiple roles, including employment. Having a full-time job may limit a daughter's ability to take on caregiving responsibilities or may place considerable strain on her should she do so (e.g., Mutschler, 1994; Scharlach & Boyd, 1989). Many caregivers leave their jobs within 3 months after becoming a caregiver, whereas others rearrange their work schedules or reduce their hours (Franklin, Ames, & King, 1994; Mutschler, 1994). Although employment can be a source of role conflict or strain, some women report that their jobs give them a break from caregiving.

Other social trends also have implications for caregiving. The century-long trend toward smaller families places the responsibility for care of a parent on a smaller number of children. In fact, midlife couples are likely to have more parents than children (Gatz, Bengtson, & Blum, 1991). Because of geographic mobility in the United States, children or their parents may move hundreds of miles away from one another, making it difficult to provide direct care. Increasing rates of divorce among parents and their children may affect who becomes a caregiver. Will children be willing to assist a parent who they did not grow up with? Similarly, higher divorce rates among the younger generation means that sons and daughters may have reduced resources for assisting their parents.

One last consideration is that caregiving takes place in a family context in which parents and children have provided, or failed to provide, various kinds of assistance for many years. In general, parents provide more help to their adult children than vice versa (Zarit & Eggebeen, 1995). Even as parents may be coping with their own disabilities, they may be assisting a child financially or in some other way. Thus, caregiving should not be seen as a one-way street. Rather, it has emerged from an ongoing history of interchanges between generations.

The end result of these social and demographic trends is that more older people need assistance than ever before, but the social resources for providing help are increasingly limited. The most likely person to provide care may be older or may have limited resources for providing assistance. It should not be surprising, then, that caring for an elder is frequently a stressful experience. The stress on families and implications for clinical interventions are described in the next section.

STRESS AND CAREGIVING

Caring for a disabled elder over a long period of time has been found to have a variety of adverse effects (for reviews, see Gatz et al., 1991; Zarit,

1994). Caregivers experience higher rates of depression and other psychiatric symptoms and may have more health problems of their own than age-matched control peers who are not caregivers. They participate less in social activities, have more problems at work, and have more frequent conflict with other family members, often over how they are caring for their relative. As caregiving expands to an all-encompassing involvement, some people may experience what has been called an "erosion of self" (i.e., the feeling of becoming trapped or that one's identity has been completely submerged into the caregiving role; Aneshensel, Pearlin, Mullan, Zarit, & Whitlatch, 1995).

Despite this overall negative picture, there is considerable variability in how caregivers adapt to stressors. One of the most enduring findings in caregiving research is that people in similar situations react in highly different ways (Aneshensel et al., 1995; Zarit, 1994). Although some people may be overwhelmed by their circumstances, others cope effectively in similar situations. Identifying the sources of variability of responses to the stressors of caregiving is the key to developing clinical interventions. By helping caregivers to control stressors that are especially problematic or by enhancing mediating factors that limit the impact of care-related stressors, clinicians can reduce the stress on primary caregivers.

The stress process model of caregiving developed by Pearlin and his associates (Aneshensel et al., 1995; Pearlin, Mullan, Semple, & Skaff, 1990) is useful for identifying sources of stress and their possible mediation (see Figure 1). In particular, two key concepts—stress proliferation and stress containment—help identify sources of individual differences in adaptation and possible points for intervention. The term *stress proliferation* refers to a process by which the effects of primary stressors associated with caregiving spill over into other areas of a person's life. Primary stressors are activities that caregivers perform directly as a result of the elder's disability (e.g., assisting with activities of daily living or responding to the agitated behavior of a patient with dementia). Within this model, primary stressors also refer to the caregiver's subjective responses to these demands, such as feelings of overload. Over time, primary stressors, particularly subjective feelings of overload or feeling trapped in the caregiving role, have been found to spill over into other areas of a person's life, leading to what Pearlin and associates have called *secondary role strains*. These strains include increases in family conflict, conflict or strain at work because of caregiving, and financial strain. In turn, primary and secondary strains can lead to the erosion of self-concept and to outcomes such as increased emotional distress and poor health. Objective stressors, such as what type and how much care is provided, have surprisingly little overall effect in this proliferation process. Rather, people respond in unique ways to the specific stressors of caregiving. Their subjective response to stressors and the extent of proliferation into other areas of the person's life ultimately determines whether

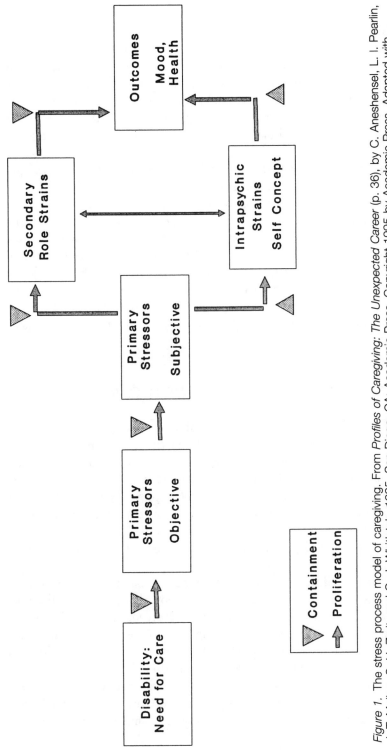

Figure 1. The stress process model of caregiving. From *Profiles of Caregiving: The Unexpected Career* (p. 36), by C. Aneshensel, L. I. Pearlin, J. T. Mullan, S. H. Zarit, and C. J. Whitlatch, 1995, San Diego, CA: Academic Press. Copyright 1995 by Academic Press. Adapted with permission.

caregivers become depressed or decide that they are unable to continue in the role (Aneshensel et al., 1995; Aneshensel, Pearlin, & Schuler, 1993; Zarit, Todd, & Zarit, 1986).

By contrast, the term *stress containment* refers to the process by which resources available to caregivers reduce the impact of primary and secondary stressors. Resources can be material, such as economic, social (e.g., social support), and psychological, including coping responses and feelings of mastery. Using longitudinal data, Aneshensel et al. (1995) found that social support, coping, and mastery were effective in containing caregiving stressors.

These findings suggest that clinical interventions with family caregivers can be effective by reducing stress proliferation and improving stress containment. Caregivers' feelings of distress, and even the breakdown of caregiving, are not attributable directly to the elder's disability or disease. Rather, disability creates a situation that may or may not be overwhelming to caregivers depending on other circumstances in their lives and the resources that they can access. Interventions that pinpoint the specific primary and secondary stressors that are troubling to a particular caregiver and that develop strategies for stress containment can be effective in reducing feelings of depression or other indicators of emotional and physical strain.

CLINICAL INTERVENTIONS WITH CAREGIVERS

Clinical interventions can help families in several ways. Clinicians can assist families on key decisions, helping them identify their options and make choices that best reflect their values and resources. Clinicians also can make interventions with the disabled older person or with the family to reduce care-related problems and improve how the situation is managed. Finally, clinicians also may function as consultant-advocates for the family, helping them to interact more effectively with formal service providers, including physicians, social service agency personnel, and nursing home staff.

To address clinical issues of caregiving competently and effectively, practitioners need specific skills and information that go beyond the usual basic training that they are likely to have received. Clinicians' own personal experiences and views about caring for an older relative can be misleading; if unexamined, they are more likely to interfere than to aid professional judgment. People vary so much in their values about how and how much care they want to provide and in their resources for providing care. Clinicians should help families plan for care in a way that implements their own values, not the clinicians'. A prime example involves decisions about nursing home placement. There is probably no other question that is as upsetting and difficult for families. Over the years, I have observed that this issue is frequently mishandled by clinicians from many different professions: physicians, psychologists, social workers, nurses—everyone. The error they make is to bully the family into making a placement decision, often couching their arguments in medical terms (i.e., it is best for the patient). However, decisions about how to provide long-term care are a matter of values. Some people may be willing to make more personal sacrifices to keep someone at home, whereas others are not willing or able. The clinician's role in this situation is to encourage the family to explore its options and to make its own decision rather than to impose a decision in an authoritarian manner.

Among the knowledge and skills clinicians need in assisting caregiving families are as follows:

- *Familiarity with the common disorders of aging and with their possibilities for treatment (see chapter 9 in this book)*. In particular, there may be reversible or treatable components of many chronic diseases.
- *Information on diagnosis and assessment of disorders of aging*. The clinician needs to know how to interpret diagnostic information (e.g., concerning diagnosis of dementia) and to identify when further assessment is needed and when it is not. (See chapter 8 of this book.)
- *Knowledge of aging services*. There often is an extensive network of services available to older people and their families, although locating them and working one's way through the confusing array of eligibilities and other requirements for these programs can be frustrating. Clinicians need a familiarity with this service system and how it works so that they can help guide families to obtain appropriate services and to deal with the frustrations they may encounter.
- *Appropriate clinical skills*. Finally, clinicians need to use appropriate clinical skills to help families accommodate effectively to the stresses and choices they face. I have found behavioral approaches very helpful, especially for helping families learn how to more effectively manage problems related to the elder's mood or behavior (e.g., Teri, 1994; Teri & Logsdon, 1990). Cognitive–behavioral approaches often are useful for helping families clarify their values and consider alternatives (see chapters 2 and 3 in this book). A family-systems perspective also is valuable because knowing when and how to involve other family members often is critical (see chapter 6 in this

book). These approaches are emphasized in the following sections, but clinicians will recognize that skills drawn from other theoretical perspectives also can be useful.

Assessment

The starting point for clinical interventions is assessment. Because of the considerable individual differences in caregiving, and the variable responses caregivers have to similar stresses, it is crucial to begin by determining what problems a particular caregiver is experiencing. The stress process model, which was described briefly earlier, provides a useful guide to conducting an assessment. The clinician can identify the specific primary and secondary stressors that are present and the caregiver's specific subjective responses to them. As suggested earlier, how someone responds subjectively to a stressful situation or event is more important for planning interventions than just knowing whether the event has occurred. For example, many people regard incontinence as a stressor that will overwhelm family caregivers, leading to nursing home placement. Although some caregivers do respond to incontinence by becoming overwhelmed, others cope with it effectively. In planning interventions, it is important to identify the problems that are stressful to this caregiver rather than assuming that a particular disability such as incontinence will be overwhelming.

Assessment also identifies caregivers' current knowledge and understanding of their relative's illness and their commitment to the caregiving role. Pearlin (1992) described caregiving as a "career," with different phases of socialization. An early period of "role acquisition" is characterized by the growing understanding of the need to provide ongoing care and making the commitment to do so. The term *role enactment* describes the period of active caregiving in the community. Institutional placement represents a key transition that alters the caregiving role but does not end it. Finally, bereavement means a formal end to caregiving activities, although there are lingering effects of one's involvement. Because interventions can be more fruitful by taking into account caregivers' understanding of their involvement and commitment, I have organized the discussion of interventions according to phases of the caregiving career.

Role Acquisition

The process by which people take on the role of caregiver is not well described in the literature, nor is it well understood. Role acquisition often has occurred long before families seek help or become involved in research. Retrospective accounts suggest that role acquisition comes about in different ways. In one pattern, the need for caregiving develops suddenly after an acute illness and hospitalization. Hospital discharge planners or social work staff sometimes will assist families in these situations, but with the trend toward shorter hospital stays, the family may have little time for practical planning or for sorting out the emotional side of this decision. Depending on the nature of the elder's problem, hospitalization may be followed up by a brief stay in a nursing home for recovery and rehabilitation services. This type of stay after an acute hospitalization is covered by Medicare (in contrast to chronic care in a nursing home). It also can provide families with more time to make arrangements for care once the elder returns to the community.

There often is no single event that triggers caregiving. Instead, the family gradually becomes involved as the elder's condition warrants. Dementia provides the most vivid example of gradual onset of disability and consequently caregiving. Families will vacillate about whether something is wrong with their relative and if help is needed. They may waver between not wanting to take away the elder's independence, not wanting to acknowledge the growing incapacity, and not wanting to give up their own independence. At this point in the development of a disability, a comprehensive assessment can provide the family with a better understanding of the elder's condition and need for assistance. It also can provide them with information about the alternatives that are available for care, such as specialized senior housing, or services that can help the elder remain in the community. Unfortunately, families often do not get much help or advice at this time.

One of the most complex situations occurs when parents with growing disabilities live far from their children. Children will be faced with the question of moving parents closer to them or into their household. They often may be concerned that their parent is no longer safe living alone. They also may have difficulty arranging for services for their parent at a distance or find that their parent will not accept the help. Like any caregiving decision, there is no "right" solution to this problem, only different options that each have advantages and disadvantages. Advantages to staying in a familiar place include having friends and neighbors around. Being in a familiar setting also can support old habits and routines. The older person may be able to find his or her way around town or may be able to carry out activities at home. Adjusting to a new setting and new routines can lead to a loss in abilities in someone with dementia or other significant disabilities. Similarly, children often expect that a parent will adjust socially after a move, finding new friends and activities, but that may be difficult because of the parent's disabilities. As a result, the parent may become completely dependent on children for social activities. The benefits of remaining at home may offset the increased safety concerns. On the other hand, moving a parent closer or into one's home makes it possible to arrange and supervise care more effectively and to have frequent social interactions. It also may be possible for a parent to adjust better to a new setting if the move is made sooner rather than later. Finally, the older person's preferences need to be taken into account as well. Whatever the decision, there is no perfect solution. The clinician's role in this situation is to help families consider the alternatives rather than to press a particular choice on them. Families need information and support at this point in caregiving to make the best decision consistent with their values.

Clinicians also may encounter situations that are presented to them as involving caregiving but in which assessment reveals that the older person is competent and largely or completely independent. These situations typically involve parents and children with long-standing conflicts and enmeshed relationships. As parents age, children relabel their ongoing emotional struggle as being caused by their parent's age, and they see themselves as their parent's caretaker. Their emotional burden is real, but the context is different from caregiving. As in any family-system problem, clinicians should not ally with one person. Rather, alliances should be used strategically. Attributing family conflict to the parent's age shifts power in the family and may inappropriately place the parent in a disadvantaged position. On the other hand, defending the parent against the child may isolate the clinician and prevent any meaningful intervention. In general, clinicians can redirect the family away from caregiving issues and toward building up the boundaries between parent and child that lessen their long-standing conflict.

Of course, families with long-standing conflicts also can find themselves as caregivers. Those cases often will be difficult and challenging because the caregiver may be resentful or try to settle old grudges or disputes with their parent or siblings. I once interviewed a daughter who had been pressed into caring for her mother, who had had a stroke. Her brother and sister-in-law had been living rent-free in the mother's house and providing care. Suddenly, they decided that they could not handle the care anymore and moved out of town, literally overnight, leaving the mother alone. Her daughter moved in and was understandably angry with her brother, whom she viewed as having taken advantage of their mother. She also was angry with her mother, who she viewed as difficult, demented, and ungrateful. She said her mother had always doted on her brother but had been critical of her. She also stated that she wanted to prove to her mother that she, not her brother, was the "good" and responsible child. Unfortunately, her anger and resentment came out when she assisted her mother. She frequently yelled at her mother and took her mother's complaints about pain as personal attacks on her. In assessing the mother, I found her to have limited mobility but to have no significant cognitive problems. Consistent with her daughter's description, however, she viewed her daughter solely in a negative light and was not at all grateful that her daughter had stepped in to take care of her. Instead, she described her son in glowing terms and hoped he would come back to assist her. The presenting problem in this situation, the daughter's anger and frustration over caring for her mother, had its origins not just in the mother's disability but in a long-standing rivalry with her brother and her mother's own obvious negativity toward her. Although clinical interventions in situations such as this can focus on the practical problems of caregiving, they must take into account how the family functions. Trying to correct long-standing problems is probably too ambitious a goal; rather, the approach should be strategic, identifying changes that can support caregiving but that are possible within this family system.

Role Enactment

The term *role enactment* refers to the phase in which caregivers are actively involved in providing help and assistance to their relative. This is the phase of caregiving in which families are most likely to seek out clinicians for help. Interventions using the stress process model can pinpoint current problems and stressors and devise strategies to alleviate these situations. The focus can be on improving the older person's functioning, behavior, or mood; improving how the caregiver manages the older person; or increasing the amount of support and assistance the caregiver receives. In cases of degenerative conditions, discussions will inevitably focus on whether and when to institutionalize the older person. Because of the importance of that issue, I discuss it in the following section.

Assessment at this point focuses on identifying particular stressors and issues facing a family. The clinician should review evidence about whether there might be medically reversible components of the situation or if other disciplines might be involved. People with symptoms of dementia, for example, sometimes have treatable illnesses or problems, with medication reactions being the most common. Treatment of these problems can reduce or sometimes totally reverse the symptoms of dementia. There also may be other approaches to improving functioning. With vision loss, for example, a variety of visual aids are available to help people with severe problems (including those who are legally blind) to use their remaining eyesight (Genensky, Zarit, & Amaral, 1992). Despite their proved effectiveness, however, these visual aids are sometimes not mentioned by ophthalmologists. This example illustrates that it is important for clinicians to obtain adequate information about the medical conditions of the older people they are treating and to work with other professionals (e.g., physicians, optometrists, audiologists) to ensure that adequate treatment is provided (see chapter 9 in this book).

Many different approaches can be helpful with family caregivers. In work with caregivers of patients with dementia, my colleagues and I have found that three types of intervention are particularly useful: providing information, developing problem-solving skills, and increasing support.

These interventions can be part of individual psychotherapy, incorporated into family meetings, or part of the agenda discussed in support groups (Zarit, Orr, & Zarit, 1985). Each of these clinical approaches has different advantages, which I discuss shortly.

A starting point for interventions often is to provide families with adequate information about their elder's condition and the care alternatives available to them. Often, they have questions that have not been answered previously. In cases of chronic conditions such as dementia, families often will not be willing to take steps to improve the caregiving situation until they understand that their elder's condition cannot be cured and will not go away. The clinician must deliver a complex message: that the medical condition is not reversible but that there are steps the family can take to improve the situation.

Besides improving families' knowledge of the underlying medical condition, clinicians also can provide a framework for understanding patients' behavior and mood. With dementia, for example, families often misinterpret common problems such as asking the same question over and over again as something that the patient does deliberately or that the patient should be able to control. It is helpful to have families relabel these problems as being caused by the dementia. Families can also learn to differentiate between the patient's overt cognitive communication and underlying feelings. It may not be possible to make sense of what patients with dementia say or to reason with them so that they change their misinterpretations of events. Because their ability to think, reason, and remember is damaged, patients often insist that they are right in the face of efforts to correct them or reorient them to (someone else's) reality. Caregivers can only lose arguments over what the facts of a situation really are. Instead, it is better to focus on what the patient might be feeling, which is valid and real, even if the cognitive component makes no sense. Families then can make a response that is appropriate to what the patient must be feeling rather than to a distorted cognition.

An example is the common request among patients to see their mothers. In my experience, no amount of reasoning with patients can dissuade them from wanting to see their mothers or can convince them that their mother is dead. Some families have even shown patients their mothers' obituaries, but to no avail. In fact, reminding them their mother is dead may cause them to grieve and become more agitated. Shortly, however, they will have forgotten the "facts" and return to their insistence on seeing their mother. The key point is that families cannot win an argument over the facts; instead, they need to respond to what they think the underlying feelings might be. Providing reassurance, comfort, or similar approaches, or even reminiscing about the patient's mother, can be effective in reducing this type of complaint. Distracting patients and involving them in activities also can be helpful for these kinds of problems.

Staff in nursing homes and other formal programs also can have this problem. A special unit for patients with Alzheimer's disease had a resident who paced the halls, wanting to see her mother. This patient was disruptive to the staff and to other patients. The staff, who were trained primarily in psychiatric nursing, wanted to reorient the woman to reality, so they confronted her, telling her that her mother was dead. On hearing that her mother was dead, she became more agitated and upset, but soon again was asking to see her mother. The consulting psychologist encouraged the staff to think about what asking to see one's mother might mean and what feelings it might convey. Still not wanting to let go of "reality," the staff decided on a diversion. When the patient asked to see her mother, they had her place a call, which was answered by a staff member in another part of the unit. The staff member informed the woman that her mother was in the bath and could not come to the phone. The patient, although profoundly memory impaired, would wait about 5 min and then start asking to see her mother again because surely she would be out of her bath by now. Finally, the head nurse tried another approach. When the patient asked to see her mother, the head nurse sat down with her and said, "Let's have a cup of tea and talk about your mother." This intervention, which addressed the woman's feelings of needing some comfort rather than the reality of whether her mother was alive, calmed her down and satisfied her need to "see" her mother. As this example indicates, it does not matter whether the patient's understanding of the facts of a situation are correct. Their requests reflect feelings, which can be addressed effectively in a variety of ways, without confronting them about their incorrect perceptions of reality.

This example provides a transition to the second component of clinical interventions with family caregivers: problem solving. Zarit et al. (1985) found that use of a problem-solving approach to help families identify and implement new strategies for caregiving stressors can be highly useful. Problem solving can have several different goals. A basic approach is to help caregivers identify antecedents and consequences of problem behaviors, such as agitation. Once a pattern is identified, it is possible to implement simple changes in routines that bring the problem behavior under better control. Agitation, for example, may follow long periods of inactivity and be reinforced by giving the patient a lot of attention. An approach that heads off the agitation by increasing attention and activity before it occurs often will be effective. A variety of problems have been found to respond to this kind of behavioral intervention, including wandering off, incontinence, and depressed mood.

Problem solving also can focus on changes the caregiver can make. Sometimes, the problem is not the patient's behavior but the caregiver's interpretation of it. For example, one caregiver complained that her mother always was asking her what time her (the caregiver's) husband was coming home. As part of problem solving, we asked the caregiver to keep a log on when and how often this problem occurred. She came back after a week surprised that the problem had not happened more often. Instead, she realized that she found her mother's question irritating because she interpreted it as a criticism of her marriage. Often, caregivers magnify or exaggerate the importance of some problems, making them unmanageable. In these situations, clinicians can help them to differentiate what the patient does from their interpretation of the event and subsequent feelings. Interventions can then be made that help manage the behavior more effectively or help caregivers explore the meaning of the situation for them.

I have sometimes used a formal approach to teach caregivers to use problem solving (see Exhibit 1). Many caregivers, however, have good problem-solving skills and need only a little encouragement and direction to bring these skills to bear on caregiving issues.

A third component of interventions with caregivers is providing support. Support can come from several sources. The clinician, of course, provides acceptance and emotional support. Other family members are an important source of emotional support and can provide tangible assistance with key problems. Finally, formal services, such as adult day care, can relieve caregivers of a part of the burden of care.

When dealing with issues of support, clinicians often must help caregivers differentiate between realistic barriers to getting help and exaggerated concerns. (I address issues of getting help from the family in the section on family meetings.) With respect to formal services, caregivers may be reluctant to get help for a variety of reasons, including believing that it is wrong to accept help, that they should do everything themselves, or that their relative will not accept help. Helping them explore these beliefs, particularly in light of the advantages of getting help and disadvantages of not doing so, can be useful. They also may have concerns about the quality and reliability of formal services. These complaints may be partly (or wholly) realistic. When clinicians have a familiarity with the aging services network, they can guide caregivers toward more reliable ser-

EXHIBIT 1
The Problem-Solving Process

1. Identify the problem
   ■ Frequency of occurrence
   ■ Antecedents
   ■ Consequences
2. Generate alternative solutions
3. Select a solution: Pros and cons
4. Cognitive rehearsal
5. Carry out the plan
6. Evaluate the outcome

vices or work with caregivers to compensate for the deficiencies in the available services.

These interventions can be made in the course of brief, problem-focused psychotherapy. On occasion, a relative's disability may bring to the forefront many complex and long-standing problems that require longer intervention. As is usually the case in psychotherapy, the therapeutic relationship is used to help caregivers make difficult changes.

For example, a therapist had been seeing a couple in which the husband was providing care for his wife, who had a vascular dementia and was increasingly unable to care for herself (Zarit & Zarit, in press). The couple had been very close, and the illness was devastating to the husband, who felt that he had lost his best friend. Over a 3-year period, a series of problems was uncovered and addressed. After a few initial sessions, it became apparent that the husband was thinking about ending his wife's life and then his own. This issue was examined for several sessions, with the therapist constantly monitoring the degree of risk. Once this crisis was over (resolved largely because of the wife's ability to say she did not want to die that way), the therapist focused on practical strategies for managing caregiving more effectively. The therapist explored getting help into the home, but the husband was resistant. After several sessions, he revealed that he and his wife were pack rats and that they had filled their house with a lifetime's accumulation of things. The house also had not been cleaned for some time. A more imminent problem was that the husband had become so overwhelmed that he was no longer paying his bills. The therapist made progress with him on paying the bills and gradually helped him overcome his embarrassment over the condition of the house. When he finally did accept help in the home, however, the effort backfired. The person sent out to evaluate the family by the local Area Agency on Aging was appalled by the cluttered conditions in the house. Rather than offering any help, she threatened to bring elder abuse charges against the husband for leaving his wife alone for a few hours a week. The husband resisted pressure from the agency to place his wife in a nursing home and, instead, with the therapist's help, found alternative sources of help to ensure that his wife had proper supervision. As he had through much of this process, he was often despondent and felt isolated from friends and family. Ongoing support from his therapist helped him manage the everyday problems of care, as well as these periodic crises. Finally, his wife's condition worsened to the point that he could no longer lift her. At this point, the therapist supported him in deciding to place her in a nursing home and helped him with the sense of guilt and loss that ensued. A last crisis occurred around her death, in which, with the therapist's help, he was able to ensure that his wife was kept comfortable and that no unnecessary or invasive medical procedures were used.

This case illustrates a long, complex therapeutic involvement. Using the therapeutic relationship, the therapist helped this caregiver through a series of crises that emerged because of the extremely close relationship he had with his wife and because of the lifestyle they had led. Ongoing support and the use of problem-solving skills were needed to help him with the series of problems and crises that occurred during the course of his caregiving.

An intervention that is uniquely suited to the stresses of family caregiving is the family meeting (Zarit et al., 1985). Because the family is the most readily available source of support, bringing everyone together to develop a plan of care can be helpful to the primary caregiver. On the other hand, family conflict is common in caregiving situations and is typically a source of great distress for the primary caregiver (Semple, 1992). Family meetings can be used to identify and relieve sources of conflict.

The family meeting can incorporate all the interventions described earlier. It often opens by reviewing medical and other assessments and bringing the rest of the family up to speed on what has been done and what alternatives are available. Once questions about assessments and cures have been answered, families can focus on the caregiving situation and how to provide relief to the primary caregiver. Typically, the family will have one person who is an organizer and problem solver, one who can get the process going. The end result is improving the help and emotional support the primary caregiver receives. A combination of individual therapy with the primary caregiver followed by family meetings has been found to be particularly effective in lowering the stress experienced by caregivers (Mittelman et al., 1993; Whitlatch, Zarit, & von Eye, 1991).

An important source of information and support is other caregivers. The popularity of support groups attests to the value of learning from other people who have gone through the same situation. A variety of groups are available to caregivers of the elderly, although the most typical are those concerning Alzheimer's disease and other dementia-related illnesses. The unique contribution that groups make is providing the opportunity to interact with and learn from other people in similar circumstances. Caregivers often will try new approaches when they hear about them from other caregivers rather than from a professional. They may, for example, be more willing to try a formal service when they hear about other caregivers' experiences. As with any group, however, support groups are sometimes not helpful (e.g., if cohesion among group members does not develop or if the group is dominated by one or two people who try to impose their own values and beliefs on the rest). My colleagues and I have found that having a clinician lead a support group is useful for establishing and maintaining therapeutic processes (Toseland, 1990; Zarit et al., 1985).

During this period of role enactment, much of the focus of interventions will be on caregivers. However, it is important not to lose sight of what might be done for patients. As an example, treatment of depression among people with Alzheimer's disease can be very helpful, both for the benefit to patients and because it may reduce the problems faced by caregivers (Teri, 1994).

The Transition to Institutionalization

Most families caring for an elder with chronic disabilities think about the possibility of placement in a nursing home or other institutional facility. The clinician can explore with them both the practical and emotional issues involved in placement. An important practical step is to provide information about the available nursing homes and alternative types of group living arrangements. Besides nursing homes, different types of specialized housing are available, including retirement homes, assisted-living facilities, and board-and-care homes. Someone who does not have extensive medical needs may be able to live in one of these less restrictive settings.

In cases of dementia, a key issue is whether the facility can accommodate that problem or whether it has a special unit or activities for patients with dementia. Nursing homes increasingly offer special programs for dementia, which sometimes involve sophisticated environmental design and programming for patients (e.g., Holmes, Ory, & Teresi, 1994; Zarit, Zarit, & Rosenberg-Thompson, 1990). An effective program uses environmental design to minimize the extent to which patients must be controlled or restrained. Patients will be able to wander freely within the unit and sometimes outside to a secured garden area. Staff in these settings work in supportive and facilitative ways rather than trying to confront or control patients. Behavioral strategies are used when possible as an alternative to medication and restraints. Sometimes, however, a dementia unit may be little more than a locked door. Less expensive facilities such as a board-and-care home sometimes can provide a positive environment for patients with dementia.

A key practical issue is how families will pay for institutional care. Medicare pays for nursing home care only for short periods of time after hospitalization for an acute medical problem. Most care of elderly with chronic disabilities is paid by the family. If the elder's financial resources become exhausted paying for a nursing home, he or she can become eligible for Medicaid. Some nursing homes, however, do not accept Medicaid, so that might necessitate moving the person from one facility to another. Legal and financial planning is important in cases of chronic disability. It is particularly so for a spouse, who, under current laws, can save a portion of assets for his or her own use (approximately 50% of joint assets up to a ceiling of $67,000 and a house). Good planning should be done as early as possible in the caregiving process to maximize the amount that a spouse will have to live on.

Placement, of course, often evokes strong emotional reactions. Caregivers may feel extremely guilty over even considering the idea of placement. One common problem is that they may feel they cannot place the elder because they made a promise never to do so. It is sometimes helpful to point out that this promise was made without either the elder or caregiver anticipating the extensive amount of care that is currently required.

Perhaps the most critical issue in discussions of placement is for clinicians not to impose their own values about when it is the best time to make this decision. I have found that many people who work with the elderly will push for placement long before the caregiver is ready and before other options have been explored. They often do so out of the mistaken belief that caregivers must overcome their denial and accept the reality of the need for placement. Although less common, the opposite also sometimes occurs: The clinician opposes placement. These attitudes represent classic countertransferences by the clinician.

The clinician's motivation behind recommending placement is the mistaken belief that it will relieve stress on the caregiver. Studies that follow caregivers from before to after placement show that institutionalization alters but does not relieve stress (Aneshensel et al., 1995; Zarit & Whitlatch, 1992). Caregivers are relieved of the pressures of everyday care after placement, but new stressors emerge. They now feel the responsibility to visit on a regular basis, sometimes traveling long distances to do so. Furthermore, they often help with many of the same activities of daily living, such as feeding the patient, that they did at home. They must figure out how to interact with staff, feeling a loss of control over what happens to their relative and sometimes powerlessness to do anything to improve care. Family conflict may increase over the placement decision, especially if it has been carried out precipitously or prematurely. Finally, there is the financial pressure of paying for care. Given these new stressors, it should not be surprising that caregivers continue to experience emotional distress after placement.

In the final analysis, clinicians need to recognize that there is no best or optimal time for placement. It is an individual matter that depends on the caregiver's resources and values. The clinician's role is to facilitate discussions of institutionalization in a nonjudgmental manner. Caregivers can be encouraged to explore the possibility of placement and to visit facilities, so that they are prepared if placement becomes necessary. Clinicians also can provide accurate information about the availability and cost of facilities and emotional support, but not their own view of when it is right to place someone in a nursing home.

The period after placement often involves a difficult adjustment for caregivers. Because people believe that stress on the caregiver will be relieved by placement, support to the caregiver sometimes is greatly diminished. Compounding this problem, there are no social norms about how to interact with the caregiver after nursing home placement. Many people do not know what to say or ask a caregiver whose relative is in a nursing home. Caregivers themselves may feel awkward, guilty, and ashamed over what they did. Spouse caregivers, in particular, are in an ambiguous situation: still married yet alone at home and in social situations. One caregiver told me that he received much more support after his wife's death than when she was in a nursing home. During that period, people did not ask how she was or even how he was doing. Because of the much better developed norms around death and bereavement, he found that his social support suddenly increased after her death.

As a consequence, it is not surprising that many caregivers will feel distressed, depressed, guilty, and alone after placement. Ongoing support from a therapist can be critical during this period. Caregivers also may experience difficulties learning how to work with the nursing home staff and physicians in collaborative rather than confrontational ways. A useful role for clinicians is to direct caregivers' concerns about how their relative is treated into effective ways of obtaining that assistance.

Nursing home placement can last several years. Most caregivers gradually make an adequate adjustment to placement, although perhaps as many as 25% have significant feelings of depression as long as 4 years after placement (Aneshensel et al., 1995). These caregivers may need long-term treatment, but some can benefit from attending a well-structured support group.

Bereavement and Recovery

The caregiving role formally ends with the elder's death, although some of the lingering effects can be seen for a year or more afterward (Aneshensel et al., 1995). As with placement, bereavement is a transition that requires a reconstruction of the caregiver's life and identity. Some caregivers may feel a sense of relief, especially after a long, debilitating illness. They may have let go of the patient emotionally a long time ago and may view death as freeing the elder from suffering. For others, however, grief may be intense and its effects felt for many months. Bereavement and its aftermath are clearly times when clinical contacts with a caregiver may resume to assist with this transition.

SUMMARY

Family caregiving has become a major social issue. Although the aging of the population has placed an increased burden on society's financial resources, it also has meant that families provide unprecedented amounts of assistance to disabled elders for longer periods of time than ever before. Most families willingly provide this help, but often at considerable personal sacrifice. Timely clinical interventions can help families sort through the difficult choices they are facing and can relieve some of the stress they are experiencing. Besides having good, basic clinical skills, clinicians working with caregivers need to be aware of the implications of many common chronic diseases and of the resources and assistance that families might use. Clinical approaches that target stressful aspects of a caregiver's situation and mobilize family resources have been successful in helping with the challenges of caring for a disabled elder.

REFERENCES

Aneshensel, C. S., Pearlin, L. I., Mullan, J. T., Zarit, S. H., & Whitlatch, C. J. (1995). *Profiles of caregiving: The unexpected career.* San Diego, CA: Academic Press.

Aneshensel, C. S., Pearlin, L. I., & Schuler, R. H. (1993). Stress, role captivity, and the cessation of caregiving. *Journal of Health and Social Behavior, 34,* 54–70.

Franklin, S. T., Ames, B. D., & King, S. (1994). Acquiring the family eldercare role: Influence on female employment adaptation. *Research on Aging, 16,* 27–42.

Gatz, M., Bengtson, V. L., & Blum, M. J. (1991). Caregiving families. In J. E. Birren & K. W. Schaie (Eds.), *Handbook of the psychology of aging* (3rd ed., pp. 405–426). San Diego, CA: Academic Press.

Genensky, S., Zarit, S. H., & Amaral, P. (1992). Visual care and rehabilitation of the elderly patient. In A. A. Rosenblum, Jr., & M. W. Morgan (Eds.), *Vision and aging: General and clinical perspectives* (2nd ed., pp. 424–444). New York: Professional Press.

Holmes, D., Ory, M. G., & Teresi, J. (1994). Dementia special care: Overview of research, policy and practice. *Alzheimer's Disease and Associated Disorders,* 8(Suppl. 1), S5–S13.

Mittelman, M. S., Ferris, S. H., Steinberg, G., Schulman, E., Mackell, J. A., Ambinder, A., & Cohen, J. (1993). An intervention that delays institutionalization of Alzheimer's disease patients: Treatment of spouse caregivers. *The Gerontologist, 33,* 730–740.

Mutschler, P. H. (1994). From executive suite to production line: How employees in different occupations manage elder care responsibilities. *Research on Aging, 16,* 7–26.

Pearlin, L. I. (1992). The careers of caregivers. *The Gerontologist, 32,* 647–648.

Pearlin, L. I., Mullan, J. T., Semple, S. J., & Skaff, M. M. (1990). Caregiving and the stress process: An overview of concepts and their measures. *The Gerontologist, 30,* 583–594.

Scharlach, A. E., & Boyd, S. L. (1989). Caregiving and employment: Results of an employee survey. *The Gerontologist, 29,* 382–387.

Semple, S. J. (1992). Conflict in Alzheimer's caregiving families: Its dimensions and consequences. *The Gerontologist, 32,* 648–655.

Soldo, B. J., & Myllyuoma, J. (1983). Caregivers who live with dependent elderly. *The Gerontologist, 23,* 605–611.

Stone, R. I., Cafferata, G. L., & Sangl, J. (1987). Caregivers of the frail elderly: A national profile. *The Gerontologist, 27,* 616–626.

Teri, L. (1994). Behavioral treatment of depression in patients with dementia. *Alzheimer's Disease and Associated Disorders,* 8(Suppl. 3), S66–S74.

Teri, L., & Logsdon, R. (1990). Assessment and management of behavioral disturbances in Alzheimer's disease patients. *Comprehensive Therapy, 16,* 36–42.

Toseland, R. W. (1990). *Group work with older adults.* New York: New York University Press.

Whitlatch, C. J., Zarit, S. H., & von Eye, A. (1991). Efficacy of interventions with caregivers: A reanalysis. *The Gerontologist, 31,* 9–14.

Zarit, S. H. (1994). Research perspective on family caregiving. In M. Cantor (Ed.), *Family caregiving: Agenda for the future* (pp. 9–24). San Francisco: American Society for Aging.

Zarit, S. H., & Eggebeen, D. J. (1995). Parent child relationships in adulthood and old age. In M. Bornstein (Ed.), *Handbook of parenting* (Vol. 1, pp. 119–140). Hillsdale, NJ: Erlbaum.

Zarit, S. H., Orr, N. K., & Zarit, J. M. (1985). *The hidden victims of Alzheimer's disease: Families under stress.* New York: New York University Press.

Zarit, S. H., Todd, P. A., & Zarit, J. M. (1986). Subjective burden of husbands and wives as caregivers: A longitudinal study. *The Gerontologist, 26,* 260–270.

Zarit, S. H., & Whitlatch, C. J. (1992). Institutional placement: Phases of the transition. *The Gerontologist, 32,* 665–672.

Zarit, S. H., & Zarit, J. M. (in press). Til death do us part. In R. P. Halgin & S. K. Whitbourne (Eds.), *Partners in change: Growth through the therapeutic process.* New York: Oxford University Press.

Zarit, S. H., Zarit, J. M., & Rosenberg-Thompson, S. (1990). A special treatment unit for Alzheimer's disease: Medical, behavioral and environmental features. *Clinical Gerontologist,* 9(3–4), 47–61.

II

SPECIAL ISSUES FOR
WORK WITH THE ELDERLY

8

TECHNIQUES AND INSTRUMENTS FOR ASSESSMENT OF THE ELDERLY

ALFRED W. KASZNIAK

Despite historical pessimism regarding the efficacy of psychotherapy with older adults (e.g., Freud, 1924), accumulating recent research (see Teri & Logsdon, 1992) has encouraged the use of various psychosocial interventions for a wide range of psychological, and select medical, difficulties of older adults. Among those applications for which there are controlled experimental outcome studies are cognitive–behavioral and interpersonal therapies for depression; reminiscence and life review therapies to reduce depression and anxiety; behavioral and cognitive–behavioral treatments for depression and behavior problems in dementia; and group psychotherapy for people with cancer, stroke, pain, and cardiac disease (for a review, see Teri & McCurry, 1994). Selection of the most appropriate intervention (whether psychologic or somatic) for any person depends not only on a knowledge of the relevant treatment theory and outcome research, but also on an assessment of the physical, mental, behavioral, and situational characteristics of the individual and his or her environment. This is particularly true in treatment planning with older adults, for whom physical and medical, developmental, psychological, social, environmental, and other factors interact in highly complex ways relevant to influence the choice of an intervention strategy (Birren, Sloane, & Cohen, 1992). The ultimate goal of clinical assessment is treatment planning, which should be guided by a dynamic understanding of how each of these factors contribute and interact to interfere with functional integrity (Caine & Grossman, 1992).

The clinical assessment of elderly individuals being considered for psychological intervention is a fundamentally interdisciplinary endeavor, with physicians and other health care providers also playing necessary roles. Complex interactions exist between medical illnesses, medications (both psychotropic and nonpsychotropic), age-related changes in pharmacokinetics and pharmacodynamics, and a variety of psychologic and social factors that influence the occurrence and nature of both cognitive and affective symptoms in older adults (for reviews, see Cummings & Coffey, 1994; Depression Guideline Panel, 1993; Fry, 1986; Kaszniak, 1990; Kaszniak & Christenson, 1994; Koenig & Blazer, 1992; Lebowitz & Niederehe, 1992). This complexity requires the cooperative interaction of various medical and mental health practitioners if the diagnostic and treatment needs of older adults are to be served adequately. A review of those medical considerations of particular importance in psychological treatment planning is provided in chapter 9 in this book. More extended discussion of this topic can be found in Coffey and Cummings (1994). In this chapter I discuss the role of psychological (including neuropsychological) assessment as one important component of an interdisciplinary clinical evaluation of older individuals.

Although identified historically with "psychological testing" (Goldstein & Hersen, 1984), psychological assessment is a broader concept, encompassing procedures such as interviews, life history record and data review, tests, and situational observations (Gallagher, Thompson, & Levy, 1980). S. H. Zarit, Eiler, and Hassinger (1985) identified four major psychological assessment objectives: (a) determination of diagnosis; (b) assessment of broad patterns of behavior, thoughts, or emotions; (c) evaluation of specific variables to assist in treatment planning; and (d) evaluation of the outcomes and effectiveness of interventions. Discussions of treatment planning and the evaluation of intervention outcomes are provided in other chapters in this book. Hence, this chapter focuses primarily on the first two objectives. The determination of diagnosis requires an appreciation of the epidemiology of mental disorder in older age because this provides the clinician with a sense of base-rate probabilities for particular disorders (Gatz & Pearson, 1988). A knowledge of diagnostic criteria and the particular difficulties inherent in arriving at accurate diagnoses of elderly individuals is similarly necessary. The assessment of psychological characteristics and patterns requires an understanding of the physical, cognitive, emotional, and behavioral changes of aging. Also required is a knowledge of the assessment procedures having empirical evidence of reliability and validity for evaluating aging individuals. Therefore, I proceed with a brief overview of relevant epidemiological data. Next, general considerations in the psychological assessment of older adults are reviewed, with a focus on aspects of aging that may pose particular risks for assessment reliability and validity. This is followed by a discussion of psychological assessment procedures for identifying some of the most prevalent mental disorders among older people, with an emphasis on particularly difficult differential diagnoses (e.g., dementia vs. depression). The role of assessment in describing patterns of behavior, thought, and emotion; the characteristics of physical and social environments; and how such information may benefit patients, clinicians, other caregivers, and family members are discussed.

EPIDEMIOLOGY

On the basis of an extensive household population-based sampling of people in five U.S. cities (National Institute of Mental Health Epidemiological Catchment Area Program; Regier et al., 1988), it has been estimated that 12.3% of older adults (those 65 years of age and older) have a mental disorder as determined by a questionnaire based on standard diagnostic criteria (third edition of the *Diagnostic and Statistical Manual of Mental Disorders* [DSM–III]; American Psychiatric Association, 1980). Making up this group are 5.5% of older people with anxiety disorders (including phobia, panic, and obsessive–compulsive disorders), 4.9% with severe cognitive impairment, 2.5% with affective disorder (0.7% with a major depressive episode and 1.8% with dysthymic disorder), 0.9% with alcohol abuse or dependence, and 0.1% with schizophrenia or schizophreniform disorder. Gender differences were found for some of these disorders. For severe cognitive impairment, men had a higher prevalence rate than women at ages 65–74, a comparable rate at ages 75–84, and a markedly lower rate at 85+ years of age. This Age × Gender interaction in the prevalence of severe cognitive impairment may reflect differential mortality, with women tending to survive longer than men. However, complex interactions between gender and different causes of cognitive impairment (e.g., cerebrovascular causes, with onset at younger ages, affecting more men than women; Alzheimer's disease, with greater prevalence at older ages, affecting more women than men) remain possibilities. As might be expected, men also had a much higher prevalence of alcohol abuse than did women (1.8% for men and 0.3% for women). The overall prevalence of all types of mental disorders for the older adults in this study was lower than that for any other age group. Similarly, the prevalence also was lower for each specific type of mental disorder, except for that of severe cognitive impairment. The prevalence of severe cognitive impairment, or dementia, is age associated, as is documented next.

The Epidemiological Catchment Area Program also conducted 1-year follow-up interviews in their population (Eaton et al., 1989) to determine the incidence of new mental disorders. It was found that the risk of developing severe cognitive impairment (approximately 5% new cases each year for those aged 65+) increased with age. The incidence of alcohol abuse also increased with age (i.e., in men aged 75+, the rate of new cases was six times higher than that for men aged 65–74; in women, the rate was twice as high for those aged 75+ than for those aged 65–74). Other disorders did not show an age-associated increase in incidence, and for some disorders (e.g., panic disorder, major depression) a new onset in older age was rare.

Cognitive impairment among older adults most frequently manifests in the syndrome of dementia. Dementia, by most definitions, involves persistent deterioration in two or more areas of cognitive functioning, including memory, language, visuospatial skills, judgment or abstract thinking, and emotion or personality (Bayles & Kaszniak, 1987; Bondi, Salmon, & Kaszniak, in press-a; Cummings & Benson, 1992; Kaszniak, 1986). In studies of dementia in various countries, prevalence rates for those older than 65 years have ranged from 2.5% to 24.6% (for a review, see Ineichen, 1987), with variability between studies likely reflecting methodological differences. Cummings and Benson (1992) calculated the average of prevalence estimates across studies to show that approximately 6% of people older than 65 have severe dementia (similar to the Epidemiological Catchment Area estimate of 4.9% with severe cognitive impairment), with an additional 10–15% showing evidence of mild-to-moderate dementia. Dementia prevalence doubles approximately every 5 years after age 65, at least until age 90 (Jorm, 1990; Jorm, Korten, & Henderson, 1987).

Thus, with the exception of severe cognitive disorders, and possibly alcohol abuse, older adults do not appear to be at increased risk (compared with younger adults) for mental disorders. However, caution must be exercised in interpreting the available epidemiological data. Although the prevalence of affective disorder was only 2.5% for older adults in the Epidemiological Catchment Area study, the elderly have been found to have one of the highest rates of suicide, involving primarily older White men, for whom suicide increases dramatically from age 65 to 85+ (National Center for Health Statistics, 1993). In addition, the prevalence of clinically significant depressive symptoms that do not meet DSM–III criteria for these diagnoses is approximately 20% among older individuals living in the community (Blazer, Hughes, & George, 1987). These individuals may be at risk for the development of major depression (Rohde, Lewinsohn, & Seeley, 1990), and this could account for many of the physician office visits of older adults involving physical complaints for which no biological cause can be found (Scogin, 1994).

Similarly, it is likely that the Epidemiological Catchment Area study underestimates the prevalence of anxiety symptoms in the elderly. First, when both anxiety and depressive symptoms are present (as often occurs in older adults; Sheikh, 1994), the distinction between anxiety and depression can be difficult to make and epidemiological studies are more likely to classify such individuals as depressed (Copeland, Davidson, & Dewey, 1987; Kay, 1988). Thus, if diagnosed independently, the prevalence of anxiety might be nearly doubled (Sheikh, 1994). It also has been suggested (Blazer, George, & Hughes, 1991) that older adults might have underreported anxiety symptoms in the Epidemiological Catchment Area study because of a higher threshold for symptom reporting among those of older age. Finally, it is interesting that physicians prescribe benzodiazepines (the most frequently prescribed anxiolytics) for elderly people at a disproportionately high rate given their percentage in the general population (Moran, Thompson, & Nies, 1988).

Another complicating factor in interpreting epidemiological data for mental disorders is that these syndromes (particularly cognitive impairment, depression, and anxiety) often coexist with chronic medical illnesses among older adults (see Kaszniak, 1986; Malmgren, 1994; Scogin, 1994; Sheikh, 1994). Estimates vary from 50 to more than 80 different causes of cerebral dysfunction that can produce or simulate the syndrome of dementia (Haase, 1977; Katzman, 1986; Office of Technology Task Force, 1988). Differentiation among these causes is important because some are treatable, and as many as 13% of all cases of dementia may be caused by potentially reversible conditions (Clarfield, 1988). The most common cause of reversible dementia appears to be drug toxicity (Katzman, Lasker, & Bernstein, 1988). Although it is clinically important to be vigilant for potentially reversible causes of dementia, Alzheimer's disease, a presently irreversible degenerative disease of the brain, accounts for the largest proportion of all causes of dementia. The relative prevalence of Alzheimer's disease among people with dementia ranges from 22% to 70% across published studies (for a review, see Cummings & Benson, 1992). However, in some community surveys, particularly those from Japan and China, multi-infarct dementia (a dementia associated with cerebrovascular disease) has been found to be more prevalent than Alzheimer's disease (Folstein, Anthony, Parhad, Duffy, & Gruenberg, 1985; Li, Shen, Chen, Zhao, & Li, 1989; Rorsman, Hagnell, & Lanke, 1986; Shibayama, Kasahara, & Kobayashi, 1986). A higher relative prevalence of vascular dementia may occur in countries where stroke risk is higher, although it remains uncertain whether differences in relative prevalence estimates reflect actual regional disparities or methodological variance across studies. What is clear, however, is that Alzheimer's disease and vascular dementia are the most common causes of age-associated dementia (Roman, 1991). In the United States, Alzheimer's disease and vascular dementia are the most frequent diagnoses made of older people referred for comprehensive neurological evaluation because of memory complaints (Thal, Grundman, & Klauber, 1988). Typically, the highest proportion of longer term residents in nursing homes have a severe cognitive disorder attributable to various neurological etiologies (e.g., stroke, Alzheimer's disease, etc.; Liu & Manton, 1984; Smyer, 1988). In population studies conducted in various countries, the prevalence of both Alzheimer's disease and vascular dementia have been found to increase exponentially between the ages of 65 and 85 (for a review, see Katzman & Kawas,1994).

Anxiety and anxietylike symptoms are a common feature of medical illness in the elderly. Angina pectoris and myocardial infarction (with their symptoms of dyspnea, palpitations, chest tightening, sweating, and fear of dying) can simulate panic attacks (Sheikh, 1994). Similarly, various endocrine (Popkin & Mackenzie, 1980), neurological (Hall, 1980), and pulmonary (Karajgi, Rifkin, Doddi, & Kolli, 1990) disorders are associated with anxiety symptoms. The side effects of certain antihypertensive drugs, withdrawal from alcohol or sedative–hypnotic medications, and toxic levels of digitalis and anticholinergic drugs also can involve anxiety (Jenike, 1989).

Elderly medical outpatients and inpatients have depression rates that range from 15% to 45% across various studies (Kitchell, Barnes, Veith, Okimoto, & Raskind, 1982; Norris, Gallagher, Wilson, & Winograd, 1987; Rapp, Parisi, & Walsh, 1988; Waxman & Carner, 1984), which are substantially higher than depression prevalence for the general population of older adults. Not surprisingly, among cognitively intact elderly people in a long-term care setting, 20% of new admissions and 42% of longer term residents were found to be suffering from either major depression or dysthymic disorder (Parmelee, Katz, & Lawton, 1989). Depression frequently coexists with neurological disorders that are particularly prevalent among older adults, including stroke, Alzheimer's disease, and Parkinson's disease (for a review, see Kaszniak & Christenson, 1994; Kaszniak, Sadeh, & Stern, 1985). In addition, a number of prescription and nonprescription medications taken by older adults for common medical conditions may either produce depressionlike symptoms, induce depression, or aggravate preexisting depression (Klerman, 1983; Salzman, 1992). Older individuals often are simultaneously taking several different medications. This further complicates assessment because drug interactions also may produce depression or depressionlike symptoms (Salzman, 1992) and contribute to cognitive dysfunction.

Comorbidity of mental and medical disorders creates problems for differential diagnosis and poses challenges for psychological intervention with older adults. Such comorbidity also underscores the fact that differential diagnosis of the mental disorders of older adults is a fundamentally interdisciplinary endeavor.

GENERAL CONSIDERATIONS IN THE PSYCHOLOGICAL ASSESSMENT OF OLDER ADULTS

Clinical Interview

Although a variety of psychological assessment instruments are available, most clinicians believe that a careful interview and history remains the cornerstone of clinical evaluation. For example, when a consensus development panel of mental health professionals considered the evaluation and diagnosis of depression in older adults (National Institutes of Health, 1991), it was agreed that the clinical interview was the most important approach. The fourth edition of the DSM (DSM–IV; American Psychiatric Association, 1994) provides guidelines on how to obtain relevant interview information and observations with a given patient. Such guidelines generally are as appropriate for the assessment of older as for younger individuals. Additional specific guidance is contained within the Structured Clinical Interview for the DSM–III–R (SCID; Spitzer, Williams, Gibbon, & First, 1990), designed to assist in making revised third edition DSM diagnoses (American Psychiatric Association, 1987). The Diagnostic Interview Schedule (National Institute of Mental Health, 1979; Robins, Helzer, Croughan, & Ratcliff, 1981), a predecessor of the SCID, has shown acceptable interdiagnostician agreement when assessing both younger and older adults (Blazer et al., 1987; Helzer et al., 1985; Robins, 1985). Although structured interview schedules such as the SCID and Diagnostic Interview Schedule play an important role in the documentation of diagnosis within research, many clinicians may not routinely administer a structured interview unless they are involved in a research protocol (Scogin, 1994). However, familiarization and preferably experience with structured interview protocols likely result in greater skill when conducting an unstructured clinical interview-based assessment of an older adult (see Kaszniak & Scogin, 1995).

In applying the DSM–IV, SCID, or Diagnostic Interview Schedule criteria for diagnosis of a particular disorder, many of the somatic and behavioral symptoms listed in the criteria actually may occur as part of the normal aging process (see Kaszniak & Allender, 1985; Scogin, 1994) or may reflect physical diseases that are common among the elderly (Klerman, 1983). For example, changes with aging or medical illness in sleep pattern, appetite, fatigue, behavioral slowing, agitation, and complaints of diminished ability to think or concentrate must be differentiated from the signs and symptoms of depression. The possible contribution of physical illness must be carefully considered when using interview-based or self-report measures for which a significant proportion of the items concern somatic symptoms. For example, because 9 questions of the 17-item version of the Hamilton Rating Scale for Depression (Hamilton, 1967) involve somatic symptoms, depression scores can be significantly elevated by the presence of physical illness in older adults (Gallagher, Slife, Rose, & Okarma, 1982). As already noted, the possible contribution of medication to depression and depressionlike symptoms also must be considered.

In obtaining a history during the initial assessment of an older adult, the clinician should include specific questioning about recent or past systemic illnesses (acute and chronic), injuries (particularly head trauma), exposure to environmental toxins, past and current prescription and non-prescription drugs, and substance or alcohol abuse because any of these can contribute to the individual's current mental status. A family history, particularly focusing on psychiatric and neurological disease among relatives, also is important given the likely genetic contribution to particular disorders (e.g., depression, Alzheimer's disease, Huntington's disease, etc.). Social and cultural history should include information about the person's education, employment and financial status, current living situation, marriage and family relations, ethnic and cultural background, religious affiliation and activity, hobbies and entertainment, and social activity.

Assessment of Functional Abilities

In addition to questioning concerning possible symptoms of mental disorders and the obtaining of a thorough history, the interview also should include inquiry about the individual's ability to maintain independent self-care and function in various environments. Traditionally, functional abilities have been divided into activities of daily living (e.g., eating, dressing, grooming, toileting, bathing, mobility, and transferring) and instrumental activities of daily living (i.e., skills and behaviors needed to survive in the community, including household chores, use of transportation, shopping, money management, health maintenance, safety, and communication). As discussed by Kemp and Mitchell (1992), functional evaluation plays an important role in the comprehensive psychological assessment for three major reasons. First, the determination of functional abilities is a critical aspect of diagnosis (e.g., impaired personal, social, or vocational functioning is one of the several criteria for dementia). Second, functional assessment is necessary for the prediction of outcome variables such as ultimate living situation and relapse and for the determination of community-service assistance needs. Third, functional evaluation enables the education of family members and others about the individual's performance capacities and support needs. A review of the reliability and validity of activities of daily living and instrumental activities of daily living assessment instruments that are appropriate for older adults can be found in Kemp and Mitchell (1992).

When no informant is available to interview about a cognitively impaired patient's functional abilities, or when a highly detailed assessment of functional abilities is desired (e.g., within rehabilitation hospitals), structured testing of function can be performed. Specific testing of functional abilities can be particularly important when the clinician is being asked to make competency decisions regarding older adults (see La Rue & Markee, 1995; Loewenstein, Rubert, Argüelles, & Duara, 1995). The Structured Assessment of Independent Living Skills (Mahurin, DeBettignies, & Pirozzolo, 1991) assesses fine and gross motor skills, dressing skills, eating skills, expressive and receptive language, time and orientation, money-related skills, other instrumental activities of daily living, and social interaction with the examiner. This instrument takes approximately 1 hr to complete and consists of 50 tasks (5 in each of the 10 areas of function), with each task being criterion referenced and specific behaviorally anchored descriptions provided for passing performance. Each task is scored on a rating scale ranging from 0 to 3 based on performance accuracy and, for some tasks, time to completion. Mahurin et al. (1991) reported high (.81 to .97) test–retest (1 week interval for 10 normal elderly persons) reliability coefficients for the total score and Motor Time score (i.e., the summed total of the time taken to perform each of the tasks in the motor domain). Interrater reliability (based on two raters of 10 patients with Alzheimer's disease) was .99 for both the Total Score and the Motor Time measures. Analysis of interitem reliability for the patients with Alzheimer's disease showed a standardized alpha coefficient of .90, and, with the exception of Social Interaction, all of the subscales for the Alzheimer's disease group were significantly correlated with the Total Score (rs = 55–94). Finally, a comparison of 18 patients with Alzheimer's disease with 18 healthy age- and education-matched community residents showed that the patients with Alzheimer's disease had a significantly lower performance on all task subgroups.

Multidimensional Interview Protocols

Several multidimensional protocols have been developed for older individuals that can assist the clinician in gathering comprehensive interview information. These protocols inquire about not only symptoms of psychopathology but also about medical, nutritional, functional independence, economic, and social concerns. The Comprehensive Assessment and Referral Evaluation (CARE; Gurland et al., 1977–1978) is a lengthy (1,500-item) questionnaire administered in a semistructured format. The interview guidance and inventory of defined ratings of the CARE provide reliable, relevant information to the psychological assessment of older adults. Because of its multidimensional content (including consideration of possible psychiatric, nutritional, medical, economic, activities of daily living, instrumental activities of daily living, and social problems), sections of the CARE can be administered by various members of a multidisciplinary clinical team. Shorter versions of the CARE also have been developed (Gurland & Wilder, 1984), including the CORE-CARE (a 314-item questionnaire retaining the conceptual framework of the original CARE) and the SHORT-CARE (limited to assessment of the areas of depression, dementia, and disability).

Another multidimensional evaluation technique is the Older Americans Resources and Services, which was developed within the Duke University Longitudinal Study of Aging for clinical, research, and policy decision making (Fillenbaum & Smyer, 1981; George & Fillenbaum, 1985). This semistructured interview format provides assessments of mental and physical health, activities of daily living–instrumental activities of daily living status, social resources and economic resources, which can be completed by different multidisciplinary team members working independently. Acceptable interrater reliability and criterion validity (criteria have included independent ratings by geropsychiatrists, physician's associates, and physical therapists) have been demonstrated (Fillenbaum & Smyer, 1981). Discriminant validity also has been shown by the instrument's ability to differentiate between different populations of community residents, clinic patients, and older adults living in institutions (George & Fillenbaum, 1985).

A third comprehensive interview protocol created specifically for application with older individuals is the Multilevel Assessment Instrument, developed at the Philadelphia Geriatric Center (Lawton, Moss, Fulcomer, & Kleban, 1982). The instrument provides evaluations of behavioral competence in the domains of activities of daily living–instrumental activities of daily living, cognition, health, time use, and social interaction, as well as measures of psychological well-being and perceived environmental quality. Test–retest and interrater reliabilities and discriminative validity, determined from the administration of the Multilevel Assessment Instrument to 590 older people from various groups (independent community residents, in-home service clients, people awaiting admission to an institution), are acceptably high (Lawton et al., 1982).

Caregiver Reports

It is often important to also interview an informant who is familiar with the individual, particularly when cognitive impairment is suspected. Various dementia-related illnesses (e.g., Alzheimer's disease, Huntington's disease, Pick's disease) can result in a lack of insight or awareness concerning the severity of the person's cognitive and functional impairment (Kaszniak & Christenson, 1996; McGlynn & Kaszniak, 1991a, 1991b). When dementia is suspected, informant reports can both corroborate and expand on the history obtained from the individual being assessed. Relatives appear able to provide generally more reliable and valid reports of progressive deterioration than are provided by individuals with dementing illness themselves. Research concerning the retrospective accounts of dementia symptoms, obtained from relatives of patients referred to a memory disorders clinic, has shown that relatives' reports are reasonably reliable over a 4- to 17-month test–retest interval (La Rue, Watson, & Plotkin, 1992). Other research (McGlone et al., 1990) has compared older adults with complaints of memory difficulty who later showed evidence of progressive dementia (as determined by 8- to 24-month neuropsychological reassessment) with those with memory complaints but no subsequent evidence of progressive dementia. Both the patients with and without dementia reported comparable numbers of memory complaints. However, when relatives rated memory change over time, the patients without dementia did not differ significantly from healthy elderly control patients (without memory complaints), whereas the patients with dementia were rated by their relatives as having become significantly worse. Furthermore, the relatives' assessments of patients' memory were significantly intercorrelated with objective memory test scores and not with patients' depression. This later observation is important because other research has shown self-reported memory complaints in older adults to often be more closely correlated with depressed mood than with objective memory test performance (e.g., Bolla, Lindgren, Bonaccorsy, & Bleecker, 1991; Kahn, Zarit, Hilbert, & Niederehe, 1975; Larabee & Levin, 1986).

There also is empirical support for the validity of family-caregiver reports of specific Alzheimer's disease symptomatology. For example, Bayles and Tomoeda (1991), in a study of 99 patients with Alzheimer's disease and their caregivers, found that caregiver reports of memory and linguistic communication symptoms were significantly correlated with patients' performance on select corresponding items of a linguistic-communication test battery. Although such research encourages the use of caregiver interview data in assessment, relatives' reports can be influenced by the specific relationship to the patient. For example, La Rue, Watson, and Plotkin (1992) found that spouses of patients with memory impairment reported lower levels of impairment than did younger relatives. Clinicians thus need to be sensitive to the possibility that the informant, particularly family members, may have mixed motives in providing information (e.g., evidence of cognitive impairment may be minimized or exaggerated depending on the perceived consequences of providing this information to the interviewer). When possible, it may be useful to include more than one family informant or a family consensus approach to increase the accuracy of conclusions about the presence and range of cognitive impairments or behavioral changes.

A clinically useful format for obtaining (from a relative or other informant) a cognitive, psychosocial, emotional or psychiatric, and medical history was provided by Strub and Black (1988, pp. 143–145). There also are caregiver-report rating scales, with some supporting psychometric data, that may be helpful in obtaining structured information about cognitive impairments and behavioral changes. The Cognitive Behavior Rating Scales (Williams, 1987; Williams, Klein, Little, & Haban, 1986) were designed to obtain structured report of the presence and severity of cognitive impairment (in different areas of cognitive functioning) and behavioral symptoms through observer ratings of everyday descriptors. The Cognitive Behavior Rating Scales consist of 104 descriptive statements (e.g., "misplaces objects," "loses the train of thought in conversations") that are rated on a 5-point scale according to how well each descriptor characterizes the individual being rated. Twelve additional items yield observer ratings of the patient's overall level of cognitive abilities. The total 116 items are grouped (via an expert judge method) into nine scales: Memory Disorder, Language Disorder, Disorientation, Higher Cognitive Deficits, Dementia, Need for Routine, Apraxia, Agitation, and Depression. Items within each scale have shown acceptable internal consistency and test–retest reliability coefficients (Williams et al., 1986). However, validity data are limited to the demonstration that family members rated patients with dementia significantly worse on all subscales (except depression) than did family members of matched normal participants (Williams et al., 1986).

Another structured caregiver-report instrument that is particularly useful in the evaluation of suspected dementia is the Memory and Behavior Problems Checklist (Zarit, Orr, & Zarit, 1985). This instrument consists of 31 items referring to the memory and behavior problems often shown by elderly patients with dementia syndromes. The caregiver or informant is asked to rate the frequency of problems encountered during the past 2 weeks on a 5-point scale ranging from 0 (*never occurred*) to 4 (*occurs daily*). A Total Problems score is generated by summing the frequencies of the encountered problems. Burdz, Eaton, and Bond (1988) found acceptable internal consistency for the checklist administered to a sample of 34 caregivers of patients with dementia. The validity of the checklist, as a measure of behavior change in response to intervention, also was supported by the Burdz et al. (1988) finding of its sensitivity (in pretest vs. posttest comparisons) to a respite care versus waiting-list intervention with elderly adults with and without dementia.

The individual being assessed should be informed that others may be questioned and should typically be interviewed alone first. However, it is often better to interview informants separately from the individual. This is important both to preserve the person's dignity and because informants may be reluctant to discuss evidence of cognitive impairment or behavior change with the person present (Butler, Finkel, Lewis, Sherman, & Sunderland, 1992). The person being assessed also may be less disclosing and less able to develop a trusting relationship with the interviewer when others are present (Green, Majerovitz, Adelman, & Rizzo, 1994). Finally, family members who are caring for a relative with dementia or mental illness may themselves be experiencing significant psychological distress, with consequent impact on their own physical and mental health (see Avison, Turner, Noh, & Speechley, 1993; Schultz & Williamson, 1994). Family caregivers may thus need psychotherapeutic or other intervention (see Light, Niederehe, & Lebowitz, 1994) and should be given the opportunity to describe their distress and caregiving burden in confidence.

Assessing Caregiver Distress

Brief self-report measures are available to assist in screening family caregivers for psychological distress. The Zarit Burden Interview (J. M. Zarit, 1982; S. H. Zarit, Reever, & Bach-Peterson, 1980; S. H. Zarit, Todd, & Zarit, 1986) is a 22-item measure concerning the perceived impact of caregiving on caregiver physical and emotional health, social activities, and financial status. The caregiver is asked to respond on a 5-point scale describing how much each statement applies to him or her, with responses ranging from 0 (never) to 4 (almost always). A Total Burden score is obtained by summing across all 22 items, with higher scores indicating greater levels of perceived caregiver burden. High test–retest reliability (J. M. Zarit, 1982) and internal consistency reliability (Burdz et al., 1988) have been reported for this measure. Its validity is supported by various observations, such as significant correlations with an index of social support (S. H. Zarit et al., 1980), prediction (in a prospective longitudinal study) of dementia patient nursing home placement (S. H. Zarit et al., 1986), sensitivity to the effects of a group support program for the family members of patients with dementia (Kahan, Kemp, Staples, & Brummel-Smith, 1985), and sensitivity to the effects of a 2-week respite care program (Burdz et al., 1988). The Life Satisfaction Index-Z (Wood, Wylie, & Scheafer, 1965) is a 13-item scale assessing perceived life satisfaction, which has been frequently used with elderly individuals. This index has acceptable internal consistency reliability, and its validity is supported by its sensitivity to the stress of caring for a patient with dementia (Haley, Levine, Brown, Berry, & Hughes, 1987) and sensitivity to change following the treatment of depression in older adults (Thompson, Gallagher, Nies, & Epstein, 1983). The index has been used in the evaluation of interventions for caregivers of patients with dementia (Haley, Brown, & Levine, 1987).

The Brief Symptom Inventory (Derogatis, Lipman, Covi, Rickels, & Uhlenhuth, 1970; Derogatis & Spencer, 1982), a 53-item brief self-report measure of psychological distress symptoms, also has been used in the screening of caregivers. Derogatis and Spencer (1982) reported acceptable test–retest reliabilities and extensive normative data for primarily younger and middle-aged adults. Hale, Cochran, and Hedgepeth (1984) extended the Brief Symptom Inventory normative database to include elderly adults.

The Brief Symptom Inventory provides scores on nine symptom dimension scales, identified by factor analysis, including Depression, Anxiety, and Hostility scales, which have been hypothesized to be sensitive to the demands of caregiving for a patient with dementia (Anthony-Bergstone, Zarit, & Gatz, 1988). In addition to the nine symptom dimension scales, the Brief Symptom Inventory provides the Global Severity Index, an overall measure of distress calculated by averaging all 53 responses. The Global Severity Index, as well as the Depression, Anxiety, and Hostility subscale scores, have shown sensitivity to professional counseling interventions in a sample of primary caregivers of frail elderly individuals (Toseland & Smith, 1990).

Contributions of Sensory Changes, Response Slowing, and Physical Disability to Psychological Assessment Results

Whether obtained from clinical interview, self-report, or cognitive testing of older adults, psychological assessment results are influenced by the sensory and response speed changes of aging. Results also are clearly influenced by physical disabilities and chronic medical conditions that increase in prevalence with older age. In the following paragraphs, I briefly review these influences. More extensive treatment can be found in Bayles and Kaszniak (1987), La Rue (1992), and Storandt (1994).

Age-related sensory changes and sensory disorders influence both the selection and interpretation of assessment data. For example, Lindenberger and Baltes (1994) showed that visual and auditory acuity measures accounted for almost half of the total variance and more than 90% of the age-related variance in the cognitive test battery performance of a sample of older adults. As reviewed by Owsley and Sloane (1990) and Schieber (1992), visual capability begins to decline during the fourth decade of life, and by 65 years of age about half of all individuals show a visual acuity of 20/70 or less. Changes in visual acuity and light transmission capability of the eye are attributable to multiple age-related physical changes. It is important to consider the possible impact of visual impairment on any assessment procedure that requires visual information processing. Older adults may require higher levels of illumination and larger print than younger adults. Uncorrected visual impairment can contribute to errors on cognitive tasks involving visual material and thus may increase false-positive rates in the identification of cognitive impairment.

Auditory functioning also changes with age (for a review, see Fozard, 1990; Schieber, 1992). The prevalence of hearing loss in those older than 75 years of age has been estimated to be 50% (Plomp, 1978). Decreased auditory acuity, particularly for high-frequency sound, affects the perception of speech. Word comprehension, because of its dependence on high-frequency auditory perception, thus becomes increasingly difficult with advancing age, and communication (including that within the clinical interview) may suffer (Pickett, Bergman, & Levitt, 1979; Plomp & Mimpen, 1979). Hearing loss in an older individual also can influence performance on verbal tests of cognitive functioning, leading to potential misinterpretations of test results (e.g., Peters, Potter, & Scholer, 1988; Roccaforte, Burke, Bayer, & Wenger, 1992; Weinstein & Amsel, 1986). In some cases, older adults with hearing loss are mistakenly thought to be confused or demented (Becker, 1981), and the association between hearing loss and emotional disturbance, particularly depression, in the elderly has been documented (e.g., O'Neil & Calhoun, 1975). Although controversial, hearing loss occurring early in life has also been thought by some to be associated with the development of late-life paranoid psychosis (Cooper, 1976).

Older people are susceptible to auditory masking, resulting in the perception of speech being particularly difficult when there is background noise (Dubno, Dirks, & Morgan, 1984; Plomp & Mimpen, 1979). The rate of auditory information processing also slows with age (Lima, Hale, & Myerson, 1991) and is slowed further in many dementia-related illnesses (Tomoeda, Bayles, Boone, Kaszniak, & Slauson, 1990). In the psychological assessment of an older person, precautions should be taken to maximize auditory comprehension. These include ensuring that the patient is wearing any necessary hearing aids, maintaining eye contact (to increase the likelihood of watching the examiner's lips), conducting the assessment in a quiet room, speaking somewhat but not markedly more slowly, and, for clinicians with high-pitched voices, possibly speaking in a lower pitched voice.

Another possible contributor to the choice and interpretation of assessment procedures is the presence of any physical disability (e.g., severe arthritis, neuromuscular disorder, etc.) or chronic medical condition (e.g., heart disease, diabetes, cancer). Brief mental status examination tests, for example, have shown a decreased ability to discriminate people with dementia from those without dementia but who have some physical disability when compared with discriminative validity for those without such disability (Jagger, Clarke, & Anderson, 1992). The contribution of physical disability is of particular concern when assessing the oldest-old because approximately 29% of all people over the age of 85 suffer from a severe disability (Kunkel & Applebaum, 1992). In psychologically assessing a person with a physical disability, the clinician should rely on the approaches less likely to be affected by the person's particular physical impairments (e.g., preferentially using verbal rather than perceptual–motor tasks when evaluating cognitive functioning in a person with impaired motoric ability). Although the presence of medically well-controlled chronic illness may make only a small contribution to cognitive test performance (e.g., Ivnik, 1991), severe and poorly controlled chronic illness can have a substantial effect on cognitive performance (see La Rue & Markee, 1995).

Reaction time (both simple and choice) and information-processing speed progressively slow from early through late adulthood (Cerella, 1990; Lima et al., 1991; Wilkinson & Allison, 1989). Older adults are therefore likely to take longer than younger adults to complete various assessment procedures (Cunningham & Haman, 1992). The slowing of performance has been demonstrated to affect cognitive tasks in ways that depend on the particular cognitive processes involved and on the format used in the presentation of test material (Hertzog, 1989). Response slowing has been shown to result in slight underestimation of ability (Storandt, 1977) on the subtests of the Wechsler Adult Intelligence Scale–Revised (Wechsler, 1981) that assign bonus points for faster performance. Examiners may therefore wish to "test the limits" by permitting the older person to continue working on the test after standard cutoff times have elapsed (see Kaplan, 1988) in order to get a more complete picture of that individual's cognitive abilities. Given the longer time it may take older people to complete various assessment procedures, the possibility of fatigue contributing to results also must be considered. It may be necessary to take more frequent breaks during an assessment session, particularly when evaluating disabled, ill, or frail older adults. Healthy older people have not been found to fatigue more rapidly than younger adults during average-length (e.g., 2.5-hr) assessment sessions (Cunningham, Sepkoski, & Opel, 1978). However, older people who are physically disabled or in poor health are likely to fatigue quickly (Cunningham & Haman, 1992).

PSYCHOLOGICAL ASSESSMENT PROCEDURES FOR IDENTIFYING PREVALENT MENTAL DISORDERS

In addition to structured and semistructured interviews, the clinician has available a large number of psychological assessment procedures for evaluating neuropsychological (see Lezak, 1995), emotional, and personality functioning (see Beutler & Berren, 1995; Maruish, 1994). Not all available procedures are, however, appropriate for the assessment of older individuals. One particularly limiting factor in the selection of assessment approaches for the elderly is the availability of age-appropriate normative data. This is of particular importance in the evaluation of intellectual and neuropsychological functioning. For both healthy individuals and those with cerebral disease, performance on many cognitive, perceptual, and motor tests is negatively correlated with adult age (for reviews, see Albert, 1988; Kaszniak, 1990; La Rue, 1992; Reitan & Wolfsen, 1986). Age relationships are particularly robust for cognitive tests of abstraction and complex problem solving (Elias, Robbins, Walter, & Schultz, 1993; Mittenberg, Seidenberg, O'Leary, & DiGiulio, 1989; Moehle & Long, 1989). As noted by various authors (Erickson, Eimon, & Hebben, 1992; Kaszniak,

1987; Lovell & Nussbaum, 1994; Zec, 1993), there has been a relative lack of adequate normative data for the oldest-old (those older than 85) on most cognitive tests. Fortunately, a few larger scale normative studies recently have been published for some of the more commonly used tests, extending norms to include people older than 90 (Ivnik et al., 1992a, 1992b, 1992c; Malec, Ivnik, & Smith, 1993; Van Gorp, Satz, Kiersch, & Henry, 1986). A comprehensive reference to neuropsychological and other cognitive test norms for older adults is contained in Erickson, Eimon, and Hebben (1994).

Assessment of Mental Status

Given the age-associated prevalence of dementia, clinicians working with older adults often are faced with the need to assess cognitive functioning. There are various indicators, obtained from the interview and history, that raise the suspicion of possible dementia (see Alzheimer's Disease Association, 1995). These include the following: (a) difficulty with learning and remembering new information (e.g., recent events, conversation, placement of objects, appointments); (b) impaired reasoning and problem-solving ability at work or home; (c) problems with handling complex tasks or following a complex train of thought; (d) impaired spatial reasoning (e.g., finding way around familiar environment); (e) word-finding difficulty; and (f) changes in behavior (e.g., increased passivity or irritability, suspiciousness). When any of these indicators of dementia are present, or when other factors raise the question of possible dementia (e.g., strong family history of dementing illness), evaluation of cognitive functioning should be initiated.

The most frequently used approach to the initial assessment of cognitive functioning is the clinical mental status examination (Sultzer, 1994) or the use of more structured brief mental status screening tests (Derogatis & DellaPietra, 1994). Because dementing illnesses affect more than one single area of cognition, it is important to select a mental status evaluation procedure that samples several different areas of functioning. Some mental status screening examinations, such as the Mini-Mental State Examination (MMSE; Folstein, Folstein, & McHugh, 1975), provide brief examination of several different domains of cognitive functioning, including memory, attention–concentration, language, and visuoconstructional ability. Examination of MMSE (or other similar mental status examination) performance across these different cognitive domains thus appears to provide an avenue for detection of multiple cognitive impairments. However, a limiting factor in such an approach is the differential sensitivity of the items representing the different cognitive domains. For example, several studies (for a review, see Tombaugh & McIntyre, 1992) have shown that the MMSE language items are too simple to detect mild impairment, even though mildly demented patients with Alzheimer's disease have been shown to have clear language impairments on more difficult language tasks (for a review, see Bayles & Kaszniak, 1987). In one study of 76 participants consecutively referred to a neuropsychology service (approximately half of whom received a diagnosis of Alzheimer's disease), four of the five MMSE language items showed low (<15%) sensitivity, and three of these language items did not correlate with language measures in a neuropsychological battery (Feher et al., 1992). In the Feher et al. study, the MMSE language items did, however, show reasonably high specificity. Thus, although the presence of impairments in MMSE memory plus at least one other cognitive area can be interpreted as consistent with the multiple cognitive impairments of dementia, the absence of deficits in areas additional to memory cannot be taken as being inconsistent with dementia.

Other characteristics of mental status screening examinations also must be considered. For the MMSE, as well as for most other mental status examinations and neuropsychological tests, performance is affected by age, education, and cultural background (see Tombaugh & McIntyre, 1992). In studies in which regression analyses are used (e.g., Brayne & Calloway, 1990; Uhlmann & Larson, 1991), education has accounted for more MMSE performance variance than other demographic variables, including race, gender, and social class. In the largest normative study of the MMSE in the United States, Crum, Anthony, Bassett, and Folstein (1993) administered the MMSE to a total of 18,056 adult participants selected by probability sampling within census tracts and households of five different communities across the United States. Significant correlations were found between MMSE scores and both age ($\rho = -.38$) and years of schooling ($\rho = .50$). Crum et al. (1993) provided MMSE mean and percentile data, stratified by age (in 4-year intervals from 18 to 85+ years) and education (0–4 years, 5–8 years, 9–12 years, and college experience or higher degree). Age-specific MMSE norms also have been provided by Bleecker, Bolla-Wilson, Kawas, and Agnes (1988), although the Crum et al. (1993) norms appear to be more generally representative of the United States.

Education-related interpretative problems may remain for the MMSE and other mental status examinations even when age-stratified norms are used. For example, in one large ($N = 1,579$) study in the United Kingdom, the MMSE showed a poorer ability to discriminate patients with and without dementia who had lower educational levels and lower occupational backgrounds from those with higher educational and occupational status (Jagger et al., 1992). The MMSE also showed significantly lower discriminative validity for those aged 80 years of age and older when compared with discrimination accuracy for younger age groups.

In interpreting the results of studies examining relationships between MMSE scores and education, it is not clear whether education represents a risk factor for dementia or MMSE measurement error (see Tombaugh &

McIntyre, 1992). Many clinicians and investigators have assumed that the effects of education represent a psychometric bias, leading to misclassification of individuals having different educational histories. Indeed, there is evidence for low education increasing the probability of false-positive errors (misclassifying normal individuals as cognitively impaired), particularly when the individual in question has less than 9 years of education (Anthony, LaResche, Niaz, Van Korff, & Folstein, 1982; Murden, McRae, Kaner, & Bucknam, 1991). Higher education levels also may result in increased false-negative errors (identifying an individual with cognitive impairment as normal). For example, O'Connor et al. (1989) found that most individuals with false-negative MMSE dementia identification had relatively high levels of education. Finally, the rate of decline in MMSE scores among patients with Alzheimer's disease has not been found to be associated with education (e.g., Burns, Jacoby, & Levy, 1991). Despite the evidence that differing educational levels can be related to MMSE misclassification, it is possible that education also may be a correlate of risk factors in the development of dementia (see Katzman & Kawas, 1994). For example, lower education could be associated with risk factors for vascular dementia, such as obesity, hypertension, and serum cholesterol. Alternatively, it has been suggested that educational and occupational attainment might be surrogate variables for a brain or cognitive reserve that delays the obvious clinical onset of dementing illnesses such as Alzheimer's disease (Katzman, 1993; Stern et al., 1994). Overall, however, the available research suggests that age- and education-stratified normative data, such as that provided by Crum et al. (1993), should be used when determining whether a particular individual's MMSE score is consistent with dementia.

In addition to educational level, cultural differences can affect performance on both mental status screening tests and particular neuropsychological tests. Escobar et al. (1986) studied more than 3,000 English- and Spanish-speaking residents of Los Angeles using both English and Spanish versions of the MMSE. The Spanish-speaking participants were found to perform significantly lower on several of the MMSE items. More recently, Loewenstein, Argüelles, Barker, and Duara (1993) studied 76 female patients who had clinical diagnoses of probable Alzheimer's disease. Half of these women were primary Spanish speakers and the other half reported English as their primary language. Spanish-speaking and English-speaking participants were matched on chronological age and severity of memory impairment. The Spanish-speaking patients with Alzheimer's disease scored lower on the MMSE and various neuropsychological measures. When scores were statistically adjusted for participant's educational attainment, significant differences between Spanish-speaking and English-speaking participants remained on 3 (of 10) of the neuropsychological tests. The education-adjusted difference for the MMSE approached but did not reach statistical significance ($p = .09$). Thus, there is the possibility of

MMSE or neuropsychological test false-positive identification of dementia in Spanish-speaking individuals, particularly for those with fewer years of formal education. Comparable data for other non-English-speaking groups are not available.

In addition to primary language, race or ethnicity (e.g., Black vs. White participants of comparable educational level), social class, and socioeconomic status have been found to be related to MMSE scores in most studies that have examined these relationships (see Tombaugh & McIntyre, 1992; for an exception, see Murden et al., 1991). Thus, a low score on the MMSE or some other mental status examination, obtained by an individual whose cultural or socioeconomic background differs from that of most individuals in the normative database, may not actually reflect dementia. In such cases, it would appear important to ascertain whether there has been any deterioration in the individual's functioning in activities of daily living. Informant-based functional assessment scales can increase the accuracy of dementia identification (O'Connor, Pollitt, Hyde, Miller, & Fellowes, 1991; Pfeffer, Kurosaki, Harrah, Chance, & Filos, 1982), particularly when mental status examination results fall into the "borderline" or "questionable" range (Hershey, Jaffe, Greenough, & Yang, 1987; Morris et al., 1991). Unfortunately, specific information is not available on whether the detection of cognitive impairment in non-White racial or ethnic groups, or in lower social class or socioeconomic status groups, would be incrementally improved by the addition of instrumental activities of daily living assessment.

Gender differences in MMSE scores have been inconsistently observed across available studies (Tombaugh & McIntyre, 1992). However, even when gender differences have been observed, they do not account for a substantial proportion of MMSE score variability and generally have not been clinically important.

Neuropsychological Assessment

When mental status examination results are inconclusive, or when a more detailed evaluation of cognitive functioning is desired for purposes of differential diagnosis or treatment or management planning, neuropsychological assessment is typically initiated. Neuropsychological evaluation may be particularly helpful when there is a history of apparent cognitive decline, but a brief mental status test is performed within normal limits. Psychometric tests used in neuropsychological assessment typically have been constructed to contain a range of task difficulty, so that test scores ideally approximate a normal distribution when administered to individuals in the general population. This yields greater sensitivity to mild or subtle cognitive deficits (e.g., Bondi, Kaszniak, Bayles, & Vance, 1993; Bondi et al., 1994; Petersen, Smith, Ivnik, Kokmen, & Tangalos, 1994) than that provided by mental status screening tests on which most healthy individuals achieve near-perfect scores (cf. Crum et al., 1993). The capability of neuropsychological assessment batteries to examine performance across different, reliably measured domains of cognitive functioning may be particularly important in examining for dementia in individuals with high premorbid intellectual functioning (Naugle, Cullum, & Bigler, 1990). Performance by such individuals can be at or above general population normative expectation on all tests, yet the pattern of performance across different tests may be consistent with deterioration from a previously higher level of functioning.

Neuropsychological assessment now plays a critical role in identifying the presence and pattern of cognitive impairment, contributes to the differential neurologic diagnosis of the many possible causes of cognitive dysfunction, and aids in the treatment and clinical management of those neurologic and neuropsychiatric disorders that affect higher cognitive processes (Lezak, 1995). Neuropsychological evaluation of the person with known or suspected cognitive impairment may be performed to address any or all of the following aims (see Albert & Moss, 1988; Bayles & Kaszniak, 1987; LaRue, 1992; Zec, 1993): (a) identification of the presence of cognitive impairment and patterns of impairment relevant to differential diagnosis; (b) provision of information to health care providers, patients, and family members concerning specific strengths and deficits in cognitive functions and their practical implications; (c) assessment of treatment effects or disease progression; and (d) provision of, or recommendations for, the treatment and management of cognitive and behavior problems.

Knowledge of the relationships between performance on neuropsychological tests and brain function has increased rapidly over the past few decades, due in large part to technical advances in neuroradiological imaging and cerebral electrophysiology, making it possible to examine human brain structure and function in relatively noninvasive and safe ways (see Albert & Moss, 1988; La Rue, Yang, & Osato, 1992). For example, recent studies using computed tomography scanning or magnetic resonance imaging procedures for the localization of structural cerebral damage in stroke patients (e.g., Anderson, Damasio, & Tranel, 1990; Beeson, Bayles, Rubens, & Kaszniak, 1993; Bondi, Kaszniak, Rapcsak, & Butters, 1993) have demonstrated consistent relationships between the location of brain damage and the pattern of deficits observed in neuropsychological test performance. Relationships between neuropsychological test performance and cerebral dysfunction in stroke patients have been further clarified by studies of regional cerebral glucose metabolism using positron emission tomography. Positron emission tomography studies (see Metter, 1991) have revealed a complex interplay between the pattern of neuropsychological test performance and regional cerebral hypometabolism that can occur in brain regions not structurally damaged by stroke (presumed because of the connections between the damaged and the nondamaged hypometabolic area).

Research in the neuropsychology of dementia has increased dramatically, particularly over the past 2 decades (La Rue, 1992; Poon, Kaszniak, & Dudley, 1992). An increasing portion of this research has focused on the diagnostic utility of neuropsychological measures in the differentiation of normal aging from dementia (for a comprehensive review, see Parks, Zec, & Wilson, 1993). Most such studies have compared healthy older adults with those with clinically diagnosed probable Alzheimer's disease (of mild-to-moderate dementia severity) on a battery of neuropsychological tests. Patients with Alzheimer's disease consistently have been shown to be impaired in two or more areas of cognitive functioning assessed by the tests, with the largest deficits observed in ability to learn and retain new information (e.g., Bayles, Boone, Tomoeda, Slauson, & Kaszniak, 1989; Eslinger, Damasio, Benton, & Van Allen, 1985; Huff et al., 1987; Kaszniak, Wilson, Fox, & Stebbins, 1986; Storandt, Botwinick, Danziger, Berg, & Hughes, 1984).

Research on the neuropsychological differentiation of mildly demented probable patients with Alzheimer's disease from healthy older adults (Knopman & Ryberg, 1989; Morris et al., 1991; Welsh, Butters, Hughes, Mohs, & Heyman, 1991) has shown measures of recent memory, especially those involving delayed recall, to be the most discriminating. It is particularly impressive that, within one study (Morris et al., 1991), the neuropsychological discrimination of healthy older individuals from those with mild cognitive impairment was supported by subsequent postmortem histopathological evidence consistent with Alzheimer's disease in all of those who were neuropsychologically classified as mildly impaired and in none of those classified as normal. Tests of recent memory also have shown high sensitivity and specificity in discriminating mildly impaired individuals who cognitively decline at 2-year reexamination from those who do not (Flicker, Ferris, & Reisberg, 1991). In addition to tests of learning and memory, other neuropsychological measures, such as those of semantic category fluency (e.g., generating as many names of animals as possible within a 60-s period; Monsch et al., 1992) and conceptual inferential reasoning or flexibility (e.g., a modified version of the Wisconsin Card Sorting Task; Bondi, Monsch, Butters, Salmon, & Paulsen, 1993), have shown a high sensitivity and specificity in the detection of mild dementia. Despite this encouraging data for the diagnostic utility of neuropsychological testing, interpretative caution must be exercised. Performance on neuropsychological assessment batteries specifically designed or selected for the detection of mild dementia is correlated with the examinee's educational level (Ganguli et al., 1991). As noted previously in this chapter, performance also can be affected by physical disability, visual or auditory impairment, and limited facility with the English language.

Overall, the available research indicates that neuropsychological assessment, particularly when measures of learning and retention are included, makes an important contribution to the identification of mild dementia (for a review, see Bondi et al., in press-a). Memory assessment instruments such as the California Verbal Learning Test (CVLT; Delis, Freeland, Kramer, & Kaplan, 1988; Delis, Kramer, Kaplan, & Ober, 1987), which distinguishes features such as learning and forgetting rates, recall versus recognition, and vulnerability to interference, are particularly well suited for evaluating memory functioning in possible dementia. The various measures provided by the CVLT have shown high sensitivity in differentiating patients with Alzheimer's disease from healthy older adults (Delis et al., 1991; Kohler, 1994). The sensitivity of the CVLT to mild impairment in the earliest stages of dementia was illustrated in a recent study by Bondi et al. (1994). In that study, three consecutive annual administrations of the CVLT were performed with 56 healthy elderly participants who were free from any clinical suspicion of dementia. Participants with a positive family history for progressive dementia performed significantly worse than did those with a negative family history on several of the CVLT indexes (including measures of delayed recall) and were more likely to show evidence of developing dementia in the subsequent annual evaluations. An even more recent study (Bondi et al., in press-b) has indicated that these memory changes are associated with the presence of a putative genetic risk factor for late-onset Alzheimer's disease, the apolipoprotein E4 ($APOE_4$) allele (for further information on $APOE_4$ and Alzheimer's disease, see Poirier et al., 1993; Roses et al., 1994; Saunders et al., 1993). Measures of delayed recall provided by other memory tests, such as the Wechsler Memory Scale (Linn et al., 1995) and the Selective Reminding Test (Masur, Sliwinski, Lipton, Blau, & Crystal, 1994), also have shown encouraging sensitivity and specificity for the detection of incipient dementia in longitudinal studies of older adults without dementia who subsequently developed it.

The severity of recent memory deficits early in the course of Alzheimer's disease renders memory tests less useful (because of basement effects) for staging the severity of dementia across individuals (Welsh, Butters, Hughes, Mohs, & Heyman, 1992) or for tracking the progression of dementia over time (Kaszniak, Wilson, et al., 1986). Neuropsychological measures of other aspects of cognitive functioning (e.g., attention, abstraction or problem solving, recognition memory, language, confrontation naming, visuospatial and constructional abilities) appear to be better for staging dementia severity or tracking dementia progression. Recommendations concerning the selection of such neuropsychological measures that are appropriate for the assessment of older adults can be found in Bayles and Kaszniak (1987), Butters, Salmon, and Butters (1994), La Rue, Yang, and Osato (1992), and Lovell and Nussbaum (1994).

Although a comprehensive review is beyond the scope of this chapter, note that etiologically and neuropathologically different dementing illnesses show different patterns of intact and impaired abilities in neuro-psychological assessment (for reviews, see Butters et al., 1994; Bondi et al., in press-a). Neuropsychological assessment therefore contributes to the differential diagnosis of dementia. For example, the CVLT has been shown to be helpful in differentiating Alzheimer's disease from Huntington's disease, in that patients with Alzheimer's disease showed a greater percentage of cued-recall intrusions (presumed to reflect susceptibility to proactive interference) and poorer recognition memory after delay (Delis et al., 1991). Such memory, as well as other cognitive differences, appear to reflect the relative neuroanatomical locus of damage in the so-called "cortical" (of which Alzheimer's disease is prototypical) versus "subcortical" (of which Huntington's disease is prototypical) dementias (see Cummings & Benson, 1992).

One frequent differential diagnostic reason for referring an older individual for neuropsychological assessment occurs when the person presents with signs of both cognitive impairment and depression. It has been estimated that between 1% and 31% of patients diagnosed as having a dementing illness may actually be suffering from depression with associated cognitive deficits (Katzman et al., 1988). Furthermore, as many as 20% of older depressed patients may have cognitive deficits severe enough to suggest the possibility of dementia (LaRue, D'Elia, Clark, Spar, & Jarvik, 1986). Mistakenly diagnosing a dementing illness in a person who is actually suffering from depression can deprive the individual of appropriate treatment (psychologic, pharmacologic, or both), risking further functional deterioration. Conversely, misdiagnosing a dementing illness as depression also can result in inappropriate treatment and the failure to provide prognostic information that would permit patient and family members to prepare and plan for the consequences of progressive dementia. In reviewing the research, Siegel and Gershon (1986) found that 25–30% of older people who were initially referred for evaluation and treatment of depression were ultimately found to have a progressive dementing illness. Of particular relevance for the differential diagnosis of dementia and depression is evidence that the symptom presentation of depression in older adults varies with the age of depression onset. Elderly people with an older age of depression onset, compared with those with younger age of onset, have shown more frequent neuroimaging abnormalities, more frequent neuropsychological impairment, and less frequent family histories of affective illness, among other differences (for a review, see Caine, Lyness, & King, 1993).

Diagnosis is particularly complicated by the possible coexistence of dementia and depression. In reviewing the literature, Teri and Wagner (1992) found the majority of studies reporting prevalence estimates in the 17–29% range for coexisting depression in Alzheimer's disease. Because patients with coexisting depression and Alzheimer's disease can benefit from treatment of their depression (for a review, see Teri & Wagner, 1992), failure to diagnose and treat depression in a patient with Alzheimer's disease can result in unnecessary suffering and excess functional impairment.

Research has supported the validity of certain patterns of neuropsychological test performance (for a review, see Kaszniak & Christenson, 1994) as important contributors in the effort to differentiate the cognitive effects of dementia and depression. Depressed patients often complain of memory and other cognitive (e.g., concentration) difficulty and also may show some evidence of impairment on neuropsychological testing (Reynolds et al., 1988). Except for the most severely depressed older patients, cognitive deficits are relatively mild for most depressed patients (Johnson & Magaro, 1987; La Rue, 1992; Niederehe, 1986). Cognitive processes that require greater attention and effort (as opposed to more "automatic" cognitive processes) are the ones generally most impaired in depression (see Weingartner, 1986). Craik and McDowd (1987), measuring performance decrement on a secondary reaction time task, showed that recall requires more processing resources (effort) than does recognition for both younger and older adults. Consistent with the expected decreased effort of memory processing in depression, depressed older adults are often impaired (relative to age-matched control adults) on free-recall tests but not recognition memory tests (Blau & Ober, 1988; Nussbaum, Kaszniak, Swanda, & Allender, 1988). Patients with mild-to-moderate dementia and Alzheimer's disease, by contrast, demonstrate deficits in both recall and recognition memory (for a review, see Kaszniak, Poon, & Riege, 1986).

In addition to comparing recall and recognition memory task performance, the qualitative analysis of error patterns in recognition memory may be helpful in attempting to differentiate persons with Alzheimer's disease from those with depression. Depressed patients typically exhibit a conservative decision criteria (i.e., a disproportionate number of false-negative errors) compared with nondepressed individuals, and this "cautious" response style appears to be greater among older depressed people (Miller & Lewis, 1977; Niederehe, 1986). By contrast, patients with Alzheimer's disease generally show a liberal response bias in their performance of both verbal (Branconnier, Cole, Spera, & De Vitt, 1982) and pictorial recognition memory tasks (Snodgrass & Corwin, 1988). The CVLT contains both free-recall and recognition memory tasks and provides for calculation of response bias. These CVLT measures have been shown to be useful in the clinical differentiation of Alzheimer's disease from older depressed patients (Massman, Delis, Butters, Dupont, & Gillin, 1992). Otto et al. (1994) provided CVLT normative data for outpatients with major depression, although their sample unfortunately included only patients in the 18- to 54-year-old age range.

Another feature of memory performance that is useful in differentiating depressed from older adults with dementia involves the rate that new information, once adequately learned, is forgotten. Hart, Kwentus, Taylor, and Harkins (1987) examined rate-of-forgetting differences between depressed older adults, mildly demented patients with Alzheimer's disease, and normal control adults after the groups had been equated for initial learning by variation of stimulus exposure time. Depressed patients and patients with Alzheimer's disease both showed learning impairments, but only the group with Alzheimer's disease showed rapid forgetting in the first 10 min after learning to criterion. These results are of particular clinical interest because the depressed patients and patients with Alzheimer's disease performed similarly on most of the rest of a set of commonly used neuropsychological tests.

Despite such encouraging data, the interpretation of neuropsychological assessment of individuals with coexistent depression and cognitive impairment, particularly those with a later age of depression onset, requires considerable caution. The long-term prognosis of these individuals is highly variable (for a review, see Caine et al., 1993). Some investigators have reported 2-year stability in posttreatment mood and cognitive improvement of older individuals with both dementia and depression (e.g., Rabins, Merchant, & Nestadt, 1984). By contrast, other investigators (Kral & Emery, 1989) have found that most (89%) successfully treated patients with evidence of concomitant depression and dementia eventually develop a progressive dementia syndrome when followed over long intervals (i.e., 18 years). Furthermore, it is possible for dementia to initially present as depression without obvious cognitive deficit. Reding, Haycox, and Blass (1985), in a 3-year follow-up study, showed that 57% of older depressed patients who were not initially thought to have dementia went on to develop it. Older age, evidence of cerebrovascular, extrapyramidal, or spinocerebellar disease, confusion, or somnolence in response to low doses of tricyclic antidepressant medication, or having more than two errors on a brief mental status questionnaire, were characteristic of those who developed obvious dementia. The mental status questionnaire difference between those depressed elderly who did and did not develop dementia in the Reding et al. study might suggest a prognostic role for mental status or neuropsychological assessment. However, other recent research has indicated that the neuropsychological assessment of older people with coexistent depression and cognitive impairment is not helpful in predicting the development of progressive dementia over an average 18-month follow-up (Nussbaum, Kaszniak, Allender, & Rapcsak, 1995). Given the state of current research, it appears advisable to periodically reassess older individuals who show both memory impairment and symptoms of depression, even when there has been apparent improvement of cognitive deficits following depression treatment.

Assessment of Depression

The *DSM–IV* (American Psychiatric Association, 1994) provides the current consensual diagnostic criteria for the depressive disorders. The diagnosis of major depression requires that a major depressive episode be documented, as defined by five of nine symptoms being present during a 2-week period. These nine symptoms include depressed mood, decreased interest in activities, insomnia or hypersomnia, significant weight loss or gain, fatigue or decreased energy, psychomotor agitation or retardation, diminished thinking or concentration ability, feelings of worthlessness or guilt, and suicidal ideation. The *DSM–IV* diagnostic criteria also specify that there must never have been a manic, hypomanic, or mixed episode and that the depressive episode must not be better accounted for by other diagnostic possibilities (e.g., schizoaffective disorder, delusional disorder, etc.).

Although, as already discussed in this chapter, the clinical interview remains the most important approach to assessment, including that for depression, various other approaches can aid in clinical screening for depressive symptoms. Several reviews are available that compare reliability, validity, and normative data for self-report depression screening instruments used with older adults (Fry, 1986; Gallagher, 1986a; Kaszniak & Allender, 1985; Yesavage, 1986). Geropsychology-specific reviews are available for the Beck Depression Inventory (BDI; Gallagher, 1986b), the Geriatric Depression Scale (GDS; Sheikh & Yesavage, 1986), the Center for Epidemiological Studies–Depression Scale (Radloff & Teri, 1986), the Zung Self-Rating Depression Scale (Zung & Zung, 1986), and the Depression Adjective Check List and Multiple Affect Adjective Check List (Lubin & Rinck, 1986). Unfortunately, reliability and validity data specific to depression-screening scale application with the oldest-old (i.e., those 85+ years) generally are not available (see Scogin, 1994; Weiss, Nagel, & Aronson, 1986).

Within general clinical psychological practice, broad-spectrum personality and psychopathology assessment instruments, such as the second edition of the Minnesota Multiphasic Personality Inventory (MMPI-2; Butcher, 1989), are frequently used in screening for depression and other mental disorders. However, caution must be exercised in using instruments such as the MMPI-2 because specific normative data on older adults are not available. The MMPI-2 normative group did consist of adults ranging in age from 18 to 89 who were selected to be representative of the U.S. population (see Greene & Clopton, 1994). Butcher et al. (1991) argued that specific older age norms are not necessary when assessing the elderly with the MMPI-2. However, as pointed out by Scogin (1994), Butcher et al. (1991) did find normal older men to have slightly, but significantly, higher MMPI-2 Depression scale (Scale 2) scores than normal younger men, likely reflecting a differential response to the items reflecting somatic complaints. There also has been a report (Harmatz & Shader, 1975) suggesting that MMPI (Dahlstrom, Welsh, & Dahlstrom, 1972) Depression scale items involving demand characteristics of social desirability (still contained within the MMPI-2 Depression scale) may be answered differently by older and younger individuals. Finally, the clinician must take into consideration the potential problems involved in asking a depressed older adult to complete the 567 questions of the entire MMPI-2 (Scogin, 1994).

As Scogin (1994) noted, the BDI (A. T. Beck, Ward, Mendelsohn, Mock, & Erbaugh, 1961) and the GDS (Yesavage et al., 1983) are widely used specific depression self-report instruments that have shown particularly favorable reliability and validity for use with older adults. Internal consistency and test–retest reliability of the 21-item BDI have been demonstrated for both nondepressed older volunteers and elderly depressed outpatients (Gallagher, Breckenridge, Steinmetz, & Thompson, 1983; Gallagher, Nies, & Thompson, 1982). Using the conventional cutoff score of 10, the 21-item BDI also has shown clinically acceptable sensitivity and specificity (against depression research diagnostic criteria) when administered to elderly medical outpatients and inpatients (Norris et al., 1987; Rapp, Parisi, Walsh, & Wallace, 1988). Although less research is available on the 13-item short form of the BDI, acceptable internal consistency reliability has been demonstrated with both nondepressed older adults (Foelker, Schewchuk, & Niederehe, 1987) and elderly outpatients with major depression (Scogin, Hamblin, Beutler, & Corbishley, 1988). Good sensitivity and specificity also have been shown for the 13-item BDI using a cutoff score of 5 (Scogin et al., 1988).

One necessary caution in using the BDI for depression screening among older adults concerns the fact that both psychological and somatic items are included in the inventory. Older adults have been shown to score significantly higher than younger adults on the somatic items of the BDI (Items 15–21) even though mean scores for the psychological items (Items 1–14) did not differ (Bolla-Wilson & Bleecker, 1989). Rapp, Parisi, Walsh, and Wallace (1988) compared the diagnostic efficiency of the psychological items portion of the BDI with that of the somatic items portion. As might be expected, given the medical inpatient population participating in their study, they found the psychological items to have better sensitivity and specificity. This underscores the difficulties encountered in interpreting possible somatic depressive symptoms, particularly among medically ill older adults. The BDI (as well as the GDS) appears to be less effective in identifying major depression in elderly men than women, at least among psychiatric inpatients (Allen-Burge, Storandt, Kinscherf, & Rubin, 1994), suggesting the need for future research to examine the validity of separate cutoff scores for older men and women.

The GDS is a 30-item questionnaire developed for use with older adults that has clearly and simply phrased items and a yes–no response format. The item content focuses on mood and mood-related symptoms and does not include somatic items that may reflect physical illness in the elderly. A score of 11 or greater is considered possible depression. The GDS has been shown to have high internal consistency (Parmelee, Lawton, & Katz, 1989; Yesavage et al., 1983) and to be valid for depression screening in older outpatients and inpatients, including those in nursing homes (Lesher, 1986; Olin, Schneider, Eaton, Zemansky, & Pollock, 1992; Parmelee et al., 1989; Rapp, Parisi, Walsh, & Wallace, 1988; Scogin, 1987; Yesavage et al., 1983).

The simple phrasing and response format of the GDS, as well as the omission of somatic items, suggests that it might be well suited for detecting possible depression among older people with cognitive impairment. Some studies have shown no difference in the reliability or validity of the GDS for patients with Alzheimer's disease compared with that for institutionalized residents with no cognitive impairment (Parmelee & Katz, 1990; Yesavage, Rose, & Lapp, 1981), although other studies have shown lower sensitivity and specificity for depression in older people with dementia (Burke, Houston, Boust, & Rosaforte, 1989; Kafonek et al., 1989). When using the GDS to screen for depression in older adults with known or suspected dementia, the clinician must be cautious to avoid false-negative conclusions. Several studies have shown that collateral sources (i.e., spouses and other relatives) and trained clinical observers report significantly higher frequencies of depression-related symptoms in mildly demented patients with Alzheimer's disease than do the patients themselves (Burke, Rubin, Morris, & Berg, 1988; Knesevich, Martin, Berg, & Danziger, 1983; Mackenzie, Robiner, & Knopman, 1989; Rubin, 1990; Teri & Wagner, 1991). As noted by Kaszniak and Christenson (1994), this relative under-reporting of depression symptoms by patients with Alzheimer's disease may reflect the progressively impaired awareness of symptoms and deficits that appears to accompany Alzheimer's disease (Kaszniak & Christenson, 1996; Kaszniak & McGlynn, 1991a, 1991b). Alternatively, it may be that ability to report the frequency and severity of depression-related symptoms is impaired by dementia-related deficits in understanding questions and recalling events and experience from the recent past (Burke et al., 1988; Teri & Wagner, 1992).

The likelihood that the severity of memory impairment of patients with Alzheimer's disease and the degree to which they are aware of their cognitive deficits both contribute to their symptom reporting on the GDS is supported by the work of Feher, Larrabee, and Crook (1992). Feher et al. administered the GDS, the Hamilton Depression Rating Scale (HDRS), and various cognitive measures to a group of patients with mild-to-moderate dementia and Alzheimer's disease. They also measured self-awareness of deficits by computing a difference score between a self-report memory questionnaire and an informant-rated memory questionnaire. In multiple regression analysis, the HDRS was the most important predictor of GDS scores, although performance on memory measures and the self-awareness of deficits index also were significant predictors. The authors suggested that the GDS should be used cautiously with patients with Alzheimer's disease who deny or minimize cognitive deficits because they also are likely to underestimate depressive symptoms.

Of course, it also is possible that in some cases discrepancies between depression symptoms reported by patients with Alzheimer's disease and their caregivers could be attributable to an overreporting of symptoms by the collateral sources. Mackenzie et al. (1989) found that family members tended to report that a patient was depressed when they were uncertain of the patient's current mood and that discrepant reports were more frequent for patients who had a prior history of psychiatric illness. Similarly, it has been suggested that collateral sources may be more sensitive to or have a "heightened awareness" of depression symptoms that occur in Alzheimer's disease and are therefore more likely to overreport depression (Burke et al., 1988).

Because both patient and caregiver bias in reporting of depression symptoms can possibly occur, depression screening in patients with known or suspected dementia optimally includes information from both the patient and caregiver, as well as the clinician's observation. The Columbia University Scale for Psychopathology in Alzheimer's Disease (CUSPAD; Devanand et al., 1992) provides one approach to obtaining caregiver reports of depression and other psychopathologic symptoms of patients with dementia. The CUSPAD is a semistructured interview protocol that can be administered in approximately 10–25 min. High interrater reliability (between a trained lay interviewer and a research psychiatrist) and divergent validity for the depression and other scale items have been reported for the CUSPAD (Devenand et al., 1992). Another promising interview protocol (requiring additional research to establish its psychometric properties) is the Cornell Scale for Depression in Dementia (Alexopoulos, Abrams, Young, & Shamoian, 1988), a 19-item instrument with which a clinician can structure interviews of both the patient and an informant.

Assessment of Anxiety Disorders

Older adults can present with any of the various different anxiety disorders (including generalized anxiety disorder, phobia, panic, and obsessive–compulsive disorders), although generalized anxiety disorder is one of the most common presentations (Blazer et al., 1991). The core feature of generalized anxiety disorder (American Psychiatric Association, 1994) include unrealistic or excessive worry about two or more life circumstances for a period of 6 months or longer. Other features include various manifestations of motor tension, autonomic hyperactivity, and vigilance.

Despite the fact that anxiety disorders are more prevalent than affective disorders in older age (Regier et al., 1988), few studies have focused specifically on the assessment and treatment of anxiety in the elderly. Consequently, relatively few empirical data are available on the psychometric properties of various anxiety measures and anxiety disorder interview protocols when used with older individuals (J. G. Beck, Stanley, & Zebb, 1995; Hersen & Van Hasselt, 1992; Sheikh, 1991). Recently, however, there has been an increased interest in assessing and treating anxiety disorders in the elderly (see Hersen & Van Hasselt, 1992), resulting in the publication of psychometric data for older adults on some of the more commonly used anxiety measures. For example, the State–Trait Anxiety Inventory (Spielberger, 1983; Spielberger & Sydeman, 1994) has been shown to have acceptable internal consistency reliability and discriminative validity in distinguishing elderly psychiatric inpatients (mixed diagnoses) from community-resident older adults (Himmelfarb & Murrell, 1983). Similarly, Matt, Dean, Wang, and Wood (1992) found that the 42-item version of the Hopkins Symptom Checklist (SCL-42; Derogatis, Lipman, Rickels, Uhlenhuth, & Covi, 1974; Derogatis & Lazarus, 1994) has validity in the symptom screening of older adults. Using factor-derived syndrome classifications (following the method of Uhlenhuth, Balter, Mellinger, Cisin, & Clinthorne, 1983), Matt et al. found the SCL-42 to produce anxiety and depression syndrome prevalence rates in a sample of 1,131 elderly community residents, which is consistent with other epidemiological data. Furthermore, Matt et al. found evidence of convergent validity, in that the elderly participants classified by the SCL-42 as showing depression or anxiety syndromes were significantly different from other participants on independent measures such as antidepressant and antianxiety medication use and recent clinical diagnoses of depression or anxiety disorder. Older adult norms for SCL-90-R (Derogatis, 1983) are currently under development (Derogatis & DellaPietra, 1994).

More recently, J. G. Beck et al. (1995) examined the psychometric properties of the Penn State Worry Questionnaire (Meyer, Miller, Metzger, & Borkovec, 1990) when used with older adults. J. G. Beck et al. administered the questionnaire to 94 healthy older adults (aged 55–82 years) and 47 older patients (aged 55–81 years) with generalized anxiety disorder (diagnosed using the Anxiety Disorders Interview Schedule—Revised; DiNardo & Barlow, 1988). They found that the questionnaire showed good internal consistency reliability (Cronbach's alphas = .887 for the clinical sample and .803 for the control sample), acceptable convergent validity (.40–.58 correlations with other independent measures of anxiety and depression) in both samples, and acceptable discriminant validity (distinct mean scores for the two samples), encouraging the use of the questionnaire with older adults.

THE ROLE OF ASSESSMENT IN DESCRIPTION

Psychological assessment clearly makes important contributions in the diagnosis of mental disorders in older age, and accurate diagnosis is critical for treatment selection (see Gatz, 1994; Perry, Frances, & Clarkin, 1990). In addition, psychological assessment has much to contribute in providing accurate descriptions of patterns of behavior, thought, and emotion, as well as the characteristics of older people's physical and social environments. Such descriptions can be valuable in the selection of particular types of psychological intervention (e.g., cognitive therapy, behavioral therapy, psychodynamic therapy) for the individual with a particular mental disorder (see Beutler, Wakefield, & Williams, 1994). As reviewed by Beutler and Clarkin (1990), relevant dimensions of patient characteristics, as assessed by standard psychological tests, for predicting the differential response to psychosocial treatment include (a) symptom severity, (b) problem-solving ability of the patient, (c) problem complexity, (d) potential to resist therapeutic influences, and (e) style of coping with threat. Unfortunately, there is a lack of research that specifically evaluates the treatment-prescriptive validity of various psychological tests with older adults. Another area of needed research is that which would relate response to different psychosocial interventions with personality traits, as measured by personality assessment instruments that have available data covering the entire life span (see McCrae & Costa, 1990). Until such research data become available, the clinician is forced to extrapolate from available studies on younger and middle-aged adults (e.g., Beutler et al., 1994).

Accurate description provided by psychological assessment also can help patients and their caregivers (both personal and professional) in understanding the patient, therefore reducing the distress associated with ambiguity. Patients and their family members are typically confused and distressed by the psychological changes that have brought the individual to professional attention. Even when there may be no available effective treatment for the disorder (e.g., as in Alzheimer's disease), patients and their family members may be less distressed when they understand what specific psychological functions are affected and which remain generally unaltered. In the case of a progressive dementing illness, it is important to accurately describe cognitive strengths and deficits as early as possible in the course of the illness. For example, individuals who are early in the course of Alzheimer's disease may have marked impairment of memory but more intact abilities in language comprehension and expression and conceptual reasoning. Thus, the person at this stage of illness may be able to competently make decisions about considerations such as their wishes concerning future medical and long-term care and the disposition of their estate. Giving the individual and his or her family members accurate assessment information can allow the making of decisions and plans before the progression of illness renders the person incompetent to do so.

It also is possible (LaBarge, Rosenman, Leavitt, & Cristiani, 1988) that people with milder cognitive impairments (e.g., in the early stage of Alzheimer's disease) may improve their use of coping strategies and identify ways of compensating for memory loss when they are given accurate descriptions of their specific cognitive strengths and deficits (derived from neuropsychological testing) within the course of brief supportive counseling. It also is important that this information be provided as early as possible to the person with a progressive dementing illness because insight and the ability to maintain awareness of cognitive deficits may be lost with further progression of their illness (Kaszniak & Christenson, 1996; McGlynn & Kaszniak, 1991a, 1991b).

Accurate description of cognitive strengths and deficits also contributes to the clinical management of individuals with dementing illness. Describing what areas of cognitive functioning remain intact can help families to formulate plans for sharing daily responsibilities between the patient and others (La Rue, Yang, & Osato, 1992). Conversely, the clear description of impaired cognitive functions can indicate areas in which the patient will likely require additional supervision or assistance. Evidence supporting the predictive validity of neuropsychological assessment for such purposes is beginning to appear. In a study of patients with probable Alzheimer's disease, Henderson, Mack, and Williams (1989) found that neuropsychologically documented visuoconstructive deficits (equating those patients with and without visuospatial deficits for severity of memory impairment) predicted "real-world" manifestations of spatial disorientation (i.e., caregiver-reported episodes of the patient becoming lost, wandering, and not recognizing familiar environments). Similarly, Persad et al. (1995), studying a group of healthy older adults, found that neuropsychological measures of abstract problem solving, response inhibition, and variability in attention, as well as a measure of general anxiety, were predictive of an impaired ability to avoid obstacles as avoidance task complexity increased. The authors suggested that the neuropsychological and anxiety measures may be useful as possible indicators of who is at high risk for tripping accidents (one of the most frequent causes of falls in the elderly). Finally, although available research results have been mixed, neuropsychological evaluation also may make a contribution to decisions about whether a person in the earlier stages of a dementing illness can continue safely in potentially risky activities such as driving (for a review, see Kaszniak, Keyl, & Albert, 1991).

Finally, it is important to evaluate the environmental context (both social and physical) in which the older individual exists, both in assessing functional abilities and in planning interventions (Lawton, 1986). Typically, the environmental context is assessed through behavioral observations or reports of the observations of others and may include a visit to the person's domicile (e.g., house, apartment, nursing home, or board-and-care home; Gatz, 1994). When a highly detailed assessment of environmental characteristics is desired (e.g., for research concerning the efficacy of psychosocial interventions across different environmental contexts), reliable and valid assessment protocols are available. Such protocols can provide the clinician with guidance concerning what aspects of environmental context might be considered in less structured clinical assessment.

For example, the Multiphasic Environmental Assessment Procedure (Moos & Lemke, 1984) was designed to assess physical and architectural features, organizational structure and policy, staff characteristics, and both staff and resident perceptions of the social climate of sheltered-care environments for older adults. The Multiphasic Environmental Assessment Procedure consists of the Physical and Architectural Features Checklist (Moos & Lemke, 1980), the Policy and Program Information Form (Lemke & Moos, 1980), the Resident and Staff Information Form (Lemke & Moos, 1981), and the Sheltered Care Environment Scale (Lemke & Moos, 1987). The Physical and Architectural Features consists of nine subscales (i.e., Physical Amenities, Social-Recreational Aids, Prosthetic Aids, Orientational Aids, Safety Features, Architectural Choice, Space Availability, Staff Facilities, and Community Accessibility), with each containing a number of items rated by a trained observer. In a study of 93 representative sheltered-care facilities, Moos and Lemke (1980) found internal consistency (Cronbach's alpha) reliabilities ranging from .58 to .75 and test–retest reliabilities (for a subset of nine facilities) ranging from .71 to .96 across the nine subscales. Relationships of the Physical and Architectural Features subscale scores to variables such as ratings by residents of facility attractiveness and pleasantness support its validity. The Policy and Program Information Form is designed to measure the policies and services of sheltered-care settings across 10 conceptually unified dimensions (i.e., selectivity, expectations for functioning, tolerance for deviance, policy clarity, policy choice, resident control, provision for privacy, availability of health services, availability of daily living assistance, and availability of social-recreational activities). Each dimension is assessed by a number of questions that are answered by the administrator or the individual identified as most closely related to that particular policy or program area. Studying the same 93 sheltered-care facilities described earlier, Lemke and Moos (1980) reported internal consistency (Cronbach's alpha) reliabilities ranging from .58 to .90 and test–retest reliabilities ranging from .74 to .96 across the 10 dimensions. Correlations among these 10 dimensions and variables such as facility size and level of care provided (Lemke & Moos, 1980) support the validity of this instrument. The Sheltered Care Environment Scale (SCES) consists of 63 yes–no questions composing seven subscales (i.e., Cohesion, Conflict, Independence, Self-Exploration, Organization, Resident Influence, and Physical Comfort). The SCES questions were designed to be completed by both sheltered-care residents and staff. However, experience has indicated that residents with marked intellectual impairment are unable to complete the SCES even with assistance (Lemke & Moos, 1987). On the basis of a study of 93 sheltered-care facilities in Northern California, Lemke and Moos (1987) reported internal consistency (Cronbach's alpha) reliabilities ranging from .56 to .79 and split-half reliabilities ranging from .59 to .83 for staff ratings across the seven SCES subscales. The ability of the SCES to discriminate between facilities (Lemke & Moos, 1987) and generally high correlations between the SCES and a parallel set of interview questions covering the SCES dimensions (Smith & Whitbourne, 1990a; see also Lemke & Moos, 1990; Smith & Whitbourne, 1990b) support its discriminative and construct validity.

SUMMARY

As documented in several chapters in this book, there recently has been a steadily increasing interest in psychological intervention with older adults. Psychological assessment plays a vital role in the planning and evaluation of such intervention. In this chapter I have provided an overview of epidemiological data on the prevalence and incidence of mental disorders in older age. I have argued that a knowledge of age-specific epidemiology is necessary in alerting the clinician to the relative probabilities of various psychological disorders among older people. The chapter also has provided a brief review of general considerations in the psychological assessment of older adults, with attention given to the aspects of aging that can pose risks to assessment reliability and validity. This was followed by a selected review of psychological assessment procedures for identifying some of the most prevalent mental disorders among older people. As described in this review, there are an increasing number of assessment tools for which reliability and validity data for older people are available, although continuing research, particularly involving the oldest-old, is needed.

In this chapter I have given particular attention to the contributions of psychological assessment to the difficult differential diagnostic question of dementia versus depression, which is frequently encountered in clinical geropsychological practice. Although much progress has been made in determining those assessment variables that are most discriminating, those few available longer term follow-up studies suggest that continued caution is necessary when interpreting psychological assessment data relevant to this diagnostic task. In addition to examining the contributions of psychological assessment to the diagnosis of mental disorders in older age, I have explored the role of assessment in accurately describing patterns of behavior, thought, and emotion, as well as the characteristics of the older person's physical and social environments, and how such information may benefit patients, professional caregivers, and family members. As the research reviewed in this chapter illustrates, a growing empirical base has developed for the clinical practice of psychological assessment with older individuals. The maturation of psychological assessment practice in clinical geropsychology will require continuing investigations that help link assessment results with the selection of psychosocial interventions that are differentially efficacious across older individuals having various biological, psychological, social, and environmental context characteristics.

REFERENCES

Albert, M. S. (1988). Assessment of cognitive function. In M. S. Albert & M. B. Moss (Eds.), *Geriatric neuropsychology* (pp. 57–81). New York: Guilford Press.

Albert, M. S., & Moss, M. B. (Eds.). (1988). *Geriatric neuropsychology*. New York: Guilford Press.

Alexopoulos, G. S., Abrams, R. C., Young, R. C., & Shamoian, C. A. (1988). Cornell Scale for Depression in Dementia. *Biological Psychiatry, 23*, 271–284.

Allen-Burge, R., Storandt, M., Kinscherf, D. A., & Rubin, E. H. (1994). Sex differences in the sensitivity of two self-report depression scales in older depressed inpatients. *Psychology and Aging, 9*, 443–445.

Alzheimer's Disease Association. (1995). *Is it Alzheimer's? Warning signs you should know*. Chicago: Author.

American Psychiatric Association. (1980). *Diagnostic and statistical manual of mental disorders* (3rd ed.). Washington, DC: Author.

American Psychiatric Association. (1987). *Diagnostic and statistical manual of mental disorders* (3rd ed., revised). Washington, DC: Author.

American Psychiatric Association. (1994). *Diagnostic and statistical manual of mental disorders* (4th ed.). Washington, DC: Author.

Anderson, S. W., Damasio, H., & Tranel, D. (1990). Neuropsychological impairments associated with lesions caused by tumor or stroke. *Archives of Neurology, 47*, 397–405.

Anthony, J. C., LaResche, L., Niaz, U., Von Korff, M. R., & Folstein, M. F. (1982). Limits of the "Mini-Mental State" as a screening test for dementia and delirium among hospital patients. *Psychological Medicine, 12*, 397–408.

Anthony-Bergstone, C. R., Zarit, S. H., & Gatz, M. (1988). Symptoms of psychological distress among caregivers of dementia patients. *Psychology and Aging, 3*, 245–248.

Avison, W. R., Turner, R. J., Noh, S., & Speechley, K. N. (1993). The impact of caregiving: Comparisons of different family contexts and experiences. In S. H. Zarit, L. I. Perlin, & K. W. Schaie (Eds.), *Caregiving systems: Formal and informal helpers* (pp. 75–105). Hillsdale, NJ: Erlbaum.

Bayles, K. A., Boone, D. R., Tomoeda, C. K., Slauson, T. J., & Kaszniak, A. W. (1989). Differentiating Alzheimer's patients from the normal elderly and stroke patients with aphasia. *Journal of Speech and Hearing Disorders, 54,* 74–87.

Bayles, K. A., & Kaszniak, A. W. (1987). *Communication and cognition in normal aging and dementia.* Boston: College-Hill/Little, Brown.

Bayles, K. A., & Tomoeda, C. K. (1991). Caregiver report of prevalence and appearance order of linguistic symptoms in Alzheimer's patients. *The Gerontologist, 31,* 210–216.

Beck, A. T., Ward, C. H., Mendelsohn, M., Mock, J., & Erbaugh, J. (1961). An inventory for measuring depression. *Archives of General Psychiatry, 4,* 561–571.

Beck, J. G., Stanley, M. A., & Zebb, B. J. (1995). Psychometric properties of the Penn State Worry Questionnaire in older adults. *Journal of Clinical Geropsychology, 1,* 33–42.

Becker, G. (1981). *The disability experience: Educating health professionals about disabling conditions.* Berkeley: University of California Press.

Beeson, P. M., Bayles, K. B., Rubens, A. B., & Kaszniak, A. W. (1993). Memory impairment and executive control in individuals with stroke-induced aphasia. *Brain and Language, 45,* 253–275.

Beutler, L. E., & Berren, M. R. (1995). *Integrative assessment of adult personality.* New York: Guilford Press.

Beutler, L. E., & Clarkin, J. (1990). *Systematic treatment selection: Toward targeted therapeutic interventions.* New York: Brunner/Mazel.

Beutler, L. E., Wakefield, P., & Williams, R. E. (1994). Use of psychological tests/instruments for treatment planning. In M. E. Maruish (Ed.), *The use of psychological testing for treatment planning and outcome assessment* (pp. 55–74). Hillsdale, NJ: Erlbaum.

Birren, J. E., Sloane, R. B., & Cohen, G. D. (Eds.). (1992). *Handbook of mental health and aging.* San Diego, CA: Academic Press.

Blau, E., & Ober, B. A. (1988). The effect of depression on verbal memory in older adults [Abstract]. *Journal of Clinical and Experimental Neuropsychology, 10,* 81.

Blazer, D., George, L. K., & Hughes, D. (1991). The epidemiology of anxiety disorders: An age comparison. In C. Salzman & B. D. Lebowitz (Eds.), *Anxiety in the elderly* (pp. 17–28). New York: Springer.

Blazer, D., Hughes, D. C., & George, L. K. (1987). The epidemiology of depression in an elderly community population. *The Gerontologist, 27,* 281–287.

Bleecker, M. L., Bolla-Wilson, K., Kawas, J., & Agnes, D. A. (1988). Age-specific norms for the Mini-Mental State Exam. *Neurology, 38,* 1565–1568.

Bolla, K. I., Lindgren, K. N., Bonaccorsy, C., & Bleecker, M. L. (1991). Memory complaints in older adults: Fact or fiction? *Archives of Neurology, 48,* 61–64.

Bolla-Wilson, K., & Bleecker, M. L. (1989). Absence of depression in elderly adults. *Journal of Gerontology: Psychological Sciences, 44,* P53–P55.

Bondi, M. W., Kaszniak, A. W., Bayles, K. A., & Vance, K. T. (1993). Contributions of frontal system dysfunction to memory and perceptual abilities in Parkinson's disease. *Neuropsychology, 7,* 89–102.

Bondi, M.W., Kaszniak, A. W., Rapcsak, S. Z., & Butters, M. A. (1993). Implicit and explicit memory following anterior communicating artery aneurysm rupture. *Brain and Cognition, 22,* 213–229.

Bondi, M. W., Monsch, A. U., Butters, N., Salmon, D. P., & Paulsen, J. S. (1993). Utility of a modified version of the Wisconsin Card Sorting Test in the detection of dementia of the Alzheimer type. *Clinical Neuropsychologist, 7,* 161–170.

Bondi, M. W., Monsch, A. U., Galasko, D., Butters, N., Salmon, D. P., & Delis, D. C. (1994). Preclinical cognitive markers of dementia of the Alzheimer type. *Neuropsychology, 8,* 374–384.

Bondi, M. W., Salmon, D. P., & Kaszniak, A. W. (in press-a). The neuropsychology of dementia. In I. Grant & K. M. Adams (Eds.), *Neuropsychological assessment of neuropsychiatric disorders* (2nd ed.). New York: Oxford University Press.

Bondi, M. W., Salmon, D. P., Monsch, A. U., Galasko, D., Butters, N., Klauber, M. R., Thal, L. J., & Saitoh, T. (in press-b). Episodic memory changes are associated with the APOE-ε4 allele in nondemented older adults. *Neurology.*

Branconnier, R. J., Cole, J. O., Spera, K. F., & De Vitt, D. R. (1982). Recall and recognition as diagnostic indices of malignant memory loss in senile dementia: A Bayesian analysis. *Experimental Aging Research, 8,* 189–193.

Brayne, C., & Calloway, P. (1990). The association of education and socioeconomic status with the Mini Mental State Examination and clinical diagnosis of dementia in elderly people. *Age and Ageing, 19,* 91–96.

Burdz, M. P., Eaton, W. O., & Bond, J. B. (1988). Effect of respite care on dementia and nondementia patients and their caregivers. *Psychology and Aging, 3,* 38–42.

Burke, W. J., Houston, M., Boust, S., & Rosaforte, W. (1989). Use of the Geriatric Depression Scale in dementia of the Alzheimer's type. *Journal of the American Geriatrics Society, 37,* 856–860.

Burke, W. J., Rubin, E. H., Morris, J., & Berg, L. (1988). Symptoms of "depression" in senile dementia of the Alzheimer's type. *Alzheimer's Disease and Associated Disorders, 2,* 356–362.

Burns, A., Jacoby, R., & Levy, R. (1991). Progression of cognitive impairment in Alzheimer's disease. *Journal of the American Geriatrics Society, 39,* 39–45.

Butcher, J. N. (1989). *Adult clinical system user's guide for the MMPI-2.* Minneapolis: University of Minnesota Press.

Butcher, J. N., Aldwin, C. M., Levenson, M. R., Ben-Porath, Y. S., Spiro, A., & Bosse, R. (1991). Personality and aging: A study of the MMPI-2 among older adults. *Psychology and Aging, 6*, 361–370.

Butler, R. N., Finkel, S. I., Lewis, M. I., Sherman, F. T., & Sunderland, T. (1992). Aging and mental health: 2. Diagnosis of dementia and depression. *Geriatrics, 47(6)*, 49–52, 55–57.

Butters, M. A., Salmon, D. P., & Butters, N. (1994). Neuropsychological assessment of dementia. In M. Storandt & G. R. VandenBos (Eds.), *Neuropsychological assessment of dementia and depression in older adults: A clinician's guide* (pp. 33–59). Washington, DC: American Psychological Association.

Caine, E. D., & Grossman, H. (1992). Neuropsychiatric assessment. In J. E. Birren, R. B. Sloane, & Gene D. Cohen (Eds.), *Handbook of mental health and aging* (pp. 603–641). San Diego, CA: Academic Press.

Caine, E. D., Lyness, J. M., & King, D. A. (1993). Reconsidering depression in the elderly. *American Journal of Geriatric Psychiatry, 1*, 4–20.

Cerella, J. (1990). Aging and information-processing rate. In J. E. Birren & K. W. Schaie (Eds.), *Handbook of the psychology of aging* (3rd ed., pp. 201–221). San Diego, CA: Academic Press.

Clarfield, A. M. (1988). The reversible dementias: Do they reverse? *Annals of Internal Medicine, 109*, 476–486.

Coffey, C. E., & Cummings, J. L. (Eds.). (1994). *Textbook of geriatric neuropsychiatry*. Washington, DC: American Psychiatric Press.

Cooper, A. F. (1976). Deafness and psychiatric illness. *British Journal of Psychiatry, 129*, 215–226.

Copeland, J. R., Davidson, L. A., & Dewey, M. E. (1987). The prevalence and outcome of anxious depression in elderly people aged 65 and over living in the community. In G. Racagnia & E. Sneraldi (Eds.), *Anxious depression: Assessment and treatment* (pp. 43–47). New York: Raven Press.

Craik, F. I. M., & McDowd, J. M. (1987). Age differences in recall and recognition. *Journal of Experimental Psychology: Learning, Memory, and Cognition, 13*, 474–479.

Crum, R. M., Anthony, J. C., Bassett, S. S., & Folstein, M. F. (1993). Population-based norms for the Mini-Mental State Examination by age and educational level. *Journal of the American Medical Association, 269*, 2386–2391.

Cummings, J. L., & Benson, D. F. (1992). *Dementia: A clinical approach* (2nd ed.). Boston: Butterworth-Heinemann.

Cummings, J. L., & Coffey, C. E. (1994). Geriatric neuropsychiatry. In C. E. Coffey & J. L. Cummings (Eds.), *Textbook of geriatric neuropsychiatry* (pp. 3–15). Washington, DC: American Psychiatric Press.

Cunningham, W. R., & Haman, K. L. (1992). Intellectual functioning in relation to mental health. In J. E. Birren, R. B. Sloane, & G. D. Cohen (Eds.), *Handbook of mental health and aging* (2nd ed., pp. 339–354). San Diego, CA: Academic Press.

Cunningham, W. R., Sepkoski, C. M., & Opel, M. R. (1978). Fatigue effects on intelligence test performance in the elderly. *Journal of Gerontology, 33,* 541–545.

Dahlstrom, W. G., Welsh, G. S., & Dahlstrom, L. E. (1972). *An MMPI handbook: Vol. 1. Clinical interpretations.* Minneapolis: University of Minnesota Press.

Delis, D. C., Freeland, J., Kramer, J. H., & Kaplan, E. (1988). Integrating clinical assessment with cognitive neuroscience: Construct validation of the California Verbal Learning Test. *Journal of Consulting and Clinical Psychology, 56,* 123–130.

Delis, D. C., Kramer, J. H., Kaplan, E., & Ober, B. A. (1987). *The California Verbal Learning Test.* New York: Psychological Corporation.

Delis, D. C., Massman, P. J., Butters, N., Salmon, D. P., Kramer, J. H., & Cermak, L. (1991). Profiles of demented and amnesic patients on the California Verbal Learning Test: Implications for the assessment of memory disorders. *Psychological Assessment: A Journal of Clinical and Consulting Psychology, 3,* 19–26.

Depression Guideline Panel. (1993). *Depression in primary care: Vol. 1. Detection and diagnosis: Clinical Practice Guidelines, No. 5* (Publication No. 93-0550). Rockville, MD: U.S. Department of Health and Human Services, Public Health Service, Agency for Health Care Policy and Research.

Derogatis, L. R. (1983). *SCL-90-R: Administration, scoring and procedures manual II.* Baltimore: Clinical Psychometric Research.

Derogatis, L. R., & DellaPietra, L. (1994). Psychological tests in screening for psychiatric disorder. In M. E. Maruish (Ed.), *The use of psychological testing for treatment planning and outcome assessment* (pp. 22–54). Hillsdale, NJ: Erlbaum.

Derogatis, L. R., & Lazarus, L. (1994). SCL-90-R, Brief Symptom Inventory, and matching clinical rating scales. In M. E. Maruish (Ed.), *The use of psychological testing for treatment planning and outcome assessment* (pp. 217–248). Hillsdale, NJ: Erlbaum.

Derogatis, L. R., Lipman, R. S., Covi, L., Rickels, K., & Uhlenhuth, E. R. (1970). Dimensions of outpatient neurotic pathology: Comparison of a clinical versus an empirical assessment. *Journal of Consulting and Clinical Psychology, 34,* 164–171.

Derogatis, L. R., Lipman, R. S., Rickels, K., Uhlenhuth, E. H., & Covi, L. (1974). The Hopkins Symptom Checklist (HSCL): A self-report symptom inventory. *Behavioral Science, 19,* 1–15.

Derogatis, L. R., & Spencer, P. (1982). *Administration and procedures: Brief Symptom Inventory manual.* Baltimore: Johns Hopkins University Press.

Devanand, D. P., Miller, L., Richards, M., Marder, K., Bell, K., Mayeux, R., & Stern, Y. (1992). The Columbia University Scale for Psychopathology in Alzheimer's Disease. *Archives of Neurology, 49,* 371–376.

DiNardo, P. A., & Barlow, D. H. (1988). *Anxiety Disorders Interview Schedule-Revised (ADIS-R).* Albany: Phobia and Anxiety Disorders Clinic, State University of New York.

Dubno, J. R., Dirks, D. D., & Morgan, D. E. (1984). Effects of age and mild hearing loss on speech recognition in noise. *Journal of the Acoustical Society of America, 76,* 87–96.

Eaton, W. W., Kramer, M., Anthony, J. C., Dryman, A., Shapiro, S., & Locke, B. Z. (1989). The incidence of specific DIS/DSM-III mental disorders: Data from the NIMH Epidemiologic Catchment Area Program. *Acta Psychiatrica Scandinavica, 79,* 163–178.

Elias, M. F., Robbins, M. A., Walter, L. J., & Schultz, N. R. (1993). The influence of gender and age on Halstead-Reitan Neuropsychological Test performance. *Journal of Gerontology: Psychological Sciences, 48,* P278–P281.

Erickson, R. C., Eimon, P., & Hebben, N. (1992). A bibliography of normative articles on cognitive tests for older adults. *Clinical Neuropsychologist, 6,* 98–102.

Erickson, R. C., Eimon, P., & Hebben, N. (1994). A listing of references to cognitive test norms for older adults. In M. Storandt & G. R. VandenBos (Eds.), *Neuropsychological assessment of dementia and depression in older adults: A clinician's guide* (pp. 183–197). Washington, DC: American Psychological Association.

Escobar, J., Buirnam, A., Karno, M., Forsythe, A., Landsverk, J., & Golding, J. M. (1986). Use of the Mini-Mental Status Examination (MMSE) in a community population of mixed ethnicity: Cultural and linguistic artifacts. *Journal of Nervous and Mental Diseases, 174,* 607–614.

Eslinger, P. J., Damasio, A. R., Benton, A. L., & Van Allen, M. (1985). Neuropsychologic detection of abnormal mental decline in older persons. *Journal of the American Medical Association, 253,* 670–674.

Feher, E. P., Larrabee, G. J., & Crook, T. H. (1992). Memory self-report in Alzheimer's disease [Abstract]. *Journal of Clinical and Experimental Neurology, 14,* 18.

Feher, E. P., Mahurin, R. K., Doody, R. S., Cooke, N., Sims, J., & Pirozzolo, F. J. (1992). Establishing the limits of the Mini-Mental State: Examination of "subtests." *Archives of Neurology, 49,* 87–92.

Fillenbaum, G., & Smyer, M. (1981). The development, validity and reliability of the OARS multidimensional function assessment questionnaire. *Journal of Gerontology, 36,* 428–434.

Flicker, C., Ferris, S. H., & Reisberg, B. (1991). Mild cognitive impairment in the elderly: Predictors of dementia. *Neurology, 41,* 1006–1009.

Foelker, G. A., Jr., Schewchuk, R. M., & Niederehe, G. (1987). Confirmatory factor analysis of the short form Beck Depression Inventory in elderly community samples. *Journal of Clinical Psychology, 43,* 111–118.

Folstein, M. F., Anthony, J. C., Parhad, I., Duffy, B., & Gruenberg, E. M. (1985). The meaning of cognitive impairment in the elderly. *Journal of the American Geriatrics Society, 33,* 228–235.

Folstein, M. F., Folstein, S., & McHugh, P. R. (1975). Mini-Mental State: A practical method for grading the cognitive state of patients for the clinician. *Journal of Psychiatric Research, 12*, 189–198.

Fozard, J. L. (1990). Vision and hearing in aging. In J. E. Birren & K. W. Schaie (Eds.), *Handbook of the psychology of aging* (3rd ed., pp. 150–170). New York: Van Nostrand Reinhold.

Freud, S. (1924). On psychotherapy. In S. Freud (Ed.), *Collected papers* (Vol. 1, pp. 249–263). London: Hogarth Press.

Fry, P. S. (1986). *Depression, stress, and adaptations in the elderly: Psychological assessment and intervention.* Rockville, MD: Aspen.

Gallagher, D. (1986a). Assessment of depression by interview methods and psychiatric rating scales. In L. W. Poon (Ed.), *Handbook for clinical memory assessment in older adults* (pp. 202–212). Washington, DC: American Psychological Association.

Gallagher, D. (1986b). The Beck Depression Inventory and older adults: Review of its development and utility. *Clinical Gerontologist, 5*, 149–163.

Gallagher, D., Breckenridge, J., Steinmetz, J., & Thompson, L. (1983). The Beck Depression Inventory and Research Diagnostic Criteria: Congruence in an older population. *Journal of Consulting and Clinical Psychology, 51*, 945–946.

Gallagher, D., Nies, G., & Thompson, L. W. (1982). Reliability of the Beck Depression Inventory with older adults. *Journal of Consulting and Clinical Psychology, 50*, 152–153.

Gallagher, D., Slife, B., Rose, T., & Okarma, T. (1982). Psychological correlates of immunologic disease in older adults. *Clinical Gerontologist, 1*, 51–58.

Gallagher, D., Thompson, L. W., & Levy, S. M. (1980). Clinical psychological assessment of older adults. In L. W. Poon (Ed.), *Aging in the 1980s: Psychological issues* (pp. 19–40). Washington, DC: American Psychological Association.

Ganguli, M., Ratcliff, G., Huff, F. J., Belle, S., Kancel, M. J., Fisher, L., Seaberg, E. C., & Kuller, L. H. (1991). Effects of age, gender, and education on cognitive tests in a rural elderly community sample: Norms from the Monongahela Valley Independent Elders Survey. *Neuroepidemiology, 10*, 42–52.

Gatz, M. (1994). Application of assessment to therapy and intervention with older adults. In M. Storandt & G. R. VandenBos (Eds.), *Neuropsychological assessment of dementia and depression in older adults: A clinician's guide* (pp. 155–176). Washington, DC: American Psychological Association.

Gatz, M., & Pearson, C. G. (1988). Ageism revised and the provision of psychological services. *American Psychologist, 43*, 184–188.

George, K., & Fillenbaum, G. (1985). OARS methodology: A decade of experience in geriatric assessment. *Journal of the American Geriatrics Society, 33*, 607–615.

Goldstein, G., & Hersen, M. (1984). Historical perspectives. In G. Goldstein & M. Hersen (Eds.), *Handbook of psychological assessment* (pp. 3–15). Elmsford, NY: Pergamon Press.

Green, M. G., Majerovitz, S. D., Adelman, R. D., & Rizzo, C. (1994). The effects of the presence of a third person on the physician-older patient medical interview. *Journal of the American Geriatrics Society, 42,* 413–419.

Greene, R. L., & Clopton, J. R. (1994). Minnesota Multiphasic Personality Inventory-2. In M. E. Maruish (Ed.), *The use of psychological testing for treatment planning and outcome assessment* (pp. 137–159). Hillsdale, NJ: Erlbaum.

Gurland, B., Kuriansky, J., Sharpe, L., Simon, R., Stiller, P., & Birkett, P. (1977–1978). The Comprehensive Assessment and Referral Evaluation (CARE): Rationale, development, and reliability. *International Journal of Aging and Human Development, 8,* 9–42.

Gurland, B., & Wilder, D. (1984). The CARE interview revisited: Development of an efficient, systematic clinical assessment. *Journal of Gerontology, 39,* 129–137.

Haase, G. R. (1977). Diseases presenting as dementia. In C. E. Wells (Ed.), *Dementia* (2nd ed., pp. 27–67). Philadelphia: F. A. Davis.

Hale, W. D., Cochran, C. D., & Hedgepeth, B. E. (1984). Norms for elderly on the Brief Symptom Inventory. *Journal of Consulting and Clinical Psychology, 52,* 321–322.

Haley, W. E., Brown, S. L., & Levine, E. G. (1987). Experimental evaluation of the effectiveness of group intervention for dementia caregivers. *The Gerontologist, 27,* 376–382.

Haley, W. E., Levine, E. G., Brown, S. L., Berry, J. W., & Hughes, G. H. (1987). Psychological, social, and health consequences of caring for a relative with senile dementia. *Journal of the American Geriatrics Society, 35,* 405–411.

Hall, R. C. W. (Ed.). (1980). *Psychiatric presentations of medical illness.* New York: Spectrum Publications.

Hamilton, M. (1967). Development of a rating scale for primary depressive illness. *British Journal of Social and Clinical Psychology, 6,* 278–296.

Harmatz, J. S., & Shader, R. I. (1975). Psychopharmacologic investigations in healthy elderly volunteers: MMPI Depression scale. *Journal of the American Geriatrics Society, 23,* 350–359.

Hart, R. P., Kwentus, J. A., Taylor, J. R., & Harkins, S. W. (1987). Rate of forgetting in dementia and depression. *Journal of Consulting and Clinical Psychology, 55,* 101–105.

Helzer, J. E., Robins, L. N., McEvoy, L. T., Spitznagel, E. L., Stoltzman, R. K., Farmer, A., & Brockington, I. F. (1985). A comparison of clinical and Diagnostic Interview Schedule diagnoses. *Archives of General Psychiatry, 42,* 657–666.

Henderson, V. W., Mack, W., & Williams, B. W. (1989). Spatial disorientation in Alzheimer's disease. *Archives of Neurology, 46,* 391–394.

Hershey, L. W., Jaffe, D. F., Greenough, P. G., & Yang, S. (1987). Validation of cognitive and functional assessment instruments in vascular dementia. *International Journal of Psychiatry in Medicine, 17,* 183–192.

Hersen, M., & Van Hasselt, V. B. (1992). Behavioral assessment and treatment of anxiety in the elderly. *Clinical Psychology Review, 12,* 619–640.

Hertzog, C. (1989). The influence of cognitive slowing on age differences in intelligence. *Developmental Psychology, 25,* 636–651.

Himmelfarb, S., & Murrell, S. A. (1983). Reliability and validity of five mental health scales in older persons. *Journal of Gerontology, 38,* 333–339.

Huff, F. J., Becker, J. T., Belle, S. H., Nebes, R. D., Holland, A. L., & Boller, F. (1987). Cognitive deficits and clinical diagnosis of Alzheimer's disease. *Neurology, 37,* 1119–1124.

Ineichen, B. (1987). Measuring the rising tide: How many dementia cases will there be by 2001? *British Journal of Psychiatry, 150,* 193–200.

Ivnik, R. J. (1991, August). *Normative neuropsychological assessment of the elderly: General considerations.* Paper presented at the 99th Annual Convention of the American Psychological Association, San Francisco.

Ivnik, R. J., Malec, J. F., Smith, G. E., Tangalos, E. G., Petersen, R. C., Kokmen, E., & Kurland, L. T. (1992a). Mayo's Older Americans Normative Studies: WAIS-R norms for ages 56 to 97. *The Clinical Neuropsychologist, 6*(Suppl.), 1–30.

Ivnik, R. J., Malec, J. F., Smith, G. E., Tangalos, E. G., Petersen, R. C., Kokmen, E., & Kurland, L. T. (1992b). Mayo's Older Americans Normative Studies: WMS-R norms for ages 56 to 94. *The Clinical Neuropsychologist, 6*(Suppl.), 49–82.

Ivnik, R. J., Malec, J. F., Smith, G. E., Tangalos, E. G., Petersen, R. C., Kokmen, E., & Kurland, L. T. (1992c). Mayo's Older Americans Normative Studies: Updated AVLT norms for ages 56 to 97. *The Clinical Neuropsychologist, 6* (Suppl.), 83–104.

Jagger, C., Clarke, M., & Anderson, J. (1992). Screening for dementia: A comparison of two tests using receiver operating characteristics (ROC) analysis. *International Journal of Geriatric Psychiatry, 7,* 659–665.

Jenike, M. A. (1989). Anxiety disorders of old age. In M. A. Jenike (Ed.), *Geriatric psychiatry and psychopharmacology* (pp. 248–271). St. Louis, MO: Mosby-Year Book.

Johnson, M. H., & Magaro, P. A. (1987). Effects of mood and severity on memory processes in depression and mania. *Psychological Bulletin, 101,* 28–40.

Jorm, A. F. (1990). *The epidemiology of Alzheimer's disease and related disorders.* London: Chapman & Hall.

Jorm, A. F., Korten, A. E., & Henderson, A. S. (1987). The prevalence of dementia: A quantitative integration of the literature. *Acta Psychiatrica Scandinavica, 76,* 465–479.

Kafonek, S., Ettinger, W., Roca, R., Kittner, S., Taylor, N., & German, P. (1989). Instruments for screening for depression and dementia in a long-term care facility. *Journal of the American Geriatrics Society, 37,* 29–34.

Kahan, J., Kemp, B., Staples, F. R., & Brummel-Smith, K. (1985). Decreasing the burden in families caring for a relative with a dementing illness. *Journal of the American Geriatrics Society, 33*, 664–670.

Kahn, R. L., Zarit, S. H., Hilbert, N. M., & Niederehe, G. (1975). Memory complaint and memory impairment in the aged. *Archives of General Psychiatry, 32*, 1569–1573.

Kaplan, E. (1988). A process approach to neuropsychological assessment. In T. Boll & B. K. Bryant (Eds.), *Clinical neuropsychology and brain function: Research, measurement, and practice* (pp. 127–167). Washington, DC: American Psychological Association.

Karajgi, B., Rifkin, A., Doddi, S., & Kolli, R. (1990). The prevalence of anxiety disorders in patients with chronic obstructive pulmonary disease. *American Journal of Psychiatry, 147*, 200–201.

Kaszniak, A. W. (1986). The neuropsychology of dementia. In I. Grant & K. M. Adams (Eds.), *Neuropsychological assessment of neuropsychiatric disorders* (pp. 172–220). New York: Oxford University Press.

Kaszniak, A. W. (1987). Neuropsychological consultation to geriatricians: Issues in the assessment of memory complaints. *The Clinical Neuropsychologist, 1*, 35–46.

Kaszniak, A. W. (1990). Psychological assessment of the aging individual. In J. E. Birren & K. W. Schaie (Eds.), *Handbook of the psychology of aging* (3rd ed., pp. 427–445). San Diego, CA: Academic Press.

Kaszniak, A. W., & Allender, J. (1985). Psychological assessment of depression in older adults. In G. M. Chaisson-Stewart (Ed.), *Depression in the elderly: An interdisciplinary approach* (pp. 107–160). New York: Wiley.

Kaszniak, A. W., & Christenson, G. D. (1994). Differential diagnosis of dementia and depression. In M. Storandt & G. R. VandenBos (Eds.), *Neuropsychological assessment of dementia and depression in older adults: A clinician's guide* (pp. 81–117). Washington, DC: American Psychological Association.

Kaszniak, A. W., & Christenson, G. D. (1996). Self-awareness of deficit in patients with Alzheimer's disease. In S. R. Hameroff, A. W. Kaszniak, & A. C. Scott (Eds.), *Toward a science of consciousness: The first Tucson discussions and debates* (pp. 227–242). Cambridge, MA: MIT Press.

Kaszniak, A. W., Keyl, P., & Albert, M. (1991). Dementia and the older driver. *Human Factors, 33*, 527–537.

Kaszniak, A. W., Poon, L. W., & Riege, W. (1986). Assessing memory deficits: An information processing approach. In L. W. Poon (Ed.), *Handbook for clinical memory assessment of older adults* (pp. 168–188). Washington, DC: American Psychological Association.

Kaszniak, A. W., Sadeh, M., & Stern, L. Z. (1985). Differentiating depression from organic brain syndromes in older age. In G. M. Chaisson-Stewart (Ed.), *Depression in the elderly: An interdisciplinary approach* (pp. 161–189). New York: Wiley.

Kaszniak, A. W., & Scogin, F. R. (1995). Assessing for dementia and depression in older adults. *The Clinical Psychologist, 48*(2), 17–24.

Kaszniak, A. W., Wilson, R. S., Fox, J. H., & Stebbins, G. T. (1986). Cognitive assessment in Alzheimer's disease: Cross-sectional and longitudinal perspectives. *Canadian Journal of Neurological Sciences, 13,* 420–423.

Katzman, R. (1986). Alzheimer's disease. *New England Journal of Medicine, 314,* 964–973.

Katzman, R. (1993). Education and the prevalence of dementia and Alzheimer's disease. *Neurology, 43,* 13–20.

Katzman, R., & Kawas, C. (1994). The epidemiology of dementia and Alzheimer disease. In R. D. Terry, R. Katzman, & K. L. Bick (Eds.), *Alzheimer disease* (pp. 105–122). New York: Raven Press.

Katzman, R., Lasker, B., & Bernstein, N. (1988). Advances in the diagnosis of dementia: Accuracy of diagnosis and consequences of misdiagnosis of disorders causing dementia. In R. D. Terry (Ed.), *Aging and the brain* (pp. 17–62). New York: Raven Press.

Kay, D. W. K. (1988). Anxiety in the elderly. In M. Roth, J. R. Noyes, & G. D. Burrows (Eds.), *Biological, clinical and cultural perspectives: Handbook of anxiety* (Vol. 1, pp. 289–310). Amsterdam: Elsevier/North Holland Science.

Kemp, B. J., & Mitchell, J. M. (1992). Functional assessment in geriatric mental health. In J. E. Birren, R. B. Sloane, & G. D. Cohen (Eds.), *Handbook of mental health and aging* (2nd ed., pp. 671–697). San Diego, CA: Academic Press.

Kitchell, M. A., Barnes, R. F., Veith, R. C., Okimoto, J. T., & Raskind, M. A. (1982). Screening for depression in hospitalized geriatric medical patients. *Journal of the American Geriatrics Society, 30,* 174–177.

Klerman, G. L. (1983). Problems in the definition and diagnosis of depression in the elderly. In L. D. Breslau & M. R. Haug (Eds.), *Depression and aging: Causes, care and consequences* (pp. 3–19). New York: Springer.

Knesevich, J. W., Martin, R. L., Berg, L., & Danziger, W. (1983). Preliminary report on affective symptoms in the early stages of senile dementia of the Alzheimer's type. *American Journal of Psychiatry, 140,* 233–234.

Knopman, D. S., & Ryberg, S. (1989). A verbal memory test with high predictive accuracy for dementia of the Alzheimer type. *Archives of Neurology, 46,* 141–145.

Koenig, H. G., & Blazer, D. G. (1992). Mood disorders and suicide. In J. E. Birren, R. B. Sloane, & G. D. Cohen (Eds.), *Handbook of mental health and aging* (2nd ed., pp. 379–407). San Diego, CA: Academic Press.

Kohler, S. (1994). Quantitative characterization of verbal learning deficits in patients with Alzheimer's disease. *Journal of Clinical and Experimental Neuropsychology, 16,* 749–753.

Kral, V. A., & Emery, O. B. (1989). Long-term follow-up of depressive pseudodementia of the aged. *Canadian Journal of Psychiatry, 34,* 445–446.

Kunkel, S. R., & Applebaum, R. A. (1992). Estimating the prevalence of long-term disability for an aging society. *Journal of Gerontology: Social Sciences, 47,* S253–S260.

LaBarge, E., Rosenman, L. S., Leavitt, K., & Cristiani, T. (1988). Counseling clients with mild senile dementia of the Alzheimer's type: A pilot study. *Journal of Neurological Rehabilitation, 2,* 167–173.

Larabee, G. L., & Levin, H. S. (1986). Memory self-ratings and objective test performance in a normal elderly sample. *Journal of Clinical and Experimental Neuropsychology, 8,* 275–284.

La Rue, A. (1992). *Aging and neuropsychological assessment.* New York: Plenum.

La Rue, A., D'Elia, L. F., Clark, E. O., Spar, J. E., & Jarvik, L. F. (1986). Clinical tests of memory in dementia, depression, and healthy aging. *Journal of Psychology and Aging, 1,* 69–77.

La Rue, A., & Markee, T. (1995). Clinical assessment research with older adults. *Psychological Assessment, 7,* 376–386.

La Rue, A., Watson, J., & Plotkin, D. A. (1992). Retrospective accounts of dementia symptoms: Are they reliable? *The Gerontologist, 32,* 240–245.

La Rue, A., Yang, J., & Osato, S. (1992). Neuropsychological assessment. In J. E. Birren, R. B. Sloane, & G. D. Cohen (Eds.), *Handbook of mental health and aging* (2nd ed., pp. 643–670). San Diego, CA: Academic Press.

Lawton, M. P. (1986). Functional assessment. In L. Teri & P. M. Lewinsohn (Eds.), *Geropsychological assessment and treatment* (pp. 39–84). Elmsford, NY: Pergamon Press.

Lawton, M. P., Moss, M., Fulcomer, M., & Kleban, M. H. (1982). A research and service oriented multilevel assessment instrument. *Journal of Gerontology, 37,* 91–99.

Lebowitz, B. D., & Niederehe, G. (1992). Concepts and issues in mental health and aging. In J. E. Birren, R. B. Sloane, & Gene D. Cohen (Eds.), *Handbook of mental health and aging* (pp. 3–26). San Diego, CA: Academic Press.

Lemke, S., & Moos, R. H. (1980). Assessing the institutional policies of sheltered care settings. *Journal of Gerontology, 35,* 96–107.

Lemke, S., & Moos, R. H. (1981). The suprapersonal environments of sheltered care settings. *Journal of Gerontology, 36,* 233–243.

Lemke, S., & Moos, R. H. (1987). Measuring the social climate of congregate residences for older people: Sheltered Care Environment Scale. *Psychology and Aging, 2,* 20–29.

Lemke, S., & Moos, R. H. (1990). Validity of the Sheltered Care Environment Scale: Conceptual and methodological issues. *Psychology and Aging, 5,* 569–571.

Lesher, E. L. (1986). Validation of the Geriatric Depression Scale among nursing home residents. *Clinical Gerontologist, 4,* 21–28.

Lezak, M. D. (1995). *Neuropsychological assessment* (3rd ed.). New York: Oxford University Press.

Li, G., Shen, Y. C., Chen, C. H., Zhao, Y. W., & Li, S. R. (1989). An epidemiological survey of age-related dementia in an urban area of Bejing. *Acta Psychiatrica Scandinavica, 79,* 557–563.

Light, E., Niederehe, G., & Lebowitz, B. D. (Eds.). (1994). *Stress effects on family caregivers of Alzheimer's patients.* New York: Springer.

Lima, S. D., Hale, S., & Myerson, J. (1991). How general is general slowing? Evidence from the lexical domain. *Psychology and Aging, 6,* 416–425.

Lindenberger, U., & Baltes, P. B. (1994). Sensory functioning and intelligence in old age: A strong connection. *Psychology and Aging, 9,* 339–355.

Linn, R. T., Wolf, P. A., Bachman, D. L., Knoefel, J. E., Cobb, J. L., Belanger, A. J., Kaplan, E. F., & D'Agostino, R. B. (1995). The "preclinical phase" of probable Alzheimer's disease: A 13-year prospective study of the Framingham cohort. *Archives of Neurology, 52,* 485–490.

Liu, K., & Manton, K. G. (1984). The characteristics and utilization pattern of an admission cohort of nursing home patients. *The Gerontologist, 23,* 92–98.

Loewenstein, D. A., Argüelles, T., Barker, W. W., & Duara, R. (1993). A comparative analysis of neuropsychological test performance of Spanish-speaking and English-speaking patients with Alzheimer's disease. *Journal of Gerontology: Psychological Sciences, 48,* P142–P149.

Loewenstein, D. A., Rubert, M. P., Argüelles, T., & Duara, R. (1995). Neuropsychological test performance and prediction of functional capacities among Spanish-speaking and English-speaking patients with dementia. *Archives of Clinical Neuropsychology, 10,* 75–88.

Lovell, M. R., & Nussbaum, P. D. (1994). Neuropsychological assessment. In C. E. Coffey & J. L. Cummings (Eds.), *Textbook of geriatric neuropsychiatry* (pp. 129–144). Washington, DC: American Psychiatric Press.

Lubin, B., & Rinck, C. M. (1986). Assessment of mood and affect in the elderly: The Depression Adjective Check List and the Multiple Affect Adjective Check List. *Clinical Gerontologist, 5,* 187–191.

Mackenzie, T. B., Robiner, W. N., & Knopman, D. S. (1989). Differences between patient and family assessments of depression in Alzheimer's disease. *American Journal of Psychiatry, 146,* 1174–1178.

Mahurin, R. K., DeBettignies, B. H., & Pirozzolo, F. J. (1991). Structured assessment of independent living skills: Preliminary report of a performance measure of functional abilities in dementia. *Journal of Gerontology: Psychological Sciences, 46,* P58–P66.

Malec, J. F., Ivnik, R. J., & Smith, G. E. (1993). Neuropsychology and normal aging: The clinician's perspective. In R. W. Parks, R. F. Zec, & R. S. Wilson (Eds.), *Neuropsychology of Alzheimer's disease and other dementias* (pp. 81–111). New York: Oxford University Press.

Malmgren, R. (1994). Epidemiology of aging. In C. E. Coffey & J. L. Cummings (Eds.), *Textbook of geriatric neuropsychiatry* (pp. 17–33). Washington, DC: American Psychiatric Press.

Maruish, M. E. (Ed.). (1994). *The use of psychological testing for treatment planning and outcome assessment.* Hillsdale, NJ: Erlbaum.

Massman, P. J., Delis, D. C., Butters, N., Dupont, R. M., & Gillin, J. C. (1992). The subcortical dysfunction hypothesis of memory deficits in depression: Neuropsychological validation in a subgroup of patients. *Journal of Clinical and Experimental Neuropsychology, 14,* 687–706.

Masur, D. M., Sliwinski, M., Lipton, R. B., Blau, A. D., & Crystal, H. A. (1994). Neuropsychological prediction of dementia and the absence of dementia in healthy elderly persons. *Neurology, 44,* 1427–1432.

Matt, G. E., Dean, A., Wang, B., & Wood, P. (1992). Identifying clinical syndromes in a community sample of elderly persons. *Psychological Assessment, 4,* 174–184.

McCrae, R. R., & Costa, P. T. (1990). *Personality in adulthood.* New York: Guilford Press.

McGlone, J., Gupta, S., Humphrey, D., Oppenheimer, S., Mirsen, T., & Evans, D. R. (1990). Screening for early dementia using memory complaints from patients and relatives. *Archives of Neurology, 47,* 1189–1193.

McGlynn, S. M., & Kaszniak, A. W. (1991a). Unawareness of deficits in dementia and schizophrenia. In G. P. Prigatano & D. Schacter (Eds.), *Awareness of deficit after brain injury: Clinical and theoretical issues* (pp. 84–110). New York: Oxford University Press.

McGlynn, S. M., & Kaszniak, A. W. (1991b). When metacognition fails: Impaired awareness of deficit in Alzheimer's disease. *Journal of Cognitive Neuroscience, 3,* 184–189

Metter, E. J. (1991). Behavioral correlates of abnormalities of metabolism in stroke patients. In R. A. Bornstein & G. G. Brown (Eds.), *Neurobehavioral aspects of cerebrovascular disease* (pp. 60–82). New York: Oxford University Press.

Meyer, T. J., Miller, M. L., Metzger, R. L., & Borkovec, T. D. (1990). Development and validation of the Penn State Worry Questionnaire. *Behavior Research and Therapy, 28,* 487–495.

Miller, E., & Lewis, P. (1977). Recognition memory in elderly patients with depression and dementia: A signal detection analysis. *Journal of Abnormal Psychology, 86,* 84–86.

Mittenberg, W., Seidenberg, M., O'Leary, D. S., & DiGiulio, D. V. (1989). Changes in cerebral functioning associated with normal aging. *Journal of Clinical and Experimental Neuropsychology, 11,* 918–932.

Moehle, K. A., & Long, C. J. (1989). Models of aging and neuropsychological test performance decline with aging. *Journal of Gerontology: Psychological Sciences, 44,* P176–P177.

Monsch, A. U., Bondi, M. W., Butters, N., Salmon, D. P., Katzman, R., & Thal, L. J. (1992). Comparisons of verbal fluency tasks in the detection of dementia of the Alzheimer type. *Archives of Neurology, 49,* 1253–1258.

Moos, R. H., & Lemke, S. (1980). Assessing the physical and architectural features of sheltered care settings. *Journal of Gerontology, 35,* 571–583.

Moos, R. H., & Lemke, S. (1984). *Multiphasic Environmental Assessment Procedure manual*. Palo Alto, CA: Social Ecology Laboratory, Veterans Administration and Stanford University Medical Center.

Moran, M. G., Thompson, T. L., & Nies, A. S. (1988). Sleep disorders in the elderly. *American Journal of Psychiatry, 145*, 1369–1378.

Morris, J. C., McKeel, D. W., Jr., Storandt, M., Rubin, E. H., Price, J. L., Grant, E. A., Ball, M. J., & Berg, L. (1991). Very mild Alzheimer's disease: Informant-based clinical, psychometric, and pathologic distinction from normal aging. *Neurology, 41*, 469–478.

Murden, R. A., McRae, T. D., Kaner, S., & Bucknam, M. E. (1991). Mini-Mental State Exam scores vary with education in blacks and whites. *Journal of the American Geriatrics Society, 39*, 149–155.

National Center for Health Statistics. (1993). *Health, United States, 1992*. Hyattsville, MD: Public Health Service.

National Institute of Mental Health. (1979). *The Diagnostic Interview Schedule*. Washington, DC: National Institute of Mental Health, Center for Epidemiological Studies.

National Institutes of Health. (1991). *Consensus development conference statement: Diagnosis and treatment of depression in late life*. Washington, DC: National Institutes of Health.

Naugle, R. I., Cullum, C. M., & Bigler, E. D. (1990). Evaluation of intellectual and memory function among dementia patients who were intellectually superior. *The Clinical Neuropsychologist, 4*, 355–374.

Niederehe, G. (1986). Depression and memory impairment in the aged. In L. W. Poon (Ed.), *Handbook for clinical memory assessment in older adults* (pp. 226–237). Washington, DC: American Psychological Association.

Norris, J. T., Gallagher, D., Wilson, A., & Winograd, C. H. (1987). Assessment of depression in geriatric medical outpatients: The validity of two screening measures. *Journal of the American Geriatrics Society, 35*, 989–995.

Nussbaum, P. D., Kaszniak, A. W., Allender, J., & Rapcsak, S. (1995). Depression and cognitive decline in the elderly: A follow-up study. *The Clinical Neuropsychologist, 9*, 101–111.

Nussbaum, P. D., Kaszniak, A. W., Swanda, R. M., & Allender, J. (1988). Quantitative and qualitative aspects of memory performance in older depressed vs. probable Alzheimer's disease patients [Abstract]. *Journal of Clinical and Experimental Neuropsychology, 10*, 63.

O'Connor, D. W., Pollitt, P. A., Hyde, J. B., Fellows, J. L., Miller, N. D., Brook, C. P. B., & Reiss, B. B. (1989). The reliability and validity of the Mini-Mental State in a British community survey. *Journal of Psychiatric Research, 23*, 87–96.

O'Connor, D. W., Pollitt, P. A., Hyde, J. B., Miller, N. D., & Fellowes, J. L. (1991). Clinical issues relating to the diagnosis of mild dementia in a British community survey. *Archives of Neurology, 48*, 530–534.

Office of Technology Assessment Task Force. (1988). *Confronting Alzheimer's disease and other dementias*. Washington, DC: Science Information Resource Center.

Olin, J. T., Schneider, L. S., Eaton, E. E., Zemansky, M. F., & Pollock, V. E. (1992). The Geriatric Depression Scale and the Beck Depression Inventory as screening instruments in an older adult outpatient population. *Psychological Assessment, 4*, 190–192.

O'Neil, P. M., & Calhoun, K. S. (1975). Sensory deficits and behavioral deterioration in senescence. *Journal of Abnormal Psychology, 84*, 579–582.

Otto, M. W., Bruder, G. E., Fava, M., Delis, D. C., Quitkin, F. M., & Rosenbaum, J. F. (1994). Norms for depressed patients for the California Verbal Learning Test: Associations with depression severity and self-report of cognitive difficulties. *Archives of Clinical Neuropsychology, 9*, 81–88.

Owsley, C., & Sloane, M. E. (1990). Vision and aging. In F. Boller & J. Grafman (Eds.), *Handbook of neuropsychology* (Vol. 4, pp. 229–249). Amsterdam: Elsevier.

Parks, R. W., Zec, R. F., & Wilson, R. S. (Eds.). (1993). *Neuropsychology of Alzheimer's disease and other dementias*. New York: Oxford University Press.

Parmelee, P. A., & Katz, I. R. (1990). Geriatric Depression Scale. *Journal of the American Geriatrics Society, 38*, 1379.

Parmelee, P. A., Katz, I. R., & Lawton, M. P. (1989). Depression among institutionalized aged: Assessment and prevalence estimation. *Journal of Gerontology, 44*, M22–M29.

Parmelee, P. A., Lawton, M. P., & Katz, I. R. (1989). Psychometric properties of the Geriatric Depression Scale among the institutional aged. *Psychological Assessment, 1*, 331–338.

Perry, S., Frances, A., & Clarkin, J. (1990). *A DSM-III-R casebook of treatment selection*. New York: Brunner/Mazel.

Persad, C. C., Giordani, B., Chen, H. C., Ashton-Miller, J. A., Alexander, N. B., Wilson, C. S., Berent, S., Guire, K., & Schultz, A. B. (1995). Neuropsychological predictors of complex obstacle avoidance in healthy older adults. *Journal of Gerontology: Psychological Sciences, 50B*, P272–P277.

Peters, C. A., Potter, J. F., & Scholer, S. G. (1988). Hearing impairment as a predictor of cognitive decline in dementia. *Journal of the American Geriatrics Society, 36*, 981–986.

Petersen, R. C., Smith, G. E., Ivnik, R. J., Kokmen, E., & Tangalos, E. G. (1994). Memory function in very early Alzheimer's disease. *Neurology, 44*, 867–872.

Pfeffer, R. I., Kurosaki, T. T., Harrah, C. H., Chance, J. M., & Filos, S. (1982). Measurement of functional activities in older adults in the community. *Journal of Gerontology, 37*, 323–329.

Pickett, J. M., Bergman, M., & Levitt, M. (1979). Aging and speech understanding. In J. M. Ordy & K. Brizzee (Eds.), *Aging: Vol. 10. Speech systems and communication in the elderly* (pp. 167–186). New York: Raven Press.

Plomp, R. (1978). Auditory handicap of hearing impairment and the limited benefit of hearing aids. *Journal of the Acoustical Society of America, 63,* 533–549.

Plomp, R., & Mimpen, A. M. (1979). Speech reception threshold for sentences as a function of age and noise level. *Journal of the Acoustical Society of America, 66,* 1333–1342.

Poirier, J., Davignon, J., Bouthillier, D., Kogan, S., Bertrand, P., & Gauthier, S. (1993). Apolipoprotein E polymorphism and Alzheimer's disease. *Lancet, 342,* 697–699.

Poon, L. W., Kaszniak, A. W., & Dudley, W. N. (1992). Approaches in the experimental neuropsychology of dementia: A methodological and model review. In M. Bergner, K. Hasegawa, S. Finkel, & T. Nishimura (Eds.), *Aging and mental disorders: International perspectives* (pp. 150–173). New York: Springer.

Popkin, M. K., & Mackenzie, T. B. (1980). Psychiatric presentations of endocrine dysfunction. In R. C. W. Hall (Ed.), *Psychiatric presentations of medical illness* (pp. 139–156). New York: Spectrum Publications.

Rabins, P. V., Merchant, A., & Nestadt, G. (1984). Criteria for diagnosing reversible dementia caused by depression. *British Journal of Psychiatry, 144,* 488–492.

Radloff, L. S., & Teri, L. (1986). Use of the Center for Epidemiological Studies-Depression Scale with older adults. *Clinical Gerontologist, 5,* 119–136.

Rapp, S. R., Parisi, S. I., & Walsh, D. A. (1988). Geriatric depression: Physicians' knowledge, perceptions and diagnostic practices. *The Gerontologist, 29,* 252–257.

Rapp, S. R., Parisi, S. A., Walsh, D. A., & Wallace, C. E. (1988). Detecting depression in elderly medical inpatients. *Journal of Consulting and Clinical Psychology, 56,* 509–513.

Reding, M., Haycox, J., & Blass, J. (1985). Depression in patients referred to a dementia clinic: A three-year prospective study. *Archives of Neurology, 42,* 894–896.

Regier, D. A., Boyd, J. H., Burke, J. D., Locke, B. Z., Rae, D. S., Myers, J. K., Kramer, M., Robins, L. N., George, L. K., Karno, M., & Locke, B. Z. (1988). One-month prevalence of mental disorders in the U.S. *Archives of General Psychiatry, 45,* 977–986.

Reitan, R. M., & Wolfsen, D. (1986). The Halstead–Reitan Neuropsychological Test Battery and aging. *Clinical Gerontologist, 5,* 39–61.

Reynolds, C. F., Hoch, C. C., Kupfer, D. J., Buysse, D. J., Houck, P. R., Stack, J. A., & Campbell, D. W. (1988). Bedside differentiation of depressive pseudodementia from dementia. *American Journal of Psychiatry, 145,* 1099–1103.

Robins, L. N. (1985). Epidemiology: Reflections on testing the validity of psychiatric interviews. *Archives of General Psychiatry, 42,* 918–924.

Robins, L. N., Helzer, J. E., Croughan, J., & Ratcliff, K. S. (1981). National Institute of Mental Health Diagnostic Interview Schedule: Its history, characteristics, and validity. *Archives of General Psychiatry, 38,* 381–389.

Roccaforte, W. H., Burke, W. J., Bayer, B. L., & Wenger, S. P. (1992). Validation of a telephone version of the Mini-Mental State Examination. *Journal of the American Geriatrics Society, 40*, 697–702.

Rohde, P., Lewinsohn, D. M., & Seeley, J. R. (1990). Are people changed by the experience of having an episode of depression? A further test of the scar hypothesis. *Journal of Abnormal Psychology, 44*, 853–857.

Roman, G. C. (1991). The epidemiology of vascular dementia. In A. Hartman, W. Kuschinsky, & S. Hoyer (Eds.), *Cerebral ischemia and dementia* (pp. 9–15). Berlin: Springer-Verlag.

Rorsman, B., Hagnell, O., & Lanke, J. (1986). Prevalence and incidence of senile and multi-infarct dementia in the Lundby study: A comparison between the time periods 1947–1957 and 1957–1972. *Neuropsychobiology, 15*, 122–129.

Roses, A. D., Strittmatter, W. J., Pericak-Vance, M. A., Corder, E. H., Saunders, A. M., & Schmechel, D. E. (1994). Clinical application of apolipoprotein E genotyping to Alzheimer's disease. *Lancet, 343*, 1564–1565.

Rubin, E. H. (1990). Psychopathology of senile dementia of the Alzheimer type. *Advances in Neurology, 51*, 53–59.

Salzman, C. (Ed.). (1992). *Clinical geriatric psychopharmacology* (2nd ed.). Baltimore: Williams & Wilkins.

Saunders, A. M., Strittmatter, W. J., Schmechel, D., St. George-Hyslop, P. H., Pericak-Vance, M. A., Joo, S. H., Rosi, B. L., Gusella, J. F., Crapper-MacLachlan, D. R., Alberts, M. J., Hulette, C., Crain, B., Goldgaber, D., & Roses, A. D. (1993). Association of apolipoprotein E allele 4 with late-onset familial and sporadic Alzheimer's disease. *Neurology, 43*, 1467–1472.

Schieber, F. (1992). Aging and the senses. In J. E. Birren, R. B. Sloane, & G. D. Cohen (Eds.), *Handbook of mental health and aging* (pp. 251–306). San Diego, CA: Academic Press.

Schultz, R., & Williamson, G. M. (1994). Health effects of caregiving: Prevalence of mental and physical illness in Alzheimer's caregivers. In E. Light, G. Niederehe, & B. D. Lebowitz (Eds.), *Stress effects on family caregivers of Alzheimer's patients* (pp. 38–63). New York: Springer.

Scogin, F. R. (1987). The concurrent validity of the Geriatric Depression Scale with depressed older adults. *Clinical Gerontologist, 7*, 23–31.

Scogin, F. R. (1994). Assessment of depression in older adults: A guide for practitioners. In M. Storandt & G. R. VandenBos (Eds.), *Neuropsychological assessment of dementia and depression in older adults: A clinician's guide* (pp. 61–80). Washington, DC: American Psychological Association.

Scogin, F. R., Hamblin, D., Beutler, L., & Corbishley, A. (1988). Reliability and validity of the short-form Beck Depression Inventory with older adults. *Journal of Clinical Psychology, 44*, 853–857.

Sheikh, J. I. (1991). Anxiety rating scales for the elderly. In C. Salzman & B. D. Lebowitz (Eds.), *Anxiety in the elderly* (pp. 251–260). New York: Springer.

Sheikh, J. I. (1994). Anxiety disorders. In C. E. Coffey & J. L. Cummings (Eds.), *Textbook of geriatric neuropsychiatry* (pp. 279–296). Washington, DC: American Psychiatric Press.

Sheikh, J. I., & Yesavage, J. A. (1986). Geriatric Depression Scale (GDS): Recent evidence and development of a shorter version. *Clinical Gerontologist, 5,* 165–173.

Shibayama, H., Kasahara, Y., & Kobayashi, H. (1986). Prevalence of dementia in a Japanese elderly population. *Acta Psychiatrica Scandinavica, 74,* 144–151.

Siegel, B., & Gershon, S. (1986). Dementia, depression, and pseudodementia. In H. J. Altman (Ed.), *Alzheimer's disease: Problems, prospects, and perspectives* (pp. 29–44). New York: Plenum.

Smith, G. C., & Whitbourne, S. K. (1990a). Validity of the Sheltered Care Environment Scale. *Psychology and Aging, 5,* 228–235.

Smith, G. C., & Whitbourne, S. K. (1990b). Validity of the Sheltered Care Environment Scale: Rejoinder to Lemke and Moos (1990). *Psychology and Aging, 5,* 572–573.

Smyer, M. A. (1988). The nursing home community. In M. A. Smyer, M. D. Cohn, & D. Brannon (Eds.), *Mental health consultation in nursing homes* (pp. 1–23). New York: New York University Press.

Snodgrass, J. G., & Corwin, J. (1988). Pragmatics of measuring recognition memory: Applications to dementia and amnesia. *Journal of Experimental Psychology: General, 117,* 34–50.

Spielberger, C. D. (1983). *Manual for the State–Trait Anxiety Inventory: STAI (Form Y).* Palo Alto, CA: Consulting Psychologists Press.

Spielberger, C. D., & Sydeman, S. J. (1994). State-Trait Anxiety Inventory and State-Trait Anger Expression Inventory. In M. E. Maruish (Ed.), *The use of psychological testing for treatment planning and outcome assessment* (pp. 292–321). Hillsdale, NJ: Erlbaum.

Spitzer, R. L., Williams, J. B. W., Gibbon, M., & First, M. B. (1990). *Structured clinical interview for DSM-III-R (SCID).* Washington, DC: American Psychiatric Press.

Stern, Y., Gurland, B., Tatemichi, T. K., Tang, M. X., Wilder, D., & Mayeux, R. (1994). Influence of education and occupation on the incidence of Alzheimer's disease. *Journal of the American Medical Association, 271,* 1004–1010.

Storandt, M. (1977). Age, ability level, and method of administering and scoring the WAIS. *Journal of Gerontology, 32,* 175–178.

Storandt, M. (1994). General principles of assessment of older adults. In M. Storandt & G. R. VandenBos (Eds.), *Neuropsychological assessment of dementia and depression in older adults: A clinician's guide* (pp. 7–32). Washington, DC: American Psychological Association.

Storandt, M., Botwinick, J., Danziger, W. L., Berg, L., & Hughes, C. P. (1984). Psychometric differentiation of mild senile dementia of the Alzheimer type. *Archives of Neurology, 41,* 497–499.

Strub, R. L., & Black, F. W. (1988). *Neurobehavioral disorders: A clinical approach.* Philadelphia: F. A. Davis.

Sultzer, D. L. (1994). Mental status examination. In C. E. Coffey & J. L. Cummings (Eds.), *Textbook of geriatric neuropsychiatry* (pp. 111–127). Washington, DC: American Psychiatric Press.

Teri, L., & Logsdon, R. G. (1992). The future of psychotherapy with older adults. *Psychotherapy, 29,* 81–87.

Teri, L., & McCurry, S. M. (1994). Psychosocial therapies. In C. E. Coffey & J. L. Cummings (Eds.), *Textbook of geriatric neuropsychiatry* (pp. 662–682). Washington, DC: American Psychiatric Press.

Teri, L., & Wagner, A. (1991). Assessment of depression in patients with Alzheimer's disease: Concordance among informants. *Psychology and Aging, 6,* 280–285.

Teri, L., & Wagner, A. (1992). Alzheimer's disease and depression. *Journal of Consulting and Clinical Psychology, 60,* 379–391.

Thal, L. J., Grundman, M., & Klauber, M. R. (1988). Dementia: Characteristics of a referral population and factors associated with progression. *Neurology, 38,* 1083–1090.

Thompson, L. W., Gallagher, D., Nies, G., & Epstein, D. (1983). Evaluation of the effectiveness of professionals and nonprofessionals as instructors of "coping with depression" classes for the elderly. *The Gerontologist, 23,* 390–396.

Tombaugh, T. N., & McIntyre, N. J. (1992). The Mini-Mental State Examination: A comprehensive review. *Journal of the American Geriatrics Society, 40,* 922–935.

Tomoeda, C. K., Bayles, K. A., Boone, D. R., Kaszniak, A. W., & Slauson, T. J. (1990). Speech rate and syntactic complexity effects on the auditory comprehension of Alzheimer patients. *Journal of Communication Disorders, 23,* 151–161.

Toseland, R. W., & Smith, G. C. (1990). Effectiveness of individual counseling by professional and peer helpers for family caregivers of the elderly. *Psychology and Aging, 5,* 256–263.

Uhlenhuth, E. H., Balter, M. B., Mellinger, G. D., Cisin, I. H., & Clinthorne, J. (1983). Symptom checklist syndromes in the general population. *Archives of General Psychiatry, 40,* 1167–1173.

Uhlmann, R. F., & Larson, E. B. (1991). Effect of education on the Mini-Mental State Examination as a screening test for dementia. *Journal of the American Geriatrics Society, 39,* 876–880.

Van Gorp., W. G., Satz, P., Kiersch, M. E., & Henry, R. (1986). Normative data on the Boston Naming Test for a group of normal older adults. *Journal of Clinical and Experimental Neuropsychology, 8,* 702–705.

Waxman, H. M., & Carner, E. A. (1984). Physicians' recognition, diagnosis, and treatment of mental disorders in elderly medical patients. *The Gerontologist, 24,* 593–597.

Wechsler, D. (1981). *Manual for the Wechsler Adult Intelligence Scale-Revised*. New York: Psychological Corporation.

Weingartner, H. (1986). Automatic and effort-demanding cognitive processes in depression. In L. W. Poon (Ed.), *Handbook for clinical memory assessment in older adults* (pp. 218–225). Washington, DC: American Psychological Association.

Weinstein, B. E., & Amsel, L. (1986). Hearing loss and senile dementia in the institutionalized elderly. *Clinical Gerontologist, 4*, 3–15.

Weiss, I. K., Nagel, C. L., & Aronson, M. K. (1986). Applicability of depression scales to the old old person. *Journal of the American Geriatrics Society, 34*, 215–218.

Welsh, K., Butters, N., Hughes, J., Mohs, R., & Heyman, A. (1991). Detection of abnormal memory decline in mild cases of Alzheimer's disease using CERAD neuropsychological measures. *Archives of Neurology, 48*, 278–281.

Welsh, K., Butters, N., Hughes, J., Mohs, R., & Heyman, A. (1992). Detection and staging of dementia in Alzheimer's disease: Use of the neuropsychological measures developed for the consortium to establish a registry for Alzheimer's disease. *Archives of Neurology, 49*, 448–452.

Wilkinson, R. T., & Allison, S. (1989). Age and simple reaction time: Decade differences for 5,325 subjects. *Journal of Gerontology: Psychological Sciences, 44*, P29–P35.

Williams, J. M. (1987). *Cognitive Behavior Rating Scales: Manual, research edition*. Odessa, FL: Psychological Assessment Resources.

Williams, J. M., Klein, K., Little, M., & Haban, G. (1986). Family observations of everyday cognitive impairment in dementia. *Archives of Clinical Neuropsychology, 1*, 103–109.

Wood, V., Wylie, M. L., & Scheafer, B. (1965). An analysis of a short self-report measure of life satisfaction: Correlation with rater judgments. *Journal of Gerontology, 24*, 465–471.

Yesavage, J. A. (1986). The use of self-rating depression scales in the elderly. In L. W. Poon (Ed.), *Handbook for clinical memory assessment of older adults* (pp. 213–217). Washington, DC: American Psychological Association.

Yesavage, J. A., Brink, T. L., Rose, T. L., Lum, O., Huang, V., Adey, M., & Leirer, O. (1983). Development and validation of a geriatric depression screening scale: A preliminary report. *Journal of Psychiatric Research, 17*, 37–49.

Yesavage, J. A., Rose, T. L., & Lapp, D. (1981). *Validity of the Geriatric Depression Scale in subjects with senile dementia*. Palo Alto, CA: Clinical Diagnostic and Rehabilitation Unit, Veterans Administration Medical Center.

Zarit, J. M. (1982). *Predictors of burden and distress for caregivers of senile dementia patients*. Unpublished doctoral dissertation, University of Southern California, Los Angeles.

Zarit, S. H., Eiler, J., & Hassinger, M. (1985). Clinical assessment. In J. E. Birren & K. W. Schaie (Eds.), *Handbook of the psychology of aging* (2nd ed., pp. 725-754). New York: Van Nostrand Reinhold.

Zarit, S. H., Orr, N. K., & Zarit, J. M. (1985). *The hidden victims of Alzheimer's disease: Families under stress*. New York: New York University Press.

Zarit, S. H., Reever, K. E., & Bach-Peterson, J. (1980). Relatives of the impaired elderly: Correlates of feelings of burden. *The Gerontologist, 20*, 649–655.

Zarit, S. H., Todd, P. A., & Zarit, J. M. (1986). Subjective burden of husbands and wives as caregivers: A longitudinal study. *The Gerontologist, 26*, 260–266.

Zec, R. F. (1993). Neuropsychological functioning in Alzheimer's disease. In R. W. Parks, R. F. Zec, & R. S. Wilson (Eds.), *Neuropsychology of Alzheimer's disease and other dementias* (pp. 3–80). New York: Oxford University Press.

Zung, W. W. K., & Zung, E. M. (1986). Use of the Zung Self-Rating Depression Scale in the elderly. *Clinical Gerontologist, 5*, 137–148.

9

THE MEDICAL CONTEXT OF PSYCHOTHERAPY WITH THE ELDERLY

WILLIAM E. HALEY

In this chapter, I examine the medical context of psychotherapy with the elderly patient. In my experience as a psychologist in a primary care geriatric medical clinic, I have found the variety of patients' cases, and the opportunity to collaborate with colleagues from other health care professions, to be both challenging and stimulating. Because the interaction of medical and psychological factors is often quite complex—as well as idiosyncratic to the specific disease picture and personality of the elderly patient—I start by presenting a case example to ground my subsequent, more general discussion in a real clinical context.

MEDICAL ISSUES AND PSYCHOTHERAPY: A CASE EXAMPLE

Mr. C. was an 88-year-old Black man who was referred from the gastroenterology department to the geriatrics clinic because of the patient's complaints of memory problems. The geriatrician saw the patient first, thought that he was depressed and not demented, and felt that he was a good candidate for psychotherapy for depression. Mr. C. then was interviewed by me and a psychology graduate student in the same clinic office where the physician saw him. Medical records stated that Mr. C. was in good health until 2 years ago, when he was diagnosed with gastric (stomach) cancer. At that time, a subtotal gastrectomy procedure was completed. At the time of his operation, Mr. C. weighed 185 lb (83.80 kg); at the time of the first geriatrics clinic visit, he weighed only 120 lb (54.36 kg) and appeared emaciated with his 6-ft 2-in. (1.88 m) frame. His medical records gave the additional diagnoses of functional diarrhea, postgastric surgery syndrome, dumping syndrome, and cataracts. His only medication was Imodium, which was taken 4 times daily.

Mr. C. had a medical chart about 6 in. (15.24 cm) thick. He had been followed at least every 3 months in the gastroenterology clinic and had been seen in several other medical clinics as well. His medical record included no previous psychiatric or psychological evaluation. Recent chart notes from the gastroenterology department showed that the physician felt that Mr. C. was currently doing well, which was defined as showing no evidence of recurrence of cancer on repeated medical tests and no further weight loss in the past year. The chart also included no mention (up until the recent evaluation by the geriatrician) of the patient's emotional state, cognitive functioning, or psychosocial issues. However, after our initial psychological evaluation, several important psychosocial problems became apparent. First, at the time of his hospitalization for his gastrectomy, the patient had been married for 15 years to his second wife. His first wife had died after 40 years of marriage, and his remarriage had been a disaster. The patient described his second wife as having been highly critical and constantly out to take his money. While he was in the hospital for his gastrectomy, this second wife attempted to remove all of the patient's funds from their bank account for her own use. After leaving the hospital, the patient separated from this wife and divorced her about 1 year later. Mr. C. was significantly depressed, best fitting criteria for adjustment disorder with depressed mood from the fourth edition of the *Diagnostic and Statistical Manual of Mental Disorders* (American Psychiatric Association, 1994). He did not appear demented; he gave accurate details about his medical and life circumstances, was fully oriented, and discussed subjective memory complaints common in depressed older patients (e.g., forgetting where he put his keys). Mr. C. was a highly religious man who felt guilty for what he considered as having had the poor judgment to marry this second wife and was preoccupied with anger at this woman, but he also felt that he should forgive her because of his religious faith. Mr. C. also had stopped attending church services because he had frequent and unpredictable diarrhea, up to 6 times per day. Thus, he rarely left his home and missed the social support of church and visiting other people. On interviewing the patient, it was clear that, despite several years of follow-up in the gastroenterology clinic, he did not fully understand the purpose of his medication and that he was not taking it as frequently as it had been prescribed. He was afraid that it would be harmful to him if he took too much medicine of any kind and averaged only two (rather than the prescribed four) doses per day. He attempted to follow a strict dietary regimen that he had been prescribed, but he did not really understand how this diet was supposed to control his diarrhea.

Because Mr. C. was seen in the primary care geriatric clinic, I was able to gain immediate consultation from the geriatrician, with whom I have collaborated with for years. She was able to explain to us (without medical jargon) that Mr. C.'s gastrectomy procedure had essentially removed most of his stomach; that careful dietary control of food and fluids could reduce the diarrhea symptoms; that his diarrhea could likely be better controlled through these dietary changes and taking four to six doses of his medication per day; and that this medication posed few risks for side effects or toxicity. The physician and psychologists were able to immediately present this patient with a treatment plan including education, dietary modification, medication, and brief psychotherapy as part of a total package to improve his well-being.

Mr. C. was seen in psychotherapy by a graduate student, who worked to help him to better understand his medical problems and to increase his compliance with the medication regimen. In addition, we targeted increasing his attendance at church and other pleasant activities and helping Mr. C. resolve his feelings about the conflicts he experienced with his second wife. After his first session, he showed immediate improvement in his compliance, diarrhea, activity level, and mood. Over several weeks of therapy, he enthusiastically came to his appointments with the psychologist and began to gain weight.

THE MEDICAL CONTEXT OF PSYCHOTHERAPY

This case illustrates five important points about the medical context of psychotherapy with the elderly. First, in older people, comorbidity of medical and psychological problems is common. Although the severity of medical conditions experienced by older patients can range from mild to severe and life threatening, most older adults have at least one chronic medical condition. Second, psychosocial and medical problems have a significant impact on each other. These reciprocal influences often operate in vicious circles, in which the medical problem exacerbates a psychological problem and vice versa. In the case of Mr. C., weight loss, stress and depression, and decreased levels of pleasurable activities were clearly closely linked.

A third point is that older patients typically present with psychological problems to medical rather than psychological settings. Mr. C. would never have considered scheduling an appointment to see a psychologist and would have strongly resisted any referral by his physician to be seen in a mental health setting. However, when approached properly in a medical setting, he engaged readily in a productive process of assessment and therapy. A fourth and related point is that many physicians are not well prepared to handle psychosocial problems in their patients or to identify common clinical problems such as depression and dementia in older adults. Mr. C.'s straightforward psychological problems, which were elicited readily during a 45-min interview, had not been identified by a series of health care professionals who, although highly competent in their specialty area (e.g., gastroenterology), failed to identify a key component of his problems. (Note that the geriatrician was an exception. This point is expanded on later.) Fifth, as a whole, psychologists and other psychotherapists are not well prepared to fully understand the complex, multiple medical problems with which older patients are likely to present. Mr. C.'s case was simple medically; he had only one major illness and one medication. However, few psychotherapists (including me) would be knowledgeable enough about this problem to fully appreciate the mechanism of his weight loss and diarrhea or would have been able to advise Mr. C. about how best to take his medications.

After presenting these five points in detail, I offer several recommendations to address these issues. Besides offering practical suggestions for psychotherapists who treat older patients, some implications for the way psychological services should be delivered to older patients, given the common medical context in which their problems present, are discussed.

Comorbidity of Psychological and Medical Problems

One of the most important ways that older people differ from younger people is the high prevalence of chronic illness among older adults. According to the 1989 National Health Interview Survey, arthritis affects nearly 50% of individuals over the age of 65 years, hypertension affects about 38%, and hearing impairments and heart disease each affect about 28% (U.S. Senate Special Committee on Aging, 1991). Among progressively older groups, percentages rise even higher. For example, among individuals over age 75, 55% have arthritis, 36% report hearing impairments, and 35% report heart disease (U.S. Senate Special Committee on Aging, 1991). Older patients commonly present with multiple chronic illnesses, complicating the medical management of their problems and requiring them to adhere to a complex regimen of medications and lifestyle changes.

Currently, the three leading causes of death in individuals over age 65 are heart disease, cancer, and stroke. These are all chronic diseases that, rather than leading to immediate death, generally result in years of progressive disability before death occurs. This represents a substantial change over the past century. In 1900, the major causes of death included acute diseases such as influenza, pneumonia, and gastritis. Few people survived to late life and experienced the chronic conditions that are common today.

Older people also use far more health services than younger people. For example, the average individual over the age of 65 filled about 15 prescriptions per year in 1987, compared with 3.8 prescriptions per year for individuals under age 65. In 1989, individuals over age 75 averaged 9.9 physician visits per year. The 12% of Americans over age 65 account for more than one third of total health care expenditures in the United States (U.S. Senate Special Committee on Aging, 1991).

Besides looking at rates of illness, functional impairment is another way of gauging the physical health of older adults. Among Americans over the age of 65 who are living in the community (not in institutions), 11.4% have impairment in at least one fundamental activity of daily living, such as bathing, dressing, or feeding, and these disabilities are more common in progressively older groups. Among individuals over the age of 85, 34.5% have difficulty with at least one activity of daily living. Many more older adults have impairments in one or more higher level instrumental activities of daily living, including problems in preparing meals, transportation, or managing finances (U.S. Senate Special Committee on Aging, 1991), with 56.8% of individuals over the age of 85 having at least one difficulty with an activity of daily living or an instrumental activity of daily living.

These figures describe the health of older people as a group. Not surprisingly, chronic illness and associated disability are associated with increased rates of depression. Studies that have examined the prevalence of psychological disorders in medical populations, or medical disorders among older people with depression, have found evidence for high levels of comorbidity. For example, Blazer's (1993) review suggests that up to 40% of older medical inpatients have significant depression and that diverse older medical populations such as patients with heart disease, cancer, and chronic pain have high rates of depression. These rates of depression are far higher than rates found in community surveys of older adults (see chapter 3 in this book).

Psychological and Medical Problems Affect Each Other

Medical and psychosocial problems have a substantial influence on each other. Irvine (1990) outlined a number of mechanisms through which psychosocial and medical problems commonly observed in older adults might influence each other. In one common circumstance, a complaint such as insomnia (which may be related to depression), if treated with a sedating tranquilizer, may place the patient at risk of subsequent delirium, a fall, and a hip fracture. Depression might affect recovery from a stroke by altering motivation for therapy and eliciting rejection from staff.

A number of researchers have reported that psychosocial variables affect recovery from a number of medical conditions. For example, Mossey, Knott, and Craik (1990) found that older people without significant depression were nine times more likely to regain full physical functioning after a hip fracture than were patients with persistent depression. Oxman, Freeman, and Manheimer (1995) found that lack of participation in social groups and low feelings of religious strength and comfort were risk factors for higher death rates after cardiac surgery in older adults.

Medication adherence also is a significant problem in individuals in all age groups. Psychological issues clearly are of great importance in adherence. Carney, Freedland, Eisen, Rich, and Jaffe (1995) found that depressed patients with coronary artery disease had lower levels of medication adherence. Older patients with undetected cognitive impairment are commonly given complex medication regimens that are far beyond their capacity to manage.

Some medical problems exert fairly clear, direct influences on psychological status. For example, patients with chronic obstructive pulmonary disease (emphysema), or congestive heart failure typically have low energy levels and have sleep disturbances related to their illness. Improved medical management can lead to rapid improvements in sleep and energy. Many medications also have psychological consequences, including sedation, or impairment of sexual functioning (Koenig & Blazer, 1990). In other cases, medical problems indirectly influence psychological adjustment. For example, a patient with heart disease may be afraid to engage in activity because of a fear that exertion will lead to another heart attack, or arthritis may make patients unable to participate in usual pleasurable activities. Psychological factors are often found to be more predictive of pain and functional impairment in older patients than are objective biomedical variables (e.g., Summers, Haley, Revelle, & Alarcon, 1988).

Psychological stress also can have direct effects on physical health. In particular, alterations of immune system regulation and cardiovascular reactivity are well-documented consequences of psychological stress (Adler & Matthews, 1994). These changes have implications for the onset and course of diverse disorders such as respiratory infections, hypertension, and cancer (Adler & Matthews, 1994).

Where Have All the Older Patients Gone?

Given these high rates of depression among older people with chronic medical problems and the prevalence of chronic disease in older adults, an important question is why these individuals do not typically present to psychotherapy settings. Epidemiological studies make it clear that by far the majority of Americans (young and old) with significant depression are likely to present their problems not to psychologists or other mental health professionals but to primary care physicians. For example, results from the Epidemiological Catchment Area Study show that Americans aged 65–74 years are five times more likely to tell a physician about a mental disorder than to present these symptoms to a mental health professional. Among those surveyed who were over the age of 75, none presented psychological symptoms to a mental health professional; instead, these symptoms were reported to physicians (Koenig & Blazer, 1990). Because of the stigma many Americans feel about admitting to a psychological problem and their fears and misconceptions about what a psychologist does, many patients present to their physicians with symptoms that include low energy, insomnia, and weight loss. Commonly, the patient presents distress in somatic terms and has little awareness of psychological symptoms (Katon, Kleinman, & Rosen, 1982). Somatization appears in many forms, which change with the patient's history and cultural and educational background (Shorter, 1992).

A patient seen through our geriatric medicine clinic provides a good example of this common process of somatization and denial of psychological symptoms. Mr. D. was a 71-year-old White man who was seen initially in the psychology department after referral for evaluation of possible depression by a medical resident who had rotated through geriatrics. This patient had had a coronary artery bypass graft 2 years previously, and had a history of two previous myocardial infarctions. His medical diagnoses included chronic atrial fibrillation, exertional angina, and congestive heart failure. Mr. D. was taking seven medications, primarily for his heart conditions.

When interviewed, this patient was somatically focused and minimized any psychological problems (e.g., he admitted feeling "down" only while he had been in the hospital and stated that his mood was fine when he felt well physically). Although he had given up nearly all activities, he felt that he was as active as possible given his health problems. His wife had taken over all of his usual chores, including care for a number of fruit and pecan trees that he had long enjoyed.

This patient was well-known by others on the geriatrics team, including a clinical pharmacist who had followed him for years in another clinic. The pharmacist noted that Mr. D. often appeared to be distressed and that he appeared to enjoy the close and overly solicitous attention of his wife, who reportedly constantly scolded him to avoid exerting himself. An interview with Mrs. D. confirmed this picture. The patient was depressed and inactive and appeared to enjoy supervising his wife's activities. Mr. D.'s physician felt that he was capable of much greater physical activity.

When the psychologist presented this patient with a treatment plan emphasizing increasing pleasurable activities, he was resistant and reiterated that he needed only medical care to improve his heart condition. He was advised that he should contact me in the future if he was interested in following through on our recommendations.

After about 6 months, the patient did initiate contact with me at the urging of his wife, physician, and pharmacist. He had become accustomed to seeing me in the medical clinic, and we had had several casual inter-actions, which seemed to make him more comfortable with the idea of seeing a psychologist. At this second appointment he was more forthcom-ing about how much he did miss his old activities, his fears about dying if he was too active, and the mixture of enjoyment and resentment he felt when his wife attempted to limit his activities. We were able to immedi-ately agree on two goals for psychotherapy: increasing his activities (within safe limits) and increasing his assertiveness with his wife. Over the next few months, Mr. D. gradually increased his walking tolerance from an ini-tial level of about a block to 1.5 miles (0.93 km). He also began being more active with his fruit trees and brought me fig preserves that he had picked and his wife had canned. He took pride in telling me that he was standing up to his wife when she told him to slow down. Mr. D. has remained active over a 4-year period, during which I have seen him monthly for brief supportive sessions and received numerous gifts of pre-serves and pecans.

Physicians as Providers of Psychological Services

Because of the recognition that many older patients present with complex, multiple medical problems and coexisting psychosocial problems, the medical specialty of geriatric medicine has been developed. Geriatri-cians have a clear philosophy of emphasizing comprehensive assessment and management of older patients, including attention to psychological issues (Besdine, 1988; Williams, 1994). In a recent study (Haley, Salzberg, & Barrett, 1993), physicians who headed geriatric medicine fellowship pro-grams were surveyed. Haley et al. found that geriatricians did indeed rate psychosocial problems as being extremely important in their older patients. These geriatricians also rated the value of psychologists in the care of older patients as high and stated that they felt that more than half of their older patients would benefit from psychological assessment or intervention. Ger-iatricians typically include assessment of older patients' cognitive and psy-chological functioning as a routine part of evaluations.

Despite these advances in geriatric medicine, the majority of physi-cians who see older patients are not specifically trained in geriatrics and not well prepared to handle the psychosocial problems of older patients. A number of studies have documented that primary care physicians fail to detect Alzheimer's disease and other dementias, in large part because of their failure to use standardized diagnostic criteria or formalized mental status examinations (Somerfield, Weisman, Ury, Chase, & Folstein, 1991). Studies also have shown that primary care physicians do a poor job of detecting and treating depression in older patients (Rapp & Davis, 1989; Rapp, Parisi, Walsh, & Wallace, 1988). Similarly, research shows that physicians in primary care usually do not make essential referrals for social services for the families of older patients (Haley, Clair, & Saulsberry, 1992).

Many primary care physicians do not have sufficient training or experience in the management of psychological problems, and other factors contribute to this failure of the medical system to adequately identify and address psychological disorders. Reimbursement is poor for physicians who spend the necessary time to elicit and fully evaluate psychological problems. Many patients who are excessively somatically focused also are found to resent any implication that their problems are in any way psychological and often resist referral to mental health professionals. When made, such referrals are commonly coached in an inappropriate manner, such as implying to the patient that their problem is "all in their head" rather than acknowledging the mutual influence of biomedical and psychosocial problems in the older person's well-being. Patients who present psychological distress to medical settings often use health care services excessively (Callahan, Hui, Nienaber, Musick, & Tierney, 1994).

Aggressive marketing of psychotropic medications by drug companies and unfounded biases toward medication are other factors decreasing referral for psychotherapy by physicians. As Barlow (1994) pointed out in a recent review, psychological interventions for depression show either comparable or better results when compared with antidepressant medications. However, practice guidelines for physicians emphasize medications as the first line of therapy. Antidepressant medications often are contraindicated for older patients with medical problems (Blazer, 1993). Physicians often have little experience with psychotherapy, may not be familiar with its effectiveness, and commonly do not have firsthand experience in which they see patients benefit from treatment.

Fortunately, there is evidence that physicians are aware of the need for greater attention to psychosocial problems in older patients (Williams & Connolly, 1990). In addition, physicians have been found to be highly receptive to behavioral interventions for older adults given the serious potential side effects of psychotropic drugs in older patients (Burgio, Sinnott, Janosky, & Hohman, 1992).

Psychologists' Knowledge About Medical Problems

Although there is little research on this topic, most psychologists and other mental health professionals appear to be poorly prepared to handle patients with comorbid medical problems in traditional practice settings. It is the rare psychologist or other psychotherapist who has sufficient training in the pathophysiology of disease, pharmacology, and geriatric medicine to fully understand the multiple and complex problems that commonly occur in older patients. Although with minimal training and experience psychologists can learn to understand common basic medical problems of older patients, numerous questions arise in evaluation and psychotherapy of older patients that depend on accurate assessment of the details of the patients' medical condition. For example, in an older patient with chronic obstructive pulmonary disease, the ability to interpret lung function tests will be informative about the functional capacity of an older patient and how much increased activity is likely to be realistic for the patient. Similarly, in patients with coronary heart disease, it will be difficult for the psychologist to gauge the extent to which increasing activity levels are dangerous for the patient as opposed to whether the patient might be capable of far greater activity. In older patients with cancer, an appreciation of the stage of their disease, and the likely prognosis of the patient, again is essential in planning psychotherapy. Medical findings also may point to the diagnosis of alcohol abuse in patients who deny such problems (Barry, 1993). It is likely that this problem also occurs for psychiatrists, many of whom do not have sufficient expertise in geriatric medical care to fully understand the complexities of these older patients.

In a recent study, James and Haley (1995) found evidence that psychologists have certain biases against people who are in poor health as potential patients. Psychologists drawn from the National Register of Health Service Providers in Psychology ($N = 371$) were asked to complete a number of ratings concerning four hypothetical patients: older and in good health, younger and in good health, older and in poor health, and younger and in poor health. Psychologists were more strongly affected by the patient's presentation with poor health than they were by the patient's age. Particularly noteworthy is that health status affected not only clinical variables such as prognosis but also biased ratings of personality characteristics, such that people in poor health were rated as being less cooperative, tolerant, and pleasant than those in good health. Psychologists also rated their subjective competence to successfully treat the patient as lower when the patient was described as in poor health. In this study, the patient was described as having only a single medical problem, far less impaired than many older people with multiple severe chronic illnesses. Similar biases are commonly found by other health care professionals, including physicians (Hall, Epstein, DeCiantis, & McNeil, 1993).

SUGGESTIONS FOR MANAGING OLDER PATIENTS

Two different perspectives are presented on what should be done to provide better psychological services to older people with comorbid medical and psychological problems. First, broader issues in the health care and mental health delivery systems, including ideas about how to alter the structure of typical service delivery to better meet the needs of older patients, are discussed. Second, practical clinical recommendations for adapting psychotherapy to the special needs of older patients with coexisting medical problems are described.

System Issues in Service Provision

One type of attempt to deal with these problems in service delivery to medically ill patients is to increase physician education about psychological disorders, including specific training in the detection of psychological disorders. In research studies, physicians have been shown to improve their detection and treatment of depression after training programs, particularly through systematic administration of brief screening inventories (e.g., Callahan, Hendrie, et al., 1994; Miller, Morley, Rubenstein, Pietruszka, & Strome, 1990). The practical clinical value of such efforts is unknown, however. One recent study indicated that such a program of physician education and screening for depression (which did not include recommending psychotherapy) led to more prescription of antidepressant medication treatment, but no change in actual levels of depression in older depressed patients treated in a medical setting (Callahan, Hendrie, et al., 1994). Given the numerous demands placed on primary care physicians and the time constraints of the typical office visit, it is probably unrealistic to expect better training of physicians alone to solve this problem.

At the practical clinical level, psychologists who are interested in serving older patients with medical problems will need to educate physicians about the benefits of referral for these problems. Many physicians, after having a successful experience with referral for psychological services, are grateful to the psychologist for helping them with some of the difficult problems that are encountered in general medical care. Primary care physicians often are less concerned with some of the "turf issues" that commonly occur in referrals between psychiatrists and psychologists. However, physicians need education in the tactful and appropriate way to introduce a psychological evaluation to the patient.

Psychologists who intend to deal with primary care physicians also must learn something about the culture of medicine. Physicians have different expectations than do psychologists about referrals, such as an expectation for feedback about the progress of a referral. Physicians also are much less interested in lengthy reports than psychologists and tend to prefer brief, practical reports and recommendations.

Another potential solution to the problems faced with older patients with coexisting medical and psychological services is for the psychologist to recommend that the older person have a physical examination as part of the evaluation process. In younger patients, such a recommendation is often made in a casual manner and has a low yield. In older patients, the common problem is that older patients have had numerous medical evaluations, but they may in fact be receiving inadequate diagnosis and treatment unless they are seen by a knowledgeable physician. For example, many physicians who are highly competent in a medical specialty area or in the general care of younger patients are not well informed about the management of older patients with complex multiple medical problems. Thus, the psychologist cannot be assured that just because the patient has had a medical evaluation, even by a well-respected physician, their geriatric medical concerns have been addressed adequately. One practical solution to this problem is for the psychologist to have a good working relationship with one or more physicians whom the psychologist has worked with closely and who can be trusted to properly evaluate the concerns of older patients. Although many physicians may have this capability, board-certified specialists in geriatric medicine are likely to be optimal for such comprehensive medical evaluation.

Another step that would improve treatment of older patients would be for psychologists to learn more about the medical problems of older patients. Some training in pathophysiology and pharmacology relevant to the problems of older patients, and clinical experience in medical settings, would make psychologists more knowledgeable about many of the common illnesses presenting in older patients. Psychologists have made important contributions toward the understanding of a number of diseases through research and clinical work in behavioral medicine (Blanchard, 1994), and clinical internships increasingly offer rotations in behavioral medicine. However, most of this work has been focused on intervention with patients with a single disorder rather than with multiple problems. Some of this knowledge can be picked up readily through brief clinical experience in geriatric settings (Haley & Gatz, 1995), particularly when interdisciplinary teams can model collaboration. Although psychologists hoping to educate themselves about geriatric medical issues will be unlikely to master knowledge about the full range of medical problems seen in older patients, they can be better prepared to communicate with health care providers and understand the psychosocial implications of disease.

A number of important basic principles about common medical problems in older patients are reviewed in several sources (Besdine, 1988; Williams, 1994). One important principle in geriatric medicine has to do with the importance of distinguishing between normal or usual aging, successful aging, and disease (Rowe & Kahn, 1987). Problems that are commonly attributed to "old age" may be the result of disease, and older people are at risk to not seek medical attention until disease is advanced (Williams, 1994). Contrary to stereotype, hypochondriasis does not increase with age (Costa & McCrae, 1985). Normal aging in the absence of disease generally leads to a reduction in reserve capacity in most organ systems, although such decrements are much smaller in individuals who age "successfully" through appropriate exercise, diet, and social support and engagement

(Rowe & Kahn, 1987). Another important principle is the altered presentation of disease in late life; for example, an older patient experiencing a myocardial infarction may present with confusion rather than chest pain (Haley & Dolce, 1986). It also is common for older patients to present with multiple chronic diseases; thus, the emphasis in geriatric medicine is on care for chronic disease, with a focus on patient functioning and well-being rather than on cure of disease (Williams, 1994).

Psychologists also can learn something about medications that are particularly problematic for use in older people, as a way of identifying medicines that can produce problems such as excessive sedation and delirium. Older patients often are increasingly sensitive to the effects of medications. The distribution of a drug may be altered because of the common loss of lean muscle mass and increased body fat found in older people. Altered hepatic (liver) and renal (kidney) functioning can reduce the clearance of drugs, leading to a longer half-life in the body and thus increasing concentrations of a drug in an older patient (Schwartz, 1994). Because older people are likely to be taking multiple medications, the potential for inappropriate drug prescription is higher (Wilcox, Himmelstein, & Woolhandler, 1994) and other problems such as drug interactions are increasingly likely (Gurwitz, 1994). However, given the common scenario of multiple illnesses and multiple medications in older patients, it will be unrealistic for most psychologists to expect to fully understand the effects of medications on their older patients, even with considerable training and experience in this area. Because older patients are much more vulnerable to serious side effects from psychotropic drugs, and psychotropic medications can interact in a dangerous manner with other medications taken by the patient, consultation with specialists in geriatric medicine will often provide optimal care for older patients.

One important alternative for the health care system to use in caring for older patients is the team approach. Geriatric teams have been developed for the optimal management of older patients with complex, multiple medical and psychosocial problems (Tsukuda, 1990). Within such a system, the psychologist can work in collaboration with a physician who is skilled in geriatric issues and other professionals, including nurses, social workers, and clinical pharmacists. There is considerable research evidence that comprehensive geriatric evaluation and treatment leads to better outcomes for frail older patients, including improved functional capacity and increased longevity (Thomas, Brahan, & Haywood, 1993). However, it would be expensive to provide every older adult with a full cadre of interdisciplinary assessments. Instead, it would be much more practical in many systems for psychologists to form collaborations or partnerships with physicians interested in geriatric care. At the clinical level, if the psychologist can arrange to see patients within the office medical setting, this adds a number of advantages to care delivery. The psychologist is seen as part of the medical team and gains from the tremendous status and esteem in which older patients often hold their physicians. Close contact between the physician and psychologist allows for ideal collaboration concerning the patient's medical and psychological problems. The more commonly used consultation model, in which physicians identify patients for referral to a mental health setting, suffers from several disadvantages. First, physicians may fail to identify appropriate referrals. Close consultative contact allows for mutual education and decreases problems in coordination of care. Because it is commonly found that less than 50% of older patients follow through on a recommendation for a mental health consultation (Callahan, Hendrie, et al., 1994), service in the medical clinic is more likely to reach patients who are in need.

Adapting Psychotherapy for the Medically Ill Patient

Although there is little research on the application of psychotherapy to older people with medical problems, I offer a number of suggestions based on the clinical literature and on clinical experience. For example, one issue that psychologists must learn to attend to in older patients in appropriately identifying and responding to hearing loss. Many older individuals suffer from presbycusis, an age-related hearing loss in which the higher pitches are not heard as well as lower pitches. One practical implication of this knowledge is that older patients with this type of hearing problem will do much better with an interviewer who pitches his or her voice low and who speaks directly in front of the patient so that lipreading cues can be used. Several psychology trainees who I have supervised could not at first be understood by their patients because of their habit of pitching their voice too high. These trainees learned to pitch their voices lower and to avoid the common problem of raising the pitch through increasing the volume of the voice, with dramatic improvement in their interviewing of older patients.

One essential point in the initial evaluation of a patient with a medical problem is that the psychologist should clearly explain the rationale for psychological evaluation. One common rationale to present is that when older people develop medical problems, many also develop psychological difficulties including anxiety, depression, or inability to carry out activities that they had previously enjoyed. Medical problems also can cause impairments in memory and thinking processes. Thus, a rationale is presented for why it would be important to inquire about psychological problems and to assess cognitive functioning. In the initial interview, it also is important to elicit the patient's perspective on his or her medical problems. If the psychologist jumps right into questions about psychological functioning, the real medical concerns of the patient will appear to be minimized to the patient. Thus, the psychologist should ask for patients to explain what kind of health problems they have and to allow the patients to explain in their words how they understand these problems. This is often informative: Many patients either fail to describe problems that are described in their medical record, have a poor understanding of the nature of their illness, or cannot accurately report on their medications or associated dietary regimens. Thus, the psychologist immediately gains some information about the patient's knowledge, competence, and compliance.

In medically ill populations, it is important to "normalize" the patient's concerns. For example, before asking questions about depression, the psychologist can preface the question with a statement that it is common for people who have medical problems to get sad or discouraged about these problems and to inquire whether this has happened to the patient. During the interview, the psychologist should be attentive to signs that the patient is resenting the personal line of inquiry and be prepared to explain the purpose of questions.

Even when the patient has considerable objective medical problems, the psychologist should not accept the notion that a poor quality of life, or depression, is inevitable given the medical circumstance. Many medically ill people who are limited in their physical activities are able to find important and valuable things in their life that give them enjoyment. In psychotherapy with the medically ill patient, a critical issue is identifying realistic activities and goals for the patient. The patient also must learn to live with limitations and to vary typical activities. For example, the older man who once enjoyed hunting and fishing may be unable to carry out these activities, but he may still be able to enjoy being outdoors or visiting with friends.

Coexisting medical and psychological problems present a number of potential complications to psychotherapy. For example, some patients will blame their psychological problems solely on their medical conditions and believe that further medical evaluation or intervention (such as surgery) is really needed. This is an instance in which the psychologist can be much more effective if he or she is in close collaboration with the patient's physician. It is extremely frustrating to the psychologist to be unsure about whether the patient's medical problems could in fact be given better attention, versus whether the patient is excessively somatically focused.

Psychotherapy with older patients also commonly involves some collaboration with family and other health care providers. Besides physicians, treatment goals can be carried out in collaboration with such professionals as dieticians, physical and occupational therapists, nurses, and social workers. Family members often provide essential care for frail older adults and may be essential in carrying out a treatment plan. Family members are at risk for depression themselves because of the demands of caregiving.

Conventional "boundaries" that are maintained by psychotherapists may be unnecessary and counterproductive when working with older patients with medical problems. For example, older patients who are frightened or in pain may be comforted by holding their hands. One psychology trainee who was working with an older patient with severe disabilities brought him small gifts and took him outdoors from the hospital for sessions; these steps allowed her to show him that her interest in him was sincere, and it presented him with much-needed opportunities for enjoyment.

Another important issue affecting psychotherapy with older patients is that facing the real possibility of death will be a common issue both for the patient and for the psychologist. Psychologists who work closely with medically ill older patients will have the experience of helping older people face their own death. Older patients also may unexpectedly die, which can be traumatic for the psychologist. Particularly when working in settings such as medical units of a hospital or nursing homes, patient death may be a common occurrence. Psychotherapy with dying patients can be gratifying and effective (e.g., Kastenbaum, 1992; Osterweis, Solomon, & Green, 1984; Worden, 1991) in helping the older person and his or her family deal with death, a fact of life faced by all older patients.

SUMMARY

Perhaps the most important way that psychotherapy with the elderly differs from psychotherapy with younger people is that significant health problems that interfere with daily activities are much more common in older adults. Understanding the health problems of older patients will be much more informative than knowing how old they are. Health problems are intimately connected with psychological functioning and vice versa. To provide optimal psychological services to older patients, psychologists must have a complete understanding of the medical context of their difficulties, which ideally can be done through collaboration with the patient's physician. Ultimately, such a change in the mindset of the psychologist—out of the traditional office and into the clinic—will have benefits not only for underserved older adults but also for a health care system that is inattentive to psychosocial issues (Gatz & Smyer, 1992). Finding creative mechanisms to reach older adults in the "front lines" of primary care potentially can provide greatly needed psychological services to a grossly underserved segment of the population.

REFERENCES

Adler, N., & Matthews, K. (1994). Health psychology: Why do some people get sick and some stay well? *Annual Review of Psychology, 45,* 229–259.

American Psychiatric Association. (1994). *Diagnostic and statistical manual of mental disorders* (4th ed.). Washington, DC: Author.

Barlow, D. H. (1994). Psychological interventions in the era of managed competition. *Clinical Psychology: Science and Practice, 1*, 109–122.

Barry, P. P. (1993). Chemical dependency. In W. R. Hazzard, E. L. Bierman, J. P. Blass, W. H. Ettinger, & J. B. Halter (Eds.), *Principles of geriatric medicine and gerontology* (3rd ed., pp. 1125–1130). New York: McGraw-Hill.

Besdine, R. W. (1988). Clinical approach to the elderly patient. In J. W. Rowe & R. W. Besdine (Eds.), *Geriatric medicine* (2nd ed., pp. 23–36). Boston: Little, Brown.

Blanchard, E. B. (1994). Behavioral medicine and health psychology. In A. E. Bergin & S. L. Garfield (Eds.), *Handbook of psychotherapy and behavior change* (4th ed., pp. 701–733). New York: Wiley.

Blazer, D. G. (1993). *Depression in late life* (2nd ed.). St. Louis, MO: Mosby.

Burgio, L. D., Sinnott, J., Janosky, J. E., & Hohman, M. J. (1992). Physicians' acceptance of behavioral treatments and pharmacotherapy for behavioral disturbance in older adults. *The Gerontologist, 32*, 546–551.

Callahan, C. M., Hendrie, H. C., Dittus, R. S., Brater, D. C., Hui, S. L., & Tierney, W. M. (1994). Improving treatment of late life depression in primary care: A randomized clinical trial. *Journal of the American Geriatrics Society, 42*, 839–846.

Callahan, C. M., Hui, S. L., Nienaber, N. A., Musick, B. S., & Tierney, W. M. (1994). Longitudinal study of depression and health services use among elderly primary care patients. *Journal of the American Geriatrics Society, 42*, 833–838.

Carney, R. M., Freedland, K. E., Eisen, S. A., Rich, M. W., & Jaffe, A. S. (1995). Major depression and medication adherence in elderly patients with coronary artery disease. *Health Psychology, 14*, 88–90.

Costa, P. T., & McCrae, R. R. (1985). Hypochondriasis, neuroticism, and aging: When are somatic complaints unfounded? *American Psychologist, 40*, 19–28.

Gatz, M., & Smyer, M. A. (1992). The mental health system and older adults in the 1990s. *American Psychologist, 47*, 741–751.

Gurwitz, J. H. (1994). Suboptimal medication use in the elderly: The tip of the iceberg. *Journal of the American Medical Association, 272*, 316–317.

Haley, W. E., Clair, J. M., & Saulsberry, K. (1992). Family caregiver satisfaction with medical care of their demented relatives. *The Gerontologist, 32*, 219–226.

Haley, W. E., & Dolce, J. J. (1986). Assessment and management of chronic pain in the elderly. *Clinical Gerontologist, 5*, 435–455.

Haley, W. E., & Gatz, M. (1995). Methods for attracting clinical psychology students to work in aging. In B. G. Knight, L. Teri, J. Santos, & P. Wohlford (Eds.), *Applying geropsychology to services for older adults: Implications for training and practice* (pp. 113–118). Washington, DC: American Psychological Association.

Haley, W. E., Salzberg, L. F., & Barrett, J. J. (1993). Psychologists in geriatric medicine: Results of a national survey. *Professional Psychology: Research and Practice, 24*, 491–499.

Hall, J. A., Epstein, A. M., DeCiantis, M. L., & McNeil, B. J. (1993). Physicians' liking for their patients: More evidence for the role of affect in medical care. *Health Psychology, 12*, 140–146.

Irvine, P. W. (1990). Patterns of disease: The challenge of multiple illnesses. In C. K. Cassel, D. E. Riesenberg, L. B. Sorensen, & J. R. Walsh (Eds.), *Geriatric medicine* (2nd ed., pp. 96–101). New York: Springer-Verlag.

James, J. W., & Haley, W. E. (1995). Age and health bias in practicing clinical psychologists. *Psychology and Aging, 10*, 610–616.

Kastenbaum, R. (1992). *The psychology of death* (2nd ed.). New York: Springer.

Katon, W., Kleinman, A., & Rosen, G. (1982). Depression and somatization: A review. *American Journal of Medicine, 72*, 127–135.

Koenig, H. G., & Blazer, D. G., II. (1990). Depression and other affective disorders. In C. K. Cassel, D. E. Riesenberg, L. B. Sorensen, & J. R. Walsh (Eds.), *Geriatric medicine* (2nd ed., pp. 473–490). New York: Springer-Verlag.

Miller, D. K., Morley, J. E., Rubenstein, L. Z., Pietruszka, F. M., & Strome, L. S. (1990). Formal geriatric assessment instruments and the care of older general medical outpatients. *Journal of the American Geriatrics Society, 38*, 645–651.

Mossey, J. M., Knott, K., & Craik, R. (1990). The effects of persistent depressive symptoms on hip fracture recovery. *Journal of Gerontology: Medical Sciences, 45*, 163–168.

Osterweis, M., Solomon, F., & Green, M. (1984). *Bereavement: Reactions, consequences, and care.* Washington, DC: National Academy Press.

Oxman, T. E., Freeman, D. H., & Manheimer, E. D. (1995). Lack of social participation or religious strength and comfort as risk factors for death after cardiac surgery in the elderly. *Psychosomatic Medicine, 57*, 5–15.

Rapp, S. R., & Davis, K. M. (1989). Geriatric depression: Physicians' knowledge, perceptions, and diagnostic practices. *The Gerontologist, 29*, 252–257.

Rapp, S. R., Parisi, S. P., Walsh, D. A., & Wallace, C. E. (1988). Detecting depression in elderly medical inpatients. *Journal of Consulting and Clinical Psychology, 56*, 509–513.

Rowe, J. W., & Kahn, R. L. (1987). Human aging: Usual and successful. *Science, 237*, 143–149.

Schwartz, J. B. (1994). Clinical pharmacology. In W. R. Hazzard, E. L. Bierman, J. P. Blass, W. H. Ettinger, & J. B. Halter (Eds.), *Principles of geriatric medicine and gerontology* (3rd ed., pp. 259–275). New York: McGraw-Hill.

Shorter, E. (1992). *From paralysis to fatigue: A history of psychosomatic illness in the modern era.* New York: Free Press.

Somerfield, M. R., Weisman, C. S., Ury, W., Chase, G. A., & Folstein, M. F. (1991). Physician practices in the diagnosis of dementing disorders. *Journal of the American Geriatrics Society, 39*, 172–175.

Summers, M. N., Haley, W. E., Revelle, J. D., & Alarcon, G. S. (1988). Radiographic assessment and psychological variables as predictors of pain and functional impairment in osteoarthritis of the knee or hip. *Arthritis and Rheumatism, 31,* 204–208.

Thomas, D. R., Brahan, R., & Haywood, B. P. (1993). Inpatient community-based geriatric assessment reduces subsequent mortality. *Journal of the American Geriatrics Society, 41,* 101–104.

Tsukuda, R. A. (1990). Interdisciplinary collaboration: Teamwork in geriatrics. In C. K. Cassel, D. E. Riesenberg, L. B. Sorensen, & J. R. Walsh (Eds.), *Geriatric medicine* (2nd ed., pp. 668–678). New York: Springer-Verlag.

U.S. Senate Special Committee on Aging, American Association of Retired Persons, Federal Council on the Aging, and U.S. Administration on Aging. (1991). *Aging America: Trends and projections.* Washington, DC: Department of Health and Human Services.

Wilcox, S. M., Himmelstein, D. U., & Woolhandler, S. (1994). Inappropriate drug prescribing for the community-dwelling elderly. *Journal of the American Medical Association, 272,* 292–296.

Williams, M. E. (1994). Clinical management of the elderly patient. In W. R. Hazzard, E. L. Bierman, J. P. Blass, W. H. Ettinger, & J. B. Halter (Eds.), *Principles of geriatric medicine and gerontology* (3rd ed., pp. 195–201). New York: McGraw-Hill.

Williams, M. E., & Connolly, N. K. (1990). What practicing physicians in North Carolina rate as their most challenging geriatric medicine concerns. *Journal of the American Geriatrics Society, 38,* 1230–1234.

Worden, J. W. (1991). *Grief counseling and grief therapy: A handbook for the mental health practitioner* (2nd ed.). New York: Springer.

10

PSYCHOLOGICAL INTERVENTIONS IN NURSING HOMES

CATHERINE SELTH SPAYD and MICHAEL A. SMYER

In this chapter we provide an introduction to the range of approaches psychologists may use in serving nursing home residents with mental illness. We begin by considering briefly a basic question: Why should psychologists worry about nursing homes at all? After sketching the need for mental health services in long-term care settings, we consider how to ply the psychologist's trade in such settings. Are adaptations of traditional service approaches necessary for successful work in nursing homes? Next, we consider the importance of "leveraging" psychological expertise in nursing homes. How can psychologists "extend" their skills by consulting with a range of participants in the setting? Finally, we consider the policy context that shapes the practice of psychology in nursing homes.

Case Example

A psychologist receives a referral from the physician at a nursing home where the psychologist consults. The note reads as follows: "Please have psychologist see him for sexual acting out."

Initial discussion with the day-shift nursing supervisor reveals the following details. Ralph Johnson is a 77-year-old retired mailman who has resided in the intermediate care section of the nursing home for 15 months. He was admitted from home because his wife was unable to care for him after he suffered two cardiovascular accidents (CVAs) over an 11-month period. Mrs. Johnson visits 1 or 2 times per week, always with their daughter, Elaine, because Mrs. Johnson does not drive.

Mr. Johnson's strokes have left him with residual right-sided weakness and somewhat slurred speech; the supervisor states that he is confused at times. Other medical problems include high blood pressure, for which he takes Capaten, and diabetes, which has been well controlled by diet until recently, when he began eating less well and losing weight. He has not been put on insulin. He also suffers from some arthritis and carries a diagnosis of "chronic anxiety," for which he takes Xanax. Ralph is able to walk with a walker, but he has been walking less and less over the past 7 months. The supervisor remembers that he was initially fairly active in the home's recreational activities program and assumes that he still attends programs regularly. He sleeps well and enjoys watching TV in his room and chatting with his one cognitively intact roommate.

Regarding the physician's referral, the supervisor states, "I really have no idea about that. We've never had any trouble with him. The nurses on the second shift got the doctor to write that order."

This case description illustrates the complexity of mental and physical health problems that nursing home residents face. Mr. Johnson was coping with the challenges of recovery from a stroke that had affected his physical capacity and orientation. His family struggled to provide care and now was searching for effective ways to be supportive while he was in the nursing home. The professional staff tried to communicate across disciplines (e.g., medicine, nursing, psychology) and across time (e.g., first shift, second shift). The referral also embodies the ambiguity of providing psychological consultation in this complex environment (Smyer, Cohn, & Brannon, 1988). For example, in Mr. Johnson's case, who is the client? How will success be defined? What is the role of the nursing assistant? What is the role of the supervisor? What are the most effective assessment and treatment strategies for the psychologist to undertake?

WHY WORRY ABOUT NURSING HOMES?

A senior colleague of ours once quipped, "Why worry about nursing homes anyway? Only 5% of the elderly are in them." Of course, she was right—partly. Only 5% of the elderly are in nursing homes at any one point in time. This cross-sectional view, however, sorely underestimates an individual's lifetime chances of using such a setting and the critical role that nursing homes have come to play as providers of mental health (as well as physical health) care for older adults.

Consider the work of Kemper and Murtaugh (1991). They estimated the likelihood of nursing home care. Basing their projections on a simulated cohort of individuals who turned 65 years of age in 1990, they estimated that 43% would use a nursing home sometime before they died. Of course, the likelihood increased with increasing age: 17% for those 65–74, 36% for those 75–84, and 60% for those 85–94. Nursing homes are therefore an integral part of older adults' health care experience, even if used only for short-term care (e.g., a 30-day intensive physical rehabilitation admission subsequent to hip fracture, or for IV therapy).

For psychologists, two other elements make nursing homes important practice settings: the high rates of mental disorders among their residents and the low rates of mental health service provision. For almost a decade, researchers have used national data sets to depict high rates of mental disorders among nursing home residents. For example, Goldman, Feder, and Scanlon (1986) estimated that there were 350,000 people in nursing homes in 1977 with primary or secondary diagnoses of mental illness. Using the 1985 National Nursing Home Survey, Burns et al. (1993) estimated that there were 275,000 nursing home residents with a mental illness. Comparable figures were reported using the National Medical Expenditure Survey of 1987, with 59% having some mental illness: twenty-nine percent of residents had dementia, 14% had dementia and other mental disorders, and 16% had other mental disorders (Lair & Lefkowitz, 1990).

These estimates were based on data gathered before the most recent major federal initiative aimed at improving the quality of care in nursing homes: the Nursing Home Reform Act, part of the Omnibus Budget Reconciliation Act (OBRA) of 1987 (Robinson, Haggard, & Rohrer, 1990; Rohrer, Robinson, & Haggard, 1990; Smyer, 1989). Through OBRA 87, Congress sought to improve the quality of care by requiring that all potential nursing home residents be screened to assess their need for mental health care. Early estimates suggested that a minority of elderly people with mental illness would be screened out because most residents with mental illness have a combination of mental and physical disorders that require both nursing care and mental health consultation (Freiman, Arons, Goldman, & Burns, 1990). Recent estimates suggest that nursing homes continue to treat older residents who are both mentally and physically ill, despite congressional efforts in OBRA 87 to shift some of that care elsewhere (Shea, Clark, & Smyer, 1995).

A minority of nursing home residents with mental illness receive mental health treatment, however. For example, Burns et al. (1993) found that fewer than 5% of mentally ill residents received mental health services in a month. Smyer, Shea, and Streit (1994) found that only 19% of residents with mental illness received mental health services at any time during their stay. Again, these trends have continued in the "post-OBRA 87 era": Five years after OBRA 87 was passed, 29% of nursing home residents with mental illness received service during the year. Fewer than 5% of these residents received services from psychologists (Shea et al., 1995).

With these trends of mental illness and inadequate service provision as a context, a recent national conference, Barriers to Mental Health Services for Nursing Home Residents, reached consensus on six general principles that should shape the development and provision of services in long-term care:

1. Mental health services are an essential component of nursing home residents' primary care.
2. Mental and physical health are integrally related, particularly for frail elders. Care for physical disorders and disabilities must be integrated with care for mental and behavioral problems.
3. Nursing homes must attend to the mental health needs of a variety of special populations, including persons with diagnosed acute depression and chronic schizophrenia, individuals without a psychiatric diagnosis but evidencing symptoms of mood problems, those with behaviors seen as problematic by the nursing home staff, those whose mental problems are caused by physical illness and medications, those with Alzheimer's disease or another dementia, and those with a history of chronic mental illness.
4. Each facility staff member should be trained, as appropriate, to either participate in providing mental health care or to help create an environment conducive to residents' mental health.
5. Families play an important role in treating residents' mental and behavioral symptoms and should be invited to participate in care planning.
6. The active involvement of mental health specialists in care planning as well as in direct treatment should be facilitated and encouraged (Lombardo, 1994; Lombardo, Fogel, Robinson, & Weiss, 1995).

These principles form a set of goals for psychologists and other mental health professionals to pursue. In the rest of this chapter we highlight different approaches to achieving better psychological services in nursing homes.

ADAPTATIONS OF TRADITIONAL PSYCHOLOGICAL SERVICES IN THE NURSING HOME SETTING

Many of the necessary adaptations of psychological services in the nursing home environment are simply extensions of concepts covered in other chapters in this book. That is, much of what the reader already has learned is applicable in this environment but more so; nursing home residents often feel more vulnerable, are more dependent, and are typically more depressed than elderly people in the community (Rovner, Kafanek, Filipp, Lucas, & Folstein, 1986). However, there are a number of particular modifications that facilitate psychological work in nursing home settings, as summarized below.

Location

Finding an optimal place for providing psychological services within the nursing home can be tricky. Typically, there are few private areas for confidential interventions. Most residents do not have private rooms; thus, if the resident is bedridden, it may be necessary to ask fellow roommates to leave the room to afford privacy for the session. At times, of course, this solution is not feasible, and a bed curtain may need to be drawn with somewhat lowered voices to offer at least some semblance of privacy. Other areas that may be able to provide a confidential setting include the nursing home chapel, a TV lounge, a doctor's examination room, a dentist office, a porch, the nursing supervisor's office, or a beauty shop. In summary, it often takes creativity to identify a private area. Once this area is identified, it also is helpful to post a "do not disturb" sign on the door or otherwise notify nursing staff not to intrude during the session.

Initial Evaluation

Once a referral is received, the psychologist's first step in a nursing home, as in other places, is to perform an initial clinical evaluation, or intake. It is recommended that a preprinted intake form, such as the sample nursing home intake form shown in Appendix A, be completed concurrently with the initial interview to expedite record-keeping time.

The first clinical evaluation should include the following steps:

- A thorough chart review must be completed, including review of medications, medical diagnoses, past psychiatric diagnoses or treatments, a psychosocial history that is often provided by social services, notes or attendance sheets regarding activities attendance, and several months' worth of nursing notes. Reviewing notes beginning several months prior to the referral problem offers a behavioral baseline of the resident's functioning. In reviewing this information, a background understanding of medical diagnoses and their psychological complications as well as the psychiatric side effects of various medications is helpful (see chapter 9 in this book for a more thorough review of these issues).

- A clinical interview of 30–45 min, if the resident is able to tolerate this length of time, is typically the next step in the evaluation process. In this interview, the psychologist should obtain a psychological history, the resident's perception of the presenting problem, other concerns he or she may have, some sense of how the resident spends his or her time in the nursing home, as well as a brief cognitive screening measure (e.g., the Mini-Mental State Examination; Folstein, Folstein, & McHugh, 1975), and a brief measure of emotional functioning (e.g., the Geriatric Depression Scale) if depression is suspected (Lesher, 1986; Yesavage et al., 1983; also see chapter 7 in this book for more detail regarding assessment issues). It often is helpful to ask "easier" or less threatening questions first, such as information about a resident's daily life, and to save queries about psychiatric history and the cognitive screening evaluation until the conclusion of the interview once therapeutic rapport is established.
- Next, it is often important to contact directly the resident's family in order to obtain their perspective on the resident's behavior and psychological functioning. Interesting confirmations or contradictions in information can be identified via this process, comparing the staff's, the family's, and the resident's own perception of his or her current situation. Collaboration with the home's social worker is important in establishing contact with the family.

However, the psychologist must obtain the resident's consent to consult with family member and other staff members (Moody, 1988). Ethical issues arise as psychologists try to balance a concern for the resident's autonomy and ability to control treatment decisions with a concern for protecting the residents and other residents from harm. In short, practice in this setting is at the intersection of ethical, legal, and moral issues (Appelbaum & Grisso, 1988; Kapp, 1988).

- The psychologist working in the nursing home setting needs to be particularly attuned to sensory and language impairments frequently encountered among nursing home residents. Often, nursing aides or other nursing staff are best equipped to give pointers or hints about how to communicate effectively with each resident.

Once this initial evaluation is completed, one can begin to formulate a treatment plan. In contrast to individual outpatient work, in the nursing home setting this plan must be coordinated with a wide variety of people and the consultant will likely need to educate not only the resident but his or her family and staff regarding the benefits of psychological intervention. Even if other staff are not requested to assist in carrying out the treatment plan, their understanding of the need for any type of psychological intervention will be helpful if the resident, for example, later questions its benefit.

Individual Psychotherapy

Although psychotherapy in nursing homes most resembles psychotherapy in other settings, some adaptations are necessary. First, it often is helpful to split therapy sessions into more frequent but briefer contacts for a number of reasons. Some residents' medical status or general physical debilitation lead them to become easily fatigued and therefore unable to focus necessary attention and thought on the therapeutic interaction for the traditional session length of 50 min or more. Physical pain associated with sitting erect and maintaining eye contact or even the effort of speaking for a lengthy interval when suffering from a pulmonary disorder are examples of medical conditions that may indicate that longer sessions are impractical. Additionally, some residents with cognitive impairments such as concentration deficits and memory loss may require more frequent and shorter sessions. For such individuals, twice-weekly, 25- to 30-minute sessions allow information to be presented more frequently and in closer proximity of time to promote greater retention over time. Also, a better sense of continuity and therapeutic rapport tend to be established using shorter but more frequent sessions with such residents.

Chapter 1 in this book, concerned with individual psychotherapeutic interventions with older adults, provides a sound overview of types of interventions that may be appropriate for older adults and common themes that arise in this therapeutic work (see also Knight, 1986). As with any population, the particular psychotherapeutic interventions used will be determined by the therapist's preference and expertise, matched with the patient's personality and intellectual characteristics and subsequent receptivity to that approach. With nursing home residents, the issue of the resident's cognitive functioning level is one such characteristic that must be considered when selecting a psychotherapeutic approach. Insight-oriented psychotherapy, for example, requires that the resident have good memory skills (to assimilate and integrate information discovered about oneself over a course of psychotherapy sessions) as well as good abstraction skills (to comprehend and mentally manipulate these complex data). Alternately, a problem-solving focus or here-and-now-focused interventions are more beneficial for residents with mild cognitive impairment who no longer have as good memory and abstraction skills. Residents with mild-to-moderate impairment also may benefit from structured behavioral interventions, whereas residents with severe impairment are likely not appropriate candidates for individual psychotherapy.

Therapeutic life review, first described by Butler (1963), is a specific psychotherapeutic intervention that is particularly beneficial to this population. A useful example is that of an elderly nursing home resident who had undergone bilateral below-knee amputations:

> Secondary to gangrene created by long-term diabetes and poor diabetic self-management, this resident had recently lost first one, then the second leg. He had become significantly depressed over the course of a 6-month period after the second amputation and was referred for the presenting problem of poor motivation to work productively in physical and occupational therapy sessions to learn adaptive ways of functioning from a wheelchair. After evaluation and initiation of individual psychotherapy for depression, the resident in an early session happened to mention his enjoyment of a previous occupation as a brickyard worker. He emphasized how much he had enjoyed working outside and the sense of productivity engendered by the physical labor of moving the bricks about. In response to a casual comment by the therapist regarding how interesting it was to hear about the resident's past occupation, he proceeded to launch into a longer description of several past jobs he had held. At the resident's initiative, this theme continued over a course of five or six additional therapy sessions. The resident, in effect, was conducting a self-initiated "life review" of his various colorful and interesting past occupations. The therapist did little to contribute to this process, but rather asked clarifying questions occasionally and reinforced the resident's descriptions of a hard-working attitude and behaviors over the course of his lifetime. On conclusion of this occupational life-review process, the patient expressed significant lifting of the depression, with demonstration of a brighter affect, less hopelessness, and otherwise general improvement of his depressive symptoms. A likely interpretation for this course of events was the particular benefit of life review and validation of the resident's valuable roles over a course of a lifetime now that he was no longer able, in the same way, to contribute "productively" to society. Once this validation was provided, the resident was more receptive to accepting adaptations in his lifestyle in order to remain active and self-directing.

Life-review techniques also may be woven into other psychotherapeutic techniques, often as initiated by the resident himself or herself, reflecting back on life's successes and disappointments. Although typically most beneficial when used with people with intact cognitive functioning, life review also can be helpful with some residents with mild impairment. With this subgroup, some factual details of past histories may be obviously inaccurate or may sound implausible. However, focusing on the underlying thematic issues raised can be helpful. For example, a resident may speak of his recently deceased wife as still alive and discuss how he misses her presence and supportive words. The therapist may choose to focus on encouraging the patient to discuss his marital history and relationship and avoid challenging him on the fact of her death.

Finally, it is vital that the psychologist practicing in the nursing home setting appreciate the flexibility required to work effectively in this setting. For example, the psychologist may identify the need to become a resident advocate, as suggested in the following case study:

> A nursing home resident was referred for clinical depression. Although the resident was clearly significantly depressed, on further investigation and psychotherapy with him, it became clear that his recently inserted tube feeding apparatus was the primary source of his depression. The resident felt he was no longer in control of his own food intake, and certainly this sense of helplessness contributed to his feeling of depression. On review of the chart, it was learned that the initial insertion of the feeding tube had been somewhat controversial and two different physicians had disagreed regarding its need. With the psychologist's encouragement, the resident eventually did insist on a third medical opinion, which clarified that the tube could be removed safely. When this removal was accomplished, the resident became significantly less depressed, more socially interactive and active, and exhibited greater vivacity and a willingness to engage in nursing home life.

The psychologist also can beneficially serve as "ghost writer" of a resident's life memoirs, consolidating and organizing the resident's stories of meaningful life events into a written narrative, or can facilitate a therapeutic intervention in which someone else performs this function. This intervention may be particularly helpful for a minimally depressed individual with, for example, an adjustment disorder to nursing home placement. These examples serve to underscore the general point that the psychologist in the nursing home will be called on to fulfill atypical roles and provide creative therapeutic techniques. He or she must be comfortable with such adaptations to the traditional 50-min talking therapy session, to be maximally effective, and to enjoy, rather than become frustrated by, working in this setting.

Group Psychotherapy

Group psychotherapy is a particularly helpful psychological intervention in the nursing home setting, and it is highly appropriate for this population (Brink, 1990). However, many practitioners and researchers in the field of geriatric mental health have suggested that it is inappropriate and ineffective to mix cognitive functioning levels within one psychotherapy group (e.g., Brink, 1990; MacLennan, Saul, & Weiner, 1988). That is, although psychotherapy groups can be designed for patients with varying levels of cognitive ability, it is best to keep these groups separate. Otherwise, lower functioning patients are unable to follow more complex conversation, whereas higher functioning patients may feel the therapist is being condescending.

Keeping this construct in mind, effective and beneficial psychotherapy groups can be led to the nursing home setting at a variety of levels with carefully selected group members. Traditional insight-oriented or group process work can be highly effective with the highest functioning residents. Other residents with early dementia and depression have been successfully grouped into a productive psychotherapy alliance using a more structured, psychoeducational group model. These groups are usually content specific, focusing on some specific mental health issue (e.g., coping with depression, improving memory skills, assertiveness training, anger management, etc.), and are led in an interactive "teacher–student" type format, with frequent opportunities for group discussions and expressions of mutual support. Residents often are more comfortable attending groups with such a clear focus, feeling less stigmatized than when attending an open psychotherapy group. Finally, the psychologist can, acting as a consultant, design and initiate other group therapy processes for individuals with cognitive impairment that may then be led on an ongoing basis by another nursing home staff member, such as the occupational therapist or recreational therapist. For example, using their theoretical knowledge base, psychologists can develop sensory stimulation groups that focus on activating all five senses via the use of concrete stimuli (e.g., songs, perfume, food, pictures, or other props) and promote positive social interaction skills in severely regressed older adults.

Group psychotherapy has several advantages over individual work with nursing home residents. First, group therapy allows an opportunity for appropriate, supportive interactions with peers that often is not otherwise found in the nursing home environment. Despite the concerted efforts of nursing homes activity therapy departments, many residents are resistant to joining in groups with their peers, fearing that they are the only "with it" (i.e., high-functioning) resident around. Group psychotherapy can allow residents to discover that other high-functioning peers also are "hiding in their rooms" and can be a support system for each other.

Group therapy also offers a model for peer-based reality testing. As any therapist doing group work knows, group psychotherapy participants typically respond better to being "called on an issue" or otherwise addressed regarding their misperceptions when such a challenge is issued by a peer.

Similarly, group psychotherapy provides positive role models of adaptive responses to aging. Just as group work with younger residents allows each resident to see how others are successfully coping with shared life issues, the same phenomenon occurs with older adults.

Group therapy also allows the resident to be an active, productive helper to others, a situation that rarely occurs in the nursing home environment. In fact, in many nursing home situations, residents are not permitted to physically "help" each other because of regulations and safety policies. However, the group therapy setting allows residents to provide emotional support and therefore to remain valuable members of their community. Additionally, the group therapy format allows the nursing home resident to give and receive mutual support to compensate for the loss of a previous support system. Professionals working in the nursing home setting will recognize the frequent resident comment that "all my friends are gone now." New relationships will not compensate fully for lifelong friendships that have ended because of death, retirement, or moving away. However, the group therapy situation allows residents to develop new friendships.

Finally, group psychotherapy discourages dependence on the therapist and instead promotes mutual interdependence on peers, a more natural, healthier support system. In addition, group therapy is an efficient use of the therapist's time. By reaching several residents at once, the therapist can "leverage" his or her time to meet more of the demand for mental health services.

Other issues frequently arise in applying group psychotherapy in the nursing home setting. Group work is typically ineffective for the socially withdrawn resident, who tends to fade into the corner when more active group members are participating. Although this concern must be considered in group psychotherapy with any age, there is a certain subset of older adults who tend to be more passive and withdrawn, secondary to depression, physical fatigue, and the effort of making a space for themselves in a group conversation. In particular, older people with communication difficulties such as hearing loss, expressive or receptive aphasia, or poor speech quality secondary to physical debilitation may be somewhat embarrassed or feel inadequate in expressing themselves in a group setting.

There also is a tendency within the group setting for residents to make superficial or polite conversation or to focus on somatic or other unproductive complaints (e.g., "the food tastes terrible here"). Again, although this tendency appears in groups of all ages, older individuals' lesser psychological sophistication and their less frequent experience with a group psychotherapy format tend to make this occurrence more likely. An effective group therapist, however, is typically able to overcome this initial tendency by repeatedly steering the group to more meaningful conversational topics.

Other modifications to the group psychotherapy process also are required in the nursing home setting. The group room must be a non-threatening, private, acoustically sound area, a set of criteria that are often difficult to accommodate in the nursing home setting. Additionally, the group room should not be too distant from the residents' living area to facilitate residents walking or being transported by wheelchair to and from the session. Hopefully, the nursing staff can assist in walking residents or pushing wheelchairs to the session. Second, it is possible to include hard-of-hearing people in the group with the help of the therapist. The use of inexpensive microphones, hearing amplification systems, and strategic resident placement are effective in this regard. It also is important to be aware of patients who have some type of secondary gain to an alleged or "selective" hearing loss and to gradually challenge patients on their hearing inconsistencies in the group setting. Thirdly, it is strongly recommended that psychotherapy groups be co-led with nursing home staff. This staffing configuration provides (a) a cotherapist, which is always helpful in a larger group setting; and (b) an individual who is more familiar with the nursing home routine, environment, and residents' recent life events within the home. Effective combinations of psychologist and nursing home staff members include a recreational therapist, social worker, or creative arts therapist. A music therapist, for example, can encourage verbal and nonverbal emotional experiences via musical lyrics and notes. The music also can be an effective conduit for residents' emotional expression as well as a sound source for "grounding" confused residents in reality.

PSYCHOLOGICAL CONSULTATION WITH NURSING HOME STAFF

In addition to working directly with residents, a significant percentage of the psychologist's time in nursing homes will be spent working with the staff. This situation occurs because of several unique features of the nursing home resident and his or her environment. Compared with the independent adult psychotherapy patient, the nursing home resident is, by definition, more dependent on others to fulfill his or her daily needs. Interactions with these caregivers have a great impact on the resident's day-to-day psychological well-being. The resident also resides in a large institution, the physical, regulatory, and social demands of which are inherently complex and difficult to negotiate. Helping the resident often requires assisting him or her to negotiate this environment, including its staff. Furthermore, residents with severe cognitive impairment, as noted earlier, will not likely benefit, if even recall, individual psychotherapeutic interventions offered once or twice weekly. Educating caregivers to provide psychologically supportive interventions on a day-to-day, and even minute-to-minute basis, clearly is a more effective way to help such residents. Finally, given the limited number of mental health professionals, and the great number of nursing home residents in need of psychological services, it is of practical benefit to train staff to become "extenders" of the psychologist's time and resources. In consulting with these staff members, it is important to understand nursing home staffing and organizational structure (Smyer et al., 1988). The following discussion identifies key personnel in the nursing home staffing structure and typical psychological consultation issues that arise with each group.

Nursing Staff

In nursing homes, "nurses run the show." Although registered nurses (RNs) often act as floor supervisors and are in positions of administrative authority, the nursing aide has the most resident contact and therefore is probably the person who has the most psychological impact on the resident. The nursing aide is both a resource for obtaining direct information regarding residents' behavior and the person who will likely carry out or (unintentionally or otherwise) sabotage the planned psychological intervention. Therefore, it is extremely important to emphasize the benefits to nursing aide staff members themselves when presenting a psychological intervention. For example, empathizing with staff that "it must feel terrible when Mr. Smith strikes out at you when you are trying to help him. That's a hard thing for anyone to deal with" can be both an empathic bond and a springboard to suggesting interventions to minimize Mr. Smith's aggression. The focus thus becomes not just helping the resident but, as important, helping staff manage that resident to minimize staff conflict and injury.

A particular difficulty in the nursing home setting is coordinating interventions between nursing shifts to provide consistent behavioral responses to residents' behaviors. For this reason, it is strongly advised that the psychologist directly meet with staff on all three shifts. When this is not feasible, calling into the third shift by telephone, or videotaping or audiotaping any presentation regarding a specialized treatment plan can be extremely effective. Not only is the psychologist's awareness of all three shifts emphasized by this strategy, but all nursing aide staff members are recognized as having important observations of and influences on the resident's behavior. An additional advantage of taping training is that not only off-shift, but also part-time, staff have consistent information that they can access any time they come to work.

Any written treatment plan must be clear, short, concrete, and direct if one truly wants the nursing aide, the primary caregiver, to read and understand it. Many nursing aides do not have a high school education and have significant difficulties reading. Foreign-born aides may not read any English. Therefore, it is typically most effective to review all interventions orally with staff and to use written plans as a backup for consistency in implementation over time. Similarly, psychological assessment reports should be brief, jargon-free, and emphasize the functional implications of one's test findings. For example, a neuropsychological assessment that examines attentional deficits may have the most practical significance if one can discuss a patient's anticipated length of attention span for a grooming activity. Similarly, if one subtype of memory is demonstrated to be more impaired than another, it may be important to point out to nursing staff that it is helpful to use pictorial cues rather than verbal prompts when attempting to remind a resident to wash his or her face each morning. Again, in addition to the written assessment report, it is essential to review findings directly with staff in simple terms.

In addition to eliciting the understanding and support of the nursing aide "line staff," one also must develop and review psychological interventions with the licensed practical nurse or RN who manages the unit and has administrative authority over the nursing aide staff. This nurse may be able to provide helpful insights into how to motivate his or her staff members and can, for example, assign particularly strong staff members to implement challenging behavioral interventions. The director of nursing or his or her assistant may be helpful facilitators when the psychologist encounters a particularly resistant nursing unit staff.

Comprehensive consultation with nursing staff is particularly important when behaviorally based psychological interventions are recommended (Smyer et al., 1988). A useful distinction here is between behavioral modification and environmental modification. We define behavioral modification strategies, also known as operant conditioning, as actual attempts to elicit the resident's modification of his or her own behavior in order to attain a reinforcer or avoid some type of aversive consequence. Environmental modification, on the other hand, is a term reserved for external (i.e., staff) interventions such as stimulus control and is designed to manage or alter the resident's behavior. This distinction is particularly important in the nursing home population, which includes a high percentage of adults with cognitive impairment. To expect the more severely impaired of these individuals to modify their own behaviors in anticipation of some subsequent consequence is unrealistic, when many times they would be unable to remember from occasion to occasion what the consequence would be. For these residents, environmental modification (i.e., altering the environment to elicit more appropriate behavior) is a more realistic and helpful intervention technique.

In one example, a psychologist worked with an elderly, highly demented, nursing home resident who had lost all impulse control and frequently attempted sexual activity with other male and female residents, staff members, and family members. The resident would wheel up to available candidates and attempt to unzip their pants, fondle them, or have them fondle him. When "counseled" regarding his behavior, even moments later, the resident would have no recall of the event, would express remorse, and would state his intention never to repeat his behavior, only for it to recur in subsequent moments. For this resident, the behavior management strategy of altering the environment to satisfy his sex drive without harming or threatening others was an effective technique. He was provided a stuffed dog, which he proceeded to hug, kiss, fondle, and lick in a manner that apparently satisfied his sexual impulses without harming other individuals.

Sometimes, however, more traditional behavioral modification techniques are appropriate in the nursing home. In particular, young-old residents with mental retardation or mild dementia are often referred for psychological intervention because of their exhibition of various inappropriate behaviors. For these individuals, a more straightforward behavioral approach can be helpful and should include the following initial steps: (a) accurately assessing and operationally defining targeted behaviors (e.g., Herman & Barnes, 1982) and (b) encouraging, persuading, and otherwise ensuring accurate staff documentation regarding the targeted behavior in a baseline condition and after the behavioral plan is enacted (Cohn, Smyer, & Horgas, 1994). In this effort, it is important to remember the staff understandably resist additional documentation. Therefore, documentation requests must be simple, not duplicate charting, and should use checklists or coding systems for various behaviors whenever possible. The less actual writing required of the nurse or nursing aide the better. Similarly, it is essential to clarify the ultimate value of the initially greater effort required in such behavioral assessments. Staff members will be more receptive to requests for additional documentation if they understand the long-term gains that will result.

As noted earlier, effective behavioral techniques include staff members' recommendations and input whenever possible. The approach should be spelled out simply in writing (see Appendix B for a sample behavioral plan), in direct meetings, and through frequent checks back with the direct line staff after the program is implemented. It also is helpful to discuss with nursing staff that behavioral interventions are necessarily a trial-and-error process and that changes to the initial plan will be necessary. Furthermore, it is important to predict to staff that the resident's targeted, maladaptive behavior will likely increase in frequency initially before extinguishing to prevent staff's premature rejection of the plan in the first few days. If this idea can be presented in a collaborative way (i.e., that the psychologist and staff are working together to develop the best plan possible), staff are typically receptive and more likely to accept changes in the program along the way (see also chapter 2 in this book, which addresses in detail modification of behavioral interventions for elderly patients).

A psychological intervention that is indirectly beneficial to residents by helping the larger nursing home community is to provide support groups for nursing staff, serving as their advocate or support group facilitator. Bereavement groups, for example, have been therapeutic in some nursing homes. In general, nursing home work is stressful for caregivers, and a high rate of "burnout" and subsequent turnover frequently results. If the psychologist can support nursing staff by providing them with a greater sense of well being and thereby promote better continuity of nursing personnel, residents certainly will benefit.

Attending Physician

The physician, although he or she often has infrequent resident contact, can be a useful support system to the psychologist in implementing interventions. When initially joining the nursing home team, the psychologist should arrange to meet at least with the physicians who provide medical care to a majority of the residents. One goal of this meeting is to educate the physician regarding the psychologist's role and the benefits of psychological interventions (including fewer telephone calls to the physician seeking psychiatric medication to manage the resident's behavior). Another goal might be to explore what level of input on the use of psychiatric medications the physician would find useful. Although the psychologist is not, of course, in the position to prescribe medications, he or she may still be of help to the physician by clarifying a psychiatric diagnosis (e.g., major depression) and suggesting a class of psychotropic medication to be considered (e.g., antidepressant). Many general practitioners appreciate the psychologist's honest and direct opinions regarding these issues. However, initial "permission" to address this somewhat sensitive issue can be helpful when approaching the topic later for specific residents.

Once the psychologist–physician alliance is established, the physician's inherent "clout" can be helpful. For example, if a consistent behavioral intervention is needed across shifts but is resisted by certain staff members, it is effective to request that the physician write an order for the intervention. Such a written order requires staff to follow that intervention or else complete an incident report to explain why they did not follow a doctor's order. For example, in one instance, a behavioral assessment strongly indicated that shaving was a clear and specific antecedent to physically aggressive behavior for a confused man. However, despite the psychologist's recommendation not to shave him, the nursing staff felt they were not adequately performing their duties if the resident was left scruffy and unshaven. Even emphasizing that their own physical safety could be augmented by not shaving him was ineffective in this case. However, a physician's order stating "do not shave patient" was effective in sparing these nurses unnecessary injury.

Furthermore, many physicians appreciate being contacted with results and recommendations regarding psychological findings rather than relying on written reports to communicate with them. This direct contact maximizes chances for physician agreement and follow-through on interventions requiring their participation, such as psychiatric medication usage or referral for psychiatric consultation. Again, initial clarification with the physician regarding his or her preference about such contacts can be invaluable.

Finally, the psychologist can suggest to the physician the need for psychiatric referral for appropriate medication management or inpatient psychiatric treatment when indicated. Staff members in the nursing home setting may not consider these more structured mental health interventions, but the physician typically will readily respond to the psychologist's recommendation for them.

Social Worker

The social worker, in his or her role as the resident's advocate, can often intervene with reluctant residents, family, or staff to promote a psychological intervention. As noted earlier, the social worker also is typically a good source of psychosocial information regarding the patient's lifelong functioning and family relationships. Social workers also usually appreciate being contacted as the intermediary in the psychologist's discussion with families because family liaison is one of their primary job roles. Depending on their training level and experience, social workers also may be appropriate providers of psychological interventions, such as supportive counseling. Indeed, master's-level clinical social workers may be uniquely qualified to provide family therapy sessions, as well as many of the interventions outlined in this chapter, and their expertise should certainly be respected and used.

Families

If such qualified clinical social workers are not available in the nursing home, however, the psychologist may be called on to provide family therapy, an area addressed in detail in chapter 6 in this book. In addition to more traditional family work, the psychologist also can provide helpful suggestions for family members' interventions with residents. Family members often have inadequate knowledge or skill in beneficially visiting a nursing home resident. Providing structured activities or encouraging the therapeutic recreation personnel to do so can promote enjoyable, thus potentially more frequent, family visits for these isolated older adults. For confused individuals, encouraging the family to record their visits, such as via use of a sign-in calendar or a picture board with photography that documents visits, can be particularly helpful in assuring the resident of ongoing family support. Similarly, requesting families to provide a photo album with captions labeling family members and the dates and occasions of special life events can be an effective intervention for residents with mild depression or mild dementia.

Another helpful family intervention is the development of a "simulated presence" audiotape (Gallagher-Thompson, 1994). In this intervention, family members are encouraged to describe, in an upbeat manner, recent or remote pleasant events that they shared with the resident (e.g., "Remember the time we went on the bus trip to Florida and it rained? But we enjoyed ourselves so much anyway"). These simulated presence tapes reassure residents of their family's interest and involvement when they are unable to visit, and, with residents with memory impairment, can be played over and over again without boredom setting in. Families are usually willing to be helpful to the resident in these concrete ways, appreciating the opportunity to help out with the his or her care.

Recreational Therapist

The recreational therapist is another useful ally, particularly in cases in which the psychological recommendations include increasing activity involvement. Telephoning or directly speaking with the recreational therapist about specific strategies and practical examples of how to engage a patient with dementia who has a poor attention span in activities is much appreciated and certainly benefits this resident in the long term. Similarly, a resident with depression may be helped by greater activities involvement but be reluctant to attend because of social withdrawal. This resident may be well served by a coordinated effort among the psychologist, recreational therapist, and nursing staff to develop a structured therapeutic activity program with gradually increasing intensity.

The psychologist also can serve as an advisor to develop effective psychosocial interventions, which are led by ongoing recreational therapy staff. Examples of this type of intervention are the sensory stimulation group, mentioned previously, and reminiscence therapy, a structured intervention for residents with mild dementia that focuses on eliciting memories of concrete life experiences while reinforcing reality orientation concepts. The psychologist may help develop a theoretical rationale for these groups and their initial design and may even co-lead a few groups with recreational therapy staff to model appropriate interventions, then allow staff to take over with periodic supervision of their efforts.

Another effective intervention is to provide recreational therapy staff education on various dementias and other psychological disturbances to facilitate their work with residents with such diagnoses. Particularly effective in this regard has been to provide staff copies of the Pleasant Event Schedule for Alzheimer's Disease (Teri & Logsdon, 1991). Recreational therapists report that this tool is helpful in developing practical ideas for simple activities that patients with dementia enjoy. This schedule often is completed using family members' identification of previously enjoyed activities (see chapter 2 in this book).

Administrator

The psychologist also can provide a unique perspective to nursing home administrative staff regarding policy changes or development via education "at the top" on various mental health issues. For example, encouraging or contributing to the development of an ethics committee, a suicide precautions policy and procedure, or similar systemswide mental health interventions may be effective preventive contributions. As another example, the psychologist might effectively persuade the administrator to minimize or eliminate "nursing rotation" scheduling, thereby maximizing continuity of resident care and a sense of stability and security for all residents of the home. Nursing home administrators also will likely be receptive to the psychologist's offers for general staff in-servicing on various topics of geropsychology, another preventive mental health technique and a way for the new consultant to promote himself or herself in the home.

Other Allies

Many nursing homes also have rehabilitation specialists such as occupational therapists, physical therapists, and speech pathologists, who can provide important information about residents' functional capacities. These consultants may be helpful in initial assessments and in carrying out interventions to promote residents' optimal independence, thereby promoting positive self-esteem and minimizing a physical sense of helplessness.

Security personnel, found in many larger facilities, can be a useful ally for the psychologist once they are convinced of their importance and influence on the resident's psychological well-being. The use of a security guard, for example, to enforce the consequence of removal of a resident from an area when he or she is physically disruptive protects nursing personnel and adds an element of authority by this uniformed individual's attendance at the scene. Security personnel also can be asked to talk with the resident about the unlawful nature and legal consequences of his or her behavior. These legal ramifications must be realistic (i.e., the local police will actually agree to charge a resident with assault, stealing, etc., with meaningful consequences, such as a fine or restitution, applied).

FINANCIAL ISSUES

Our final area of discussion is the practical issue of how the interventions outlined earlier are to be reimbursed. As elsewhere, psychological practice in the nursing home is shaped by the fiscal environment of federal and private insurance programs. The direct consumer costs of mental illness in 1985 (the most recent year with published estimates) were $42.5 billion, with $10.6 billion attributable to nursing home care (Rice, Kelman, & Miller, 1992). It is estimated that the direct costs had risen to $67 billion by 1990 (cited in National Advisory Mental Health Council, 1993).

Even when nursing homes are the only focus, the costs of mental health care are substantial. For example, Shea, Smyer, and Streit (1993) estimated that the cost of providing the mental health services mandated by OBRA 87 would be between $311 million and $1.34 billion per year depending on the definition of those in need and the form of service provision.

However, adequate funding for mental health services in nursing homes must depend on Medicare and Medicaid as the major sources of revenue. In their report from a national conference on barriers to care, Lombardo et al. (1995) summarized the need for improvement in this area:

> Medicare and Medicaid payment policies must be amended to provide adequate funding to support regular, ongoing visits of mental health professionals to nursing homes. For years, payments for mental health services under these programs have taken a low priority as compared with funding for general medical services. For example, Medicare typically reimburses 50 percent of approved rates for ambulatory mental health services compared to 80 to 100 percent for other medical services. Medicaid in most states also reimburses at relatively low rates for mental health services, and some states do not reimburse at all for some mental health services or for the services of mental health providers other than psychiatrists. The program's payments do not reflect the cost of caring for behavioral and mental health problems that occur in nursing homes. When per diem Medicaid rates for nursing homes are too low to cover all needed services, mental health services included or bundled into global rates are often never performed because of the lack of funds. Medicaid rates must no longer be set so low that it is difficult for staff to individualize care. (p. 187)

Recent revisions to Medicare reimbursement regulations have allowed psychologists and clinical social workers to be reimbursed as independent mental health practitioners for older adults. Medicare is thus likely to be the consultant's primary payment source for psychological interventions in nursing homes. It is therefore important to understand the Medicare program's operating mechanisms to successfully access these payments. Medicare, a federally funded program, is run under the auspices of the national Health Care Finance Administration (HCFA), which establishes federal policy regarding reimbursement for elderly people's medical and mental health care. However, local fiscal intermediaries (the insurance companies that process Medicare claims) interpret these policy decisions and operationally define them as various rules and guidelines that individual professionals must follow to receive payment for claims submitted to that intermediary. Each fiscal intermediary manages and interprets Medicare regulations regarding reimbursable psychological interventions somewhat differently. It is therefore advisable to contact one's local fiscal intermediary to be sure the complexities of Medicare billing are understood.

There are some general HCFA guidelines, however, of which it is important to remain aware. Medicare regulations, for example, require documentation of coordination of psychological services with the patient's attending physician unless the patient refuses such coordination. In the nursing home setting, it is advisable to obtain a routine physician's order for psychological intervention as a simple way to clarify and document physician acceptance of one's work.

Similarly, Medicare regulations do require that the provider routinely bill a patient for his or her copayment for each service, the portion of the bill that will not be reimbursed by Medicare. This copayment may be waived by the provider on an individual basis because of lack of patient finances; however, such a decision by the provider requires careful documentation of the financial justification to not attempt collection of the portion of the bill for which the resident is responsible. This awkward situation is further confused in the nursing home setting, where many residents have the nursing home accounting staff or family members serve as their representative payees. Thus, the resident himself or herself may not see the bill, yet one needs to negotiate with him or her regarding its payment. It is most helpful to discuss and decide this issue directly with the cognitively intact resident, document this decision, and then request his or her written permission to inform the payee of that decision. For confused residents, this initial discussion should be held with the resident's power of attorney, if one exists, or family members, when available. As with other populations, the therapist also must remain attuned to possible psychological meanings or interpretations residents may have regarding these financial negotiations.

Medicare categorization of psychological interventions does allow one to bill for a "short session" (of 20–30 min), which can be particularly helpful in providing the briefer but more frequent model of psychotherapy sessions mentioned earlier in this chapter.

Finally, Medicare regulations do not allow one to bill for some of the nontraditional services, discussed earlier, that the psychologist may feel are essential in providing quality psychological interventions in the nursing home. Extensive staff consultations, such as are required in behavioral modification programs, designing and establishing groups, staff support, and administrative guidance are not Medicare-reimbursable services. One may need to clarify and even negotiate understandings with one's local fiscal intermediary about allowable costs. Additionally, some nursing homes are receptive to paying the psychologist directly for needed psychological services; the homes then will bill Medicare themselves for allowable costs.

SUMMARY

Nursing homes are mental health and physical health care settings. Psychologists have a range of skills—assessment, therapy, and consultation—that can make important contributions to mental health treatment in nursing homes. Currently, however, psychologists are underrepresented in this setting.

In this chapter, we have outlined the need for psychological intervention and possible ways of adapting psychological techniques for use in nursing homes. The current national policy context may provide either incentives or barriers for service provision. However, the final determinant of psychologists' involvement in nursing homes will be the skills and motivation of the individual practitioner. It is essential that psychologists bring their skills to this mental health treatment setting.

REFERENCES

Appelbaum, P. S., & Grisso, T. (1988). Assessing patients' capacities to consent to treatment. *New England Journal of Medicine, 319,* 1635–1638.

Brink, T. L. (Ed.) (1990). Group therapy in the nursing home. *Clinical Gerontologist, 9,* 109–217.

Burns, B. J., Wagner, H. R., Taube, J. E., Magaziner, J., Permutt, T., & Landerman, L. R. (1993). Mental health service use by the elderly in nursing homes. *American Journal of Public Health, 83,* 331–337.

Butler, R. N. (1963). The life review: An interpretation of reminiscence in the aged. *Psychiatry, 26,* 65–76.

Cohn, M. D., Smyer, M. A., & Horgas, A. L. (1994). *The ABCs of behavior change: Skills for working with behavior problems in nursing homes.* State College, PA: Venture Publishing.

Folstein, M. F., Folstein, S. E., & McHugh, P. R. (1975). Mini-Mental State: A practical method for grading the cognitive state of patients for the clinician. *Journal of Psychiatric Research, 12*, 189–198.

Freiman, M. P., Arons, B. S., Goldman, H. H., & Burns, B. J. (1990). Nursing home reform and the mentally ill. *Health Affairs, 9*(4), 47–60.

Gallagher-Thompson, D. (1994, April). Short-term therapy for later life depression. Paper presented at the "Shades of Gray: Depression Among the Old and Frail" Conference, sponsored by the Philadelphia Geriatrics Center.

Goldman, H. H., Feder, J., & Scanlon, W. (1986). Chronic mental patients in nursing homes: Reexamining data from the national nursing home survey. *Hospital and Community Psychiatry, 37*, 269–272.

Herman, S., & Barnes, D. (1982). Behavioral assessments in geriatrics. In F. J. Keefe & J. A. Blumenthal (Eds.), *Assessment strategies in behavioral medicine* (pp. 473–507). New York: Grune & Stratton.

Kapp, M. B. (1988). Decision making by and for nursing home residents: A legal view. *Clinics in Geriatric Medicine, 4*(3), 667–679.

Kemper, P., & Murtaugh, C. M. (1991). Lifetime use of nursing home care. *New England Journal of Medicine, 324*, 595–600.

Knight, B. (1986). *Psychotherapy with older adults*. Beverly Hills, CA: Sage.

Lair, T., & Lefkowitz, D. (1990). Mental health and functional status of residents of nursing and personal care homes. *National Medical Expenditure Survey research finding 7* (DHHS Pub. No. PHS-90-3470). Rockville, MD: Agency for Health Care Policy and Research.

Lesher, E. L. (1986). Validation of the Geriatric Depression Scale among nursing home residents. *Clinical Gerontologist, 4*, 21–28.

Lombardo, N. E. (1994). *Barriers to mental health services for nursing home residents*. Washington, DC: American Association of Retired Persons.

Lombardo, N. B. E., Fogel, B. S., Robinson, G. K., & Weiss, H. P. (1995). Achieving mental health of nursing home residents: Overcoming barriers to mental health care. *Journal of Mental Health and Aging, 1*, 165–211.

MacLennan, B. W., Saul, S., & Weiner, M. B. (1988). Group psychotherapies for the elderly. *American Group Psychotherapy Association Monograph Series, 5*, 1–290.

Moody, H. R. (1988). From informed consent to negotiated consent. *The Gerontologist, 28*(Suppl.), 64–70.

National Advisory Mental Health Council. (1993). Health care reform for Americans with severe mental illnesses: Report of the National Advisory Mental Health Council. *American Journal of Psychiatry, 150*, 1447–1465.

Rice, D. P., Kelman, S., & Miller, L. S. (1992). The economic burden of mental illness. *Hospital and Community Psychiatry, 43*, 1227–1232.

Robinson, G. K., Haggard, L., & Rohrer, C. F. (1990). *Nursing home reform and its implications for mental health care*. Washington, DC: Mental Health Policy Resource Center.

Rohrer, C. F., Robinson, G. K., & Haggard, L. (1990). *Provisions of the Nursing Home Reform Act relevant to mental health care.* Washington, DC: Mental Health Policy Resource Center.

Rovner, B. W., Kafanek, S., Filipp, L., Lucas, M. J., & Folstein, M. F. (1986). Prevalence of mental illness in a community nursing home. *American Journal of Psychiatry, 143,* 1446–1449.

Shea, D. G., Clark, P., & Smyer, M. (1995, November). *Treatment of persons with a mental illness in nursing homes after OBRA 87.* Paper presented at the annual meeting of the Gerontological Society of America, Los Angeles, CA.

Shea, D. G., Smyer, M. A., & Streit, A. (1993). Mental health services for nursing home residents: What will it cost? *Journal of Mental Health Administration, 20,* 223–235.

Smyer, M. A. (1989). Nursing homes as a setting for psychological practice. *American Psychologist, 44,* 1307–1314.

Smyer, M. A., Cohn, M. D., & Brannon, D. (1988). *Mental health consultation in nursing homes.* New York: New York University Press.

Smyer, M. A., Shea, D. G., & Streit, A. (1994). The provision and use of mental health services in nursing homes: Results from the National Medical Expenditure Survey. *American Journal of Public Health, 84,* 284–287.

Teri, L., & Logsdon, R. (1991). Identifying pleasant activities for individuals with Alzheimer's disease: The Pleasant Events Schedule-AD. *The Gerontologist, 31,* 124–127.

Yesavage, J. A., Brink, T. L., Rose, T. L., Lum, O., Huang, V., Adey, M., & Leirer, V. O. (1983). Development and validation of a geriatric depression scale: A preliminary report. *Journal of Psychiatric Research, 17,* 37–49.

APPENDIX A
SAMPLE INTAKE FORM

Date of consultation: Age:

Referral question:

Chief complaint:

Initial impressions:

    Level of consciousness: Attitude toward interview:

    Unusual behaviors:

Emotional status:

    Affect:

    Mood:

    Symptoms of depression:

        Anxiety:
        Psychosis:
        Mania:
        Other psychiatric disturbance:

    Previous psychological and psychiatric history:

Cognitive status:

    Mini Mental State score:

    Deficits:

Psychosocial status:

    Marital status: Date of nursing home admission:

    Education:

    Employment history:

    Recreational activities:

    Social supports:

    Influence of religion:

    Previous or present history of drug or alcohol use:

Other observations:

Diagnostic impressions:

Therapeutic goals:

Psychology treatment plan:

                            _____   _____

                            Psychologist   Date

APPENDIX B
BEHAVIORAL TREATMENT PLAN

A. Rationale

This treatment plan is designed to provide a consistent staff approach to M. _____'s infrequent but disruptive verbal outbursts and physical aggression. The goal is to teach M. _____ that such behavior is inappropriate and has consequences. Similarly, appropriate (nondisruptive, nonaggressive) expressions of anger or distress have positive consequences.

B. Responsible staff

A-Wing nursing staff, all shifts

A-Wing activity worker

A-Wing social worker

Consulting psychologist

C. Targeted behaviors

1. Prolonged or highly offensive verbal abuse, including

   a. Yelling of more than a few words

   b. Threatening harm to another

   c. Repeated swearing

2. Any attempted or actual physical abuse toward any other person

D. Materials needed

1. Monthly activities/"Fifth Ward" calendar (in resident's possession; replacement obtained from Activities Dept. if lost)

2. Gold star stickers (at nursing station)

3. "Solutions" logbook (in resident's possession; spare at nursing station)

E. Behavioral approach

1. Appropriate behavior equals verbal praise, daily star, restaurant outing with activities staff every 2 weeks:

   a. Before bedtime, second-shift nursing staff will praise the resident if only appropriate behavior (calm, controlled handling of upsets or no upsets) has been exhibited that day. Identify the appropriate behavior and the positive reinforcer earned (e.g., I noticed how calm you were today—you did a good job" or "I was pleased with the way you controlled your anger at _____ today—you handled that problem well. Here's a star for your calendar; only _____ more days (14 in a row) until you get to go out with Shirley for a meal!"

b. Encourage the resident to use her "Solutions" logbook to deal with her distress. When she is calm, offer her some time to talk about the issue and listen supportively.

c. All staff will remind the resident of these techniques and encourage, then praise, her use of them when she is angry.

F. Staff training

1. The consulting psychologist will train all staff in the above plan and will review it with the resident. She also will monitor its effectiveness over time in decreasing abusive behaviors.

G. Documentation

1. Nursing staff will document all incidents of inappropriate behavior (prolonged or offensive verbal abuse and any attempted or actual physical abuse) in nursing notes. Each lost star incident should have corresponding documentation in nursing notes.

2. Each evening the assigned nurse will document receipt or denial of daily star on the Behavioral Treatment Plan Documentation Form (see Appendix C).

3. For each outing, the assigned activities worker will document the one-on-one outing provided to the resident.

APPENDIX C
BEHAVIORAL TREATMENT PLAN DOCUMENTATION FORM

Targeted behaviors (= loss of daily star)

1. Prolonged or highly offensive verbal abuse, after one warning
2. Any attempted or actual physical abuse (no warning given)

All other behaviors (= daily star placed on resident's activity calendar, before bed, by nurse)

Date	Check one:		14 consecutive stars = outing earned	Staff initials
	Star given	Star lost		

Note. To be used with the behavioral treatment plan (see Appendix B).

11

ETHICAL CONSIDERATIONS IN THE TREATMENT OF OLDER ADULTS

JUDY M. ZARIT and STEVEN H. ZARIT

The practice of psychotherapy continuously raises a myriad of ethical issues. As they do when working with younger clients, psychologists need to place treatment with older people within the framework of ethical principles and the code of conduct that has been developed to guide the profession (American Psychological Association [APA], 1992). A theme of the chapters in this book has been that psychotherapy with older clients is often highly similar to that with other adult clients but that sometimes different issues or processes are involved. The same tenet holds for ethical matters. All of the varied ethical dilemmas that arise with younger clients also arise with older clients, but some concerns are more frequently encountered or require special deliberation that goes beyond standard training in ethical conduct.

For the purposes of this chapter, we have chosen the two most frequently encountered ethical dilemmas in a geriatric practice: confidentiality and end-of-life issues. In both instances, the competency of the identified client can be in question, and the clinician often finds himself or herself doing a difficult balancing act between representing the client's wishes and working with the family or with other health care providers, whose interests or desires may be much different. The challenge in these situations is to uphold the ethical standards set out by the APA. These standards are built on a foundation of six general principles: competence, integrity, professional and scientific responsibility, respect for people's rights and dignity, concern for others' welfare, and social responsibility (APA, 1992). Our goal is to examine how these established ethical standards can be applied to the complex situations that can be encountered with older clients around confidentiality and at the end of life.

CONFIDENTIALITY

In a geriatric practice, there are many potential threats to confidentiality. Confidentiality can be differentially affected by the client's living situation (independent community dwelling, assisted living, nursing home, hospital), by the nature of the psychological problem (functional vs. organic), and by whether family members are involved in the therapy. Furthermore, there is a much higher incidence of concurrent medical treatment with older than younger clients, which requires frequent consultation between the psychologist and a variety of physicians. Because there are such important differences in the kind of confidentiality issues that arise, depending on the setting in which the older person lives, we have organized our discussion according to place of residence, whether people live independently in the community, in assisted-living settings, or in an institution.

Older People Living in the Community

When working with older adults who live independently in the community, confidentiality issues are generally the same as they would be for a younger client, provided that the diagnosis is functional in nature. In other words, the depressed older person is entitled to the same confidentiality as any other client. For example, if a concerned son or daughter calls about his or her mother who is in treatment, a release must be obtained from the client before a conversation with her children can take place. A decision will have to be made with the client whether to allow unlimited consultation with family members or to confine the communication to specific domains.

Family members are much more likely to contact therapists about elderly clients than in a general adult practice, as are neighbors and other interested community members, so a well-thought out response when calls arise is essential. When an unexpected call occurs, the best tactic is to listen to the information being given without divulging whether the person is in one's care, then advise the caller that he or she may wish to raise this concern with the person and that any professional who is involved with that person will need a signed release to communicate directly with the caller. This tactic allows the clinician to assess whether there is a dangerous situation without compromising the client's confidentiality.

The psychologist's dilemma then becomes how he or she uses that information. Of course, if the situation involves imminent danger to one's client or other people, confidentiality is no longer an issue. In other situations, the clinician may judge that it is in the client's best interest to talk with the caller. The therapist must then find a way to steer the client toward the information, hopefully resulting in a signed release. The Ethical Principles of Psychologists and Code of Conduct (APA, 1992), especially the specific tenets regarding confidentiality, should guide all such decision making.

The situation is slightly different when the client either has been referred for evaluation of an organic impairment or a dementing illness (Alzheimer's disease, vascular dementia, or some other memory impairment) is known to be present. It usually is critical to coordinate this kind of assessment with the client's physician and to exchange information that can clarify the diagnosis. If a power of attorney (POA) for health care has been executed by someone other than the client, releases to obtain information from or to send reports to physicians or other professionals must be signed by that person. This is one of the most troubling of situations for therapists, particularly because many patients with dementia retain some awareness of their intellectual deficits. When the clinician's observations in the initial interview lead to the opinion that the patient retains some capacity for decision making, it is also advisable to obtain signed releases from the patient, even though they may not be considered legally binding in the face of the POA. (Guardianship is used rarely as a legal device for older people with compromised intellectual functioning; a POA is the most typical way this situation is handled, but clinicians need to be aware of the specific legal mechanisms available in the state in which they practice. Usually, a POA must be specific for health care. Someone with the POA to manage finances is not automatically permitted to take over management of health affairs.)

A common dilemma for clinicians arises when a client has been referred for an initial evaluation of memory impairment and competency has been found to be significantly compromised, yet no POA exists. Some clients in those circumstances will willingly sign releases to allow the psychologist to talk with their physician when their specific purpose is explained to them. Others may not be willing to sign releases at all. If a client is reluctant to sign a release to his or her primary physician on an initial visit, it is advisable to develop a therapeutic relationship and then reintroduce the release when some trust has been established.

One way to circumvent this problem is to include in intake documents a release of information based on Medicare's requirement that psychologists must offer to consult with the primary physician at the onset of treatment. It is often that same physician who has referred the client, but a signed release is still mandated. An example of this release is shown in Exhibit 1. This release, of course, does not resolve the problem of sharing information with the family, which can be done only with the client's consent. In almost all cases, however, that will not be a problem and clients will give permission to talk with their family. Information should be shared with the family only when it is relevant and in the client's best interests (e.g., when the family is providing care for the client and the results of an assessment will help them plan how to do that more effectively).

A tricky ethical dilemma is whether a release signed by someone who is believed to be incompetent is valid. From a legal perspective, until an individual has been declared legally incompetent, which requires a court

EXHIBIT 1

Sample Release-of-Information Form

Medicare Consultation Release

It may be beneficial for me to contact your primary care physician regarding your psychological treatment or to discuss any medical problems for which you are receiving treatment. In addition, Medicare requires that I notify your physician, by telephone or in writing, concerning services that are being provided by me unless you request that notification not be made.

Please check one of the following:

_____ You are authorized to contact my primary care physician, whose name and address are shown below, to discuss the treatment that I am receiving while under your care and to obtain information concerning my medical diagnosis and treatment.

_____ I do not authorize you to contact my primary care physician with regard to the treatment that I am receiving while under your care or to obtain information concerning my medical diagnosis and treatment. I am providing you with the name and address of my primary care physician only for your records.

_____

Signature and date

---

appearance, they are considered competent. That does not, however, relieve clinicians of their obligation to weigh conflicting ethical concerns. The decision to obtain a consent to release information from a client with questionable competency must be based on the evaluation that doing so is in the client's best interest. This problem fortunately occurs only rarely in practice. Instead, individuals usually have been encouraged to sign POAs by physicians and attorneys while they are still (sometimes marginally) competent. We should add that a finding of dementia or other type of cognitive deficit does not necessarily mean an individual is no longer legally competent. Rather, competency depends on understanding the specific issues involved, in this case, giving consent for release of information (see Grisso, 1994).

The following example indicates the kind of complications that can arise regarding confidentiality when several members of a family are involved.

> The initial contact was made by John K., a 48-year-old attorney who had POA for his father, Harry, who had developed clear organic impairment following open-heart surgery. Although the main focus was on his father, John requested help for both of his parents. He had observed that his mother, Mary, was not coping well with his father's impairments. The initial evaluation was made on the father, although the mother (who also had POA for her husband) was present. That was done because Mary did not consider herself in need of any help, but simply wanted her husband restored to his former self. From a practical perspective, beginning with an assessment of Harry would clarify the extent of his deficits and the kinds of problems his wife had to cope with. As often happens in caregiving situations, Mary could then be brought into treatment as the focus shifted from finding out what was wrong to identifying what the family could do to manage these problems more effectively. Mary signed consent forms for communication about her husband to be freely shared with her son and all of the physicians involved in her husband's care.
>
> After a few visits, John called and wanted a summary of the treatment. Because a release had been signed by his mother to discuss his father, this was done. However, in the course of that conversation, it became clear that he wanted to talk as much about his mother's functioning as he did about his father's. He expressed concern that she was becoming overwhelmed by having to care for her husband and that she was behaving oddly (e.g., kicking her husband under the table if he said something she objected to). As it became apparent that the focus of the discussion was now going to shift from the father to the mother, it was necessary to obtain a release from her. Through the process of assessment of her husband, Mary had become engaged in trying to understand his difficulties and her reactions to them. At this point, she was eager for open communication among everyone and

gave the release for the therapist to talk with her son. This step became important later when a decision had to be made to place Harry in a nursing facility, which required many conversations with John about what would be in both Harry's and Mary's best interest.

In general, if the clinician anticipates a need to speak with family members, it is wise to obtain releases early in treatment. When dealing with a frail older person, questions about moving to a more protective setting are common, and families are naturally going to want to be involved in that decision making. The therapist can be helpful in this situation because the family often turns to him or her for an expert opinion in choosing among the options available to them. The therapist also can ensure that the client's best interests are taken into account rather than letting the decision be made by the most forceful person in the family. Institutionalization can occur prematurely (i.e., before the older person needs or wants to move to a protected setting). In other situations, however, institutionalization can be a preferred alternative to a deteriorating or unsafe home setting.

That example raises another issue. It is preferable that therapists do not treat more than one person in a family, except when explicitly conducting marital or family therapy. With older clients, however, there are special circumstances in which one therapist will be involved with two or more family members. These situations typically involve dementia and other chronic disabilities. Issues that may be discussed include arranging and coordinating care for the person with the disability, making long-term plans for care, and the impact that the disability has on the primary caregiver and other family members. The use of multiple therapists in that situation would unnecessarily complicate the treatment process for the family.

The therapist who is seeing multiple family members must take steps to avoid the pitfalls inherent in this type of arrangement. The therapist must consider whether he or she can take a position that is in everyone's best interests. That may require being able to reconcile different viewpoints about issues such as placement. The therapist also must be sure not to reveal anything said to him or her in confidence by one family member to anyone else in the family. In general, tactfulness and respect for each person's opinions are critical in this situation. Although the communications can become complicated, it remains preferable to channel everything through a single therapist than to add more specialists to a situation in which the family already is overburdened with doctors. Of course, the usual constraints about seeing more than one person in a family would apply when treating an older person who functions independently.

Older People in Assisted-Living Situations

When one's client lives in an assisted-living situation, confidentiality issues can become tricky. Many different types of specialized housing are available to older people, which provide assistance when they are not able to function independently. Assisted living usually implies that the person has relinquished control over certain aspects of daily living, such as meals, housekeeping, bathing, or the administration of medication. In its simplest form, assisted living may be a board-and-care facility, boarding home, or residential hotel. In some states, retirement hotels and residences that previously catered to the well elderly are adding services so that people can remain in the facility despite declining functioning. Services will vary as will cost. In a more formalized "personal care residence," there will be nursing care available, although it is not usually routinely provided. These facilities differ, however, from nursing homes, which are licensed and regulated as medical facilities, and in which different rules for confidentiality apply.

Residents of assisted-living facilities also vary considerably in their functioning. Some may be fully competent and seek out a therapist. Or they may be physically or intellectually compromised. The referral may come from the client, their family, their physician, a community agency, or the facility.

Consistent with the APA's Ethical Principles, it is best to limit the transmission of information to the least number of people who need to know and whatever is in the best interest of the client. Although some facilities keep a chart that resembles exactly a nursing home or hospital chart, the psychologist is under no obligation to write confidential information in the chart. It is advisable for therapists to keep all records confidential, as would be done with any other client. A self-referred client should be asked whether he or she wants the primary physician kept informed and a release either signed or denied. Beyond that, the only time the facility needs to know about therapy is in a situation of dangerousness or whether competency becomes an issue. When the family requests treatment, an assessment should be made as to whether the family should be involved in treatment and whether it is in the client's best interest for the therapist to stay in communication with the family. In either case, releases must be signed to allow free exchanges of information. Occasionally, a physician will refer a client who does not have any identified family members. Again, if the client is competent, the only release necessary is for the physician. However, if the client is not competent, it may be necessary to communicate with the facility to determine whether the client has or needs the involvement of a geriatric case manager or if the Area Agency on Aging or other appropriate public agency could assume guardianship to ensure that the person's best interests are being protected. In this case, a release from the patient to communicate freely with the facility would still be necessary.

There may be situations in which the clinician would like to share findings of his or her evaluation with the facility but the resident refuses to give consent. This problem can be especially troubling when the resident has dementia and is having some obvious difficulties in the facility. We have often encountered older clients who are early in the dementia process and are aware of some of their deficits. Because of their anxiety and fear over what is happening to them, they refuse to allow any communication to occur between the therapist and the facility. Their right to confidentiality must be respected unless the situation is or becomes dangerous. Usually, if the relationship is continued, it will be possible to obtain the release at a later time in such a way that clients will agree to at least a limited communication with the facility that would be in their own best interest. As an example, the clinician might talk to the manager of the facility about things that would be helpful to the client in that setting, but without divulging personal information or problems discussed with the client.

Nursing Home or Hospital

In these settings, Medicare requires that each visit be documented with the date, type of service provided, length of service, some indication of the content of the service, and a signature. Because these records are open to all medical and ancillary personnel who have access to records, and because security of those records is light, it is preferable to make only the necessary entries to ensure continuity of care in the facility and to keep extended notes in more secure confidential files in one's own office. For example, if one's client is depressed, that would be the notation in the chart in the facility, along with any suggestions for how staff might assist the client or recommendations that the patient be evaluated for antidepressant medication. In one's own files, one would document exactly what the client said, whatever tests might have been used, and so on.

Patients in nursing homes and hospitals usually have signed a blanket release from confidentiality that pertains to all who treat them, allowing free communication among professional staff. It still is important for psychologists to consider the client's privacy and best interests. Just because it is permissible to communicate with staff members does not mean that it is in the client's best interest that everything be communicated. The psychologist should take care to communicate only what is necessary for the staff to know about his or her client, with emphasis on preserving the client's privacy. Bear in mind that residents in nursing facilities and patients in hospitals feel intruded on and powerless, and the psychologist may be the only person with whom they discuss those feelings.

One of the most useful roles for psychologists in the nursing home is consultant to staff about behavior problems of patients, particularly patients with cognitive impairment, but also those with severe personality disorders that put undue stress on the staff caring for them. The best way to protect client confidentiality in these situations is to make positive suggestions to staff in general terms rather than discussing a particular patient. When the psychologist talks about a class of patients, rather than an individual, it allows the staff member to think about applying his or her suggestions across a variety of patients, which helps them stay oriented to the psychologist's suggestions in a professional way. Often staff members will consult with the psychologist about a patient with whom they are personally having difficulties. In this case, it is still best to move the discussion to the general level, although the psychologist may mentally be using information he or she knows about that particular patient to guide his or her suggestions.

Although patients or the person holding the POA have released the psychologist to communicate freely within the nursing home or hospital, it is still necessary to obtain a specific release before the psychologist can communicate with family members other than those with the POA. Although this step sounds obvious, it is not always possible to anticipate the variety of family structures (or dysfunction) that the psychologist will encounter. Therefore, a certain amount of vigilance is necessary when responding to family members who may inquire about assessment or treatment of their relative.

Confidentiality issues, then, can arise in a variety of different ways for older people depending on the setting in which they live, the client's competency to give consent, the involvement of family, and the need to exchange information with other health care providers. Situations will arise in which clinicians must weigh the competing demands of different ethical principles. The clinician's responsibilities to clients, particularly around protecting confidentiality, should remain in the forefront, guiding decisions about treatment and release of information.

END-OF-LIFE ISSUES

We begin this discussion with an example that illustrates the complexity of end-of-life decisions. The clients were Bess, a 70-year-old woman with Alzheimer's disease, and her 72-year-old husband of 45 years, Frank. Bess was referred by a neurologist, who requested a neuropsychological evaluation after diagnosing her dementia. In the course of the evaluation, it became apparent that Bess was acutely and painfully aware of her deficits and clinically depressed as a result. Psychotherapy was initiated with her and continued until her memory deficits became sufficient to contraindicate talking therapy. As she declined, treatment shifted to Frank, who had become increasingly depressed and angry about the hopeless deterioration he saw taking place in his wife. They were seen together and separately over a 5-year period, both in the office and later at home, when Bess was no longer able to leave the home because of degenerative arthritis and increased fear of falling outside the home. Finally, she started falling helplessly to the floor at night, and Frank had to call the police and neighbors to help get her up. When he realized that he could no longer take care of her, he placed her in a nursing home. Three months after she went to the facility, and on the urging of his son-in-law who was a physician, Frank asked that Bess be coded as do not resuscitate (DNR) and that no extraordinary means be used to prolong her life.

Bess was severely aphasic but was able to communicate her unhappiness about her situation both through an anguished expression, and occasionally, by asking plaintively, "Why me?" During the first year of therapy with Bess, we established that although her first choice was to be cared for at home, she would accept a nursing home if it became necessary. She also talked at great length about how unhappy she was with what had become of her. She did not want to be a burden to Frank and worried about his depression. While she was still able to, she granted Frank POA, including responsibility for health care decisions.

About 6 months after she entered the nursing home, Bess suddenly became ill. Tests showed that she had been bleeding internally, probably secondary to the nonsteroidal anti-inflammatory medication she had been taking for her arthritis. This is where the ethical dilemmas begin. When is a situation to be defined as "end of life," which then triggers the prohibition on using extraordinary means, and what are the hidden implications of decisions that physicians ask families to make about treatment?

The physician, Dr. Smith, explained the situation to Frank and gingerly asked him whether he wanted Bess to have a transfusion. Frank responded by asking Dr. Smith what he would normally do. The physician interpreted that as an indication that he wanted treatment started, so Bess was transferred to the hospital for the transfusion. Once the transfusion was started, she immediately had an allergic reaction, which is rare. The physician stopped the transfusion. Bess was running a temperature of 102 °F, and the physician asked Frank whether he wanted an intravenous [IV] hookup started to hydrate her. He agreed so that Bess did not get dehydrated. She was then returned to the nursing home.

At the nursing home, some of the staff were upset that the IV hookup had been started in light of Bess's no extraordinary measures status. Given her physical situation, they felt that she was clearly in decline and would die soon. Without the IV hookup, the process would take 5–14 days, but with the IV hookup, she could linger for much longer. That had not been explained to Frank by Dr. Smith. The nursing staff asked the psychologist to discuss this dilemma with Frank given the length and nature of their relationship. Frank was distraught by the turn of events, so the options were delicately explained to him. The psychologist then called the physician and asked what his intentions were. (It was helpful that the psychologist and physician had already worked together on several cases and had developed a good collaborative relationship.) Dr. Smith explained that when he started the IV hookup in the hospital, it would be in place only for 4 days, just to rehydrate Bess after the transfusion reaction. After that, once her physical status was stabilized, it would be removed. Indeed, on the third or fourth day, when the IV hookup came loose, the nurses were instructed not to replace it. At that point, Bess was in a coma, was non-responsive, and was dying. She lingered for another 5 days and was kept as comfortable as possible. She died peacefully.

The psychologist's role in this situation was complex. Because of the nature and longevity of her relationship with Frank, the psychologist was thrust into the role of the person who could best delineate the choices that were being made. The physician was prepared to abide by Frank's wishes not to prolong Bess's life needlessly, but he did not make explicit exactly what each choice meant. Frank was relying on the physician to make the decisions for him, including determining the point when no further treatment should be given, but the physician was bouncing the decision making back to him. The choice had been made not to resuscitate, not to take extraordinary steps to prolong life, but Frank was put in the position of determining whether the transfusion and then the IV hookup were extraordinary steps. After the psychologist intervened, Frank was able to defer to the physician, who followed the original plan of removing the IV hookup after 4 days. Frank felt that a medical protocol had been followed rather than that he had made a decision that might prematurely shorten his wife's life.

In this example, the psychologist put herself in the situation of advising the caregiver on these decisions. The psychologist had to remain neutral, representing what would be in Frank's best interest and what would represent Bess's preferences best. The psychologist's own personal biases could not enter into the decision. Psychologists have tremendous power to influence their clients, and, in a situation like this, they have to continuously assess whether their own values and biases are entering into the decision-making process.

A major question is whether that is a role one wants to assume. Because of the nature of the psychotherapeutic relationship, which involves talking extensively to one's clients and getting to know their beliefs, attitudes, and values, psychologists may be in a unique position to address these end-of-life issues. Physicians rarely have the time to spend with their patients or the patients' families to explore these issues in any depth. Consequently, many geriatricians and family practice physicians are eager to collaborate in this kind of decision making and even to defer some of the explanation of alternatives to the psychologist. Occasionally, the physician may make a referral to a psychologist specifically to determine what the individual's wishes are, particularly when there is some question about competency or whether depression or anxiety might be clouding the patient's decision-making abilities. As in the example just presented, the intervention with a patient can gradually include a widening circle of involved family members who can be involved individually or in a family session. This role can be emotionally demanding and includes knowing the explicit and implicit medical, legal, and ethical considerations for addressing end-of-life situations.

There is a growing body of legal and ethical writing that addresses end-of-life issues. Most writers on these issues make a distinction between active euthanasia and passive approaches that involve withholding procedures that might prolong life (Thomasma, 1992). Active approaches such as performed by Jack Kevorkian are clearly more controversial. Whatever one's personal opinion of euthanasia, psychologists have a legal and ethical obligation to prevent suicides, whether assisted or otherwise.

Legal and ethical issues concerning the decision to cease or withhold active treatment of terminally ill individuals are complex and evolving. There has been considerable debate over whether decisions should be made according to principles of beneficence (i.e., having appropriate people choose what is in the patient's best interest) or based on the principle of autonomy whereby the patient or his or her proxy makes the decision. The Cruzan case has had a large influence on legal standards for cessation of treatment (see White, 1992). Nancy Cruzan was a young woman who fell into a persistent vegetative state as a result of injuries suffered in a serious automobile accident and who was kept alive on life supports. Her family sued to have her life supports removed. The courts eventually ruled in favor of the family, largely on the basis of testimony that the patient had stated in conversations before the accident that she preferred not to be kept alive in that kind of condition. In deciding for the family, the court endorsed the principle of autonomy.

The principle of autonomy in end-of-life decisions is supported by passage of the Patient Self-Determination Act, which was part of the Omnibus Budget Reconciliation Act (OBRA) of 1990 (Sections 4206 and 4751 of OBRA, 1990, Public Law 101-508). Under the provisions of this act, all Medicare and Medicaid provider organizations, including hospitals and nursing homes, must obtain at the time of admission advanced directives that indicate the patient's preferences about terminating treatment. When the patient is not able to respond, the closest family member indicates a preference, as in the DNR order that was given in the previous example. A concurrent trend that has grown out of the publicity received by the Cruzan case and similar situations is for people to execute advanced directives (sometimes called *living wills*) that indicate their preferences concerning medical treatment in extreme situations.

Although these approaches offer people some degree of control over end-of-life decisions for themselves or for close family members, there remain many problems and questions. From a practical perspective, most people do not have advanced directives (Moore et al., 1994). Complicating the situation is the fact that health care providers will often do what they believe to be appropriate, regardless of an advanced directive or POA. That will especially be the case if the family is divided over what the appropriate treatment should be (Moody, 1992). Some ethicists raise serious objections to the principle of autonomy. Dresser (1992), for example, argued that the patient's prior choices should not influence current decisions because the person may not have foreseen this particular situation and might now make a different choice. Proxy decisions by family members are criticized even more strongly because, in the absence of an advanced directive, the family cannot truly know what the patient wanted (Rhoden, 1988).

The importance and complexity of these issues have grown out of the long-standing trend in medicine in which what were previously considered heroic or extraordinary measures are becoming standard procedures for care. An obvious example is the use of hydration and feeding tubes for late-stage patients with dementia, which are increasingly being implemented in end-stage cases. Are these kinds of procedures heroic measures, or have they become routine and expected care? Does hydration or a feeding tube contribute to the comfort of an end-stage patient, or do these procedures needlessly prolong suffering? As Nuland (1993) observed in his powerful book, *How We Die*, the medical technology exists to do all sorts of amazing things, but at the end of life, should people be made uncomfortable rather than helped to die peacefully? Thomasma (1992) made a powerful critique of this trend in medicine, arguing that current premises need to be reversed in end-of-life situations. Rather than assuming that everything must be done to prolong life, Thomasma proposed that the "default mode" of modern medicine should be to do nothing to extend life in a hopeless situation, except when requested by the patient, family, or an advanced directive. While the debate among medical ethicists continues, medical technology is extending the boundaries of life-and-death decisions in new and unexpected ways, placing families in situations in which they are not prepared.

Beyond the ethical dimensions involved in these situations, psychologists also need to be aware of the practical implications of medical decisions in life-threatening situations in order to help patients and their families obtain the kind of care that they prefer. As illustrated in the case example, medical personnel have developed a set of implicit rules in end-of-life situations, in which each decision has certain consequences. Families will be asked to make decisions but often without being aware of the long-term implications. The most important feature of the decisions posed to families is that once procedures to manage an acute situation are started, physicians will usually feel obligated to continue them. It is difficult to discontinue some procedures such as feeding tubes and respirators after they have been started if the patient cannot survive independently without them. In the previous example, the physician could have argued for the need for continued hydration or might have encouraged the use of a feeding tube. Indeed, the decision to cease hydration would have been controversial in many medical settings. In some nursing homes or hospitals, staff will actively oppose removing these treatments and have gone to court to prevent it. The result is that families who do not want to prolong suffering sometimes find themselves on an irreversible course of doing just that because they have made decisions without a full understanding of what their choice meant.

A related consideration is that physicians, hospitals, and nursing homes need to support the decisions reached by patients and their families. Some physicians will not agree to follow specific advanced directives or to implement the treatment plan proposed by the family, or a facility will have its own guidelines. Once a terminal phase of care has begun, it may be impossible to reconcile these differences in beliefs. Families caring for someone with a predictable course of decline, such as dementia, should be encouraged to talk about terminal-stage care ahead of time with the patient's physicians to make sure the patient's preferences are likely to be implemented.

One of the more problematic aspects of these situations is determining whether a patient has entered a final terminal phase. Physicians may be reluctant to make this determination, and, as in the previous example, turn to the family for guidance about whether to continue treatment. In other instances, physicians will insist on initiating treatment in situations that the family may regard as terminal. As physicians' skills in prolonging life continue to improve, the decision that a situation is terminal may become increasingly social, not medical.

One additional consideration is that older people and their families need to understand the implications of their decisions concerning use of different types of medical facilities. Specifically, the patient's preferences as indicated by DNR orders, "no extraordinary measures" orders, or by living wills (also called *advanced directives*) are all invalid in the emergency room and in situations in which the paramedics have been called. In these emergency situations, emergency medical technicians and physicians need to be able to respond to the crisis immediately before them, and they will not honor advanced directives or DNR orders.

Most families of older clients are not aware of this situation. As a result, a severely impaired patient with dementia who has a significant medical event, such as a myocardial infarction or cardiovascular accident, may be taken to the emergency room and resuscitated contrary to the wishes of the patient and family. The only physician who can honor advanced directives is the primary care physician, so in these situations it is advisable for family members to consult with this doctor first before making a trip to the emergency room. When the older person resides in a nursing home, the family should make similar arrangements with the staff. Some nonmedical programs, such as adult day care or assisted-living facilities, may feel obligated to call for emergency help despite the presence of a DNR order. It might fall on the psychologist to make explicit to the family what the consequences will be of using emergency services, as opposed to calling the patient's physician, and to help them discuss these issues with nursing home staff or other people involved in the patient's care.

The psychologist's role in these situations is not to decide what is best for the patient or family but to help families understand the implications of their decisions and to help them make decisions that reflect their preferences and those of the patient. To be effective and helpful in the decision-making process, psychologists need to be able to present the various choices in a nonjudgmental and clear manner. That will depend on understanding their own values and clearly differentiating them from their clients' values. For example, one may believe that people deserve a natural death, unencumbered by technology, except to keep someone as comfortable and free from pain as possible. Some patients and families may instead value prolonging life as long as possible. Families must find their own answer to the dilemma of knowing that they have done everything that should be done but without needlessly prolonging suffering. Whatever the situation, the psychologist's role is to help people articulate their values and then to make decisions in a manner that is consistent with those values.

SUMMARY

Beyond the basic issues of becoming competent and comfortable in treating older people, clinicians need to develop an understanding of the complex legal and ethical issues that can arise. Foremost among these are confidentiality and end-of-life issues. The APA's Ethical Principles and Code of Conduct of Psychologists provides a framework and set of principles for addressing the dilemmas that are encountered. However, because the principles are broad and abstract, clinicians often find themselves in situations in which they must apply and extend these basic tenets in situations for which there are no specific precedents. It is important for clinicians to approach these decisions carefully, getting input from colleagues, and examining their own biases and values so that they are able to differentiate what they would want for themselves from their clients' best interests. There clearly is a need for more education in this area and for development of forums for discussion of ethical dilemmas in the care of older people by psychologists and between psychologists and other health care professionals.

REFERENCES

American Psychological Association. (1992). Ethical principles of psychologists and codes of conduct. *American Psychologist, 47*, 1597–1611.

Dresser, R. S. (1992). Autonomy revisited: The limits of anticipatory choices. In R. H. Binstock, S. G. Post, & P. J. Whitehouse (Eds.), *Dementia and aging: Ethics, values and policy choices* (pp. 71–85). Baltimore: Johns Hopkins University Press.

Grisso, T. (1994). Clinical assessments for legal competence of older adults. In M. Storandt & G. R. VandenBos (Eds.), *Neuropsychological assessment of dementia and depression in older adults: A clinician's guide* (pp. 119–140). Washington, DC: American Psychological Association.

Moody, H. R. (1992). A critical view of ethical dilemmas in dementia. In R. H. Binstock, S. G. Post, & P. J. Whitehouse (Eds.), *Dementia and aging: Ethics, values and policy choices* (pp. 86–100). Baltimore: Johns Hopkins University Press.

Moore, K. A., Danks, J. H., Ditto, P. H., Druley, J. A., Townsend, A., & Smucker, W. D. (1994). Elderly outpatients' understanding of a physician-initiated advance directive discussion. *Archives of Family Medicine, 3*, 1057–1063.

Nuland, S. B. (1993). *How we die: Reflections on life's final chapter.* New York: Knopf.

Rhoden, N. K. (1988). Litigating life and death. *Harvard Law Review, 102*, 375–446.

Thomasma, D. C. (1992). Mercy killing of elderly people with dementia: A counterproposal. In R. H. Binstock, S. G. Post, & P. J. Whitehouse (Eds.), *Dementia and aging: Ethics, values and policy choices* (pp. 101–117). Baltimore: Johns Hopkins University Press.

White, P. D. (1992). Essays in the aftermath of Cruzan. *Journal of Medicine and Philosophy, 17*, 563–571.

INDEX

informant reports, 192
interpersonal problems, 85–86
interpersonal psychotherapy, 83–99
maintenance therapy, 87–97
medical disease comorbidity, 168,
    224–225
physical disease interactions,
    225–226
physician detection and treatment
    of, 228–229
Depression Adjective Check List, 189
Desipramine, 75–76
Diagnostic Interview Schedule, 169
Disability. *See* Physical disability
Divorce, 122–123
Do not resuscitate orders, 278, 280,
    282–283
Drug interactions, 233
Dying patients, 236
Dysfunctional thoughts, 49, 67–68

Early maladaptive schemas, 73
Educational approach. *See* Psychoeduca-
    tional approach
Educational level, and assessment,
    180–181
Emergency services, ethics, 282–283
Emotions, developmental changes, 22–24
End-of-life issues, 277–284
Enmeshment issues, 125
Environmental factors
    and assessment, 195–197
    nursing homes, modification,
        254–255
Epidemiological Catchment Area Study,
    165–167
Epidemiology, 165–168
Erectile dysfunction, 52–53
Ethics, 269–284
    confidentiality issues, 270–277
    end-of-life issues, 277–284
Ethnicity, and assessment, 181–182
Euthanasia, 280
"Expert system" program, 20

Facial expression, 24
Family caregivers, 139–159
    anger treatment, 54–55, 77
    assessment, 146, 175–176
    bereavement, 157

"career" aspects, 146
clinical interventions, 139–159
coping variability, 142
"erosion of self," 142
family meeting function, 154
family therapy, 127–128, 134
group psychoeducational classes,
    76–77
as informants, 172–175
informational interventions,
    150–151
interpersonal psychotherapy, 91–92
nursing home placement decision,
    145
problem-solving approach, 151–153
role acquisition, 146–149
role transitions, 91–92
social and demographic trends,
    140–141
strategic therapy approach, 149
stress, 141–144, 175–176
support issues, 152–154, 157
Family conflicts, and depression, 62–63
Family consultation, 257–258
Family meeting, 154
Family myths, 130–131, 133
Family-of-origin therapy, 127
Family themes, 124
Family therapy, 121–137
    assessment phase, 129–131
    benefits, 128–129
    definition, 122
    disadvantages, 129
    history, 126–128
    indications for, 125–126
    least intrusion principle, 133–134
    rationale, 122–126
    systems model, 128, 131–132
Fluid intelligence, 20
Following the contact function, 107
Forgetting rate, 188
Free-recall tasks, 187
Freud's treatment view, 104
Functional abilities
    assessment, 170–171
    and chronic illness, 225

Gender differences
    life expectancy, 8
    mental disorders, 165
Gender role stereotypes, 23

Schema change therapy, 73–74
SCL-42, 193
Secondary role strains, 142
Selective Reminding Test, 185
Semistructured interviews, 172
Senior centers, 27
Sensory changes, 176–178
Sensory stimulation groups, 250
Separation issues, 125
Sexual dysfunctions, 52–53
Sheltered Care Environment Scale, 196–197
SHORT-CARE, 172
Silence, and psychoanalytic therapy, 107
"Simulated presence" audiotape, 258
Sleep-maintenance insomnia, 51–52
Social context, 27–28
Social isolation. *See* Interpersonal deficits
Social services, 5
Social workers, consultation, 257
Socioeconomic factors, 182
Somatization, 227
Spousal caregivers. *See also* Family caregivers
    and nursing home placement, 157
    trends, 140–141
State–Trait Anxiety Inventory, 193
Stimulus-control techniques, 53
Stress
    family caregivers, 141–144, 146
    physical health effects of, 226
Stress containment, 142–144
Stress proliferation, 142–144
Structured Assessment of Independent Living Skills, 171
Structured Clinical Interview for *DSM-III-R*, 169
Structured interview assessment, 169–170
Successful aging, 232–233

Suicide
    epidemiology, 166
    ethical obligations, 280
Support groups, caregivers, 154
Support services, caregivers, 152–154, 157
Systems model, family therapy, 127–128

Team approach, 233–234
Terminal patients, ethics, 282
Termination, psychotherapy phase, 68
Therapeutic relationship, 73
Therapists
    as change agents, 133–134
    "expert consultants" role, 132
    in family therapy, 132–134
Training manuals, 39
Transference, 96, 107
Treatment contract, 67
Treatment manuals, 39
Tricyclic antidepressants. *See* Antidepressant medication

Vascular dementia, 167–168
Visual aids, 149
Visual changes, 176

Wisconsin Card Sorting Task, 184
Wisdom, 42
Women
    life expectancy, 8
    personality development, 22–23
Working memory, 21

"Young-old," 8

Zarit Burden Interview, 175
Zung Self-Rating Depression Scale, 189

ABOUT THE EDITORS

Steven H. Zarit, PhD, is Professor of Human Development and Assistant Director of the Gerontology Center, Pennsylvania State University, as well as Adjunct Professor at the Institute of Gerontology, University College of Health Sciences, Jönköping, Sweden. Zarit received his degree from the Committee on Human Development, University of Chicago, with emphases in adult development and aging and clinical psychology. He has held faculty positions at City College of New York and the University of Southern California (USC). While at USC, he founded the program for mental health of older adults (now the Tingstad Older Adult Counseling Center).

Zarit has conducted research on problems of mental health and aging and is known for his research on family caregiving and on the oldest-old. He has authored several works, including *Aging and Mental Health* (Free Press, 1980), *The Hidden Victims of Alzheimer's Disease: Families Under Stress* (with N. K. Orr and J. M Zarit; New York University Press, 1985), and *Profiles in Caregiving: The Unexpected Career* (with C. Aneshensel, L. I. Pearlin, J. Mullan, and C. J. Whitlach; Academic Press, 1995).

Bob G. Knight, PhD, is the Merle H. Bensinger Associate Professor of Gerontology and Psychology at the Andrus Gerontology Center, University of Southern California (USC). In this position, he serves as Director of the Tingstad Older Adult Counseling Center and Co-Director of the Los Angeles Caregiver Resource Center. Knight received his PhD in clinical psychology from Indiana University, Bloomington. His professional experience in working with older adults began at the Urban League of Madison County, Indiana, where he organized and served as first president of the Madison County Council on Aging in 1973. Prior to joining the USC faculty, from 1980 to 1988, he managed the Senior Services Program at

Ventura County Mental Health Services. In Fall 1995, Knight was a Visiting Professor at Sheffield University, England.

Knight has published extensively on mental health and aging, including *Psychotherapy With Older Adults* (Sage, 1986, 1996), *Outreach With the Elderly* (New York University Press, 1989), and *Older Adults in Psychotherapy: Case Histories* (Sage, 1992). In addition, with L. Teri, P. Wohlford, and J. Santos, he was editor of *Mental Health Services for Older Adults: Implications for Training and Practice in Geropsychology* (American Psychological Association, 1995).